# The Political Economy of
# SOCIAL WELFARE POLICY IN AFRICA

## Transforming policy through practice

Edited by
VIVIENE TAYLOR & JEAN D. TRIEGAARDT

*With contributions from*
Ndangwa Noyoo
Rinie Schenck
Mimie Sesoko

**OXFORD**
UNIVERSITY PRESS
SOUTH AFRICA

# OXFORD
## UNIVERSITY PRESS

Oxford University Press is a department of the University of Oxford.
It furthers the University's objective of excellence in research, scholarship,
and education by publishing worldwide. Oxford is a registered trade mark of
Oxford University Press in the UK and in certain other countries.

Published in South Africa by
Oxford University Press Southern Africa (Pty) Limited

Vasco Boulevard, Goodwood, N1 City, Cape Town, South Africa, 7460
P O Box 12119, N1 City, Cape Town, South Africa, 7463

The Political economy of social welfare policy in Africa: Transforming policy into practice

ISBN 978 0 19 907647 5

First impression 2018

Typeset in Utopia 9.5pt on 12pt
Printed on 70gsm woodfree paper

## Acknowledgements
Publishing manager: Alida Terblanche
Publisher: Marisa Montemarano
Project manager: Gugulethu Baloyi
Editor: Revenia Abrahams
Designer: Jade Benjamin
Typesetter: Chris Leo
Indexer: Tanya Paulse
Cover design by: Judith Cross
Printed and bound by: ABC Press
6061

The authors and publisher acknowledge the following parties for the images used in this book:
p. 18 Drum Social Histories/Baileys African History Archive/Africa Media Online; pp. 39 & 205 Artist James Berrang
Commissioned by OUPSA; p. 42 Historic Images/Alamy Stock Photo; pp. 13 & 151 source: https://www.sahistory.org
za/people/krotoa-eva and https://www.sahistory.org.za/people/frantz-fanon; p. 44 Greg Marinovich/South Photos/
Africa Media Online; p. 52 cartoonPolyp.org.uk/polyp@polyp.org.uk; p. 63 Sueddeutsche Zeitung Photo/Alamy Stoc
Photo; p. 72 Bongiwe Gumede/Gallo Images; p. 85 Marion Kaplan/Alamy; p. 87 Langgong Vectorist/Shutterstock;
p. 94 POOL Old Gallo Images; p. 115 Georg Berg/Alamy Stock Photo; p. 120 magic pictures/Shutterstock; pp. xiii,
134 & 301 Allan Taylor; p. 87 magic pictures/Shutterstock; p. 139 Sylvie Bouchard/Shutterstock; p. 157 Gallo Images
Alamy Stock Photo; p. 180 ACIFIC PRESS/Alamy Stock Photo; p. 181 Steve Estvanik/Shutterstock; p. 213 Shutterstoc
p. 227 source: https://www.parliament.gov.za/parliaments-photos; p. 241 Paul Weinberg/South Photos/Africa Media
Online; p. 245 Pictorial Press Ltd/Alamy Stock Photo; p. 246 Sowetan/Times Media Digital Archive/Africa Media
Online; p. 262 Graeme Williams/South Photos/Africa Media Online; p. 291 Adwo/Shutterstock.

# Abridged table of contents

# Table of contents

## Part 2 Using evidence to shape transformative social welfare policy

## Part 3  Making social welfare policy

# Foreword

I appreciate the opportunity to write the foreword for this book, *The Political Economy of Social Welfare Policy in Africa* 1st edition, and to explain why I consider it important and timely, and why, in my view, it is destined to be a reference for social service professionals, scholars, and policymakers in years to come.

First, the chapters in the first part of the book argue for a paradigm shift in how social welfare policy is understood and explain why a transformative approach is essential. This is done by using a political economy framework to analyse the evolution of social welfare policy as a response to the most pressing social and economic deprivations experienced by people in Africa. Using some countries in sub-Saharan Africa as examples, and particularly South Africa, it points out the intersections among political and economic choices made by governments over time and the consequences of these choices when governments and states fail people. Chapters in this book highlight the complexities of the political economy of Africa with its roots in a long history of conquest and struggles against imperialism, colonial and postcolonial processes. However, despite the history and complex political and economic features that make life incredibly hard for the poorest people on the continent, some chapters point out that there is growing impetus towards a more human rights and transformative approach to social welfare policy in countries in the region.

Chapter 1 of this book makes explicit that the basis of transformative social welfare policy and practice is social justice and human rights. This chapter questions technical policy processes as being deeply political using South Africa's experiences to illustrate the mix of economic exploitation and social and political disempowerment. This conceptualisation impels us as policymakers, scholars of social policy and practitioners to adopt a human rights approach to social welfare policy in Africa and especially in countries such as South Africa. Such an approach would do much to ensure that policies and social service practice are directed at addressing inequalities, discrimination, and multiple deprivations that people experience as a consequence of oppressive regimes, exploitative production and market systems, and structural inequalities. It breaks new ground in how we understand the links between macro structural factors and micro level household experiences of people in a regional and global context that is dominated by neoliberal financial and economic globalisation.

Second, the political economy approach used to analyse social welfare policy is not only groundbreaking but also moves away from conservative and orthodox approaches that do not effectively tackle structural forces and other impediments to societal well-being, especially those which are embedded in countries' colonial and postcolonial histories. This book is ambitious on another level. It squarely addresses the questions that, to a large extent, explain the social welfare policy failures of governments in eradicating poverty, and reducing inequalities, unemployment, hunger, and malnutrition. Instead of maintaining the status quo with regard to policies and professional practice in the social services, this book provides the knowledge base and techniques to enable policymakers and scholars to critique inequitable and unjust systems and to propose alternatives to such systems.

Third, chapters in this book argue for a new approach to scholarly work in social welfare policy and social development and provide the theories, experiences and knowledge that provide a much needed shift away from palliative and status quo approaches to an approach that critically engages with why poverty, inequalities, vulnerabilities and risk persist in postcolonial, independent African countries. The historical analysis that comes with this political economy approach to social welfare empowers policymakers, practitioners, and students to understand the ravages of capitalism and political intolerance in Africa and counter these with a transformative approach.

The editors of this book compel us to look beyond the surface and to change the way we understand social welfare policy and the paradigms we use to address the persistent problems of poverty, social inequalities, and vulnerabilities in our country. This is not surprising. Viviene Taylor is one of the foremost social policy experts in South Africa and has shaped democratic South Africa's social policy significantly. Her pioneering work on comprehensive social security for South Africa laid the basis for a transformative social protection system that improves the lives of the majority of the poorest citizens. Given her work on social protection in Africa for the African Union, on the National Planning Commission, her role as Chair on the Review of the White Paper for Social Welfare Policy (1997), and her work on the High Level Panel Review of Key Legislation in South Africa, Prof Viviene Taylor is particularly well placed to identify and analyse policy, legislative and accountability gaps in social welfare policies and provisions. Her research experience on social policy, poverty, and inequalities, and her wide-range of policy knowledge are evident in the chapters of this book and reveal her commitment to transforming social policy and social protection systems to reduce poverty and inequalities in South Africa and on the continent.

Jean Triegaardt is Professor and Senior Research Associate at the Centre for Social Development in Africa (CSDA), University of Johannesburg, and has more than 25 years of experience as a social work academic and 12 years as a social work practitioner. She has worked in both South Africa and internationally and has researched and written on social protection; social policy; poverty, unemployment and inequality; refugees and migrants; and restorative justice. Her contributions to the field of social work and social policy influence thinking and practice in South Africa. Most recently, she served on the Ministerial Committee on the Review of South Africa's White Paper for Social Welfare and continues to influence social work education in South Africa.

This book takes us beyond contemporary discourses and policy perspectives on social welfare, social protection and social development to critique and find alternatives that focus on how to transform structural inequities through policies that ensure universal and humane systems of social development. It has both theoretical and real world practical application and adds new insights, knowledge and approaches to promote social transformation in Africa.

**Kgalema Motlanthe**
**Former President, Republic of South Africa**

# Acknowledgements

This book is an outcome of contributions made by many individuals through research, consultations, workshops, and collaborative engagements. We had the privilege of working with many committed individuals and we thank them for the many different ways in which they worked with us. We acknowledge in particular all the contributing authors who worked tirelessly to complete their chapters during various review processes, the peer-reviewers who provided invaluable insights and appreciation for the paradigmatic shifts in thinking and practicing social welfare policy from a political economy perspective. As always many individuals provided behind the scenes support throughout the process of producing this book. Our publisher Marisa Montemarano from Oxford University Press provided support, encouragement, and measured guidance whenever we needed this. Others within the OUP team who provided technical support include Ilka Lane, former Development Editor for her guidance, wisdom and advice; Jeanne Maclay-Mayers who speedily ensured that the draft manuscript was sent to the peer-reviewers; Gugulethu Baloyi; and most recently the copy editor, Revenia Abrahams.

Viviene Taylor: a special acknowledgement for exceptional support, love and forbearance received over the years from my husband Allan Taylor. As our social and family time decreased because of research and writing he was remarkably patient and understanding. Not only is he a source of emotional support but his technical and research help was invaluable in ensuring that I was able to cross check and verify data for chapters in this book and many others. Allan patiently filled the vacuum created by my absence from many family events and activities while I was glued to my computer and research. In addition, special mention must be made of the administrative and research assistance provided by Crystal Kleinhans. She diligently arranged meetings with the publishers and kept track of all the processes for me. Her role was invaluable. Both deserve my unreserved thanks and appreciation for their roles in my life and work. Many social policy and social development scholars influenced my work over the years and I owe them my appreciation. I had the privilege of working with Prof Amaratya Sen and engaged with many eminent scholars from the global south. Their work continues to inspire me to pursue both epistemic and social justice as we seek to advance the transformation of Africa's political economy.

Jean Triegaardt: I especially acknowledge with sincere gratitude and thanks the following individuals for the assistance and support given during the research and writing of my chapters for this book. Special mention and thanks to Connie Nxumalo (DDG for Welfare Services, National Department of Social Development), Monitoring & Evaluation Unit in the Presidency, and Godfrey Ngobeni (Library Assistant, University of Johannesburg Library Services). Over the years, my thinking on social policy has been cultivated and honed by colleagues such as Professor Emeritus David G. Gil (Brandeis University) – my former professor at Washington University, Saint Louis; Professors Buford Farris, Jack Stretch, and William Hutchison; and the late Professor Joan Smith at Saint Louis University School of Social Service. The debates in the doctoral classroom, particularly on the Frankfurt School of Thought, were inspiring. My thinking on social development has been influenced by Professors James Midgley (University of Berkeley, California); Leila Patel (Centre for Social Development in Africa, University of Johannesburg); and the late Edwell Kaseke (formerly at University of the Witwatersrand, Johannesburg). Finally, to my husband, Dwight, and our two daughters, Allison and Melanie, for their understanding of the family time that they sacrificed during my involvement in writing this important book. And then there is our granddaughter Maya, who is too young to know and understand the rigours of academia but is such a joy and inspiration.

Editors

**Viviene Taylor and Jean Triegaardt**

# List of contributors

**Assoc Prof Ndangwa Noyoo** is an Associate Professor and the Head of Department of Social Development, Faculty of Humanities, University of Cape Town. He holds a Doctor of Philosophy (Ph.D) from the University of the Witwatersrand, a Master of Philosophy (M.Phil.) in Development Studies from the University of Cambridge and a Bachelor of Social Work (BSW) from the University of Zambia. He was a Post-Doctoral Fellow at the *Fondation Maison des Sciences de l'Homme*, Paris, France, 2005–06. Previously, he worked for the University of Johannesburg as an Associate Professor in the Department Social Work; for the South African government as a Senior Social Policy Specialist/Chief Director in the National Department of Social Development; and as a Senior Lecturer in the Department of Social Work at the University of the Witwatersrand. His research interests are social policy, social development, Indigenous Knowledge Systems (IKS), and public policy. He is the author of 33 peer reviewed journal articles and book chapters. An accomplished writer in Africa's experiences and challenges in development, he also authored eight books, which include, among others, *Wrong things about Africa* (2016) and *Social Welfare in Zambia: The Search for a Transformative Agenda* (2013).

**Dr Catherina (Rinie) Schenck** is the DST/NRF/CSIR Chair in Waste and Society at the University of the Western Cape. She was previously the Head of the Department of Social Work at the University of the Western Cape, and taught at the University of South Africa and the University of Pretoria. She has published many articles in the field of social welfare and development in scholarly journals, and authored a book titled *Introduction to participatory community practice* (2010). In addition to her interest as SARChI Chair, her research interest is people in poverty and unemployment.

**Dr Mimie Priscilla Sesoko** is the Head of the Social Work Department at the University of South Africa. She completed her PhD in Social Policy at the Heller School of Social Welfare at Brandeis University in Massachusetts USA. Her research interest is social policy, community development, youth, and women, rural and economic development. Before joining UNISA, she was the program director at W.K Kellogg foundation and worked as social specialist at the Development Bank of Southern Africa (DBSA). She has vast experience in development, leadership, management and organisational development as she worked in government, the private sector, and at a number of non-governmental organisations as a social specialist and a Chief Executive Officer. She started at UNISA as a senior lecturer before she was appointed the Head of the department.

**Prof Viviene Taylor** is a specialist in comparative social policy, development planning, and social and economic development. Her research focus addresses poverty and social inequalities using a political economy and human rights perspective. She is a social science graduate with postgraduate qualifications in Social Planning and Administration and Social Policy from the University of Cape Town. Taylor's career consists of both national and international development experience spanning more than 35 years. She has researched and written numerous publications on social policy and development related issues. Books she authored include *Social Mobilisation: Lessons from the Mass Democratic Movement* (1997) and *Gender*

*Mainstreaming in Development Planning: A Reference Manual for Governments and other Stakeholders* (1999). She was principal author and researcher of a 50-country research study for the African Union called *Social Protection in Africa* in 2008, which contributed to the Social Policy Framework for Africa. She served as Adviser to South Africa's Minister of Social Development and chaired the Committee of Inquiry into Comprehensive Social Security in South Africa during 1999–2002. The Report of the Committee of Inquiry into Comprehensive Social Security (Taylor Report, 2002) constitutes South Africa's policy framework for social protection. She worked at the UN with Professor Amartya Sen, as Deputy Director in a global Commission on Human Security. More recently, she chaired the Ministerial Committee on the review of South Africa's White Paper on Social Welfare. She has also served on international Expert Groups of the United Nations Division for Economic and Social Affairs on themes such as Social Security/Protection, Social Policy, Civil Service Reform, and Social Exclusion. She currently serves as a Commissioner on the National Planning Commission in South Africa.

**Prof Jean D. Triegaardt** is Senior Research Associate at the Centre for Social Development in Africa (CSDA), University of Johannesburg, South Africa. She obtained her PhD from Saint Louis University, USA. Her research interests are social protection, social policy, poverty, unemployment and inequality, refugees and migrants, and restorative justice. She was a social work academic for twenty-five years at various South African universities and practised as a social worker for twelve years in Canada and the US. Previously, she served as the Head of the Department of Social Work at the University of Johannesburg. In 2003, at the University of California, Berkeley, she spent a sabbatical as a Fulbright scholar. Formerly, she was the editor of the South African journal titled *The Social Work Practitioner-Researcher* for six years (now known as the *Southern African Journal of Social Work and Social Development*). She served as a member of the Ministerial Committee to Review the Implementation of the White Paper for Social Welfare (1997). This was a two-and-a half-year review process that included research in all South Africa's nine provinces. The outcome of this review culminated in a report with policy recommendations which was launched on the 4 October 2016.

# List of acronyms

| | |
|---|---|
| **ACHPR** | African Charter on Human and Peoples' Rights |
| **ACRWC** | African Charter on the Rights of the Welfare of the Child |
| **ANC** | African National Congress |
| **AU** | African Union |
| **BCM** | Black Consciousness Movement |
| **BUSA** | Business Unity South Africa |
| **BWF** | Black Women's Federation |
| **CA** | Capability Approach |
| **CBO** | Community-based Organisation |
| **CEDAW** | Convention on the Elimination of All Forms of Discrimination against Women |
| **CGE** | Commission on Gender Equality |
| **COPE** | Congress of the People |
| **CORMSA** | Consortium for Refugees and Migrants in South Africa |
| **CSG** | Child Support Grant |
| **CSI** | Corporate Social Investment |
| **CSO** | Civil Society Organisation |
| **CSW** | Concerned Social Workers |
| **DA** | Democratic Alliance |
| **DPLG** | Department of Provincial and Local Government |
| **DPO** | Disabled Person's Organisation |
| **DPSA** | Disabled People South Africa |
| **ECA** | Economic Commission on Africa |
| **ECOWAS** | Economic Community of West African States |
| **EFF** | Economic Freedom Fighters |
| **ESAP** | Economic Structural Adjustment Programme |
| **FAMSA** | Families South Africa |
| **FBO** | Faith-based Organisation |
| **FMSP** | Forced Migration Studies Programme |
| **FRELIMO** | *Frente de Libertação de Moçambique* |
| **FSAW** | Federation of South African Women |
| **GEAR** | Growth, Employment and Redistribution |
| **HDI** | Human Development Index |
| **IDP** | Internally Displaced Persons |
| **IFI** | International Financial Institution |
| **ILO** | International Labour Organisation |
| **JRC** | Jesuit Refugee Centre |
| **LFA** | Logical Framework Approach |
| **LHR** | Lawyers for Human Rights |
| **MDG** | Millennium Development Goal |
| **MOST** | Management of Social Transformation |
| **MPLA** | *Movimento Popular de Libertação de Angola* |
| **NA** | National Assembly |
| **NAC** | Nyasaland African Congress |

NAM ................................................................................................ Non-Aligned Movement
NASW, SA ............................................... National Association of Social Workers, South Africa
NCOP ................................................................................... National Council of Provinces
NDP ................................................................................... National Development Plan
NEDLAC ............................................ National Economic Development and Labour Council
NGO ................................................................................ Non-governmental Organisation
NPA ................................................................................ National Prosecuting Authority
NPC .................................................................................. National Planning Commission
NRC .................................................................................. Northern Rhodesia Congress
OAU .................................................................................. Organisation of African Unity
OPEC ............................................................ Organisation of Petroleum Exporting Countries
PAC .................................................................................... Pan Africanist Congress
PDO ................................................................................ Parliamentary Democracy Offices
PPP ................................................................................ Public–Private Partnerships
PRSP .................................................................................. Poverty Reduction Strategy Paper
RDP ................................................................................ Reconstruction and Development Programme
RENAMO .................................................................................. *Resistência Nacional Moçambicana*
SABSWA ...................................................... South African Black Social Workers Association
SADC ............................................................ Southern African Development Community
SADCC .......................................... Southern African Development Co-ordination Conference
SAP ................................................................................ Structural Adjustment Programme
SASPCAN ................... South African Society for the Prevention of Child Abuse and Neglect
SASSA ................................................................................ South Africa Social Security Agency
SERI ................................................................................ Socio-economic Rights Institute of South Africa
SOAP ................................................................................ Social Old Age Pensions
SPF ................................................................................ Social Policy Framework
SRANC .................................................... Southern Rhodesia African National Congress
Stats SA ................................................................................ Statistics South Africa
SWAPO ................................................................................ South West African People's Organisation
TAC ................................................................................ Treatment Action Campaign
UDF ................................................................................ United Democratic Front
UDHR ................................................................................ Universal Declaration of Human Rights
UDM ................................................................................ United Democratic Movement
UN ................................................................................ United Nations
UNCRPD ................... United Nations Convention on the Rights of Persons with Disabilities
UNDP ................................................................................ United Nations Development Programme
UNESCO .......................... United Nations Educational, Scientific and Cultural Organisation
UNHCR ................................................ United Nations High Commissioner for Refugees
UNICEF ........................................ United Nations International Children's Emergency Fund
UNOCHA ..................... United Nations Office for the Coordination of Humanitarian Affairs
UNRSD ........................... United Nations Research Institute for Social Development
UWCO ................................................................................ United Women's Congress
ZANU ................................................................................ Zimbabwe African National Union
ZAPU ................................................................................ Zimbabwe African People's Union

# PART
# 01

# Thinking policy:
# the political economy of
# social welfare policy

# Transforming social welfare policy: Africa and South Africa

*Viviene Taylor*

Chapter 1 provides a detailed discussion and analysis of social welfare policy within the context of a political economy framework. It provides knowledge and critical understanding of social welfare policy development in Africa. Using South Africa as a recent example, it illustrates how analysing social welfare policy through a political economy lens reveals the structural forces and other impediments to societal well-being, especially those that are embedded in countries' political economies. The objectives and outcomes for this chapter are set out below.

## Objectives

✓ Clarifying and defining social welfare policy, and discussing how social welfare policy differs from other types of policy that, at times, are used interchangeably with social welfare policy, but are not the same.

✓ Explaining the significance of using a political economy framework to analyse how social welfare policy has changed over time in response to the political, economic, and social contexts in Africa and South Africa.

✓ Highlighting some of the main features of the evolution of social welfare policy in Africa, and providing a more detailed analysis of the political economy of South Africa's evolving social welfare policy – history, politics, economics, and social impacts.

✓ Providing a critical overview of the paradigmatic shifts in social welfare policy over time, relating these shifts to changes in the ideological, political, and economic thinking in different periods.

✓ Providing an analysis of the main features of transformative social welfare policy and its relevance for contemporary postcolonial African states.

## Outcomes

✓ Understanding and explaining the meaning of social welfare policy and related concepts, and identifying the values and theories that influence social welfare policy.

✓ Describing and critically analysing the political economy of social welfare policy and its evolution in Africa and South Africa.

✓ Identifying and understanding the features of transformative social welfare policy, and discussing critically the relevance of such features of social welfare policy for postcolonial and post-development countries.

✓ Applying an understanding of transformative social welfare policy in professional social service practice to enhance the well-being of people and promote policy advocacy for a human rights approach to achieve equity and change.

# 1.1 Introduction

Social service professionals, students, and policymakers will be able to draw on this chapter to expand their knowledge and professional understanding of how social welfare policy applies in real world situations. It also provides an understanding of the ways in which transformative understandings of social welfare policy, and the approaches that emerge from this, can address some of the most pressing social conditions that lead to poverty, inequalities, vulnerability, and risk in countries in Africa.

Social welfare policies and the study of social welfare policy as a discipline are gaining traction on the continent of Africa for a number of reasons. Among these reasons are the urgency to respond to conditions of extreme poverty and the realisation that traditional support systems such as the family, community, and kinship are being eroded and are no longer able to cope with the heavy burden of care imposed on them. Recurring social crises in the form of *structural unemployment*, chronic conditions of poverty, and *epidemiological* crises as a result of diseases such as HIV and Aids, famine, and food insecurity highlight the significance of transforming traditional social welfare policy in response. The systematic and violent disruptions to black family life as a project of political and economic subjugation of the majority during colonial and postcolonial white rule in Africa, particularly in South Africa, continue to limit the life chances and well-being of the majority of people on the continent.

> **structural unemployment:** Structural unemployment means that people are unable to obtain employment because there are not enough jobs available due to lack of skills, declining economic growth, bad policies, and barriers to economic participation of people over a long period of time.
>
> **epidemiological:** Epidemiological means that people or regions suffer from an extensive and significant burden of disease such as HIV and Aids that affects large parts of the population in a country or region.

Political emancipation in countries in Africa and more recently in South Africa – which was only achieved just more than two decades ago – has not brought the social and economic freedoms that inspired struggles for national liberation. Poor, inadequate and, at times, corrupt systems of governance with ineffective policies combined with *neoliberal* economic globalisation influence social welfare policy development. Neoliberal economic globalisation creates conditions that change patterns of production (how goods and services are produced), employment opportunities, and development, and undermines the coping abilities and resilience of individuals, households, and societies. New technologies and information systems also create new risks and vulnerabilities for people who remain outside of mainstream economic and social processes because they are excluded and continue to be marginalised from the benefits of development.

## Politics, governance and social welfare policies in Africa

Policies and systems of social welfare are ways in which *states* respond to social crises and to the inability of individuals, families, and societies to cope with the changes and resulting hardship from such structural conditions. *Systems of social welfare* emerge as outcomes of political and economic decision-making processes (governance regimes) with the aim of providing social and economic support to individuals, families, households, and communities who experience multiple deprivations that undermine their social functioning. Social welfare policies and the systems that result from these policies change over time as political and economic regimes change in countries. Social welfare policy – as a professional field of study and a field of practice – some theorists argue (Gilbert and Specht, 1986), has many dimensions. It can be applied narrowly (in a piecemeal and residual manner that does not bring about fundamental transformative change) or social welfare policies can be transformative (when using normative approaches progressively and developmentally to achieve the human rights of citizens) and result in comprehensive change that improves the well-being of people. Most governments in Africa use a residual, incremental, and piecemeal approach to social welfare policies (Taylor, 2008) as social welfare and social development services are assumed to be the responsibility of families and communities, and that of economic markets rather than that of the state.

At times social service professionals[1] and policymakers work within the existing structures (including the family and economic structures) of society as if these structures are fully functioning and serve the interests of all in society. The structures and systems in many of our societies are not functioning, or function only for a select few, which result in a breakdown of family life with high levels of unemployment and poverty. This breakdown of social and economic structures contributes to and exacerbates poverty; unemployment; the abuse of women, children, and the elderly; and the abuse of people experiencing conditions such as mental illness, addictions, and crime, among many others. Systems of social welfare and the social welfare policies that arise in countries are usually introduced when primary institutions such as the family, religious institutions, educational institutions, economic, and political institutions are unable to meet the needs of members of their societies to function effectively. In most societies it is assumed that the family as an institution performs the function of socialisation and social integration of all its members. Although religious and educational institutions also enable the socialisation and social integration functions, it is the family that traditionally assumed this function as its primary role (Gilbert and Specht, 1986). Contemporary societies in Africa now recognise that social institutions such as families and capitalist economic and financial markets can fail, and when they fail, the social impacts for the poorest people are devastating.

Governments and non-governmental organisations respond to these conditions in many different ways. When institutions such as the family and educational systems are destroyed or undermined, the state and government make policy choices on how to intervene to ensure that socialisation and social integration into society take place. Family life and educational, religious, and political institutions in Africa had to conform to colonial and postcolonial government administrative pressures. In South Africa, black family life came under attack from one of the most repressive and dehumanising processes of governance characterised by the apartheid system. Institutions such as the family, traditional institutions of governance, and livelihood systems were wantonly destroyed or undermined to advance the hegemony of the white ruling class at the time. It was amidst the political and economic state project of exploitation, subjugation, and 'divide and rule' that social welfare as a system of policies, structures, and processes evolved in Africa.

**hegemony:** Hegemony means having either economic or political power that is used to dominate and rule people and economic processes in countries and regions.

Democratic and socially responsive governments acknowledge that social welfare policies and social protection measures not only improve conditions for the poorest and most vulnerable but can also act as a springboard for economic and social inclusion. Using a political economy framework, the chapter provides a critical analysis of how social welfare policy has changed over time in response to the political, economic, and social pressures within states and external to states. The pressures to modernise, to comply with international markets and a global trade regime through the World Trade Organisation (WTO) that privileges the industrial north, and to adhere to the prescriptions set by the International Monetary Fund (IMF) and the World Bank (WB) are enormous and can constrain governments' policy action. These institutions are considered global institutions of economic and trade governance, and complying with their rules leads to a competitive environment in which economic, social, and political choices are traded off against each other by governments in power during different periods.

The chapter also provides a critical overview of the paradigmatic shifts in social welfare policy over time and relates these shifts to changes in the ideological, political and economic thinking during different periods. A critical synopsis of the main features of social welfare policy is also provided, as well as the ways in which social welfare was used during various periods to provide care and support to people to enable them to overcome personal hardship and deprivation.

# 1.2 Conceptualising and defining social welfare policy, social policy, and transformative social welfare policy

This section defines concepts of social welfare, social policy, and transformative social welfare policy. It also provides a conceptual analysis of how these terms relate to one another and how they differ from one another. It discusses how the concept of transformative social welfare policy emerges and why this shift in understanding of social welfare policy provides a different lens through which we both understand conditions affecting people and how these conditions can be addressed to empower and protect people. The section further provides an analysis of the values and ideas that underpin government action in social welfare and why it is necessary to move from remedial to transformative interventions in the field of social welfare. Social welfare policy is defined and discussed in more detail below.

## 1.2.1 Social welfare policy

Social welfare policy is understood as responses to people's needs and the programme measures taken to address these needs. The aim of social welfare policy is usually to improve the well-being of people and enhance their ability to cope and function in society, despite extreme hardship, poverty, vulnerabilities, and risks throughout people's life cycles. Social welfare policies and legislation in most countries are approved and enacted by governments through parliamentary processes. They are directly influenced by the values and principles of the political regime in power and by the economic approach to development that governments adopt and promote. Social welfare policies and programmes are put into place when governments make decisions about whose needs should be addressed and the programmes and processes that should be established to provide for these needs. A significant aspect of social welfare policy includes making decisions about the resources that should be allocated to finance social welfare services, social welfare benefits and other forms of provision to address needs, issues, and social problems. The choices governments make about these dimensions[2] or domains of social welfare are part of the broader political and economic process. The type of values and ideologies that political regimes adopt influence both the social and economic policy choices they make. A number of liberation movements adopted socialist policies prior to gaining independence but very few governments retained such policies in the post-independence phase in part because of internal factors and international pressures to comply with prescriptions and regulations set by the international community.

The scope of social welfare policy in African countries that have a low revenue earning capacity, are highly indebted, have national budget deficits, and have extreme poverty (refer to Chapters 5 and 6) is usually limited to providing services and benefits within a residual approach (refer to Chapter 3). The services and benefits are thus minimal and means tested, and are responses to social crises and emergencies and not part of a comprehensive social welfare policy approach. South Africa, Mauritius, and Seychelles differ from many countries in Africa by providing more comprehensive social welfare services. Social welfare policy, for example, in South Africa, provides for social security (social assistance in the form of cash grants and social insurance); social services and in-kind benefits in the form of access to primary health care, education, and food; protection measures for children, youth, and adults; and trauma counselling and other forms of psychosocial support.

South Africa's Constitution (Act 108 of 1996) makes the provision of primary health care and education universal. This means that everyone is entitled to have access to health care and education. Section 27 of the Constitution also makes the provision of social security to those who are unable to provide for themselves an entitlement. In this way, South Africa ensures that some forms of social welfare (such as health, education, and social security) are available to provide for people's basic needs. Other social welfare services that focus on addressing the psychosocial needs of people are not universally available. Such social welfare service provision is directed at specific categories of people who may be exposed to various risks or may be vulnerable at different times during their life cycles.

Some examples of specific categories of people in all countries in Africa who may require social welfare services during their life cycle or when they are exposed to risks include:

- People who are vulnerable throughout the life cycle – from birth through the early and middle developmental stages of growth, and through aging.
- Children in need of care and protection because of violence and neglect.
- People with physical and mental disabilities – those who are differently abled.
- People with addictions such as substance use disorders.
- People living in poverty and destitution.
- Children and young people in trouble with the law.
- The chronically unemployed who experience social marginalisation.
- Women and people who experience violence and discrimination.
- Households and families experiencing trauma and disruptions.
- Refugees and migrants whose human rights are violated.

In summary, social welfare policy is government action taken to regulate the social provision of social services and benefits to address needs and improve social conditions affecting the well-being of all people. These services and benefits can be targeted at vulnerable and at-risk individuals and groups and can be limited in scope, or they can be universal, framed within a human rights approach, and available to all who need such services. Social welfare services that are limited and narrow in scope are usually only available in situations of emergency and offer temporary relief rather than pathways out of poverty towards sustainable human development. Such interventions provide temporary relief or amelioration of social conditions only to those who are unable to cope; this is understood as a residual approach to social welfare policy. A human rights and development-oriented approach (refer to Chapter 3) is one way through which governments as institutions provide social welfare services based on normative criteria (such as approved international standards of human rights and values) to ensure goods and services are available to all those who live in a country and who meet such criteria.

Take, for example, South Africa's approach to social welfare policy which is framed within the Constitution and the *White Paper for Social Welfare* of 1997 and differs from the residual and institutional approaches because it takes a normative and developmental approach (refer to Chapter 3). On the one hand, the approach is normative because it is based on standards and rights established through the values in the Constitution and in legislation. It is developmental, on the other hand, because government has to ensure that the social and economic rights enshrined in Chapter 2 of the Constitution are progressively realised within available resources. Social welfare needs are addressed comprehensively, and goods and services are available to those who need them as a right of citizenship, or residence when it comes to the rights of children.

Besides national constitutions, countries in Africa can also use the African Charter on Human and Peoples' Rights (ACHPR) of 1981 as an international human rights instrument to ensure the promotion and protection of people's human rights on the continent. States can use the African Charter on Human and Peoples' Rights as a guideline to align social welfare policies and legislation to respond to the human development needs of their citizens. The African Charter recognises people's economic, social, and cultural rights, and came into effect in October 1986. This was followed by the establishment of the African Commission on Human and Peoples' Rights whose role is to provide guidance on how the articles in the ACHPR are interpreted and to oversee its implementation by African states (African Union, 1981). The adoption of the ACHPR was in part a response to the imposition of *Economic Structural Adjustment Programmes* (ESAPs) in Africa that were accompanied by cutbacks in social expenditures and led to deepening poverty and social crises in many African countries. The ACHPR is an international human rights instrument which all 54 African Union (AU) member states ratified by 2016. When people's human rights and needs are violated and social welfare policies are not aligned to the ACHPR, social service professionals can use the channels of the African Commission on Human and Peoples' Rights to bring these violations to the attention of the relevant institutions and authorities.

The preceding subsection highlighted the context within which social welfare policy emerges in Africa and South Africa's approach to social welfare policy. It discussed the links between politics, economics, and governance and social welfare policies. The introduction of social welfare policies as a response to state and market failures was also discussed. It is in response to regional and global governance failures that we note the emergence of international human rights instruments to promote social welfare and development of people in Africa. The next subsection analyses the distinction between social welfare policy and social policy and defines social policy.

## 1.2.2 Social policy

Some policymakers and practitioners refer to social welfare policy and social policy as if they mean the same thing, and as if these terms can be used interchangeably. Social policy, however, is broader than social welfare policy because it goes beyond the provision of direct social welfare services and benefits to include other areas such as housing, defence and security, work, and income security. The aims and consequences of social policies are much broader and are directly influenced by social, political, economic, and environmental conditions in any society. As a discipline, social policy draws its intellectual and theoretical influences from social, political, and philosophical traditions. In its broadest sense, social policy can refer to aims and objectives of social action concerning needs as well as the structural patterns or arrangements through which needs are met in a society (Mishra, 1977).

Social policy includes government social policies and social welfare activities as well as other government-defined aspects related to human well-being that are provided by public funds allocated through the fiscus or national budgets of governments. Such provision and services can include social assistance, transport, housing, health care, education, public works, and social security (Gil, 1992). Social policy further differs from social welfare policy because of its broader scope – it can include government action, private sector arrangements, and non-governmental action. Social policies are reflected in laws, policies, and practices that provide guidelines on how to address needs and social conditions in societies. Some features of social policy that overlap with social welfare policy are indicated below:

- They provide courses of action for government and non-government sectors in meeting human need.
- They enable policy planning to respond to existing and future needs.
- They ensure the equitable distribution of goods, services, and benefits.
- Social policy enables the establishment, maintenance, and legal enactment of social services and benefits.
- They relate government and non-governmental action (including that of the private sector) within agreed constitutional mandates, policy frameworks, and institutional arrangements of countries and regions.

The next subsection explains why countries in Africa are moving towards a transformative social welfare policy approach, and the concept of transformative social welfare is analysed and defined.

## 1.2.3 Defining transformative social welfare policy in Africa

Countries in Africa are moving away from a Eurocentric approach to social welfare policy to one that is appropriate for postcolonial and developmental contexts. This rethinking of social policy and social welfare policy comes out of the recognition that there are distinct historical, political, social, economic, and cultural differences between Africa and Europe and America. Such rethinking of both social policy and social welfare has set the basis for a transformative perspective that is more appropriate to the context, relevant and applicable to the lived experiences of people in Africa, and responsive to the imperatives of protection and empowerment. Theorists in Africa (Mkandawire, 2001; Adesina, 2008) refer to transformative social policy being grounded in the norms of equality and social solidarity. According to these theorists, social welfare policy provisions in the form of services and benefits are transformative if they apply to all on a universal basis. This understanding of transformative social welfare policy fits with a normative and developmental commitment to meeting human needs as a right of citizenship. It also aligns with South Africa's Constitution (Act 108 of 1996) and with the African Charter on Human and Peoples' Rights (African Union, 1981).

Social welfare policy tends to be transformative when it serves critical functions in society that include production, protection, reproduction, redistribution, and social cohesion or nation-building. Transformative social welfare policy is therefore designed to ensure that all people living in a given country are able to participate in economic activity (production) irrespective of their race, gender, status, geographical location or disability. Reproductive functions of social welfare are transformative when care is provided to ensure that women are supported and empowered through antenatal and postnatal processes, as well as when the bodily integrity of women and children is protected from violence and abuse, and exploitation. Protecting the bodily integrity of girls, women, and boys requires care in the prevention of violence and abuse against them as well as ensuring that women have the freedom to make choices about their reproductive health and care. Social welfare policy is transformative when it enables the equitable redistribution of services, provisions and income to members of society who are the poorest, most vulnerable and at risk.

Ensuring that social welfare provision empowers those who have been historically excluded from the benefits of society, promotes a shift in power relations in society. It enables redress that allows for gender and race-based equity, and also addresses spatial differences arising from rural-urban bias and apartheid or discriminatory spatial planning. An important feature of transformative social welfare policy is the focus on both the care of human beings and the integration of members of society into inclusive and fair economic and political activities (Taylor, 2014).

The basis of transformative social welfare policy and practice is social justice and human rights. A human rights approach to social welfare policy in Africa links directly to addressing inequalities, discrimination, and multiple deprivations that people experience.

A summary of the features of transformative social welfare policy and how it differs from other types of policy is listed below.

---

**REFLECTION**  **FEATURES OF TRANSFORMATIVE SOCIAL WELFARE POLICY**

Transformative social welfare policy and practice in Africa:
- Recognises the psychosocial effects of colonial and postcolonial patterns of development and institutional forms of violence on people and makes adequate social service provision to mitigate such effects.
- Shifts social welfare interventions away from blaming the 'victim' or the 'exploited' for their circumstances and focuses on addressing the structures that cause deprivations through macro and micro policy and programme interventions that improve the quality of life of the poorest.
- Focuses on structural conditions that keep people trapped in poverty while also addressing vulnerabilities and risks people experience through the life cycle.
- Restores the dignity of individuals and communities through social welfare policy and social service practice that embeds constitutional and human rights and delivers on these.
- Defines the framework for professional social service practice within human rights practices and protocols.
- Ensures democratic participation of professionals and social service providers as well as social service users in policymaking processes that aim to address the needs and welfare of people.

---

An analysis of social welfare policy and how it differs from social policy is provided above. Importantly, the concept of transformative social welfare policy was analysed and a definition of transformative social welfare policy provided. In the next section we take a closer look at the political economy approach to understanding transformative social welfare policy.

# 1.3  The political economy of social welfare policy

The evolution of the social welfare system in any country cannot be divorced from other aspects of social, economic, political, cultural, and environmental life. A political economy approach to understanding social welfare in Africa, and especially in South Africa, highlights the many ways in which specific historical contexts and political, economic and social conditions can lead to agreements or social contracts that influence responses to people's social needs. A political economy approach to social welfare policy provides a better understanding of:
- why countries respond to social needs and conditions in either narrow or comprehensive ways;

- the forms of social welfare provision that are available to assist people (for example, social work services, health care, education, social cash grants, housing, food, etc.);
- the criteria used to determine how state social allocations will be made to meet the social needs and conditions of people;
- who benefits from social welfare and social services;
- the criteria according to which people in need receive benefits;
- the structure of the social welfare delivery system – whether social welfare is provided through government, through the private sector on the basis of fees, or through non-governmental organisations on a non-profit basis;
- the mode of financing social welfare and social work services – through government revenue earned from taxes, through fees paid by those who receive services, or through donations and grants; and
- how decisions are made about social welfare arrangements and who influences such decisions.

Find below an explanation of the meaning of the political economy of social welfare policy.

## Political economy approach

## WHAT IS A POLITICAL ECONOMY APPROACH TO SOCIAL WELFARE POLICY?

The term political economy usually refers to the study of relationships between individuals and society and between the state and markets (sometimes referred to as the private sector or business). In this chapter and book, we use a political economy framework to understand how countries introduce policies to influence both economic and social well-being of people. It involves looking back over time to understand the politics and economics that led to social welfare policies that influence the life chances of people. In summary, this approach to understanding social welfare policies in your country requires:

1. a historical view that looks at what has changed and what remains the same for people, and how these changes reflect in policies and programmes;
2. a review of how individuals, families and broader parts of society interact with the state and with business/the private sector to improve the quality of their lives; and
3. an explanation of how political power is used through the state and economic power is used through business or the private sector to implement policies and legislation that ensure people's well-being or, at times, restrict their development.

Unlike most countries in Africa, South Africa is not a typical example of a postcolonial, post-independent African country because of the form of racial politics and monopoly capitalism that continues to shape a skewed, exploitative and unequal pattern of development for black people. These patterns of development can be traced to the seventeenth century when the first Dutch settlers arrived in the country and began a process of subjugation of the indigenous Africans. At the time, the British also adopted a process of industrial imperialism to extract the country's resources, especially the mineral wealth that was discovered in the late nineteenth century (Marais, 1998). The British and Afrikaner settlers combined forces and interests during different political periods to consolidate power to control and exploit migrant black labour (Webster, 1978). A dual system of economic and social rights, which was exploitative and discriminated against African people, was spawned through early industrialisation and agricultural developments in South Africa, especially visible after the Second World War when the largely Afrikaner-led National Party came into power. White workers' economic and social rights were protected and enhanced, while black workers and their families in rural areas were exploited under the terms and conditions legitimated by apartheid.

Although an exceptional situation in South Africa began in the seventeenth century (Samir Amin cited in Marais, 1998: X), it was under successive colonial governments from the late nineteenth to the twentieth century that such 'exceptionalism' became evident in social welfare policy with whites benefitting from social welfare provisions and Africans being excluded from such benefits. Marais (1998: 29) notes that after the Second World War:

> '... [the] accumulation strategy established for whites an affluent welfare state. White workers were guaranteed access to jobs, experienced rising wages and were cushioned by a wide-ranging social security system.'

The state at the time also invested significant resources in education, health care, housing, recreational and sports infrastructure for whites. These policy interventions led to the rapid economic and social development of whites which could be understood as a significant and comprehensive programme of affirmative action according to some theorists (Mkandawire, 2010). This programme started the basis for South African 'exceptionalism' when it comes to welfare provision for whites in Africa (Seekings, 2002). In the end, these social welfare policy interventions resulted in the emergence of a strong white middle class with significant protections from the state. White workers lobbied for and were granted wage increases and improvements in working conditions through collective bargaining processes. The counterpoint to this historical development and accumulation of privilege for whites was that black people were systematically and violently repressed, dispossessed from their land, and impoverished. The terms under which black people worked, lived, and interacted were prescribed by a set of apartheid laws.

It was such discriminatory and wide-scale repression of black people that led to political, social, and economic resistance in South Africa. South Africa provides an example of how, during the twentieth century, social movement activism converged with national liberation struggles to achieve a just, non-racial, and equitable society to advance transformative social welfare policy within a human rights framework.

The following section provides an analysis of the development of social welfare policies in Africa and draws on South Africa to illustrate how politics and economics influence and shape social welfare policy and development outcomes for people.

# 1.4 Africa and social welfare policies

The development of social welfare policies in Africa links directly with the history of political, economic and social processes during periods of colonialism, postcolonialism, and more contemporary post-independence contexts. Although responding to people's needs predates colonialism (refer to Chapter 2), social welfare emerges more formally and is more visible in African countries from the colonial era to the present period. Policy discourses on social welfare crystallised in Africa and other countries during periods when the political legitimacy of states was challenged by popular uprisings for improvements in the quality of life, especially of previously disenfranchised people. At times, struggles for such improvements led to the establishment of social welfare policies and programmes. These social welfare policies and programmes were reinforced in the twenty-first century by regional policy processes within Southern Africa and the African Union (African Union, 2008). Social welfare policies, and more generally social policies, are outcomes of political processes through which a state or regime responds to people's demands to address conditions affecting them and their unmet social needs. A brief overview of some of the main turning points that led to the introduction of social welfare policies in Africa is provided below.

## 1.4.1 Social welfare policy in Africa's post-independence period of the 1960s and 1970s and beyond

In post-independent, postcolonial African states, especially in the Southern African region, social welfare policy was not high on the agenda until the late 1990s. Countries in Africa in recent modern history were colonised and occupied by the British, French, and Portuguese. Belgium and Germany were also involved in the colonisation project to a limited extent. After many struggles led by national liberation or freedom movements in countries that had been colonised, some gained independence from the colonial rulers and began to organise their own systems of governance. Most countries gained independence from colonial rule in Africa in the late 1950s and early 1960s (Young, 1994). Among those that gained independence in the 1960 period were Ghana, Tanzania, and Zambia. After successive wars in the 1970s, Mozambique, Zimbabwe, and Angola gained independence. Portugal conceded independence to Mozambique and Angola in the 1970s, but for Zimbabwe it was different. A white ruling minority government under Ian Smith 'unilaterally declared independence' (UDI) from Britain in 1965 and thereafter there were intense struggles for liberation. Zimbabwe gained political independence from white minority rule in 1980. Namibia, after a protracted struggle, gained political independence from South Africa in 1990. South Africa's struggles for freedom also differed because not only was the country colonised by Britain during various periods, but it was also occupied by a settler community that put into place a government that was responsible for heinous atrocities against the majority of black people. South Africa attained its independence after years of struggle as recently as 1994. This was through a negotiated settlement with the apartheid government.

Note that social welfare policies and practices in the form we know these today were virtually nonexistent during the precolonial and colonial periods.

During the 1960s and 1970s, post-independent African states placed emphasis on: developing infrastructure; agrarian (mainly agricultural) reform; extractive industries such as mining; the export of raw materials; transitioning from colonial rule to building national governments; and addressing the postcolonial aspirations of their citizens. Colonial powers retained links with countries in Africa through administrative and economic relationships. On the administrative side, many governments adopted a philanthropic or charitable approach to social welfare that was a hybrid of traditional kinship and communal systems as well as adaptations of religious and missionary approaches. Social development was strongly influenced by the political and economic drive to build self-reliance independent from control by colonial powers to replace former colonial systems with precolonial or new systems (Fanon, 1967).

The need to address the psychosocial effects of colonialism and to rebuild communities led to social welfare and community development programmes that included education and health care as part of these social welfare systems. Traditional or indigenous forms of kinship support systems (refer to Chapter 2) at individual, family and community levels in some countries were linked to religious and emerging state systems of social welfare and community development. These systems were incorporated into existing indigenous village and urban systems. They are called hybrid systems because they combined indigenous social welfare responses with missionary-based systems of social welfare as well as systems of community development introduced by colonial regimes.

Fanon's critique of decolonisation and the processes that evolved in Africa are explained in the box below.

---

**REFLECTION**     **FANON'S CRITIQUE OF POSTCOLONIALISM IN AFRICAN STATES**

Frantz Fanon's writing on decolonisation in Africa in the 1960s says that:

> '*At whatever level we study it ... decolonisation is quite simply the replacing of a certain 'species' of men by another 'species' of men. Without any period of transition, there is a total, complete and absolute substitution*' (Fanon, 1967: 27).

The importance of a transition period is that it enables the colonised to determine their own programme of change from one order to a new order and, as part of this programme, to put into place checks and balances to prevent the abuse of political and economic power and prevent the 'absolute substitution' of one oppressive regime with another. He cautions that such substitution can replace the old colonial order of political and economic power and privilege with a new order that entrenches privilege for itself and betrays the national liberation mission of the restoration of nationhood and welfare of the people. The relevance of Fanon's analysis for social welfare policy is the importance he places on the need for postcolonial states to ensure their programmes include at the very least the minimum demands of the colonised and achieve these demands by changing the whole social structure from the bottom up.

Frantz Fanon was a psychiatrist, writer and freedom fighter

---

In South Africa, an example of such a comprehensive programme referred to by Fanon above is the Reconstruction and Development Programme (RDP) that was put together by the national liberation movement in consultation with progressive, democratic alliance partners prior to 1994. The RDP was approved as the National Programme during the first democratic South African Parliament (RSA – RDP, 1994). This comprehensive programme called for a complete transformation of the social, economic, and political systems and institutions in South Africa. It included a comprehensive overhaul of the social welfare and social security system to ensure that the needs of those who were experiencing multiple deprivations and exclusions would be prioritised. The period from the 1980s is dealt with next.

## 1.4.2 The period of structural adjustment of the 1980s and declines in social welfare

During the 1980s, the failure of effective decolonisation became apparent when governments in Africa were unable to assert economic independence from former colonial powers. The prices of African exports in the form of oil, minerals and other products fell and governments had to borrow money from the World Bank (WB) and the International Monetary Fund

(IMF)[3] – at times referred to as International Financial Institutions (IFIs) – to implement their programmes. As a result of the pressures from these financial institutions to make the interest payments on the loans according to the deadlines set, postcolonial governments usually cut back on social spending and other vital services. Government spending on health care, education, social services, and basic infrastructure were reduced and there were declines in all human development indicators with hunger, famines and conflict rising. This period was characterised and affected by:

- The consequences of the fuel crisis and higher prices of goods and services.
- Increasing debt and crises of poverty and lack of human development.
- Greater influence of IFIs as advisors from these agencies provided indebted countries with macroeconomic policy prescriptions to ensure that governments could pay the debt. These prescriptions became known as Structural Adjustment Programmes (SAPs).
- Social policy and social welfare response were couched in a basic needs approach to poverty, with free education and health care being replaced with fee-paying schools and health care services.
- At the same time the demands from people to expand education and health care interventions to reach the poorest members were increasing.
- Increasing and deepening poverty as well as declines in health and education, and hunger and famines, led to a call by some progressive organisations to address 14
- the human impacts of SAPs and a phrase often articulated at policy discussions was the 'human face of structural adjustment'.

In the 1980s, South Africa was not affected by SAPs since it was isolated by the international community for its apartheid policies and there were no approved engagements – including borrowing from these institutions – with the International Monetary Fund or the World Bank at the time. The mobilisation of anti-apartheid international solidarity movements against the repressive South African regime forced some governments to impose international financial sanctions against South Africa. The apartheid government could not borrow from the IFIs and instead borrowed from national banks to fund its activities. The pre-1994 South African government had a huge internal debt that the post-1994 government had to pay back to the national banking sector (UNDP – South African Human Development Report, 2000). Paying back this debt meant that there was limited revenue to fund social welfare programmes and other priorities in the RDP. Post 1994, South Africa also saw the impacts of the period of neoliberalism and globalisation, which are discussed below.

## 1.4.3 The 1990s and 2000s: Neoliberal globalisation pushing against universal social welfare policy in Africa

As mentioned above, the 1980s were characterised by poverty, declines in education and health care, and crumbling social infrastructure (e.g. schools, clinics, roads, water, and sanitation) which led to a refocus on meeting basic needs of people in African countries. Furthermore, the economic interdependence of African countries on Europe and the United States of America (USA) through the IFIs and export of raw materials meant that any instability in Europe or the USA affected Africa. However, as wages and demands of workers for better working conditions increased in industrial countries (i.e. Europe and the USA) the profits decreased and led industrial countries to seek cheap labour to manufacture their goods. Britain and the USA took a policy approach to allow the free movement of finance capital across countries and to deregulate business activities so that manufacturing and other industries could be moved out. This led to the emergence of transnational corporations that could move their money and establish manufacturing industries in free trade zones in China, India, and other countries where labour costs were cheap and tax on such foreign companies were extremely favourable. This type of trade and movement of finance across national borders – without government regulations to ensure the safety and welfare needs of workers and the protection of public goods such as education, social welfare services, and health care – is referred to as *neoliberal globalisation*.

During the 1990s and 2000s, as part of the neoliberal process, countries across the world were influenced to privatise social services and other essential government-subsidised services such as transport, electricity, water, and roads. As more workers were pushed into casual and informal labour the ability of households to pay for health care and education dropped and the coping mechanisms of poor and vulnerable households were eroded. Social welfare care and services were increasingly left to the non-governmental sector and religious organisations. Some governments developed partnerships with the non-governmental sector to assist in the care of people who experienced extreme hardship and who were at risk.

Some of the features of this period that influenced social welfare policy and conditions of poverty, social fragmentation, and deprivations are highlighted below:

- Neoliberalism promoted the expansion of markets in the provision of core public goods and services such as water, sanitation services, postal services, health care, education, and social welfare, effectively privatising some of these services.
- More people who could not afford to pay for services were excluded from the benefits of post-independent developments.
- The promotion of the privatisation of services and growth in provision of private fee-paying services led to cutbacks in the provision of state-run social services.
- Imports of cheap products undermined the manufacturing sector and national economic development processes.
- Low levels of technical skill and employability of African workers in high technological industries led to higher levels of unemployment and increasing poverty.
- Social protection measures in the form of income support for poor and vulnerable children, aging individuals, and people with disabilities as well as households increasingly became governments' response to failures of markets to provide work and security.

Many governments in Africa adopted a neoliberal economic agenda to comply with international prescriptions so that they could be seen as good performers within the international community. They opened up their local markets for the import of cheap goods and services produced by transnational corporations and lowered barriers to imports and tariffs (charges for imports). Because transnational corporations produced goods and products in countries in which there was a supply of surplus workers (such as China and some South Asian countries) they paid low wages and produced these goods more cheaply, and as a result the prices of these goods were much lower than it would have been if it were produced in Africa. Consequently, manufacturing in Africa declined, especially in countries like South Africa. As manufacturing declined, unemployment increased and more workers were pushed into casual and informal work. This process of deindustrialisation in African countries continually leads to a breakdown between formal employment and access to work-based social security in these countries.

South Africa, for example, was significantly affected by the uncritical adoption of a neoliberal agenda that was espoused by dominant powers such as Britain and the United States of America, through the IMF and the World Bank, during the 1990s.

As part of its transformation, South Africa adopted the Reconstruction and Development Programme (RDP) which was an outcome of agreements with all progressive social partners and provided a comprehensive framework to address the historic legacy of apartheid and its effects on the majority (more details on the RDP are provided later in this chapter). At the time, the South African government placed emphasis on strong state intervention through a mixed-economy approach supported by basic welfare rights for all during the period 1994 to 1996. The post-liberation agenda for the social and economic transformation of South Africa expressed in the RDP was crafted before neoliberalism gained traction. South Africa unfortunately did not escape the negative effects of the wave of neoliberalism that pressured African governments to change their social and economic policies in accordance with the international trend of free market capitalism, less state intervention, and cutbacks in social welfare expenditure. The South African response was to shift the policy agenda from one that focused on economic development with the promotion of redress and equity to one that focused on economic growth within an unrestricted free market.

This shift in policy, as a response to neoliberalism, emerged during the period from 1996 to 2002 as the Growth, Employment and Redistribution (GEAR) strategy (Department of Finance, 1996). GEAR shifted the emphasis of the RDP by focusing on creating an environment that would promote investment and employment. Alongside this, there were reductions in corporate taxes, removal of barriers to trade between countries, relaxation of exchange controls to promote the movement of finance capital across borders, and incentives for business investors. The main feature of neoliberalism evident in GEAR (Department of Finance, 1996) was a withdrawal of the state from the economy and from social welfare through fiscal austerity. This led to significant downsizing of government institutions and the contraction or cutting back of state expenditure for social services (e.g. health, education, housing, social security, and social welfare).

Besides South Africa's GEAR strategy, other countries in Africa went through similar shifts in their macroeconomic policies and plans. They introduced a set of prescriptions that was consistent with a neoliberal economic development approach. At a time when most countries were attempting to reduce pervasive poverty and inequalities, they found themselves cutting back and decreasing government expenditure on critical areas of social service provision. A more detailed overview of the historical, political, and economic factors that shaped South Africa's social welfare policy formation follows in the next section to illustrate how political and economic changes influence social policy and provisions.

## 1.5 The political economy of South Africa's social welfare policy

South Africa's struggles for freedom happened in a different context. Not only was the country colonised by Britain during various periods but it was also occupied by a settler community that put into place a government responsible for the worst atrocities against the majority of black people. An important focus is the shifts in policy, in approach, and in issues of distribution and redistribution of social services against both historical and contemporary struggles for social welfare rights in South Africa.

South Africa's social welfare policy and social provisions were strongly influenced by political and economic processes during particular periods of the country's history as well as by events that took place on the African continent. As mentioned previously, it was among the last of the countries in the southern part of the continent to gain its independence from white minority rule by the end of the twentieth century (1994). This section elaborates on some of the main historical influences of colonialism, and independence and post-independence processes in shaping pre- and post-1994 social welfare policies. It looks at some of the main characteristics of social welfare policy and how economic and political developments shape these characteristics.

## 1.5.1  Historical characteristics of South Africa's political economy

The intersections among the historical experiences of people, the economy, and politics in South Africa predate the discovery of gold and the beginning of the gold mining industry in the 1800s. Gold mining in the early days relied on a ready supply of cheap black African migrant labour. The emergence of social policy interventions by employers, as enacted through the government at the time, can be traced to early stages of capitalist industrial development in South Africa, especially through the mining sector. This is not unusual as the links between social security as a policy intervention and work emerged internationally alongside the beginnings of the modern capitalist industrial mode of development. Historically, South Africa's social welfare policy arose in the context of struggles waged by white workers and it was the influence particularly of white mineworkers that prompted both employers and the government at the time to introduce social policies to protect the rights of white workers. At the same time, black miners and their families experienced terrible conditions but were restricted through law and the state security apparatus from protesting, organising, and collective bargaining for improvements in their welfare and wages.

Already by 1886 issues affecting black mineworkers could be linked to three main factors which illustrate the convergence of white postcolonial ideological and economic interests through state-led processes in the nineteenth and early twentieth century. These factors were the institutionalisation of the migrant labour system, the promotion of the objective of ensuring a cheap black labour supply to minimise wage costs of white monopoly capital, and the monopoly of the recruitment and later the control of black mineworkers, through government restrictions (laws), on the formation and membership of black worker organisations (Webster, 1978: 9).

Early industrialisation in South Africa was based on the use of largely male migrant labour, and the movement of black workers from their homes in villages was controlled by the pass law system. Laws introduced by the National Party government after the Second World War legitimated an explicitly racist and brutal ideology designed to extract the economic resources of the country under exploitative and dehumanising conditions for black workers. These laws also introduced a gender bias and differentiation in black worker relations, and ensured that traditional systems of support were eroded and the family as a core institution of socialisation was broken by the removal of black men to the mines and farms (Bernstein, 1985).

There were two measures through which the apartheid South African state at the time achieved the growth of the mining industry and the control and containment of black mineworkers. These two measures reflected the politics of economic and racial dominance and took the form of, firstly, using the state's legislative power to support the economic objectives of the mine owners, and, secondly, establishing monopolistic recruiting organisations solely to recruit black mineworkers from within South Africa and the neighbouring areas or protectorates (Webster, 1978: 10). The social welfare consequences of these measures led to the breakdown of family and kinship support systems in villages. At the same time, it led to black workers either living in hostels or in shack settlements near the mines. Black mineworkers were not allowed to bring their families with them because they were considered migrants and not given residential status.

Among the draconian policy or legislative measures taken by the apartheid state in the early days of the gold mining industry was the introduction of the 'pass law'. This law stated that 'the Natives on the Rand must be in the employ of a master and wear a metal plate or badge on the arm in token of such employ' (Bransky, 1974: 10). A key organisation representing employers' interests at the time was the Chamber of Mines. Pressure was exerted by the Chamber of Mines to prevent black mineworkers from leaving the mines before their twelve-month contract was completed. Important pieces of legislation that served to push black people to seek work on the mines included The Glen Grey Act 25 of 1894 which imposed a labour tax on black workers. This was followed, a few years later, by the Natives Land Act 27 of 1913 which limited African land ownership to 13% of the country's total land area, and led to Africans living in reserves. The erosion of mutual aid and support through families and communities was accelerated through race and gender, and economically discriminatory social policies.

Women in South Africa marched to the Union Buildings to protest against the pass laws on 9 August 1956

Besides the pass laws, 'the most devastating aspect of apartheid has been the programme of mass removals, the uprooting and relocation of people through forced evictions in order to achieve the territorial segregation of the population according to the polices of apartheid' (Bernstein, 1985: 9). Many other pieces of legislation were put into place to control, subjugate, and discipline the African majority, especially the working class, and to protect and advance the well-being of whites. Since the early days of South Africa's economic development in the mining, agricultural and industrial sectors, white and black workers engaged in strikes for better working and living conditions. The difference was that while white workers achieved significant advances in their living conditions because of strike action, black workers were brutally repressed by government action (Terreblanche and Nattrass, 1990). The subsection below focuses on turning points in South Africa's economic and political history and relates these to the emergence of a dual system of social policies based on racial differentiation.

## 1.5.2 Some turning points in the political economy of social welfare

Historical turning points that shaped social welfare policy resulted from a convergence of the political and economic interests of the English and Afrikaner settlers, and white and black mineworkers on the gold mines. These turning points include briefly the historical influence of mining and trade union organisation on early social welfare policy development, and the struggles of the disenfranchised black majority for human well-being and fundamental freedoms. Factors that contributed to the development of early and contemporary social welfare policy emerged in more prominent forms during colonial, early industrial and post-democratic processes. Inferior education, influx control, the Group Areas Act 41 of 1950, and a range of other policy instruments adopted and enforced by the apartheid government undermined the ability of black people to earn decent wages and hampered their social development.

It was after the Second World War that the agricultural and mining sectors in South Africa experienced shortfalls in low-waged labour. The combination of coercive labour legislation, restrictions on movements, and inferior education was used to channel African labour (mostly unskilled) where it was needed most – into mining, domestic labour, and onto farms. In contrast, there was massive investment in public education for white children in the 1950s and 1960s which resulted in white workers securing skills that enabled them, in the 1970s and 1980s, to command high incomes in free labour markets. This apartheid strategy largely removed white workers' dependence on direct state interventions (such as job reservation through the 'colour bar'). Apartheid social welfare for whites was based on a combination of income (cash) measures through job reservation and social grants for single mothers and pensions for the elderly as well as benefits through education, health, transport, and housing. This could be characterised as a state-driven or institutional approach to social welfare policy for whites. Some social grants, such as the old age pension, were extended and proved to be an important lifeline for poor African individuals from the 1970s onward. However, because of the structural conditions including inequities in education, housing, health care and incomes, by the end of apartheid, the gap between the incomes of the employed and the unemployed remained a significant driver of inequality.

Social work was experienced by the majority of South Africans (categorised as black African)[4] as a handmaiden of the apartheid state. Social welfare and social work systems were fragmented along racial lines, and were characterised by inequities. For the black majority social welfare services were of a low standard or entirely nonexistent. Discriminatory practices and inequities existed in all social services including social work, education, health, access to basic services such as water and sanitation, housing, and access to income support and social security. The majority of people experienced the brutality of the state in many ways. The denial of citizenship to black[5] people alongside the denial of human rights was part of a deliberate apartheid political and economic strategy designed to exclude black people from access to resources and at the same time to exploit their labour. Social workers were viewed with suspicion because they were identified as professionals who carried out state regulations designed to control and discipline black people using apartheid laws and regulations. After apartheid was abolished, the new democratic government adopted the Reconstruction and Development Programme, which is discussed next.

## 1.5.3 Transforming social welfare policy: The Reconstruction and Development Programme (RDP)

Between 1992 and 1994, a wide range of progressive organisations – African National Congress (ANC), Congress of South African Trade Unions (Cosatu), South African National Civic Organisation (Sanco), and women's and environmental movements, among others – contributed to policy discussions and processes for a transformative vision and national development programme after 1994.[6] These contributions were included in a policy document and book called the *Reconstruction and Development Programme (RDP)* (ANC, 1994a) and the *National Social Welfare and Development Plan* (ANC, 1994b). These two documents were the national policy frameworks that contributed to significant changes in how social welfare was understood and translated into policy, and they were aimed at addressing the deprivations, vulnerabilities, and risks that undermined people's human development.

The RDP is explicit about the causes of social and material conditions that kept people trapped in poverty and states that it aims to transform existing social welfare policies, programmes and delivery systems to ensure basic welfare rights for all South Africans, prioritising those who were historically disadvantaged. It goes further in redefining social welfare and indicating that the goals of a *developmental social welfare* programme are to ensure the attainment of basic social welfare rights for all South Africans – irrespective of race, colour, religion, gender, and physical disability – through the establishment of a democratically determined, just and effective social delivery system (ANC, 1994a: 52).

Other transformative elements in the RDP include redressing past imbalances through a deliberate process of affirmative action in respect of those who were historically disadvantaged, especially women, children, youth, the disabled, and people in rural communities and informal settlements. It includes an emphasis on ensuring that individuals, families, and communities are enabled to participate in decision-making processes on the range of needs and problems to be addressed through local, provincial and national initiatives.

The section in the RDP on social welfare and social security reflects the contents of the National Social Welfare and Development Plan (ANC, 1994b). This document was also an outcome of research and consultative processes conducted with a range of progressive social formations and included women's organisations, progressive social workers, youth and civic movements, and a range of trade unions. Arising from these processes, the National Social Welfare and Development Plan (ANC, 1994b) was developed and presented at the ANC's Policy Conference. It helped to clarify the role of social welfare, social security, and social work in a democratic state. The plan included the values and principles that would inform future social service provision and the approach that should be taken to restructuring and transforming the apartheid welfare system.

The aims of the National Social Welfare and Development Plan were to ensure that, within a future democratic society, a social welfare system was developed that would be based on values and principles such as '*equity, social justice and the protection of human rights and fundamental freedoms*' of all South Africans (Taylor, 1994: ii cited in ANC, 1994b). The values and principles adopted by the democratic government which influenced changes in social welfare policy were made explicit in the first State of the Nation Address by the late President Nelson Mandela when he said:

> *'My Government's commitment to create a people-centred society of liberty binds us to the pursuit of the goals of the freedom from want, freedom from hunger, freedom from deprivation, freedom from ignorance, freedom from*

*suppression and freedom from fear. These freedoms are fundamental to the guarantee of human dignity. They will therefore constitute part of the centrepiece of what this government will seek to achieve, the focal point on which our attention will be continuously focused'* (Nelson Mandela, State of the Nation Address, Parliament, 1994: 10).

It was the National Social Welfare and Development Plan that articulated a transformative vision for social welfare policy that (a) would be developmental and (b) would act as a redistributive means to empower and include the majority of people into social and economic processes and institutions. This definition states that:

> *'Social welfare within a developmental approach is understood to be a comprehensive, integrated system of social services and benefits acting as a redistribution mechanism to bring about a progressive change in the social, economic, political, cultural and physical conditions of people, especially the poorest'* (ANC, 1994b: 6).

This definition of social welfare after 1994 shifts the emphasis from social welfare seen as a charitable response to one that is development oriented. The emphasis on redistribution also implies a shift from the former system of paternalistic and discriminatory processes towards a system that is located within a human rights-based approach. Developmental social welfare focuses on linking and changing the social and economic conditions to enable people to build their capabilities to lead lives that free them from poverty and deprivations. Significantly, developmental social welfare framed within a transformative and human rights agenda does not blame poor people for their poverty but promotes basic social welfare rights for all and prioritises the needs of those who are the poorest and most marginalised. A developmental approach also acknowledges the role of the state in ensuring the progressive realisation of people's rights to social services and benefits.

Developmental social welfare is (a) normative because it sets minimum standards and norms according to which people's basic needs are addressed and (b) developmental because it recognises that the process of realising the rights and entitlements of people will be attained through a programme of phased interventions in accordance with available resources. A normative approach to social welfare policy thus shares similar features with a transformative and developmental approach (refer to Chapter 3 for more details on the different approaches to social welfare policy).

The subsection that follows foregrounds transformative social welfare policy within a developmental approach and within the constitutional provisions contained in the Bill of Rights, Chapter 2 of South Africa's Constitution of 1996. It also looks at the alignment of transformative social welfare policy with and the issues raised in the most recent macro policy and planning framework – i.e. the National Development Plan (NDP) which was produced by the National Planning Commission in 2011 (NPC, 2011).

## 1.5.4 Transforming social welfare policy to align with the Constitution and the National Development Plan

The founding provisions of the Constitution of the Republic of South Africa (Act 108 of 1996) focus specifically on the importance of values of human dignity, the achievement of equality, and the advancement of human rights and freedoms as well as non-racialism and non-sexism.

The supremacy of the Constitution is explicit and all laws or conduct inconsistent or not aligned with the Constitution are invalid. In Chapter 2 of the Constitution, the Bill of Rights, section 7 (2) identifies the role of the state and explains that 'the state must respect, protect, promote and fulfil the rights in the Bill of Rights'. It reflects the intent for the state to play a strong role in protecting and promoting the rights of citizens. Such a role does not place limitations on what the state should and should not do. Nor does it leave the responsibility for the delivery of social and economic development services solely to the non-profit or business sectors. The case for change from a race-based, discriminatory, narrow and fragmented system of social welfare services to one which is comprehensive is thus supported by the South African Constitution. The state has the responsibility of ensuring access to social and economic rights, and these rights are understood as the measures that will be progressively realised in the context of extreme hardship and deprivations of the majority, and increasing levels of social inequality.

Social and economic rights in South Africa are justiciable[7] and have the same status as civil and political rights. Importantly, the South African Constitution mandates the right of access to health care, food, water, and social security in Chapter 2, the Bill of Rights. Specifically, section 27(1)(c) states that everyone has the right of access to social security, including, if they are unable to support themselves and their dependents, 'appropriate social assistance'. Subsection 27(2) states that:

> *'The state must take reasonable legislative and other measures, within its available resources, to achieve the progressive realisation of each of these rights'* (RSA, 1996: 13).

The progressive realisation of socioeconomic rights contained in the Constitution distinguishes South Africa as a developmental state. The notion of 'developmental' is one that reflects the aim of systematically advancing a rights agenda over time with a predetermined plan that gives programmatic effect to the realisation of human rights. While the Constitution provides support for social and economic rights, a political mandate also exists for the realisation of social rights. In 1994, the ANC campaigned for political power under an election manifesto that included 'welfare rights for all'. In addition, the RDP policy framework of the tripartite alliance,[8] launched that same year (ANC, 1994b: 52), identified a main goal of a developmental social welfare programme as the attainment of a democratically determined just and effective social delivery system. Furthermore, South Africa became a signatory to the Universal Declaration of Human Rights (1948) and is also obliged to ensure access to social and economic rights for its citizens. The transformation of social welfare policy thus has a clearly defined historical base, a political mandate adopted through democratic processes and social movements for change, and the constitutional and normative policy imperatives to develop a social and economic development system that is responsive to peoples' needs and grounded in human rights.

The values and principles of transformative social welfare policy and an inclusive social delivery system include principles of equality, equity, access, user involvement, empowerment, and public accountability (RDP, 1994: 52). To address the challenges of poverty and inequality, the democratic government adopted an integrated developmental vision of social development. The aim is to promote human development, economic inclusion, and social stability. South Africa's *White Paper for Social Welfare* (1997) incorporated the approach and definition of social welfare as stated in the ANC's National Social Welfare and Development Plan (ANC, 1994b: 6) and states that:

*'... social welfare is understood as a comprehensive, integrated system of social services and benefits acting as a redistribution mechanism to bring about progressive change in the social, economic, political, cultural and physical conditions of people, especially the poorest.'*

This definition of social welfare has two central components: a recognition of structural inequalities and the need for equitable redistribution of social welfare benefits and services; and the prioritisation of the needs of those most deprived.

The next subsection focuses on more recent national policy and planning processes in South Africa to illustrate how some countries in Africa engage in national development processes that include a focus on both social and economic development. In the first part of the chapter the significance of a political economy approach to transformative social welfare was analysed as critical to reversing and redressing the inequities of the politics and economics of apartheid. The section below explains how South Africa, through its first National Development Plan (NPD), links economic and social development to eliminate poverty and reduce inequalities to ensure that the well-being of its citizens is protected, promoted through a developmental process, and ultimately leads to social transformation.

## 1.5.5 South Africa's National Development Plan and transformative social welfare policy

A number of initiatives were developed since the RDP and GEAR to provide a development path that would guide the country towards economic growth and employment creation. However, unlike these initiatives that were driven by technical processes within government South Africa's first National Development Plan (NPC, 2011) was produced through a consultative process and written by the National Planning Commission (NPC, an independent Commission of experts). The National Development Plan provides a vision for the future of the country and explicitly states that the objectives of the plan are the elimination of poverty and the reduction of inequality by:

- Uniting South Africans of all races and classes around a common programme to eliminate poverty and reduce inequality.
- Encouraging citizens to be active in their own development, in strengthening democracy, and in holding their government accountable.
- Raising economic growth, promoting exports and making the economy more labour absorbing.
- Focusing on key capabilities of both people and the country.
- Building capabilities through the development of skills/education, infrastructure, social security and welfare, strong institutions, and partnerships both within the country and with key international partners.
- Building a capable and developmental state.
- Encouraging strong leadership throughout society to work together to solve problems (NPC, 2011: 1–27).

Using a capability approach (Sen, 1999), the NDP sets a number of priorities to work towards eliminating poverty and reducing inequalities that in part have their roots in the politics and economics of the country's past and the deliberate underdevelopment and marginalisation of the majority of black citizens. Chapters nine, ten and eleven of the NDP focus on education, health, and social protection. While all the chapters in the NDP are interlinked, these three chapters prioritise the development of the capabilities and social protection of especially people living in poverty who are denied access to their constitutional rights. Chapter eleven, under the theme of social protection, includes social security benefits and social welfare services as part of a range of social provisions for all those who live in South Africa. Social security benefits include (a) social assistance in the form of grants from the state for people who are living in poverty, and (b) social insurance in the form of contributions made by workers, usually in formal employment, for health care, retirement, death, and other emergencies. Social welfare services include services to a range of people through their life cycles who are experiencing difficult conditions that expose them to risk and make them vulnerable (refer to Chapter 4 in this book).

South Africa, in common with other countries in Africa, decided to frame its social assistance and social welfare services as a set of measures that broadly contributes to the social development of people. The NDP (NPC, 2011) recognises social development as the ultimate goal that seeks to integrate social and economic development processes through which people are able to enhance their capabilities and lead lives that they value with dignity and as full citizens. Pathways to achieve social development by 2030 include social protection (social assistance and developmental welfare services) and social insurance through comprehensive social security. The NDP in Chapter eleven provides a set of priority actions within a social protection framework that the country needs to implement to ensure that people who are living in poverty – and who are at risk and vulnerable – are able to meet their basic human needs (NPC, 2011).

Social Protection is one of the key priorities identified in the NDP and is central in ensuring the links between social and economic policy goals. Implementation of Chapter eleven of the NDP links with objectives in other chapters that also address elements of social protection, including the economy and employment, education, health, and infrastructure, among others, as all of these contribute to social protection. Taking a transformative approach to social welfare policy that includes protective and developmental measures, the NDP (NPC, 2011) indicates that by 2030 South Africa must achieve a defined social protection floor with social welfare as an explicit element, and social assistance must be provided for households that have not achieved the basic standard of living.

**social protection:** Social protection ensures inclusive social development by ensuring that protective, preventive, transformative, and generative measures are in place for human well-being across all sectors of society.

**mixed economy of social welfare:** A combination of services provided by the state, usually to all those who need such services, and by the market, for those who can afford to pay for their services, is referred to as a mixed economy of social welfare provision.

A combination of public and private services will be needed to attain a vision of universal and inclusive systems of social protection with an agreed social floor being the central platform.

The goal of establishing a social protection floor is to create a caring nation that has a defined social minimum or social floor with a prescribed standard of living below which no one should fall, whether they can pay for services or not. The social protection system for 2030 should include developmental social welfare services and social security and must have a defined social floor in order to assist households that have not achieved the basic standard of living. It should be responsive to the needs, realities, and livelihood conditions of those who the system is intended to benefit. Furthermore, the social protection floor must be inclusive and address the needs of all. It must reinforce the principle of building and enhancing the capabilities of individuals, households, and communities towards self-reliance and sustainability. To achieve a social protection floor, the following principles are important:

- Redistribution – allocating services and benefits to those who need them and who were historically denied access to services under apartheid.
- Subsidiarity – the state and employers should provide subsidies for low-income and poor people to access services such as transport, health care, and pensions on retirement.
- Social solidarity – transforming and unifying the country requires all those who live in it to agree on a common vision and especially on how to achieve the vision with everyone contributing to such a vision.

## 1.5.6 How does the National Development Plan and the White Paper for Social Welfare Policy of 1997 link?

The goals of the White Paper for Social Welfare Policy (1997) include a programme of developmental social welfare services to address the needs of people who experience psychosocial problems and conditions, and need social grants and social security to address income poverty and a range of other aspects related to vulnerabilities experienced by them through their life cycles. These are also the aspects that the NDP identifies as critical in eliminating poverty. However, the NDP's diagnosis is that developmental social welfare services lag behind other measures implemented by government to address the social needs and conditions of the poorest people. The NDP also highlights differences in the distribution and quality of social development services available to those who need them (including women, children, youth in trouble with the law, people with disabilities, and the elderly).

Implementation of NDP priorities (NPC, 2011) and the goals of the White Paper for Social Welfare Policy (1997) have many aspects that are common but the pathways to achieving social development as envisaged by the NDP are comprehensive. These pathways include the integration of interventions at household level with interventions at macro policy level to ensure the political economy of apartheid social welfare policy is transformed. Refer to Figure 1.1 below.

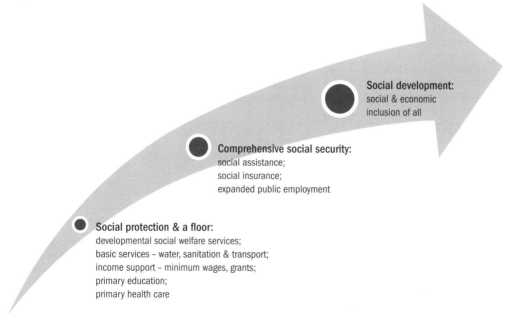

**Social development:**
social & economic
inclusion of all

**Comprehensive social security:**
social assistance;
social insurance;
expanded public employment

**Social protection & a floor:**
developmental social welfare services;
basic services – water, sanitation & transport;
income support – minimum wages, grants;
primary education;
primary health care

Figure 1.1 Pathways to social development and transformation

## 1.6 Working towards a transformative social welfare policy agenda

This section of the chapter provides a framework to enable social service professionals to work towards a transformative social welfare policy agenda in Africa and elsewhere using a political economy approach that applies human rights and social justice principles to achieve social development. It draws on South Africa's experiences as discussed in previous sections. Figure 1.2 illustrates how pre- and post-1994 processes have shaped the political economy of social welfare processes in South Africa. It identifies some of the historical processes, the social and economic contexts, the policy context, and the need for policy makers as well as professionals to engage in reflexive policy processes to transform unjust social welfare systems to achieve human rights for all.

South Africa's social work and social welfare system, with its historical basis in oppressive and discriminatory policies, required changes to enable it to contribute to social transformation of society within a rights' based framework. A social development perspective recognises that barriers to human well-being are not only economic but also social, political, military, and environmental. Within this perspective, the links among social and economic policy goals are understood as important for individual and societal well-being. Social welfare policy interventions that focus on human well-being, by ensuring structural barriers to human development are addressed through macro policy analysis and change, work within a social development paradigm. Addressing issues that affect individual welfare, household and community well-being, and social inequalities are part of the social development terrain within which social service professionals practice.

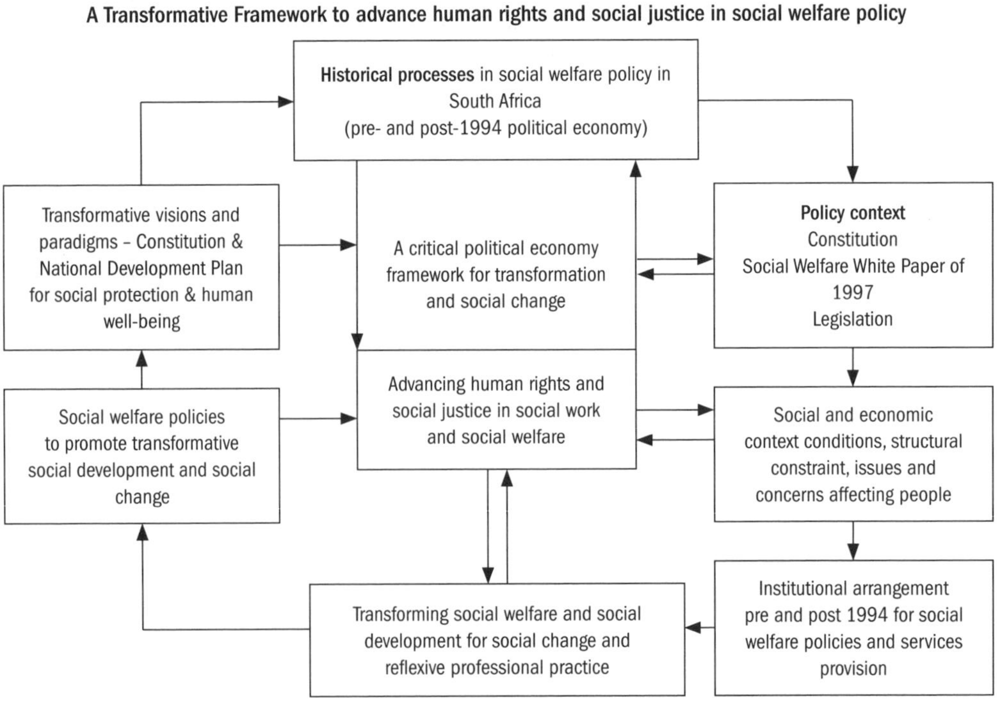

A Transformative Framework to advance human rights and social justice in social welfare policy

Source: Adapted from Taylor, 2014: 251 in Libal et al.

Figure 1.2  Transformative framework for social welfare policy

Transformative social welfare policy, as illustrated in Figure 1.2, embeds principles of human rights and social justice in its content and professional practice. Developmental social welfare includes the basic rights to welfare, shelter, food, health, employment, education, and those aspects that promote the physical, social, and emotional well-being of all in society. Just as our liberation path took its own course, South Africa's current development path differs from that of other countries in Africa. South Africa's Constitution provides a framework to make human rights understood, lived, and experienced by all its citizens. The entrenchment of social security rights in the Constitution requires the state to provide comprehensive social protection to all those who qualify for such protections. A distinguishing feature of developmental social welfare is that it is an outcome of democratic processes. It requires state and citizenship interaction in many ways. Participation from below involves decision-making that includes service beneficiaries and service providers who are in the frontline of struggles to achieve social and economic rights. Together these social and economic rights are mutually supportive and have a significant impact on the dignity of people and their quality of life – on their social welfare.

In the next section we take a closer look at the political economy of social welfare policy in South Africa.

## 1.7 Main features of the political economy of social welfare policy in South Africa

The connection between economic policies and social welfare policies can be found in the way income is distributed in a society. This distribution is influenced by states and governments through indirect and direct ways as indicated below:

- **Income distribution through indirect ways**: Some indirect ways are the regulation of labour market processes (this is the availability, supply, and regulation of and demand for labour –skilled, semi-skilled and unskilled – and the wages paid to workers) and formulation of economic policies that promote growth and development and lead to changes in the levels and patterns of income in any society.
- **Income distribution through direct ways**: Direct ways through which states and governments influence the distribution of income are taxation and the public or state provision of social services (such as public education, health care, food subsidies, transport subsidies, and housing programmes) as well as income support (such as old age pensions, child support grants, disability grants, and unemployment benefits). The state's revenue earning capacity and ability to provide for its citizens are determined by the level and types of taxes it has in place. The types of taxes that people pay include value added taxes (VAT) on goods, services and food, which everyone in a country has to pay, and personal income taxes, which are paid by all those who are usually in formal waged jobs. One's ability to contribute to personal income tax and to buy goods and services and pay VAT is directly affected by one's employment status, factors such as wages and working conditions in the labour market, and social welfare policies. The connections or relationships between work or labour and social welfare, sometimes referred to as the 'labour-welfare nexus', are breaking down as more people work in the informal sector or as casual labourers because of changes to manufacturing processes.

## 1.7.1 Inequities in social welfare provision in South Africa

As discussed in previous sections, before 1994, social welfare for whites was based on a combination of income (cash) measures through job reservation and other forms of assistance and in-kind benefits through education, health, and housing to name a few. The government invested extensively in public education for white children in the 1950s and 1960s which enabled white job seekers to acquire the necessary skills so that, by the 1970s and 1980s, they could secure high wages in free labour markets. A universal social welfare provision in the form of the social old age pension was provided for whites. This was a feature of a state-driven or institutional approach to social welfare for whites. By the 1980s, white workers were integrated into the economy in high-paying jobs and were not as dependent on direct state interventions (such as job reservation through the 'colour bar') for their social welfare. Poor African elderly received old age pensions from the 1970s and these were racially discriminatory in value, frequency, and access. Nevertheless, these benefits became an important lifeline for poor African families.

## 1.7.2 Inequities in social services in South Africa

Apartheid discriminated along racial lines with especially poor white people benefitting. Education, health, and housing benefits were biased towards whites and black South Africans were subjected to extensive labour-market discrimination and disadvantage.

Table 1.1 provides a summary of the main features of the pre- and post-1994 political economy of South Africa's social welfare policy. It includes some of the historical, political, economic, and social features and characteristics of a transforming social welfare policy and system, using South Africa as an example. In the left column the main features are identified and on the right these features are discussed in relation to the pre- and post-1994 regimes (regimes are used to describe the system of governance and rules that are in place). These main features can be identified and analysed in any country in Africa.

**Table 1.1 Transforming social welfare policy and services in South Africa**

| The political economy of transforming social welfare policy and services in South Africa | | |
|---|---|---|
| Main features | Pre 1994 | Post 1994 |
| Characteristics and adopted values | • Government led by National Party since 1948.<br>• Race-based and discriminatory provision with the state providing comprehensive institutional provision for whites and minimal welfare relief services for the black majority.<br>• Universal provision for whites.<br>• Lack of transparency in policymaking and lack of accountability in use of government revenue and resources. | • Constitution of 1996 promotes a human rights framework.<br>• The state has the duty to respect and uphold the dignity and rights of all.<br>• Non-racial, universal access to basic social welfare services.<br>• Social and economic rights are justiciable.<br>• Participation of citizens in policymaking promoted.<br>• Violation of rights taken to the Constitutional Court and other bodies. |

| The political economy of transforming social welfare policy and services in South Africa | | |
|---|---|---|
| Main features | Pre 1994 | Post 1994 |
| Concept of social welfare | • Social services to categories of people who are seen as weak and not able to cope; promotion of self-help for black majority, charity-based; the family, religious institutions and communities expected to provide help to those in need; people need to modify their behaviour and adjust to the systems and structures of the country – dealing with symptoms; psychosocial therapy focus. | • Transformative and developmental social welfare responsive to social economic and environmental concerns of all people.<br>• Dealing with underlying systems and structures that cause poverty, vulnerability as well as symptoms of social problems – development oriented.<br>• Empower and build capabilities of individuals, families and communities to change their circumstances. |
| Socioeconomic context | • Use of black migrant labour despite a labour surplus within South Africa.<br>• Unemployment.<br>• Race-based inequalities.<br>• Mass-based poverty and multiple deprivations due to divide and rule apartheid policies.<br>• Social and economic exclusions.<br>• Closed monopolistic economy.<br>• Internal debt crisis limits revenue for social spending. | • Unemployment and poverty.<br>• Intra-racial inequality.<br>• Mass-based income poverty.<br>• Deprivations in access to primary health, education and basic services being addressed.<br>• HIV/Aids.<br>• Open free market economy – with emphasis on promotion of small, medium and micro enterprises to democratise economy.<br>• Increased revenue. |
| Approach and funding | • Paternalistic, racist and patriarchal.<br>• Residual for the black majority and based on affirmative action, universal and institutional social provision for whites.<br>• Underpinned by a set of labour and welfare policies that were racially biased and premised on full employment.<br>• Based on assumption that existing institutions such as the family and economy are intact and effective in meeting people's needs<br>• State funding through tax system for whites and minimal state funding for blacks with charitable support. | • Comprehensive, normative and developmental.<br>• Social welfare policy focuses on basic needs of all through progressive realisation in line with resource availability.<br>• A mixed economy – the state pays for services and benefits for the poor, and those who can afford to pay for services and benefits do so through the market.<br>• Based on understanding that existing economic, social and governance institutions need to be transformed to respond to inequities and exclusions.<br>• State funding through tax system for free primary services in health, education, social assistance and housing to the poor.<br>• State subsidies provides for psychosocial services that are provided by the NPO sector.<br>• International and national donor organisations provide additional sources for capacity-building, HIV/Aids and youth programmes, etc. |

| The political economy of transforming social welfare policy and services in South Africa | | |
|---|---|---|
| Main features | Pre 1994 | Post 1994 |
| Services provided | • Comprehensive for whites and residual and minimal for blacks.<br>• Social work services to children, the aged, people living with disabilities, and indigent.<br>• Social grants, pensions, education and health care for whites with limited basic provision for blacks. | • Comprehensive social security to all to ensure social protection – social grants, school feeding programmes, child support, early childhood development, amongst others.<br>• Resources to address poverty through public works programmes.<br>• Free primary health care, schooling, and housing for poor people. |
| Implications for social service practice | • White professionals provide services to white people, and black professionals to black people.<br>• Fragmented and uneven, with high quality services provided to whites and poor quality provided to blacks.<br>• Black people experienced social work services as punitive (removal of children, and undemocratic).<br>• Status of social work and social workers was low since social workers seen as implementers or handmaidens of an illegitimate state.<br>• Progressive organisations, e.g. advices offices emerged outside of the state to assist people. | • Emphasis on constitutional and human rights of citizens and a shift away from 'client' orientation.<br>• National policy, norms and standards link to the Bill of Rights in Chapter 2 of the Constitution.<br>• Administrative structures for service delivery.<br>• Training and education of social service professionals are relevant for Africa.<br>• Consult with people to be served – negotiate with service users on what is to be provided, how, and with what outcomes; ensure participation of all stakeholders.<br>• Social service workers uphold rights of people and ensure access to services – knowledge of rights and services essential to monitor implementation and service delivery. |

Source: Taylor, V (2017)

# CONCLUSION

• There are five main themes in this chapter. Firstly, it explains how a political economy framework can be used to provide an analysis of the changes and the critical challenges in social welfare policy for contemporary social work and broader social service professional practice.

• Secondly, the chapter provides conceptual understandings and definitions of social welfare policy, social policy, and transformative social welfare policy, and explains the thinking that informs these definitions.

• Thirdly, the chapter traces the history or evolution of social welfare policy in Africa during different periods and compares and contrasts this history briefly with turning points in social welfare policy developments on the African continent and in South Africa.

• Fourthly, using African experiences of transforming social welfare policy, the chapter illustrates how policy environments are shaped from the period of postcolonial white rule to democratic rule in countries. It further shows how such changes can influence welfare policies, programmes, and outcomes.

- Finally, the chapter illustrates how macro policies interlink with political processes to determine how social needs and conditions are addressed and explains the implications these have for social welfare policy and social service practice in South Africa. It does this by providing an overview of macro development plans such as the RDP (ANC, 1994), GEAR programme (Treasury, 1996), and the NDP (NPC, 2011). The ideas, theories, values, and principles that shape social welfare policy arising from the National Development Plan (NPC, 2011) and the implications for social welfare development and professional practice are a part of the chapter.
- The evolution of transformative social welfare policy and practice in Africa remains an on-going project. The current context of deepening poverty, increasing social inequalities, and wide-scale social disintegration in Africa reveals the urgency for social welfare policies to be framed within a human rights and social justice approach so that people's human needs and rights can be achieved.
- The chapters that follow expand on some aspects in this chapter and add further knowledge and understanding to issues of transformation in the social welfare policy field.

## QUESTIONS

1. How did social welfare policy emerge historically in your country?
2. Describe and analyse critically some of the main political, economic, and social features that influence social welfare policy using Table 1.1 as a guideline.
3. What are the distinguishing features of transformative social welfare policy in comparison to traditional social welfare policy?
4. Apply the features in the 'Transformative framework to advance human rights and social justice in social welfare policy' as indicated in Figure 1.2 to discuss how transformative social welfare policy changes can be introduced in your country.

## REFERENCES

ADESINA, JO (2008) *Transformative Social Policy in Africa's Development* (contribution to UNDP's Human Development Report for Sub-Saharan Africa 2008). New York: UNDP/ Palgrave Macmillan.

AFRICAN NATIONAL CONGRESS (1994a) *The Reconstruction and Development Programme* (RDP). Johannesburg: Umanyano Publications (for the African National Congress).

AFRICAN NATIONAL CONGRESS (1994b) *National Social Welfare and Development Plan.* Bellville (Cape Town): Southern African Development Education Programme (SADEP).

AFRICAN UNION (1981) *African Charter on Human and Peoples' Rights.* Banjul: African Union.

BRANSKY, D (1974) *Causes of the Anglo Boer War.* Unpublished paper. Oxford.

FANON, F (1967) *The Wretched of the Earth* (English translation) Great Britain: Penguin Books.

GIL, DG (1992) *Unravelling Social Policy – Theory, Analysis, and Political Action towards Social Equality* (fifth edition). Rochester: Schenkman Books.

GILBERT, N & SPECHT, H (1986) *Dimensions of Social Welfare Policy* (second edition). USA: Prentice-Hall.

MARAIS, H (1998) *South Africa Limits to Change: the political economy of transformation.* Cape Town: University of Cape Town Press.

MISHRA, R (1977) *Society and Social Policy: Theoretical Perspectives on Welfare.* London: The MacMillan Press.

MKANDAWIRE, T (2001) 'Social Policy in a Developmental Context' *Social and Development Programme – Paper Number 7.* Geneva: United Nations Institute for Social Development.

SEEKINGS, J (2002) 'The Broader Importance of Welfare Reform in South Africa' *Social Dynamics* 28(2 - Winter), pp. 1–38.

SOUTH AFRICA. Constitution of the Republic of South Africa Act 108 of 1996. Cape Town: Constitutional Assembly of the Republic of South Africa.

SOUTH AFRICA. Department of Finance (1996) *Growth, Employment and Redistribution. A macro-economic strategy*. Available: www.treasury.gov.za/publications/other/gear/chapters.pdf.

SOUTH AFRICA. Department of Social Development (2016) *Comprehensive Report on the Review of the White Paper for Social Welfare, 1997*. Available: www.dsd.gov.za.

SOUTH AFRICA. Ministry for Welfare and Population Development (1997) *White Paper for Social Welfare* in GN 1108 in *GG* 18166 of 8 August 1997. Pretoria: Government Printer.

SOUTH AFRICA. National Planning Commission (2011) *The National Development Plan, Vision for 2030*. Pretoria: Government Printer. Available: http://www.gov.za/sites/www.gov.za/files/devplan_2.pdf.

TAYLOR, V (1997) 'The Trajectory of National Liberation and Social Movements' *Community Development Journal*, 32(3), pp. 252–265.

TAYLOR, V (1997) *Social Mobilisation – Lessons from the Mass Democratic Movement*. Cape Town: SADEP (UWC).

TAYLOR, V (2008) *Social Protection in Africa: An Overview of the Challenges*. (Research Report prepared for the African Union). Available: www.eprionline.com/wpcontent/uploads/2011/03/Taylor2008AUSocialProtectionOverview.pdf.

TAYLOR, V: 'Human Rights, Social Welfare and Questions of Social Justice in South Africa' in Libal et al. (eds.) (2014) *Advancing Human Rights in Social Work Education*, pp. 247–270. USA: International Council for Social Work Education.

TERREBLANCHE, S & NATTRASS, N: 'A periodization of the political economy from 1910' in Nattrass, N & Ardington, E (1990) *The Political Economy of South Africa* at pp. 6–23. Cape Town: Oxford University Press.

UNITED NATIONS DEVELOPMENT PROGRAMME (2000) *South Africa Human Development Report 2000*. Pretoria: UNDP.

YOUNG, C (1994) *The African Colonial State in Comparative Perspective*. New Haven and London: Yale University Press.

# Glossary of terms

**neoliberal:** when used in this book it refers to new (neo) forms of opening up economic and financial systems so that business activities and the flow of financial resources move across national borders without regulations or restrictions from governments. It is based on the thinking that free market capitalist production systems create a competitive environment that reduces the costs of products and in turn reduces the prices at which these products are sold thereby generating huge profits for shareholders and companies. Among the ways through which companies' costs are cut include paying very little for labour and not putting into place health and safety standards for workers or getting tax exemptions from governments.

**states:** when used in this way, includes government, parliaments and other constitutional institutions that are established to protect and promote human rights, good governance and freedoms. In South Africa, these institutions are referred to as Chapter 9 institutions because Chapter 9 of the Constitution makes provision for the Human Rights Commission, The Office of the Public Protector, The Gender Commission, the Fiscal and Financial Commission and a range of others.

**systems of social welfare:** it includes policies, legislation, procedures programmes, projects with structures or organisations that provide the delivery of social welfare goods and services. They include professionals such as social workers, social development workers, child and youth care workers, community development workers, and specialist social workers in the treatment of substance addiction care, trauma counselling, criminal justice social work, and psychiatric social work, among others.

**Economic Structural Adjustment Programmes (ESAPs):** these were imposed on governments in Africa after many governments were forced to borrow money from the International Monetary Fund and World Bank due to declining commodity prices, the oil crises and policy failures. The prescriptions imposed on these countries included cut backs on social services, privatisation of state-owned enterprises, currency deregulation, and the relaxation of financial and tariff controls. ESAPs in Africa preceded the neoliberal free trade and free movement of finances across borders. The social impacts of ESAPs included wide scale and deepening poverty, food insecurity and starvation, health, and education declines, displacement and migration in Africa.

**neoliberal globalisation:** it refers to new (neo) forms of opening up (liberal) global finance and economic development processes with as little government intervention as possible. It is usually led by transnational global corporations in the industrial or manufacturing sectors and in the service sectors. This type of globalisation has also led to the establishment of new markets for new information technologies, policy advice services, privatisation of core public services in some countries, and new partnerships between governments and the private sector referred to as public private partnerships.

## Endnotes

1 Social service professionals include social workers, youth and child care workers, social development workers, community development workers, health care professionals, and educators and teachers, among others. They are involved in the care and service provision for the well-being and development of people, and implement policies and processes within a professional code of ethics.

2 While the author of this chapter refers to aspects of social welfare, Gilbert and Specht, 1986 use the term dimensions of social welfare and Gil, 1992 uses the functions of social welfare to distinguish how these influence economic, social, environmental, and cultural arrangements or ways of life.

3 The World Bank and International Monetary Fund are financial institutions that were established after the Second World War in Bretton Woods by countries in Europe, the United States of America, Canada, and Australia to fund the reconstruction and development of countries that were destroyed physically and economically during the war. These institutions continued and extended their loans to countries in Africa, Latin America and Asia to finance infrastructure needs of postcolonial states. However, the conditions under which such loans were granted and the interest payments were extremely harsh and led to most countries becoming highly indebted. An increasing percentage of the national budgets of African countries went to servicing the debt and left little money available for health, social welfare, education, and food.

4 Racial categories such as Black African, Coloured or mixed race, Asian and White were used to provide differential and discriminatory access to resources, and economic and political power under the apartheid state before 1994. These categories (population groups) are still in use to ensure equity in allocation of resources and access to opportunities for all those historically disadvantaged.

5 In this sense the author uses black to denote all people of colour not only those categorised as African. In the 1970s, a conscious attempt was made to redefine all those who experienced institutionalised racism and discrimination under the collective term black to build unity against apartheid and reaffirm being black.

6 At the time of writing this book, the author of this chapter was the Social Welfare Policy Coordinator for the ANC and was the policy contributor for the section on Social Security and Social Welfare in the RDP (1994a) and led the research and process as well as wrote the *ANC Ready to Govern National Social Welfare and Development* Plan (1994b).

7 'Justiciable' means that the public or an individual can take the government or any state or non-state actor to the Constitutional Court for either violating their constitutional rights and entitlements. The state or any other actor will then have to show that it intends to deliver such rights and entitlements over a period of time and within its' available resources.

8 The tripartite alliance at the time included the African National Congress, the South African Communist Party and the Congress of South African Trade Unions. On specific issues this alliance included in various forums the South African National Civic Organisation and Women's Organisations.

# CHAPTER 02

# The evolution of social welfare policy in Southern Africa

*Ndangwa Noyoo*

'Never before in history has such a sweeping fervor for freedom expressed itself in great mass movements which are driving down the bastions of empire. This wind of change blowing through Africa, as I have said before, is no ordinary wind. It is a raging hurricane against which the old order cannot stand [...] Hence the twentieth century has become the century of colonial emancipation, the century of continuing revolution which must finally witness the total liberation of Africa from colonial rule and imperialist exploitation.'

– Kwame Nkrumah, *Africa Must Unite*

Chapter 2 sheds light on the concept of social welfare policy and explains how it took shape in Southern Africa. The chapter bases its analysis on a political economy approach (as introduced in Chapter 1). It also looks at how social welfare systems evolved under colonial rule. The chapter's objectives and outcomes are provided below.

## Objectives

✓ Tracing and discussing the development of social welfare policy in Southern Africa.

✓ Discussing the history and political economy of Southern Africa in relation to how it influenced the development of social welfare policies in the region.

✓ Explaining patriarchy as a colonial construct which eroded the important role African women played in governance before colonialism.

## Outcomes

✓ Having a firm grasp of the history of Southern Africa's social welfare systems and of the region.

✓ Having a deeper understanding of the region's political economy and how it influences each country's social welfare outcomes.

✓ Understanding the contemporary social welfare policy trends of Southern Africa.

✓ Identifying the manner in which the political and economic forces shaped social welfare processes in Southern Africa – in the precolonial, colonial and postcolonial periods.

## 2.1 Introduction

When discussing social welfare policy, it is important to note that it is usually a by-product of a political economy and a specific welfare regime that is unique to a country. A political economy approach recognises the critical role of politics and the economy in shaping the social welfare system and other processes in a particular country. Therefore, political and economic factors are given significant attention by analysts when using this approach as they endeavour to understand a country's development prospects.

With regard to Southern Africa, the term social welfare policy will be used in the plural form because the area that is being examined is a region and not a specific country. This chapter adopts an overarching approach because it attempts to shed light on the evolution of social welfare policy in the Southern African region and not in an individual country. At the outset, it must be stated that Southern Africa is not homogenous but it is in many respects a diverse area especially in relation to: economic, environmental, ethnic, political, and social aspects, among others. It is important to highlight that countries in the region have different colonial traditions which continue to shape and influence their present-day governance and administrative styles as well as their institutional, policy and legislative frameworks. Despite this, there are many similarities between the different Southern African countries, such as cultural, linguistic, and governance aspects, to mention just a few.

## 2.2 Southern Africa in perspective

Presently, all Southern African countries have a wide array of natural resources which ideally should be harnessed for the benefit of their peoples. Not only is the region rich in minerals, but it has arable land. In the recent past, a country like Zimbabwe was referred to as the 'breadbasket' of Africa. But in the last decade it has been food insecure. The main reason for this was the deplorable political situation which emanated from increasing authoritarianism on the part of the president and the ruling party. In the process, many sectors of the economy were negatively impacted, especially agriculture. More tellingly, Zimbabwe had instituted a chaotic and violent land reform programme which led to the confiscation of land from white Zimbabweans. The land was supposedly redistributed to deserving black Zimbabweans. However, this process was marred by cronyism, inefficiencies and political patronage. This is how politics, bad governance and material conditions intersect to make people's lives insecure. Nevertheless, in the last decade, some of the countries in the region have managed to almost become food secure, while the majority are still food insecure despite having fertile land.

Southern Africa straddles two oceans, the Atlantic and Indian Oceans, which provide many coastal countries with various marine resources that are vital for their economic growth and social development. Despite the many resources at the disposal of countries in this region, the majority of its people are poor. There is, therefore, a disjuncture between Southern Africa's natural resources endowment profile and the low quality of life of the majority of its people. Many countries have low-quality or even non-existent infrastructure. This adds to the burden of development as there is a high cost in the way countries harness their natural resources and how they conduct their business.

Economically and politically, South Africa is the dominant country in the region – and also on the continent. However, despite its purported wealth, the majority of South Africans are also poor and unemployed. According to new data released by Statistics South Africa (Stats SA), poverty is on the rise in South Africa. The latest Poverty Trends in South Africa report by Stats SA, (2017a) shows that, despite the general decline in poverty between 2006 and 2011, poverty levels in South Africa were rising by 2015. More than half of South Africans were poor in 2015, with the poverty headcount increasing to 55,5% from a series low of 53,2% in 2011 (Stats SA, 2017a). In the first quarter of 2017, South Africa's unemployment rate peaked at 27,7%. This is the highest unemployment rate observed since September 2003 (Stats SA, 2017b). In the same breath, South Africa remains one of the most unequal countries in the world (Stats SA, 2014). This reveals that the social welfare of the majority of citizens is a serious concern. Social welfare policy does and should play a redistributive role by providing goods and services to those who are poor and economically excluded.

Despite these challenges, South Africa still fares better in comparison to the standard of living of other Southern African countries. Botswana, Mauritius, and the Seychelles are also better off economically than other countries since many of their citizens enjoy a higher standard of living than those of other Southern African countries. On the other hand, Angola, despite its huge oil reserves and the fact that it has exported oil for decades, has low human development levels. Angola's Human Development Index (HDI) value for 2015 was 0.533 – which put the country in the low human development category – positioning it at 150 out of 188 countries and territories (United Nations Development Programme, 2016).

Apart from poverty, the Southern African region has a very high disease burden and HIV/Aids and malaria are the main contributors to its high mortality rates. Some countries like Swaziland and Lesotho exhibit very high HIV infection rates and the epidemic is not diminishing in these countries. In regard to the Democratic Republic of the Congo (DRC), insecurity is a major problem with an unending war unfolding and different forms of armed insurrection and violence taking place in some parts of this vast country.

Currently, Southern Africa is facing major challenges relating to undemocratic political regimes, bad governance, and human rights violations. These issues are eroding the region's social and economic development prospects. See below for some examples of these issues:

**EXAMPLES**    **ISSUES THAT HAVE A NEGATIVE IMPACT ON SOCIAL AND ECONOMIC DEVELOPMENT IN SOUTHERN AFRICA**

- Zimbabwe has consistently been undemocratic for almost 20 years now with its 93-year-old president, Robert Mugabe, steadfastly clinging to power. However, he was forced to resign on 21 November 2017 following a bloodless military intervention on 14 November 2017. It remains to be seen whether or not Zimbabwe will follow a democratic path after its former Vice President Emmerson Mnangagwa was sworn in as president on 24 November 2017.
- Angola has an equally dismal record in governance and human rights. In Angola, journalists and other critics are arbitrarily arrested and jailed without due process. The ailing president, 74-year-old Jose Eduardo dos Santos, decided not to stand for re-election and ended his term of office in September 2017. His presidency lasted almost four decades.
- In the DRC, Joseph Kabila has refused to hold elections or step down after his term of office elapsed.
- Madagascar has just been readmitted to the Southern African Development Community (SADC) after it was expelled in 2009 for deposing a democratically elected president via a military coup.
- Swaziland is still an absolute monarchy where its citizens are being denied civil liberties and political rights (Freedom House, 2013).
- In Zambia, the democratic dividends that were steadily building up after the country reverted to multiparty democracy in 1991, after the defeat of its founding president Kenneth Kaunda, are being eroded. Since coming to power in 2011, the Patriotic Front-led government has been overseeing human rights violations as well as undermining civil liberties in the country. People are detained arbitrarily while the police perpetrate violence against the citizens. Also, the president, Edgar Lungu, recently invoked emergency powers (Africa Liberal Network, 2017).
- Mozambique has experienced reversals in its democratic gains with violence flaring up in 2015. The former rebel group, the Mozambican National Resistance (**RENAMO** or *Resistência Nacional Moçambicana* in Portuguese), led armed attacks against the ruling Mozambique Liberation Front (**FRELIMO** or *Frente de Libertação de Moçambique* in Portuguese) party supporters and structures due to an election dispute. The political situation still remains volatile and fragile.

These deplorable socioeconomic and political conditions have triggered migrations in the region as people search for a better life and the means to survive. In addition, the social impacts of poverty and destitution in Southern Africa have spurred disproportionate migrations to South Africa as many see it as a land of opportunity. This has resulted in South Africa carrying an extra burden of responsibility as it looks after citizens of some countries in the region with failed political and economic systems.

## 2.3 The making of postcolonial societies in Southern Africa

Today, all countries of Southern Africa are independent nation-states. This was not the case four decades ago when some were still under colonial rule. Many of these countries had to resort to armed struggle to gain their independence. A good number of these countries belonged to the political grouping referred to as the Frontline States. The sole purpose of the Frontline States was to ensure that the countries in the region which remained under colonial rule gained their independence. To this end, it provided moral and material support and other forms of solidarity to the liberation movements of the region, namely: the People's Movement for the Liberation of Angola (MPLA or *Movimento Popular de Libertação de Angola* in Portugese); FRELIMO in Mozambique; African National Congress (ANC) and Pan Africanist Congress (PAC) in South Africa; South West African People's Organisation (SWAPO) in Namibia; and Zimbabwe African People's Union (ZAPU) and Zimbabwe African National Union (ZANU) both in Zimbabwe.

Heading the Frontline States were the first presidents of Botswana, Tanzania, and Zambia, namely, Seretse Khama, Julius Nyerere, and Kenneth Kaunda, respectively. The Frontline States raised the issue of independence for the Southern African countries at African and world fora such as the Organisation of African Unity (OAU), the United Nations (UN) Security Council, and the Non-Aligned Movement (NAM). Most of the liberation movements and freedom fighters from the countries under colonial domination made their way to Tanzania and Zambia where they established bases and military camps and waged the armed struggle against Portuguese, Rhodesian, and apartheid colonial regimes. While some of the political exiles, who were mostly civilians, were trained in guerrilla warfare in the military camps, others worked as professionals in government departments or parastatal organisations, or furthered their education at Tanzanian and Zambian institutions of higher learning. Due to their proximity to apartheid South Africa, Botswana, Lesotho, and Swaziland provided covert support to the liberation forces of South Africa for fear of military reprisals. Political exiles also studied at their institutions of higher learning. Many citizens of Botswana, Lesotho, and Swaziland died after South African assassins or 'death squads' as they were known, carried out military and bombing raids whilst pursuing ANC and PAC freedom fighters who were in exile in these countries.

The country that bore the brunt of Portuguese, Rhodesian, and South African military raids was Zambia. Many lives were lost in Zambia, and infrastructure was destroyed because of this country's support for the liberation movements and the struggle for independence. As countries gained independence, beginning with Angola and Mozambique in 1975, they joined the Frontline States and provided support to the countries remaining under colonial rule.

In 1980, the Frontline States was reconstituted as the Southern African Development Co-ordination Conference (SADCC) in Lusaka, Zambia, to act as a bulwark against apartheid

South Africa's economic and military hegemony in the region. This was because all countries of Southern Africa depended on South Africa economically, either through trade or trade routes, or directly through the remittances of migrant workers as in the case of Lesotho and Mozambique. Malawi was the exception as it had diplomatic ties with South Africa and traded openly with the apartheid regime. Its president, Hastings Kamuzu Banda, did not support the struggle for independence in the region and was friendly with the colonial regimes of Southern Africa.

Map of SADC countries

By 1990, when Namibia became independent, many people in the region called the relevance of the SADCC into question and thereafter it was dissolved. In 1992, in Windhoek, Namibia, the SADCC became the Southern African Development Community (SADC). When South Africa became a free and democratic country in 1994, it joined the SADC. Therefore, for this chapter's purposes, a political definition of Southern Africa is proffered and adopted. It is based on the landscape that encompasses the 15 countries that make up the regional economic bloc of the SADC. These countries are Angola, Botswana, the DRC, Lesotho, Madagascar, Malawi, Mauritius, Mozambique, Namibia, Seychelles, South Africa, Swaziland, Tanzania, Zambia, and Zimbabwe (SADC, 2017). Each of these countries has their unique precolonial, colonial and postcolonial experiences and social welfare systems. Their social welfare policies emanated from different socio-political and economic conditions. Southern African countries were once British, Belgian, Dutch, German, French, or Portuguese colonies. South Africa and Namibia have Dutch, English, and German influences. Namibia, which was known as German South West Africa, was handed over to South Africa by the League of Nations – a forerunner of the United Nations –when Germany was defeated after the First World War in 1918. Another German colony in the region, Tanganyika, or present-day Tanzania, became a British colony after this same war. All these countries would later fight for their freedom and gain independence. Once they became independent, they used instruments such as social welfare policy to create better lives for their citizens. In this section, we have discussed how countries which were under colonial rule in Southern African fought for their independence.

Now that we have covered the decolonisation of Southern Africa, we move on to discuss the precolonial era in the section below.

## 2.4 The precolonial era

Prior to Europeans' incursions into Africa, Africa's precolonial, socio-political landscape was linked to the various indigenous polities, which were usually kingdoms. They were overseen by different kings and queens – as in the case of Queen Nzinga of the Mbundu people of present-day Angola who ruled in the 17th century. It is noteworthy that the history of Southern Africa predates European colonial occupation. Archaeological findings indicate that Southern Africa is the land from which human kind's ancestors evolved between 3 million and 1 million years ago (McKenna, 2011). It is probable that the indigenous San, Pygmy and Khoikhoi peoples of the region are genetically linked to that earlier, ancient population (McKenna, 2011). In the same vein, state formation in precolonial Southern Africa had preceded colonial rule and resulted in the establishment of, in certain places, sophisticated indigenous polities. For example, the kingdoms of the Basotho, Bamangwato, Bulozi or Barotseland, Gaza, Kongo, Mapungubwe, Mwenemutapa, among others, were highly organised politically and economically, and had created complex political bureaucracies and trade routes with other kingdoms to safeguard the security and livelihoods of their peoples. Unlike other parts of Africa, Southern Africa experienced significant and profound social upheavals in the mid-19th century which reconfigured this area's polities as well as its cultural, linguistic ties and other aspects. These upheavals that took place approximately between 1790 and 1830 are referred to as the *Mfecane* (meaning 'crushing' in the Nguni languages) or *Difaqane* (translated as 'scattering' or 'forced dispersal' in Sotho). They were a violent process that transformed the whole region. The aftermath of the Mfecane saw the birth of new powerful and centralised nations as well as the collapse of others.

Previous Eurocentric historical accounts of Southern Africa attributed the Mfecane to the 'callous' destruction of several Southern African polities by Shaka's Zulu nation. However, these accounts are being challenged by African scholars who argue that it was the annexation of African lands by the Europeans, in the first instance, that triggered the Mfecane. In fact, as Europeans made their way from the coastal areas to the hinterland of the region, a domino effect saw African nations also moving northwards and encroaching on other nations' lands which resulted in them fighting each other for the control of the remaining land and other resources.

The ripple effects of the Mfecane were profound as whole nations migrated northwards and displaced others. These include the following:

- Mzilikazi, a general in Shaka's army, fled northwards after he had differences with his leader and created a new nation of the Ndebele in present-day Zimbabwe. In the process, the Ndebele pillaged and subdued weaker nations.

- The Ngoni who broke away from the Ndwandwe of Zwide, with their ruler Zwangendaba, trekked from today's KwaZulu-Natal and settled as far as Tanzania. However, the bulk of the Ngonis settled in Eastern Zambia and Malawi. The Ngoni were one of the most scattered tribes of the Nguni stock during the Mfecane. Previously, Zwide had constantly engaged in military campaigns against Shaka who eventually routed the Ndwandwe.
- From Zwide's Ndwandwe another branch of the Ngonis also migrated under the leadership of Soshangane and established the Gaza Kingdom in Mozambique.
- From present-day Free State in South Africa migrated a Sotho group of the Fokeng stock who were led by Sebetwane. This group migrated all the way to present-day Western Zambia and defeated the Aluyi people of the Bulozi kingdom or Barotseland. After 30 years, the Sothos were defeated by remnants of the Aluyi who were by then referred to as Barotse or Lozi. However, the Sotho and Aluyi had blended and morphed into the Lozi people of Zambia.

Due to these upheavals, many ethnic groups in the region have cultural and other ties with each other. For example, the Sotho and Tswana groups in South Africa have a common heritage with the Sotho and Tswana in Lesotho and Botswana. Similarly, the Tsonga and Swati of South Africa have familial ties with the Tsonga and Swati of Mozambique and Swaziland. Furthermore, the Lozi in Zambia have links with the Sotho and Tswana of Lesotho, South Africa and Botswana, whilst the Ngoni of Zambia, Malawi, and Tanzania, and the Ndebele of Zimbabwe trace their roots back to KwaZulu-Natal in South Africa (Noyoo, 2013: 106).

The rulers of the above indigenous polities and others played crucial roles in the day-to-day affairs of their nations. They also created political systems and social networks that responded to the needs of the people. In this regard, it can be said that communal systems of support and governance acted as precolonial social welfare mechanisms. A significant part of these polities was the extended family which met the needs of people through mutual-aid systems, strong bonds of solidarity, and networks of reciprocity. The African family was the cornerstone of precolonial African societies and women were its pillars. Unlike the conventional narratives that typify African societies as inherently patriarchal, it is contended here that actually women in precolonial Africa in general, and Southern Africa in particular, occupied important positions in their societies and played critical roles in running its affairs.

It was not coincidental that many family systems in Southern Africa were matrilineal, where descent was traced from the maternal side of the family as opposed to the paternal side. Although patrilineal families (where descent was established from the father's side) existed, they did not dominate. The matrilineal family system still endures in this region and many other parts of Africa. Many feminist scholars (some of whom are not African) who decry Africa's supposed dominant patriarchy fail to see this anomaly in a historical analysis that takes into critical cognisance the statuses of women in precolonial Africa. Women not only assumed high political positions – such as Queen Nzingawho who was the ruler of the Ndongo and Matamba kingdoms or Mbuyamwambwa who established the kingdom of Bulozi or Barotseland – but were also revered as Priestesses in some nations. Women were also warriors in the Kingdom of Dahomey (now Benin), and Shaka had an army of women. In Barotseland, women had a democratic voice in the precolonial era and some were rulers. For instance, the post of the third senior chief and ruler of the southern part of the kingdom – which was occupied by Mukwae Mbowanjikana – has been reserved for women for centuries and they continue to occupy it to this day (Noyoo, 2014).

Queen Nzinga who was the ruler of the Ndongo and Matamba kingdoms

To the contrary, colonialism was the main propagator of patriarchy and undermined and weakened the roles of women in African societies. The colonial master was always a male who in most cases had left his wife and children in Europe. Apart from the missionaries who came with their wives or families, most Europeans in Africa who were in positions of authority, either as traders, hunters or political representatives, rarely had their families with them on the continent, especially in the early years of colonial rule. To this end, the Europeans patterned the colonial outpost along patriarchal lines similar to the social relations existing in Europe at the time. The colonialists then elevated males in the colonial social order and relegated women to play only nurturing roles. Patriarchy is thus a colonial construct which must be seen for what it is.

Unfortunately, as with the case of most things that are foreign to and endured in Africa, patriarchy has been embraced and entrenched by Africans despite being engendered by colonialism. The historical evidence on this matter clearly shows the importance that was accorded to women in precolonial African societies. In the precolonial period women were able to balance their nurturing and socialising roles, on the one hand, with other roles at family, community, and societal levels, on the other. The advent of colonial rule diminished this central position that women had occupied in precolonial Africa.

In ending this section, it is important to note that in precolonial Africa the politics and economic influences of the time shaped social welfare responses. During this era the elders and chiefs in villages were responsible for making decisions about individual, household, and clan well-being. There was a collective approach to problem solving and dealing with the grievances and needs of those members who could not fend for themselves. This system was eroded by the imposition of colonial rule, forced labour migration, and wars. Now that you are acquainted with the precolonial era, the next section focuses on the colonial era.

## 2.5 **The colonial era**

Due to Southern Africa's great riches, namely gold, diamonds, ivory, land, and distressingly, the very people themselves (McKenna, 2011), it attracted a large number of European colonists who quickly became settlers. Southern Africa's colonisation took its own form as it was more embedded and penetrating than in other parts of Africa, perhaps only rivalled by the European colonial foray into East Africa. One key characteristic of colonialism is exploitation. However, a distinction can be drawn between what is termed 'exploitation colonies' and those called 'settler colonies'. The difference between the two types of colonies deserves some attention, particularly because of the implications of this difference for public policymaking, power struggles, and social control in the colonies (Njoh, 2007). In 'settler colonies':

> *'... the "settlers" tended to remain permanently. Thus, in formulating laws, acquiring real property, and cultivating land, the settlers gave no thought to their place of origin. Rather, they typically made every effort to annihilate, displace, usurp and/or marginalise members of the indigenous population through institutional and other means. The situation was little different in 'exploitation colonies' or 'colonies of occupation'. In such colonies, particularly those of West Africa, the European population was usually insignificant and was comprised mainly of colonial government officials, plantation farmers, managers, and businessmen concerned exclusively with protecting their individual interests or those of the colonial empire'* (Njoh, 2007: 147).

Settler colonialism gave birth to settler capitalism. The salient historical feature of the regional political economy of Southern Africa is the penetration of settler capitalism. The spirit of settler capitalism was personified by the prototypical imperialist Cecil Rhodes. The expansion of mining capitalism and the recruitment of circular migrants for super-exploitation shaped the regional pattern of capital accumulation (Moyo and Mine, 2016: 208). Settler domination in Southern Africa implied an exclusive form of capitalism which was based on race right from the beginning (Mhone, 2001). As a consequence, Africans were reduced to marginal participants in the new economic system. Therefore, capitalism emerged as a racial type of capitalism, which was superimposed over pre-capitalist social relations, entailing unequal relations of domination and subjugation.

In many respects, it can be argued that the foregoing events discussed above served as precursors to the type of decolonisation that unfolded later in most of Southern Africa, in that it had to take a violent form through armed struggles or wars of liberation. Since settler colonialism was deeply entrenched in the region, the settlers were unwilling to relinquish power without a fight, before the indigenous people could be granted their independence. Needless to say, the starting point of this violence was colonial pacification (referring to the ruling of the local people and keeping them in their place) which took on genocidal proportions where settlers had set out to seize indigenous land in the region (Mamdani, 2014). Thus, violence characterised the anti-colonial struggles of Angola, Mozambique, Namibia, South Africa, and Zimbabwe.

Colonial rule had engaged in the exploitation of the natural resources of Africa and Southern Africa in particular. Commercial enterprises set up mining, farming and some manufacturing enterprises in the burgeoning urban enclaves where most of the Europeans resided. Africans still lived in their villages or the remaining semblances of their former kingdoms (in some parts where they had existed) before colonial rule destroyed or diluted them. At first, Europeans tried to entice Africans into the new money economy but when their labour was not forthcoming for the new commercial enterprises (because people did not want to move away from their villages), the colonial authorities resorted to draconian means to force Africans into the money economy. One of the ways in which the Africans were coerced to participate in the European or so-called modern economy was by imposing the hut tax which compelled them to pay tax to the colonial authorities. The tax was used to run the colonial state. Initially, Africans were allowed to pay the tax in kind, for example, grain, fowls, cattle, sheep, and goats were accepted as payments. Those who did not have such assets had to move to the urban centres to sell their labour or they were forcefully conscripted into labour gangs.

As the need for labour in the colonial economy grew, the colonial authorities only accepted money as a means of paying tax and banned other forms of payment. After this, Africans had no choice but to go and work in the colonial enterprises in order earn a wage for the purposes of paying the hut tax. Thus, the migrant labour system came into being. As it became more pronounced, it was defined by the recruitment of thousands of African males from the hinterland, usually on a six months' basis. After six months, the workers were returned to their villages and 'fresh' labour was recruited – a cycle which continued throughout the colonial period. While such labour migrations were taking place in particular countries, there were also transborder recruitment of African labour for the labour-intensive mining industries of South Africa and the Belgian Congo (now the DRC) with devastating social consequences. The Witwatersrand Native Labour Association (WNLA) recruited labourers from neighbouring British colonies of Lesotho, Malawi, Swaziland, Zambia, and Zimbabwe, while other organisations recruited from Mozambique.

Migrant workers living in compound away from their families

Not only was African labour exploited but it had now become commodified to suit the needs of colonial domination. Precolonial Southern African economies were effectively dismantled and Africans had no skills but their labour to sell to the Europeans. The main casualty of the migrant labour system was the African family that had not only played a role in the socialisation of its younger members, but had acted as an indigenous social welfare system to meet the needs of Africans as earlier explained. With mostly productive young males being uprooted from their villages to unknown urban destinations, the villages were left with only women, the elderly, and infirm. Agricultural production at village level dwindled, whilst the 'returnees' came back with urban social mores such as disrespect for elders or the undermining of the indigenous value systems. The migrant labour system also led to the breakdown of African values. Thus, the advent of colonial rule resulted in either the weakening or obliteration of indigenous systems altogether.

Twikirize notes that colonialism:

> '... [eroded] the ways of helping and solving problems practised in pre-
> colonial Africa, which were largely informal, micro-level operations
> carried through the family, kinship, and local chiefdoms and based on
> mutual-aid and collective action facilitated by the traditional customs
> and culture. Once these systems had been weakened through colonisation
> and modernisation, there was a gap in service provisioning and problem-
> solving' (Twikirize, 2014: 76).

However, it should be remembered that every precolonial community or society had its own way of responding to human needs (Mwansa, 2007). In most cases, European missionaries preceded other Europeans who came later to enforce colonial rule in this region. Different missionary groups came to Southern Africa to convert Africans into Christianity.

Nevertheless, it was the missionaries' insistence on undermining African religions – which in this case were also strong pillars of indigenous social welfare systems – that also undermined precolonial polities. This stance was justified by their crusade against 'paganism' and African 'backwardness'. In their quest to 'civilise' Africans, some missionaries were complicit to the genocide that was perpetrated by the colonialists' political and military structures against the indigenous peoples.

This was especially true in the case of the Catholic Church in Angola that had a close relationship with the colonial regime. Colonial rule in Angola and Mozambique was very harsh and characterised by a system of forced labour which was only abolished in the early 1960s. African labour was required on the coffee and other plantations as well as in the mines. The former system was then replaced by the migrant labour arrangement. This period also coincided with the onset of liberation wars that were waged by freedom fighters in all the Portuguese territories.

However, the Protestant Churches were more progressive and provided education and health care services to the Africans in Angola. Due to this, the Protestant missionaries were viewed with suspicion by both the colonial authorities and the Catholic Church. In most British colonies the Protestant missionary societies created the rudiments of a modern social welfare system which provided education services and health care to the indigenous peoples. In this regard, religion played a crucial role in the development of social welfare systems in Southern Africa. As the colonies became more established and many Europeans began to reside permanently in the region, formal social welfare systems were created mainly for the Europeans.

After looking at how the colonies were established, the next section explains how social welfare systems were established in these territories.

## 2.6 The role of the First and Second World Wars in shaping welfare issues and calls for self-rule in African colonies

The First World War (1914–1918) was an important milestone in the march towards self-rule in Southern Africa and the rest of Africa. It also had implications for the development of formal welfare systems by the colonial authorities. At the time, social welfare services to Africans were being provided by missionaries. Nevertheless, the First World War saw close to one million Africans, who were conscripted by Britain and France, being killed in the war against Germany. Since Britain and France were allies, soldiers were conscripted from their African colonies to fight and provide labour in this war. Some fought in Europe while others fought in Africa. East Africa and northern Zambia were battlefronts where Southern African black soldiers were deployed. After this war, only white war veterans were recognised and rewarded with benefits for the service. Africans, on the other hand, were not given anything and were expected to get on with their lives. This violent and humiliating treatment from the colonialists generated a lot of resentment from the Africans which also sowed seeds for future rebellions. Unbeknown to the colonisers, the war had made many Africans become militant and increased their yearning for self-determination.

During this period, the first organised formations against colonial rule were established by Africans which later changed into fully fledged nationalist movements. However, it was the religious sects in colonial Malawi, or Nyasaland, and Zambia (Northern Rhodesia) that initially ignited rebellions against colonial rule. In 1915, John Chilembwe, a Baptist Minister who was educated in America, organised a rebellion which resulted in the deaths of several Europeans. It was immediately crushed by the colonialists and Chilembwe was killed in the process. However, this uprising would be the rallying call for future resistance against colonial rule in Malawi. In Zambia, the religious sect of the Watch Tower openly challenged colonial rule in 1918 and led similar disturbances in Southern Rhodesia (Zimbabwe).

In the 1920s, various Native Welfare Associations were formed in Zambia, Malawi and Zimbabwe to press for better living conditions for the Africans in these colonies. The Native Welfare Associations evolved into the first nationalist parties in Malawi, Zambia and Zimbabwe. In 1944, the Nyasaland African Congress (NAC) was formed in Malawi. In Zambia, the Northern Rhodesia Congress (NRC) was formed in 1948, and in Zimbabwe the Southern Rhodesia African National Congress (SRANC) was formed in 1957. As stated above, before they became nationalist parties, these congresses were first Welfare Associations. From this it is clear that social welfare matters and politics were intertwined in colonial Southern Africa. Note also that it was not only in Nyasaland or the two Rhodesias where there were increasing calls for self-rule. Earlier, In Botswana or Bechuanaland rising nationalism and the quest for self-rule became evident in the late 1940s and early 1950s.

After the First World War, the Great Depression ensued and led to the collapse of major economies at the time. The economies of the colonies were also negatively affected as they were directly linked to those of the imperial countries. The colonial powers increased their exploitation of the colonies' resources to stave off their own economic ruin. During this period, the urban landscape changed dramatically with more Africans residing permanently in the urban areas. The urban conditions created many social ills that indirectly affected the Europeans, for example, youth in conflict with the law, prostitution, and urban squalor. The Depression also led to the unemployment of migrant labourers resulting in high poverty levels in the colonies.

Colonial authorities could not ignore these problems and reluctantly started responding to them. For example, investigations into the former problems in Malawi led to the establishment of a pioneer Native Welfare Committee in 1935. Initially, Britain's policy towards its colonies was that they were expected to be self-sufficient and not rely on Britain for their development. The Colonial Development Act of 1929 changed this and funds were disbursed to the colonies to facilitate their development. This signified a major shift in British policy towards its colonies. After the Depression, the Second World War (1939–1945) erupted and it resulted in not only increased African militancy – during and after the war – but also led to the colonial powers losing their colonies after its cessation. In 1940, the second Colonial Development and Welfare Act was passed and more money was allocated to the colonies in contrast to the first Act. Coincidentally, the *Beveridge Report on Social Insurance and Allied Services*, which made proposals for creating Britain's welfare state, was completed by William Beveridge in 1942 during the war. In 1943, a Social Welfare Advisory Committee was appointed by the Secretary of State for the Colonies to advise him on the social welfare of urban and rural communities in the colonies and on the training of social welfare workers and allied matters.

## 2.6.1 Changes in post-war Europe and its impact on social welfare in the colonies

It can be argued that the Second World War had changed social relations in both the European countries and in the colonies. This war had also forced the colonial powers to shift from crude colonialism to paternalism. Crude colonialism was exemplified by rule by force, and through militarisation and the suppression of indigenous people, while the paternalistic form of colonialism treated indigenous people as if they were children without the ability to think and determine their own futures. Also, the colonialists were compelled by global conditions and African anti-colonial struggles to begin to 'prepare' Africans for self-rule. They also undertook development projects in the colonies. Therefore, social welfare policy was viewed by the colonialists as a vehicle to develop the colonies. After the war, it became very expensive for the colonialists to keep their colonies while their chief benefactor, America (that was financing the reconstruction of Europe through the Marshall Plan), was reluctant to finance the colonial enterprise.

More importantly, after the end of the Second World War, the general atmosphere in Europe seemed to have changed. For instance, it saw the emergence of dissenting voices from citizens of the imperial countries against the status quo in Europe as well as the continued colonial occupation of African and Asian territories by the colonial powers. Post-war Europe was experiencing critical changes that threatened the old way of life. There were strident demands on the state by many sections of the European nations, especially in most of Western Europe, for social citizenship to be entrenched in such places. Some progressive Europeans also called on their governments to make provisions for better entitlements to their colonial subjects.

Against this backdrop, the third Colonial Development and Welfare Act was passed in 1945 and its budget was increased taking into account the role of social welfare in development. To this end, British colonial social welfare policy was mainly expressed through social welfare services, community development initiatives, and, to a lesser extent, nutritional programmes. After the Second World War, all the British colonies had established social welfare systems and were being guided by social welfare policies that drew their essence from the Colonial Development and Welfare Acts. This resulted in a lot of activities happening in the social welfare arena during the 1940s and 1950s. For example, in Northern Rhodesia (present day Zambia), the colonial government established a Department of Social Welfare in 1950. Prior to this, it had approached the South African government and solicited both advice and help in order to constitute an organisation that would oversee welfare matters in the country. The South African Director of Social Welfare had visited Northern Rhodesia in order to conduct a survey of welfare services in the country and make necessary recommendations on how they could be organised, co-ordinated and developed. The findings of the survey were published by the South African Department of Social Welfare in a report, Social Welfare Services in Northern Rhodesia: A Report Presented to the Government of Northern Rhodesia (1950), by Graham C. Bain. It is interesting to note that during this period, South Africa was already entrenching institutionalised racism or apartheid (Noyoo, 2013).

In the same period, the Federation of Rhodesia and Nyasaland was declared in 1953 by the settlers of the former three territories who wanted to be 'independent' from Britain but all the same continued with the subjugation of Africans. Such a stance was motivated by fear of the rising African nationalism in the three territories. The Federation only heightened tensions between the indigenous people and the settlers. In 1963, when the Federation was dissolved, Malawi and Zambia were on the verge of independence. It would take another 17 years for Zimbabwe to become independent in 1980 because the settlers in this country had effectively rebelled against Britain and unilaterally declared their 'independence' in 1965.

## 2.6.2 The emergence of Public Welfare Assistance Programmes in colonies

From the 1950s onwards, all the British colonies developed Public Welfare Assistance Programmes which responded to the neediest and most vulnerable individuals, for example, the aged, people with disabilities, orphans and the chronically ill, among others. Also, a significant shift that occurred during and after the Second World War was the extension of welfare services to Africans in the Belgian, British, and French colonies. The Portuguese colonies lagged behind in this respect. Social security and social insurance as well as residential care for the elderly who were poor and neglected were extended to the white populations only in colonial Southern Africa. Social welfare policies discriminated on the basis of race and adopted a residual approach for the majority. Yet, for white people or those who were part of the colonisers, welfare and social provision became a part of government institutional arrangements through wide-ranging affirmative action programmes. With only slight variations in particular British colonies, social welfare services encompassed the following:

- general welfare and relief;
- specialised services for people with physical and mental disabilities (those who are differently abled), the elderly, children and youth;
- services for ex-service men;
- national, racial and denominational groups;
- marriage guidance;
- road safety;
- community development and group work;
- personal services;
- housing and hostel services;
- employment and delinquency services;
- places of safety and correctional institutions;
- legal aid;
- prisoner care;

- mental health; and
- recreational and educational services (Northern Rhodesian Council of Social Services, 1962:1).

There were also specialised services for alcohol addicts which were solely for Europeans. In the British colonies of Southern Africa, social welfare policies classified services based on the *colour-bar system* in the following way:
- people of European descent or white people who occupied the highest position in this hierarchy and were entitled to all the privileges and opportunities available in the colonial territories;
- people of mixed-race origin or 'Coloured' people who were a level lower than Europeans and had certain privileges;
- Asian or Indian people were below mixed-race people; and
- African people were at the bottom of this pyramid.

Due to the racial stratification of society under colonialism and apartheid, and the effects of deliberate separation and underdevelopment of the black majority, social welfare initiatives were underpinned by residual interventions with the bulk of such services mainly available to the white population. Thus, colonial social welfare policies were driven by racial discrimination, social exclusion, and elitism. Inevitably, social welfare systems in Southern Africa were transplanted from Europe by Europeans and replicated in the region. This was due to the fact they had initially responded only to the needs of settlers and not those of the indigenous people.

### 2.6.3 Link between social welfare concerns and political concerns in African colonies

Before ending this section, it should be borne in mind that the colonial era had effectively created subdued and conquered Africans who were forced into creating wealth for the colonisers through an exploitative migrant labour system. Their indigenous social welfare systems were eroded by colonialism and the new welfare systems which were created by the colonialists responded to the needs of the settler population. However, Africans would reassert themselves later, especially after the First and Second World Wars. They began agitating for self-rule and better socioeconomic conditions. In response to the latter concern, Welfare Associations were established to press for better socioeconomic conditions in the colonies. Eventually, the Welfare Associations were changed into nationalist parties that fought against colonial rule and eventually led their countries to independence. Therefore, it can be seen that social welfare concerns in colonial Southern Africa were inextricably linked to political concerns. The next section examines Southern African social welfare policies shortly after countries won their independence in the 1960s.

## 2.7 The immediate post-independence and postcolonial periods

The first countries to gain independence in Southern Africa were the DRC and Madagascar in 1960; Tanzania in 1961; Malawi and Zambia in 1964; Botswana in 1966; and Lesotho, Mauritius, and Swaziland in 1968. Most of the other countries became independent in the 1970s, Zimbabwe in 1980, and Namibia and South Africa (the last countries to become independent) in 1990 and 1994, respectively. In the immediate post-independence period, countries of the region were faced with high levels of underdevelopment and attendant shortfalls of high illiteracy levels, high infant and adult mortality rates, poor or nonexistent infrastructure, and many other challenges. Some countries had no health and education infrastructure and had to build them. Other countries did not have a single university while the private sector was almost nonexistent. Countries in the region had to embark on state-led development processes which were mainly predicated on National Development Plans. Thousands of schools, clinics, hospitals, and houses were built by the new African governments that sought to raise the quality of life of ordinary citizens of the region. Rural development initiatives were also initiated by regional governments.

In these early years of independence, former national liberation leaders retained their political will and commitment to ensure the political, economic and social liberation of their citizens. Where there was no private sector, the states created parastatals which served a dual function of offering subsidised services to the poor, on the one hand, and playing a central role in social investment, on the other. For example, transport, electricity, and food (mainly maize meal) were provided by parastatals at subsidised prices to the poor. There were even price controls in favour of the poor in some countries. At this stage, many of the countries sought to create welfare states in an African context. Countries such as Tanzania and Zambia provided universal coverage in education and health-care services. Their social welfare policies extended their scope beyond the inherited social welfare system. These former systems were limited in focus and had only responded to the needs of the European population, through, for instance, homes for the aged. The postcolonial social welfare policies incorporated nation-building and developmental objectives of eradicating hunger, ignorance, disease, ethnic rivalries, and the exploitation of people. The next section looks at how some countries in the region radically responded to human needs.

## 2.8 Radical government approaches in response to human needs

Tanzania and Zambia had a radical approach to transforming the inherited former colonial territories and nationalised foreign-owned enterprises in order to indigenise their modes of production. Other measures were the indigenisation of the civil service which was predominantly still run by expatriates. In Zambia, the process was known as Zambianisation. Also, these two countries were guided by ideologies in their social welfare endeavours which leaned on indigenous structures. In Tanzania, Ujamaa or family-hood (in Swahili) underpinned social and economic policies as well as its development plans. Ujamaa also spoke to each person's humanity, whereby an individual was expressed through other people or his or her community and not only pursuing his or her self-interest. All forms of exploitation were discouraged and challenged at all levels of the society. This was the same in Zambia where the ideology of Humanism espoused similar ideals as those of Ujamaa. This approach to development was extended to the fight for the liberation of Southern Africa from colonial rule and settler domination. Thus, political refugees and freedom fighters also benefitted from the universal coverage in these two countries.

For the better part of the 1960s, most of the countries that first became independent were on an upward trajectory in regard to social and economic development. It must be noted that this type of development was founded on a robust process of economic development of which the dividends were then redeployed into social investment endeavours. Arguably, social welfare policies were transformative as they helped to create new societies altogether and moved millions of people out of poverty, ignorance, and debilitating diseases in a short period of just 10 years. Transformative social welfare policies, as explained in other parts of this book, are not only progressive but are informed by normative positions. These normative positions reflect values and standards that uphold the well-being and human rights of people. That is why countries were able to dictate the content and pace of development through social welfare policies and other public policies. States had played overt roles in navigating development in the region. All these countries, however, were mono-commodity producers and exporters and relied on Western and foreign markets to sell their exports such as minerals, natural resources like timber, or agricultural produce. They were, therefore, heavily dependent on foreign markets, especially of the West, for their economic development.

Another critical issue was that state agendas had not been taken over by sectional interests and other negative forces such as ethnic mobilisation, corruption, or autocracy. This heavy dependence on primary commodities for exports and reliance on foreign markets for export earnings destabilised the postcolonial development agenda after the 1960s. In 1973, after the Israeli-Arab war, the Arab oil producing countries that were members of the Organisation of Petroleum Exporting Countries (OPEC) imposed an oil embargo on the United States of America because of the military support it had provided to Israel, which helped Israel to win the war. The embargo triggered a world recession which impacted negatively on African economies. At the start of the recession African and Southern African countries had unwisely borrowed from Western financial institutions with the mistaken notion that the crisis was only temporary. After the second international financial crisis that emanated from the Iran revolution and the deposing of its leader, the Shah, regional countries such as Zambia were heavily indebted to the World Bank and International Monetary Fund (IMF).

This section showed how the newly independent countries made significant progress in meeting the needs of their citizens. However, this situation did not last and the next section explains why.

# 2.9 Economic decline and the onset of the Structural Adjustment Programme (SAP)

From the mid-1980s onwards, regional countries were made to strictly implement austerity measures referred to as the Structural Adjustment Programme (SAP). SAPs were introduced by the IMF and World Bank in countries that had borrowed funds from these financial institutions. Countries that had received loans had to pay interest on these loans as a loan condition. However, because they could not pay the interest, the IMF and World Bank put pressure on these countries to introduce SAPs which then cut back on social expenditure (such as welfare, health, and education) and required countries to sell their assets (such as land and industries) to earn money to pay back the loans. There were concerted efforts by the Bretton Woods institutions such as the IMF and World Bank to coerce countries in the region to adopt free-market policies which only increased the rolling back and delegitimisation of the state in Africa. Non-governmental organisations (NGOs) and self-help initiatives were now expected to play the critical role of social welfare provision. The IMF and World Bank's interventions had disastrous effects on social development and increased poverty in the region. This contrasts sharply with the decades of the 1960s and 1970s when social welfare policies shaped health and education outcomes in the region. Previously, the social welfare systems of these countries were expansive, universalistic, and promoted development and nation-building. With the implementation of SAPs, citizens became heavily reliant on social services in general and the colonial Public Welfare Assistance Scheme – which was almost wholly inherited and never changed by postcolonial governments – as more and more people became poor and destitute.

SAPs had also resulted in massive job losses that emanated from the retrenchment of workers and the downsizing of the public sector which was crucial in creating employment opportunities for the people. Due to the social impacts of the SAP, the family and other networks were expected to provide 'cushioning' mechanisms against the negative effects of the austerity measures. However, the extended family had already been eroded by new threats of globalisation and the HIV/Aids pandemic. In the mid-1990s, it became clear that SAPs were only increasing poverty levels in Africa and not helping countries to develop. Scholars and activists alike began to challenge the relevance of the SAP. Even some of the strident supporters of the SAP were beginning to call for 'SAP with a human face'.

Structural Adjustment Programmes increased poverty levels in Africa

By the end of the 1990s, the IMF and World Bank had begun to backtrack on this economic austerity measures and started implementing the Poverty Reduction Strategy Papers (PRSPs). Specific countries had to prepare PRSPs and show that they were going to reduce poverty. However, they were still following the prescripts of the IMF and World Bank. At this stage, most countries in the region had become extremely impoverished and had weakened social welfare systems that could not meet the needs of poor citizens due to a lack of finances stemming from fragile economies. Social welfare policies were no longer transformative but more residual and reactive in line with the neoliberal agenda of the IMF and World Bank. The next section examines the contemporary social welfare policy across the region.

# 2.10 Contemporary trends in social welfare provision in Southern Africa

The new millennium signalled a change of fortunes for Africa and the region of Southern Africa in particular. This was based on the increased prices of Africa's raw materials that countries exported. The situation had changed and a new actor, China, had emerged to buy Africa's resources for its industrialisation and modernisation processes. Many countries that had not experienced any growth or had negative growth in the 1980s and 1990s suddenly found themselves with economic growth rates of not less than 5%. Some countries such as Angola were even posting 7% economic growth rates.

However, apart from Mauritius and Botswana, there were no efforts made to make economic policies complement social welfare policies in furtherance of social development objectives. Unlike in the 1960s and early 1970s where economic dividends were used to expand social development, the social development agenda was not vigorously pursued by countries in the region. Despite their purported growth, many African countries and some countries in the region were experiencing growth which was not inclusive, with a minority segment of the population becoming immensely rich while the bulk of the population remained poor. The social indicators in these countries were dismal.

For example, apart from the period when Zambia was ruled by its late president, Levi Mwanawasa (2002–2008), much of the cited growth in the economy did not and does not seem to percolate down to the poorer sections of the society. The living conditions of the poor remain deplorable. This is also the case in Angola where oil revenues are not creating social well-being. Mozambique's growth in the last couple of years seems not to have benefitted every citizen in that country but only a select few.

With few social investment efforts being propelled by Southern African governments, social welfare policies are mainly defined by Public Welfare Assistance Schemes which have not changed much since the colonial days. This type of social assistance cannot be equated to transformative social policies which are more comprehensive and based on the redistribution of resources. Thus, in the past, most of the revenue from these countries' exports was used to expand their social welfare systems. Therefore, the social welfare policies of most countries in the region had responded to a broad range of needs, and the state had provided coverage which was comprehensive. Universal access to health care and education were guaranteed in most countries. This agenda has never been revisited by Southern African countries since the period when they had implemented SAPs.

What is gaining momentum nowadays is the drive for social security which is based on social cash transfers. Even though they have been lauded for their poverty reduction abilities, they cannot be compared to the comprehensive state-led social welfare policies of past decades which were transformative. Previous efforts had lifted significant populations out of poverty through high quality universal education, health, and other measures. Cash transfers cannot do this and arguably are residual. But they are popular as they can easily placate the masses and also seem to satisfy the Western donors supporting this programme, justifying the view that poverty is being reduced in the region.

# CONCLUSION

- Chapter 2 provides a historical analysis whilst bringing to the fore the development of social welfare systems and social welfare policies in the region.
- This is important because most of the issues raised by the chapter are not being given prominence in social welfare and social work discourses these days. For example, a contemporary challenge that transformative social welfare policy could address in the region is patriarchy. This pattern of social interaction has not changed much since it was entrenched by colonialism. It seems to define contemporary regional social welfare policy choices. Hence, in tackling patriarchy, a transformative social welfare approach would effectively respond to the reproductive health rights and choices of both men and women in this contemporary time. Also, in removing patriarchal influences in service provision, transformative social welfare policies could adapt some of the positive social relations of the precolonial era for contemporary times.
- Another deficit that can be cited is that social welfare policies in the region seem not to have reverted to their comprehensive and transformative nature, as was the case in the immediate post-independence period of the 1960s. They seem to be reactive as was the case when SAPs were defining countries' development efforts.
- There is also the key challenge of political will in this equation which is very weak and not as strong as in the immediate post-independence period. Many political actors are not predisposed to effect economic growth processes that have built-in mechanisms of wealth redistribution. This is a major shortfall in social welfare policies of the region as services that accrue from the former are limited in scope due to a lack of funding from the state, coupled with a lack of capacity due to few skilled welfare personnel.
- Given the foregoing, an imperative for transformative social welfare policy is an inclusive economic policy. This would respond to the minimal funding and few skilled welfare personnel in SADC countries. These countries would have to grow their economies to the benefit of their citizens. In this way, economic growth should be redistributed to the rest of the population via welfare programmes and services. Some of the high growth forecasts of the region have not translated into a better quality of life for most of the peoples of Southern Africa.
- In addition, state capacity remains a challenge in achieving the goals of social welfare policies. Many states remain weak and, in some cases, incapable. Another imperative for transformative social welfare policy is a capable state. States in the region need to be predicated on strong and functioning institutions. These would act as the vehicles for meeting the needs of the citizens.
- Therefore, for social welfare policy in the region to be transformative, there is a need for robust political and economic development, hinging on extensive redistributive mechanisms.
- Lastly, efforts to transform social welfare policy and practice from colonial and postcolonial industrial influences need to embrace the values, visions, and aspirations that were central to the struggles for liberation on the content.

# QUESTIONS

1. How did social welfare systems evolve in the precolonial era?
2. Can you describe the forces that influenced the development of social welfare policy in the colonial era in Southern Africa?
3. In Southern Africa, what were the main features of social welfare policies in the postcolonial era in the 1960s and 1970s?

# REFERENCES

AFRICA LIBERAL NETWORK (2017) 'State of Emergency in Zambia: An Attack on Democracy' [Online]. Available: https://www.africaliberalnetwork.org/2017/07/state-emergency-zambia-attack-democracy/ [27 July 2017].

FREEDOM HOUSE (2013) 'Swaziland: A failed feudal state' [Online]. Available: https://freedomhouse.org/sites/default/files/Swaziland-%20A%20Failed%20Feudal%20State%2019%20September%202013.pdf [27 July 2017].

MAMDANI, M (2014) *When victims become killers: Colonialism, Nativism, and the Genocide in Rwanda*. Princeton, NJ: Princeton University Press.

MCKENNA, A (2011) *The Britannica Guide to Africa: The History of Southern Africa*. New York, NY: Britannica Educational Publishing.

MHONE, G (2001) *Labour Market Discrimination and its Aftermath in Southern Africa*. Paper prepared for the United Nations Research Institute for Social Development (UNRISD) Conference on Racism and Public Policy, Durban, South Africa.

MOYO, M & MINE, Y (2016) *What Colonialism Ignored: 'African Potentials' for Resolving Conflicts in Southern Africa*. Bameda: Langaa RPCIG.

MWANSA, L-K: 'Six decades of Social Work in Botswana: Challenges of training and praxis' in Rehklau, C & Lutz, R (2007) *Internationale Sozialarbeit: Sozialarbeit des Südens, Band 2 – Schwerpunkt Africa* at pp. 93–108. Oldenburg: Paulo Freire Verlag.

NJOH, AJ (2007) *Planning Power: Town Planning and Social Control in Colonial Africa*. London: University College London (UCL).

NORTHERN RHODESIA COUNCIL OF SOCIAL SERVICES (1962) *Directory of Social Services*. Lusaka: Northern Rhodesia Council of Social Services.

NOYOO, N (2013) *Social Welfare in Zambia: The Search for a Transformative Agenda*. London: Adonis & Abbey.

NOYOO, N (2014) 'Indigenous systems of governance and post-colonial Africa: The case of Barotseland' [Online]. Available: http://bnfa.info/wp-content/uploads/2014/05/Ndangwa-Noyoo.pdf [6 June 2017].

NOYOO, N: 'Social Development in Southern Africa' in Calvelo, L, Lutz, R & Ross, F (2015) *Development and Social Work: Social Work of the South*, Volume VI at pp. 167–185. Oldenburg: Paulo Freire Verlag.

SOUTHERN AFRICAN DEVELOPMENT COMMUNITY (SADC) (2017) 'Who are SADC Member States?' [Online]. Available: http://www.sadc.int/media-centre/frequently-asked-questions [7 June 2017].

STATISTICS SOUTH AFRICA (Stats SA) (2014) *Poverty trends in South Africa: An examination of absolute poverty between 2006 and 2011*. Pretoria: Stats SA.

STATISTICS SOUTH AFRICA (Stats SA) (2017a) 'Poverty on the rise in South Africa' [Online]. Available: http://www.statssa.gov.za/?p=10334 [23 August 2017].

STATISTICS SOUTH AFRICA (Stats SA) (2017b) 'Quarterly Labour Force Survey – QLFS Q1:2017' [Online]. Available: http://www.statssa.gov.za/?p=9960 [23 August 2017].

TWIKIRIZE, JM: 'Indigenisation of social work in Africa: Debates, prospects and challenges' in Spitzer, H, Twikirize, JM & Warire, GG (2014) *Professional Social Work in East Africa: Towards Development, Poverty Reduction and Gender Equality* at pp. 75–90. Kampala: Fountain Publishers.

UNITED NATIONS DEVELOPMENT PROGRAMME (UNDP) (2016) *Human Development Report*. New York, NY: Oxford University Press.

# Approaches to social welfare policy: characteristics, values and principles

*Jean D. Triegaardt*

Chapter 3 explains the different approaches and theories related to social welfare policy. Discussing how social welfare policy evolved over time and the roles played by various stakeholders, it specifically analyses the challenges faced by South Africa in transforming a former discriminatory welfare system into one that is equitable and just. In the discussion on the feminist approach, the manner in which systems perpetuate violence against women and children and the subjugation of women is explained. The main objectives and outcomes for this chapter are set out below.

## Chapter objectives

✓ Clarifying the theoretical approaches to social welfare which include the residual, institutional, normative, developmental social welfare, and feminist approaches.

✓ Elaborating on the philosophies and values underlying these approaches which ultimately impact on the social welfare policy of a country.

✓ Describing the role of government and other stakeholders in each of these approaches, and explain how it affects the welfare of people.

✓ Considering the relevance of some of the issues that women and children are facing in order to transform social welfare policy to promote their well-being.

## Chapter outcomes

✓ Demonstrating knowledge and understanding of the different approaches and the characteristics associated with social welfare policy.

✓ Understanding the philosophies and values of different approaches and how these approaches impact on the welfare of people.

✓ Critically evaluating the role and responsibilities of government and other stakeholders in relation to social welfare based on these approaches.

✓ Appreciating the values and principles embedded within each of the approaches.

## 3.1 Introduction

This chapter provides an overview of the various approaches and theories associated with social welfare policy. Over decades the thinking on social welfare policy has evolved taking into consideration the context of global, national, political, and social issues. Social welfare policies set the parameters and provide the authorisation for welfare organisations, government agencies, the private sector, and social service professions to function. The evolution of theory on social welfare policy also manifests governments' involvement in the welfare of people to a minimal or larger extent, the prevailing norms and values, and reflections on issues of social justice, human rights, and empowerment.

In South Africa, the conceptual underpinning of its social welfare policy has shifted from the apartheid era which lacked rights for the majority of citizens to the post-apartheid era of a democracy with citizenship rights. The South African Constitution (Act 108 of 1996) and Bill of Rights (Chapter 2 of the Constitution) made provision for these rights with the advent of democracy in 1994. Policies which were subsequently formulated reflected these rights, and this includes social welfare policy. In addition, the new democratic government also developed strategic plans to improve the well-being of its citizens.

One such strategic plan is the National Development Plan 2030 (NDP) (National Planning Commission (NPC), 2012) for South Africa that was published and launched in 2011 by the then Minister of Planning in the Presidency, Trevor Manual. It provides for two overarching goals which are to eliminate poverty and reduce inequality by the year 2030. The Commission's Diagnostic Report (NPC, 2011 25), released in June 2011, identified the achievements and shortcomings since 1994 when the ANC-led government came into power. It identified a failure to implement policies and an absence of broad partnerships as the main reasons for slow progress, and provided nine primary challenges:

- Too few people work.
- The quality of school education for black people is poor.
- Infrastructure is poorly located, inadequate and under-maintained.
- Spatial divides hobble inclusive development.
- The economy is unsustainably resource intensive.
- The public health system cannot meet demand or sustain quality.
- Public services are uneven and often of poor quality.
- Corruption levels are high.
- South Africa remains a divided society.

This policy document chartered the way forward for macroeconomic and social concerns related to structural conditions such as, *inter alia*, economic growth, poverty, and employment, particularly youth employment. Building on the diagnostic report, the plan added four additional themes: rural economy; social protection; regional and world affairs; and community safety. A core vision identified in the NPC's report is that of enhanced capabilities and an active citizenry. This contributes to a developmental state which builds the capabilities of people to improve their own lives, while intervening to correct historical inequalities (NPC, 2012: 27). The NDP 2030 takes into account that millions of South Africans live in poverty, and that short-term and long-term strategies are required to obviate the large-scale effects of poverty. Some of the plans (NPC, 2012: 28) include the following:

- Introducing active labour market policies and incentives to grow employment, particularly for young people and in sectors employing relatively low-skilled people.
- Expanding public employment programmes to 1 million participants by 2015 and 2 million by 2020. As the number of formal and informal sector jobs expands, public work programmes can be scaled down.
- Expanding welfare services and public employment schemes, enabling the state to service and support poor communities, particularly those with high levels of crime and violence.
- Introducing a nutrition programme for pregnant women and young children and extend early childhood development services for children under five.

The vision of the National Development Plan (NPC, 2012: 20–38) is to build national consensus. It promotes a framework for the consolidation of a current, somewhat fragmented anti-poverty policy, and is a planning mechanism for addressing poverty and inequality. Chapter 4 of this book discusses the NDP in more detail.

In his 2014 Budget Speech, the Minister of Finance announced that there was a need to contain the public sector wage bill in order to allow space for the budget in social spending. The growth of public sector wages not only limited the expansion of public sector employment, but also narrowed the space available for pro-poor initiatives (Seekings and Nattrass, 2016: 107). This indicated the South African government's concern for promoting a budget that supported pro-poor initiatives in addition to economic growth. This Budget Speech announcement appeared to be an acknowledgment that some balance needed to be obtained with the budget, although it did not imply cutting back in critical areas such as public health professionals, social workers, and teachers.

Historically, many Western governments played a limited role in social welfare, relegating the responsibility of individual welfare to families and kin (Midgley, 2009: 182). Thus, welfare reform in many Western countries meant that government played a less significant role in addressing welfare needs. Seekings and Nattrass (2016: 31) provide a perspective which gives insight into the role of Western governments by suggesting that with most advanced capitalist countries, the state shapes 'who gets what' through redistribution as well as policies affecting the structure of employment and earnings.

In contrast to developed countries, in Brazil, a developing country, President Ignacio Lula da Silva increased minimum wages and social security payments in the mid-2000s, which contributed to economic growth and poverty alleviation (ILO, 2011). These universal social protection measures with economic strategies were effective in reducing poverty and inequality. Unemployment decreased and the government initiated educational reforms and rural projects to the benefit of some of Brazil's poorest citizens.

Apart from government's role, norms and values are also intrinsic to social welfare policy since these are reflective of society. Norms provide an indicator of the expectations within a society, while values give expression to a vision of what 'ought' to be. Normative theories are associated with social welfare policies. People will have different approaches that are dependent on their political or ideological persuasions, which may vary from extreme right to extreme left. These approaches are relevant to those who benefit from the welfare system in any society.

As we explore each of these approaches in this chapter, the processes will be discussed, and the impact on the welfare of people will be revealed. We consider the role of government and its contribution to the agenda of each of these approaches, and particularly the role of government in terms of social welfare. The approaches that will be dealt with are the residual, institutional, normative theory, developmental social welfare, and feminist approaches. As mentioned before, these approaches and theory vary from conservative approaches to liberal, social democratic, and more radical approaches. Each approach merits a chapter on its own but because of limitations of space a brief discussion and analysis of each will have to suffice.

## 3.2 Theoretical approaches and perspectives to social welfare policy

The influence of theory with its accompanying ideological underpinnings on social welfare policy is widely acknowledged. Theory has provided a way of classifying different approaches and perspectives and facilitated understanding of the models or typologies of social welfare policy. Social welfare may be viewed as a nation's system of programmes, benefits, and services that assist people to meet those needs such as social, economic, educational, and health needs that are fundamental to the maintenance of society (Zastrow, 2014: 3). Early attempts at devising models of social welfare policy were Wilensky and Lebeaux's residual-institutional models (1965). These two models were developed in the United States and are discussed below. Titmuss (1974) sought to identify social policy approaches being used in other countries. More recently, other models were introduced such as developmental social welfare and feminist models. In addition to the residual-institutional approach, normative theory, developmental social welfare, and feminist approaches are discussed in this chapter.

### 3.2.1 Residual approach

The residual approach was introduced by many colonial authorities before the independence of colonies with the purpose of minimising government intervention (Hardiman and Midgley, 1982). This approach to social welfare is characterised by minimal state intervention in the provision and financing of social welfare services and social security (Rautenbach and Chiba, 2010: 8). At the time, the view was held that the onus falls on the individual for taking care of their own and their family's needs – this conservative approach is underpinned by the premise of 'blame the victim'. In essence, this approach promotes the idea that welfare is not a right, and generally there is an antipathy to government welfare programmes. Social welfare institutions are used to meet family and social needs when the market fails. Government intervention is minimal but would devote its attention to crime and prostitution, and to the most disadvantaged such as older persons, persons with disabilities, and orphaned and vulnerable children (Hall and Midgley, 2008: 4).

Residualism as an approach in the welfare sector in South Africa was introduced by the pre-apartheid government. Only certain constituencies qualified for welfare resources, that is, poor white and coloured people in the 1920s. Seekings and Nattrass (2016: 141) observe that since the 1920s, South Africa has endeavoured to build a welfare state that has weak public contributory programmes, but strong social assistance programmes with substantial provision through the market, along the broadly 'liberal' lines identified by Esping-Andersen. A more detailed discussion of Esping-Andersen's typology on the different welfare states in industrial nations is provided in the section on the 'Institutional approach'.

In order to address the 'poor white problem' in the 1930s, social pensions and disability grants were provided by the South African government. The Department of Welfare was formed in 1937 with the express purpose of assisting poor white people with welfare services. Therefore, the pre-apartheid government only recognised the rights of white people to the exclusion of other race groups. Later, social grants were gradually expanded to include other race groups such as Indians and black Africans (Seekings and Nattrass, 2016; Patel and Triegaardt, 2008). Social assistance was racially differentiated, with white people receiving the largest portion, and black Africans the smallest share. Given that welfare resources were based on a principle of exclusion, this approach is considered to be conservative (or neoliberal), and, as indicated above, government's role was minimal. According to writers such as Hall and Midgley (2008), the residual welfare model proved to be unworkable for a range of reasons. First, economic growth did not guarantee improved standards of living and welfare for poorer people. The assumption is that this model is not equipped to deal with mass poverty and unemployment. Second, social and political demand for basic services such as health, education, and housing grew exponentially.

Later, when apartheid became institutionalised by the government, the model of welfare service delivery remained unjust, discriminatory, inappropriate, and unsustainable. As a residual model it promoted intervention at the micro level (casework and group work), but could not effectively deal with mass poverty and unemployment at the macro level. Therefore, post-apartheid welfare policy required intervention methods which were non-discriminatory, equitable and rights-based.

According to the residual approach, if the market fails and social welfare institutions also do not provide any social welfare assistance, the onus falls on individuals and families to meet people's welfare needs, with the assistance of charitable or voluntary organisations such as faith-based organisations (FBOs). Therefore, even though there are various systems and mechanisms which may provide assistance to an individual, ultimately the responsibility resides with the individual for social welfare.

From a transformative perspective, the residual approach targets only a certain sector of the population which was screened for income testing, but it does not target the wider populace who are the working poor and the structurally unemployed in South Africa. According to Statistics South Africa (Stats SA), the unemployment rate was 27,7% in the third quarter of 2017 (Stats SA, 2017). While some of those unemployed benefit from social protection, there is a gap in the social protection system because those who are structurally unemployed (individuals who are unemployed for a long time) do not qualify for unemployment insurance fund (UIF) benefits. UIF benefits only apply when a worker loses his or her job because of dismissal, contract termination by the employer, or the employer's insolvency and fails to find another job within 14 days.

Some believe that a typical example of 'residual' social welfare is social grants and social welfare services which are targeted at poor people only (Wilensky and Lebeaux, 1965). These are considered to be residual because the reach of these services and grants are limited and discriminatory. Critics would refer to this as resulting in a social stigma.

If one reviews the social and political situation in South Africa since 1994, the demands for housing, health, and education have grown considerably, particularly in the urban areas. Increasingly, more people have gained access to basic services such as electricity, water and sanitation, telecommunications, housing, and primary health care. Although these have been hard-fought gains, this expansion of services has been undermined by an inability of the poor to afford payment for them (Taylor Report, 2002: 32). Furthermore, this expansion of basic services has not satisfied many of the electorate since there are frequent protests about inadequate housing and the nondelivery of essential services such as electricity or water, and the frequency of protests increases as the winter period approaches (Mail and Guardian, 2017). This is characteristic of a residual approach – it does not provide adequate welfare services to the populace who are marginalised and impoverished. An analysis of the residual model reveals that it is discriminatory, inegalitarian, and punitive. In contrast, the institutional approach is inclusive and nondiscriminatory. This model is discussed below.

## 3.2.2 Institutional approach

The institutional approach is associated with countries in Western Europe, particularly Scandinavian countries such as Sweden, Norway, and Finland. These industrialised countries have a particular ethos about the well-being of people. Because these Scandinavian countries introduced a range of social service programmes which catered for the entire population, they are referred to as welfare states (Midgley, 2009: 182). This approach, which emphasised government's intervention in social welfare provision, became known as 'institutionalism' or 'welfarism' (Hall and Midgley, 2008: 29). The institutionalist agenda is spurred by the belief that the enhancement of people's well-being is best supported by the agency of government. Sweden remains one of the most comprehensive and generous welfare states in the world (Mishra, 1999: 77) and is viewed as the welfare state ideal as reflected in the Scandinavian social democratic model (Gilbert, 2002: 136).

Government's involvement in social welfare can be traced to the enactment of the Elizabethan Poor Laws in the sixteenth century in Britain and the Bismarck social insurance schemes in the nineteenth century in Germany. The Elizabethan Poor Law of 1601 is regarded as a milestone in the development of public welfare, and laid the foundation for the expansion of state involvement in Britain and the United States of America (USA) (Midgley, 2009: 182, 183). In Germany, social insurance started in the 1880s and was soon adopted in other European countries (Midgley, 2009). Later, social insurance was introduced in the USA through the enactment of the Social Security Act of 1935. The social security system in the USA includes social insurance programmes to provide economic security for older persons, workers with disabilities, and workers' dependents and survivors (Ozawa, 2009). Social insurance programmes are based on the contributions of employers and employees to a fund which makes provision for workers and employees for contingencies such as injury or disability, unemployment, maternity and paternity leave, and retirement. According to Midgley (2009: 183), social security is one of the few social programmes in the USA which is based on institutional ideas. Although some believed that the introduction of social security in the USA epitomised institutionalism as a principle of government responsibility (Dolgoff and Feldstein, 1980), others believed that the American people never fully accepted the principle of government welfare responsibility, and they suggest that the USA is a 'reluctant welfare state' (Jansson, 2005).

Progressive liberal ideas and social democratic ideologies have influenced the institutional approaches to social welfare policy. One of the components of the institutional approach is full employment, or certainly very low unemployment rates. Therefore, this approach would have difficulty functioning in a capitalist society (since unemployment is integral to a capitalist society) and functions well in welfare states. The criterion which epitomises a welfare state is that the welfare system is separated from the market economy. Esping-Andersen (1999) developed a classification for the different welfare states in developed industrial nations. These include social democratic socialist, corporatist, and liberal welfare regimes. Some examples are listed below:

- As mentioned in the opening paragraph in this section, Scandinavian countries such as Norway, Sweden, and Finland are known for their 'welfarism' because of their comprehensive and generous welfare benefits to their citizens, particularly Sweden. These countries espouse social democratic ideals because of the redistributive nature of their welfare resources. Resources are considered to be redistributive because the principle is that a social welfare system should redistribute income from those who have more to those who have less.

- Germany is considered to be corporatist because of the nature and range of agreements with labour, the government, and the business sector on policies such as social protection, wages and conditions of service, and fiscal issues.
- An example of a liberal welfare regime would be that of the United States of America because of its less expansive public programmes and greater involvement of the market in social provision.

Welfare states make provision for all its citizens irrespective of income. Fundamental to the welfare state is what one refers to as 'welfarism" or the institutional approach which has at its core an acknowledgement of the rights of all people, altruism, and social justice. The most prominent feature of the social democratic welfare model is universal access to publicly provided benefits that offer strong protection of labour as social rights of citizenship (Giddens, 2009: 44).

The institutional approach is underpinned by values and principles which are illustrative of concern by government about how to enhance the well-being of its people. The fundamental premise here is that government has a major involvement in ensuring the welfare of its people, and even for people beyond its borders in developing countries. Midgley (2009: 181) observes that supporters of the institutional approach believe that social welfare can best be enhanced through the agency of government.

Conservatives critiqued the institutional approach as encouraging dependency, being too exorbitant since the resources could be utilised for other sectors of the economy, and paternalistic, meaning that it is overly protective or authoritarian. Of course proponents of the institutional approach defended their position as promoting the principle of human rights of people, altruism, social justice, and inclusiveness.

Depending on whether the overall approach is liberal or conservative, welfare benefits may be distributed according to the principles of universalism or selectivity. These are discussed below.

### 3.2.2.1 Universalism
*Universalism* means that welfare benefits should be available to all citizens as a social right. Thus, *universalism* means that all South African citizens would qualify for social grants and social welfare services irrespective of income, and will be protected against any unexpected contingencies of life. Patel (2015: 19) notes that universalism refers to the right of all citizens in a country to universal coverage and access to services and benefits such as income security, medical care, education, and housing on an ongoing basis. The theory of social rights is based on the rationale of the institutional approach. Marshall (1950) proposed that intrinsic to citizenship, civil and political rights must be in tandem with social rights. By the provision of social rights, governments will promote social justice and meet the ideals of the welfare state (Midgley, 2009: 189). Much of the discussion on social rights occurs in the section on the rights-based approach under 'Developmental social welfare'.

### 3.2.2.2 Selectivity
*Selectivity* is associated with the proposition that benefits should be distributed on the basis of individual need, as determined by a test of income (Gilbert, 2002: 135). Those who support selectivity suggest that means testing (that is, screening for income) not only dispenses benefits according to financial need, but also ensures that spending is curtailed, and that funds are targeted at those in dire need. Critics of the selective means test see this approach as stigmatisation of citizens, demeaning, and punitive (Titmuss, 1968). However, Gilbert

(2002: 144) observes that with the increasing prevalence of means testing, new distinctions are being introduced into the discourse that pay tribute to universal orientation by soliciting the terminology of universalism in the service of selectivity. This means that some of the language of universalism is being introduced into the language of selectivity or income testing (means testing). One such example contrasts 'liberal universalism', which means flat rate benefits for all, with 'socio-democratic universalism', which allows for regulating benefits for vertical redistribution purposes, and it incorporates targeting in the perspective of equal outcomes. Vertical redistribution is the principle that a social welfare system should redistribute income from those who have more resources to those who have less. The main method of modifying benefits for vertical redistribution is through means testing, either at the point of distribution or consumption (Gilbert, 2002).

As indicated previously in an earlier section, social security was introduced in South Africa in the 1920s when maintenance grants and family support were provided to white and coloured people (Patel and Triegaardt, 2008: 90). Later, because of the 'poor white problem', pensions and disability grants were initiated in the 1930s. In addition to social grants being distributed on the basis of race, and predominantly poor white people qualified, they were based on the principle of *selectivity* because a means-tested approach was utilised. In 1993, social grants were provided to all races irrespective of race, colour or creed. However, they were still based on the principle of selectivity because income played a major role in the decision about who qualified for social grants. The South African Constitution (1996) does provide for social security to all but it is largely dependent on the availability of resources. Social pensions are provided to all but it is available on a sliding scale with respect to income.

The institutional approach certainly lends itself to being transformative since it is pro-poor and will provide care and well-being to all people irrespective of income. At the core of the institutional approach lies the principle of universalism.

The following subsection deals with normative theory and its influence on social welfare policy.

### 3.2.3 Normative theory

There are a range of normative positions which are portrayed in social welfare policy and these policy positions are proposed by a variety of writers and schools of thought. These writers can be grouped according to the normative influence which they exert on social welfare policy. The first group referred to as 'individualists' includes writers such as Milton Friedman and Frederick von Hayek. The second group known as the 'reformists' includes people such as William Beveridge, John Maynard Keynes, and Richard Titmuss. The third group referred to as the 'structuralists' includes writers such as Jurgen Habermas (the Frankfurt School of Thought) and Michel Foucault (Hall and Midgley, 2008: 28). The latter are often referred to as critical theorists since their focus is analysing forms of domination and oppression associated with capitalism, Fascism and Nazism.

Normative theory plays a crucial role in the formation of social welfare policy. It influences decisions of political parties, governments, non-governmental organisations, social movements, and international organisations. The role of normative theory in influencing social welfare policy is

Jurgen Habermas is a German sociologist and philosopher

also shaped by ideological traditions which can be ascribed to three distinctive positions, namely, 'individualism', 'collectivism', and 'populism' (Hall and Midgley, 2008: 28). These three traditions give rise to approaches that contribute to the role of the market, the state, and the community. If one examines each of these approaches, then it becomes clear how each of these traditions impacts and shapes social welfare policies.

### 3.2.3.1 The enterprise approach

This enterprise approach is based on an individualistic ideology which stresses that the individual has agency in social and economic life. It stresses the dominance of the market in social welfare. With individualistic ideology as a premise, some governments have abandoned 'institutional welfarism' and instead have chosen to minimise government's role in social welfare (Hall and Midgley, 2008: 31). In addition to government's minimal role in social welfare, strict budgeting controls have been imposed with cutbacks in welfare services, and this has led to welfare services being contracted out to commercial enterprises. The thinking behind this is that the market should as far as possible take care of social needs. An example of a commercial enterprise which seems to have worked effectively for youth in conflict with the law is that of BOSASA Youth Development Centre which has facilities across South Africa.

### 3.2.3.2 The populist approach

This approach is premised on populist ideology that focuses on the involvement of people together with their common values, beliefs and culture in social welfare. An observation is that populist political leaders often use anti-establishment rhetoric to secure electoral support and they often agitate for expansion of social programmes which serves the needs of the people. Populist ideas often inform social movements which emerge in response to socioeconomic and political issues and these social movements garner support for particular causes. The women's movement has brought about changes by challenging patriarchal systems and not only effected changes in the status of women, but policy changes to health, education, and welfare policies and practices. More discussion on social movements is provided in Chapter 11. In South Africa, an example of a social movement garnering support from civil society was the emergence of the 'Save South Africa' movement which gained momentum rallying people around one of their demands which was for former President Jacob Zuma to step down. President Zuma stepped down on the 14 February 2018 as a consequence of pressure from various quarters including his own party, the ANC.

### 3.2.3.3 The statist approach

This approach is underpinned by a collectivist ideology which suggests that the ideal way to achieve common goals is for people to co-operate to meet their common needs. The ultimate collective is the state that, according to collectivist thinking, is not a remote and bureaucratic organisation, but a body consisting of all citizens which is answerable to the citizens and which serves their interests (Hall and Midgley, 2008: 29). Normative ideas formed the basis of formalised social welfare provision known as 'institutionalism' or 'welfarism, which is discussed above. Wilensky and Lebeaux's (1965) work took a normative position (discussed earlier) and they asserted that the nature of institutionalism was superior to that of residualism. Critics of institutionalism suggested that government's assistance to those in need created far too much dependence and irresponsibility. This led to the demise of institutionalist theory, but created the space for what is referred to as the 'Third Way' theory (Giddens, 1998) and Midgley's developmentalist theory. In addition to these two theories, the New Way theory promotes the idea that the state emphasises a pluralist welfare system that includes individual responsibility, community participation, market involvement, and voluntary provision in social welfare. Developmentalism is based on social development thinking that first emerged in the South and was actively promoted by the United Nations. It offers a macro perspective on policy which integrates social and economic policies within a comprehensive, state-directed development process, involving both civil society and business organisations in promoting development goals (Hall and Midgley, 2008: 30). The developmental social welfare approach is discussed next.

## 3.2.4 Developmental social welfare

According to Gray (2006), developmental social welfare is the name given to South Africa's post-apartheid welfare system informed by the theory of social development as discussed in the *White Paper for Social Welfare* (Ministry for Welfare and Population Development (RSA), 1997). Developmental social welfare was introduced in South Africa because it was considered to be more inclusive and egalitarian, and would reach the majority of poor people in contrast to the apartheid system of welfare which was punitive, illegitimate, and focused on the minority of poor people (that is, residualism). The White Paper for Social Welfare (1997) provides the national policy framework for social welfare which rests on two pillars, namely, social security or social protection, and social welfare services. Social security commands the larger portion of the social development budget, and welfare services have a far smaller portion. More discussion on the budget is provided in the subsection on 'Social development partnerships or welfare pluralism' below.

The policy which was adopted in the White Paper for Social Welfare (1997) is indicative of being pro-poor and is rights-based. A discussion of the latter term is provided in a later discussion. The principle of the policy is people-centred and is founded on core values such as democracy, equity and social justice. These principles are aligned with the requirements of the South African Constitution (1996). Patel (2015: 82) observes that South Africa's developmental approach to social welfare evolved from the country's unique history of inequality and the violation of human rights as a result of colonialism and apartheid.

The idea of a developmental state in South Africa gained traction after 2005. A developmental state means that 'appropriate interventions in economic policy will allow for the promotion of economic growth and social development' (Naidoo, 2006: 124). From 2005, the ANC at its National General Council committed itself to constructing a developmental state which would intervene to restructure the South African economy (ANC, 2005 in Edigheji, 2010). This commitment was reaffirmed at its 52nd national conference in Polokwane, Limpopo, in 2007, as well as in the ANC's manifesto for the 2009 general election (ANC, 2009 in Edigheji, 2010).

More recently, the *Review of the Implementation of the White Paper* (RSA, 2016) and the vision of the NDP 2030 reinforced the policy of developmental social welfare since these are supportive of the poor in South Africa. The NPC (2012: 357) conceptualises social protection as addressing South Africa's legacy of apartheid. Social protection includes reducing the cost of living for low-income people and working-class households (with regard to the cost of food, energy, and transport), redistributing wealth, and stimulating the economy, particularly that of rural areas (NPC, 2012: 116, 198, 283). Social protection as a concept is broader than social security and is considered to provide the basic socioeconomic necessities for people to function, which, by the same token, will enable them to contribute to the social and economic development of the country.

Developmental social welfare as a concept comprises five themes. These include the following:

- A rights-based approach
- Social and economic development
- Democracy and participation
- A pluralist approach
- Bridging the micro and macro divide.

Each of these themes is explored below.

### 3.2.4.1 A rights-based approach

The rights for citizens are embedded in the Constitution of the Republic of South Africa (Act 108 of 1996) and the Bill of Rights as indicated earlier in the chapter. The rights-based approach is concerned with the rights of all citizens and meeting the needs of people, particularly those who are disadvantaged. Intrinsic to these rights are issues of social justice, a minimum living standard for all people, equitable access to services and benefits, and equal opportunity for all.

Marshall (1950) proposed certain ideas on citizenship and a progression of rights. These ideas on citizenship and progression of civil, political, and social rights also informed the perspective on social development in South Africa. These rights can be described in the following way:

- Civil rights – this right relates to the freedom to dissent and take action.
- Political rights – this right translates into an individual having the opportunity to influence political decisions and political power.
- Social rights – these rights are substantive and necessary in that individuals are afforded the necessary opportunity to achieve a minimum social status in society (Marshall, 1963).

The philosophical foundation of the rights-based approach is found in John Rawl's Theory of Justice (1971). This theory acknowledges the importance of material and non-material resources. His argument proposes that primary social goods such as liberty, opportunity, income and wealth, and the basis for self-respect should be fairly and equally distributed. As a consequence, for such distribution to be just, it must benefit the least disadvantaged. He further argues that a just society can allow for the differences in the distribution of resources provided that it benefits the least advantaged, and there is equal opportunity for access to resources. Dominelli (2010: 89) critiques John Rawls' notion of individually held rights, and suggests that his ideas deal inadequately with issues of diversity and oppression based on identity traits that have collective dimensions as well as individual ones.

South Africa's Constitution (1996), and the Bill of Rights in particular, provides for several rights and therefore obligates the state to give effect to these rights. At the heart of these rights resides the acknowledgement of the right to dignity, a recognition of the worth and value of all human beings. These rights include the economic and social rights of the right to housing (section 26); other rights such as the right to health care, food, water, shelter, and social security (section 27); and the right to education (section 29). The Bill of Rights notes that the state must take reasonable legislative and other measures, within its available resources, to achieve the realisation of these rights (RSA, 1996). Social welfare policy in South Africa is thus founded on a rights-based approach and is inclusive.

### 3.2.4.2 Social and economic development

In 1995, the United Nations convened the World Summit on Social Development which was held in Copenhagen. One hundred and twenty-seven Heads of State, including South

Africa's, affirmed the Copenhagen Declaration which subscribed to key development social policies and goals. These goals included: the eradication of poverty; reducing unemployment; promoting gender equality and empowering women; reducing child mortality; achieving universal primary education; combating HIV/Aids, malaria, and other diseases; ensuring environmental sustainability; and developing a global partnership for development (Midgley and Sherraden, 2009). The goals were assigned specific targets which were reviewed in 2015. South Africa has progressed in reducing extreme income poverty due to a progressive, pro-poor tax system which provides a basic social protection, while providing jobs has remained a challenge (Stats SA, 2017).

Sen (1999) promotes the idea that development requires the removal of major sources of unfreedom such as poverty, poor economic opportunities, social deprivation, neglect of public facilities, and the insensitivity of repressive states. A developmental state must be able to balance economic growth with social development, or it will morph into distorted development. The theory of social development provides for integrated social and economic development. The fundamental tenet of this theory is that economic growth on its own is insufficient for improving the quality of life of all citizens. This approach to social welfare proposes a macroeconomic policy framework for alleviating poverty which combines social and economic goals (Gray, 2006: S53). Social or human development is about increasing the capacities and functioning of people, and this is viewed as an investment in human beings. Significant human development features are characterised by the fundamental needs of sustenance, primary health care, literacy, and basic housing. There is considerable evidence that investments in nutrition, primary health care, education, and basic housing yield positive returns in increased participation, increased connectedness, increased cohesion, and increased social stability (Midgley and Sherraden, 2009: 286). Investments in people promote their capabilities and contribute to economic development and vice versa. Midgley and Sherraden (2009: 283) stress that social development advocates do not merely urge social welfare clients to become economically productive; they argue that adequate investments should be made to ensure that people obtain the requisite skills, knowledge, resources, opportunities, incentives, and subsidies to participate productively in the economy.

### 3.2.4.3 Democracy and participation

Democracy means rule by the people, for the people, and of the people. Democracy is a form of government in which the people have a voice in the exercise of power, and it is exercised usually through elected representatives (Soanes and Stevenson, 2008). Democracy is a system which involves competition among different political parties for positions of power (Giddens, 2002: 68). According to Patel (2015: 91), democracy means the striving for political equality, protection of liberty and freedom, and the defence of interests of the society. In a democracy, regular and fair elections are held and all citizens have the right to participate. The right of participation is accompanied by civil liberties which uphold freedom of expression and discussion, in addition to the freedom to form and join any political group or association (Giddens, 2002). Every five years national general elections are held in South Africa, and, at the time of writing this book, the next one would be held in 2019. Currently, the majority party which holds power in the country is the African National Congress (ANC). It has been the dominant party since the first democratic elections in 1994. As part of the electoral system, there are other political parties which are represented in Parliament such as the Democratic Alliance (DA), the Economic Freedom Fighters (EFF), the United Democratic Movement (UDM), Congress of the People (COPE), and other smaller parties.

### 3.2.4.4 Social development partnerships or welfare pluralism

Social development partnerships or welfare pluralism describes the engagement of a range of stakeholders in the mutual promotion and achievement of common development goals and outcomes for the marginalised sectors of society. Welfare pluralism may be viewed as the way in which welfare services are structured, organised and delivered, taking into consideration the roles and responsibilities of various sectors of society. These are the commercial or business sector, government sector, and the voluntary and non-governmental organisation (NGO) sectors which provide assistance to needy citizens (Patel, 2015: 93). Welfare pluralism may be referred to as the 'mixed economy of welfare' and has played an increasingly important role in social welfare policy discourse since the late 1970s (Gilbert, 2009: 236).

The discourse of social development partnerships or welfare pluralism recognises that the financing and delivery of welfare services occur through the domain of both the private and public sectors. The social market of the welfare state awards goods and services according to human needs, dependency, social obligations, altruistic sentiments, charitable motivations, and desires for communal security (Gilbert, 2009). This differs from a capitalist society where goods and services are distributed in an economic market by way of a profit motive, an ability to pay, productivity, consumer choice, and entrepreneurial initiative.

Figure 3.1 below illustrates the structure of welfare pluralism in the context of social and economic markets.

| Social market of the welfare state | | Economic market |
|---|---|---|
| Public domain | Private domain | |
| • Direct provision of transfers by national, provincial, and local government. <br>• Indirect transfers through tax expenditures. <br>• Regulatory transfers. | • Informal services and support by family and friends. <br>• Services by voluntary and non-profit organisations. <br>• Services by for-profit agencies. | • Goods and service produced for profit-making by agencies. |

Figure 3.1 Welfare pluralism in the social market (adapted from Gilbert, 2009: 237)

The above figure indicates that there are social aspects related to the welfare state, and then there is the economic market. It shows the two sides of the welfare state – the public and private domains. The public domain makes provision for direct and indirect transfers such as the collection of taxes which contributes to the fiscus. These taxes provide for the financing of education, health, social security, and welfare services, amongst others, which will be included in the government's budget. On the other hand, the private domain comprises the informal assistance provided by family and friends, such as groceries or money; services by non-profit organisations, for example, care of children and older people; and services provided by for-profit organisations such as corporate social investment (CSI). Corporate social investment is discussed below under the 'Voluntary sector and non-profit organisations (NPOs)'. Lastly, the economic market contributes to the welfare state by making provision for companies that produce goods and services with the intention of making a profit.

There are different sets of stakeholders who can be identified in the social welfare policy field. These include government and the state; the commercial or business sector; civil society which will include non-governmental organisatios (NGOs), faith-based organisations (FBOs), and community-based organisations (CBOs); and informal, voluntary, and international development or funding organisations. The state and government have been perceived to be the main driving force in changing social conditions, or social reform, and the major architect of social welfare policy constructs (Hall and Midgley, 2008: 11). These stakeholders are discussed in turn below.

## a)     *Government and the state*

As mentioned earlier in the chapter, governments are involved in the welfare of their citizens to a greater or lesser extent. In South Africa, the approach to developmental social welfare is envisaging government as taking the leading role in a collaborative relationship with other partners in the delivery of welfare services. South Africa's Constitution (1996) makes provision for cooperative governance which entails that the three spheres of governance – national, provincial, and local government – will co-operate even though these spheres are distinct. National, provincial, and local governments provide direct and indirect transfers. Welfare resources are provided for service delivery by means of government's allocation of funds through the budget and other fiscal mechanisms such as subsidies.

The Social Development budget allocation for the 2017–18 financial year is R148 billion in total (Minister of Social Development's Budget Speech, 25 May 2017). Of this amount, R140 billion is provided for social grants to older persons, people with disabilities, and children. Social assistance is provided to 17 million beneficiaries, of which children are the largest benefactors. In comparison with other middle-income countries, the South African government obtains much of its income from personal income tax and corporate taxes, and relies less on indirect transfers. Indirect transfers occur through special tax subsidies and tax exemptions, and the regulatory power of government. By 2014, South Africa had reduced income poverty (and inequality) through taxation and cash transfers more than other similar economies like Brazil (Seekings and Nattrass, 2016: 25).

The processes involved in developing policies are multilayered and complex. Given that the government is expected to enhance the well-being of its people, an effort is made to solicit support for the policy at hand, and obtain the input from a range of constituencies. For example, in South Africa public hearings may be held to solicit input and opinions on a draft policy from different organisations and stakeholders. More discussion on this topic is provided in Chapter 10 on 'Social welfare policy and the transformational participatory processes in South Africa'.

## b)     *Voluntary sector and non-profit organisations (NPOs)*

There are differences between the voluntary welfare sector and the NPO sector since their origins are from different historical contexts. Voluntary welfare organisations were more charity oriented, less formal, and were responsive to human needs at the coal face. NPOs are more formal, service oriented, and governed by boards within the legislation (for example, the Non-Profit Organisations Act 71 of 1997) that applies to them for registration, funding, and matters pertaining to corporate governance.

Gilbert (2009: 237) notes that the voluntary sector comprises non-profit social welfare agencies and the business sector comprises profit-oriented firms. Each is discussed below:

## c)     *The NPO sector (this term is used interchangeably with NGO)*

The relationship of NPOs with the government is a major determinant of what NPOs contribute to development. This depends upon whether voluntary organisations act in tandem with the government, in direct opposition to the government, or as a vehicle for strengthening the representation and bargaining power of weaker groups in society (Hall and Midgley, 2008: 16). In South Africa, there is a partnership between the different sectors, particularly government and non-government organisations, in delivering welfare services to its citizens.

For example, Child Welfare (an NPO) delivers foster care services to children and is subsidised by the national Department of Social Development to carry out such services.

The NPO sector and faith-based organisations provide welfare services in a range of fields such as child and family services, disabilities, substance abuse, crime prevention, rehabilitation services to ex-offenders and restorative justice, mental health, and chronic illnesses. In addition to the subsidies provided by the state, NPOs raise funds on their own in order to survive in the present restricted economic climate. Therefore, welfare pluralism can be viewed as various modes of meeting people's needs through the various sectors, but also as a system for the finance and delivery of social provisions that functions outside of the market economy (Gilbert, 2009: 236). During the Review of the Implementation of the White Paper process, there was wide acknowledgement that the NPO sector in South Africa plays a crucial role in service delivery (RSA, 2013).

## d)    *Business sector*
The business sector contributes to the welfare of people at two levels, that is, direct contributions or regulatory transfers through taxes, or indirect transfers through Corporate Social Investment (CSI) programmes. Trialogue (a company that has conducted annual research into CSI since 1998) estimated that total CSI expenditure in South Africa was R8,1 billion for the 2014–15 financial year (Mathews, 2014). Education received the biggest portion of CSI spending. The business sector works in conjunction with government in what are referred to as public–private partnerships (PPP). However, the relationship between government and the business sector is not a strong one. According to Seekings and Nattrass (2016: 240), this relationship in post-apartheid South Africa is not that different from the relationship during the apartheid era in that the combination of a (mostly) strong state and marked social distance between political and economic elites poses sharp limits to co-ordination between state and business overall.

## e)    *Informal sector*
The informal sector refers to individuals, friends, and family who provide assistance to individuals in need. These are social networks of family and friends who give mutual aid and support, for example, stokvels and burial societies. The discourse in social protection refers to this as informal social protection or social security.

## f)    *Faith-based sector (FBO)*
Many faith-based institutions have provided services to needy and disadvantaged people throughout the ages. In South Africa, during the apartheid years, faith-based organisations provided assistance to the most disadvantaged. In more recent times, both the faith-based sector and NPOs continue to provide services to people in need when welfare services have not been provided to certain groups of people, for example, refugees and migrants. Some of these organisations include, *inter alia*, the South African Red Cross, Legal Resources Centre, the Central Methodist Church, Anglican Church, and many other churches. For example, the Central Methodist Church provides counselling and educational services, as well as referral services for employment opportunities to refugees and migrants (Triegaardt, 2009). Since South Africa subscribes to the principle of non-discrimination, refugees and asylum seekers do benefit from social welfare, social assistance, and social insurance schemes, and are entitled to basic health care services and education (Mpedi and Ross, 2013: 212).

## g) *International development/countries or funding organisations*

Many international development organisations or funding bodies have provided charters or guidelines and/or funding to assist the South African welfare sector over the years.

First, the charters or guidelines provide the direction for particular welfare policies and legislation that have been formulated. South Africa supported the Copenhagen declaration of eradicating poverty at the World Summit on Social Development in 1995. In addition, South Africa also agreed to the Millennium Development Goals (MDGs) of halving poverty by 2015, the provision of universal primary education in all countries, the reduction of the infant and under-five child mortality rate by two thirds, and the reduction of maternal mortality by three fourths. Meeting the MDGs could make a positive difference to the lives of many impoverished women, men, and children. A critique of the MDGs has been that one goal has been allocated to gender equality and empowerment of women, but this goal does not address issues of social and political marginalisation of women.

### 3.2.4.5 Macro and micro divide

Bridging the macro and micro divide means that, in the past, it was difficult to bridge this chasm in social work intervention between individual and group work at the micro level, community work at the mezzo level, and policy work at the macro level. Without bridging this divide, intervention would be limited and shortsighted. The purpose of developmental social welfare is to bridge this dichotomy in order to enhance the functioning and empowerment of individuals, groups, and communities. Patel and Hochfeld (2012: 692) note that it is important to bridge the chasm between the micro interventions, aimed at individuals and families, and macro interventions to transform the structures and institutions that promote social and economic injustice.

Developmental social welfare is distinctly different from the residual approach because it is inclusive and pro-poor, with government playing a major role in the delivery and transformation of welfare services. Government plays a major role in both developmental social welfare and the institutional approaches, whereas a minimal role is played by government in the residual approach. Weyers (2013: 452) is critical of the application of the developmental social welfare approach since he thinks that it is more about rhetoric and macro policy statements, and that the South African welfare policy's trajectory is more aligned with the institutional approach.

One has to be prudent about the discourse since the analysis provided by Gilbert (2009) about the institutional approach vis-à-vis the residual approach demonstrates a more nuanced approach. Of course the central tenet of the institutional approach is universalism which means that welfare resources are provided to all people irrespective of income. In addition, the institutional approach supports full employment, and the socio-political context would be a welfare state which has been classified into three typologies by Esping-Andersen (1999). These have been discussed in the previous section. In contrast to the residual and institutional approaches, the social development partnership or welfare pluralism theme discussed previously is unique to the developmental social welfare approach.

## 3.2.5 Feminist approach

There are many interpretations of feminism. Feminism is considered to be an awareness of the oppression, exploitation and/or the subjugation of women within society, and the consciousness and action to change and transform this situation (Reddock, 1988: 53, cited by Msimang, 2002: 7). Feminist thinking became more prevalent in the twentieth century and has contributed to development discourse by firmly embedding issues of gender oppression in the public space (Hall and Midgley, 2008). Feminist approaches to social welfare policy are necessary in that the analysis and solutions will have both intended and unintended consequences for policy design and implementation. Welfare discourse has differentiated between 'deserving' and 'undeserving' women – the former perform society's roles of wife and mother, while the latter (for example, a woman with children who are born out of wedlock) do not (Hyde, 2009: 248). In the past, women who had children out of wedlock were considered to be 'undeserving' and stigmatised, and thus the term 'illegitimate' was used. Therefore, the discourse for single parents was pejorative. The feminist approach has relevance for social welfare policy because of the concern with the political, economic, and social well-being of women and their families, and the structural forces and collective processes that contribute to the oppression and disempowerment of women. Even though the Constitution and Bill of Rights provides the context for South African welfare policy with the concomitant protection of women and children, and the acknowledgement and recognition of the worth and dignity of women and children, there is increasing violence towards women and children in South Africa.

### 3.2.5.1 Violence towards women and children
Violence occurs at different levels in society. There is violence at micro levels (i.e. individual and family), mezzo or institutional levels (i.e. community or organisational), and macro or societal levels, for example:
- At a micro or interpersonal level, individuals may act violently towards one another by being physically and/or emotionally abusive. These may include setting up conditions to enforce oppression, exploitation or deprivation (Gil, 1979).
- At a mezzo or institutional level, policies and practices may set up conditions to inhibit the flourishing or the potential of human beings, e.g. corporal punishment at schools can result in inhibiting the development of a learner(s).
- At a macro level, violence is a consequence of policies which either sanction or result in deficiencies in the socioeconomic conditions of citizens (including women and children) which are needed for their optimal development.

Both mezzo and macro levels of violence are also referred to as structural violence. As a result of the lacuna in macroeconomic policies, many citizens are impoverished, unemployed, and lack decent housing. Personal violence and structural violence interact and reinforce each other (Gil, 1979: 62). Personal violence is usually 'reactive' violence rooted in structural violence, and an urge to retaliate by inflicting violence on others rather than initiating violence, because experiences which inhibit a person's development will result in stress and frustration. As structural violence increases, violence

People in South Africa have been calling for harsher sentences for child abusers and child killers

increases towards vulnerable sectors of society such as families, women, and children. Fester (2015: 283) observes that treating women equally to men and not interrogating factors such as culture which negatively impact on women's equality will perpetuate women's subordinate status. At the core of this are patriarchal views towards women (see Chapter 2) with accompanying notions of gendered roles and responsibilities.

### 3.2.5.2 Women, children and social grants

Many South African women and children benefit from the allocation of social grants. The Constitution requires that social grants are provided to poor people. Section 27(1)(*c*) of the Constitution of the Republic of South Africa (Act 108 of 1996) states that:

> *Everyone has the right to have access to … social security, including, if they are unable to support themselves and their dependants, appropriate social assistance.*

Section 28(1)(*c*) gives children 'the right to basic nutrition, shelter, basic health care services, and social services'. Social grants such as the Child Support Grant (CSG) have made a considerable difference to impoverished children. Research has demonstrated that children have benefitted from the CSGs since they are not malnourished and attend school, and that the CSGs meet the basic needs of vulnerable children (Patel and Triegaardt, 2008). The impact of the CSG has been experienced by impoverished children and their families, and it has been beneficial in the provinces with the poorest children (i.e. Eastern Cape, KwaZulu-Natal, and Limpopo) (Triegaardt, 2005). However, there are feminist writers who have suggested that although welfare benefits, that is, social grants, have alleviated poverty in the short term, they are critical of the sustainability of social grants since they believe that women need to be empowered through skills and wage labour (Fester, 2015; Hassim, 2014). This critique is not antithetical to the vision of developmental social welfare since the medium to long-term vision is the empowerment of individuals, the building of social capital by capacity-building, and development of skills through training.

### 3.2.5.3 Women's realities

Many women and children live in poverty in South Africa. Poverty, inequality, and unemployment impact directly on this marginalised sector of the population. Feminists charge that the approach to poverty does not take into consideration gender-specific aspects of women's experiences of poverty (Sweetman, 2005: 3). Many families are headed by single parents, who are predominantly black women and poor. The unemployment rate in the third quarter of 2017 was 27,7% (Stats SA, November 2017). It is the highest jobless rate since the first quarter of 2004 as unemployment rose faster than employment and more people joined the labour force. More women than men are unemployed; and more black women are unemployed than black men. The expanded definition of unemployment, which includes people who have stopped looking for work, rose to 36,4% from 35,6% (Stats SA, 2017). The South African economy moved into recession after the economy shrank in two successive quarters of 2016 and 2017. This move into recession meant that there was a reported decrease of 0,7% in GDP during the first quarter of 2017, following a 0,3% contraction in the fourth quarter of 2016 (Stats SA, 2017).

The developmental social welfare approach does consider that social grants provide assistance to women and children during their most difficult times when they are impoverished. But this perspective also allows for the enhancement of individuals through the provision of skills, training, and empowerment so that they can participate in the productive economy. According to Midgley and Sherraden (2009: 283), social welfare programmes are investment oriented and contribute positively toward economic development.

In the above section, the various political, social, and economic realities women have to face on a daily basis were discussed. These realities contribute to the oppressive and discriminatory conditions of women in spite of the protective measures of human rights legislation and the Constitution.

## 3.3  An emerging paradigm

South Africa's economy is in a state of flux. The high unemployment rate and the fact that its credit rating was downgraded to junk status by rating agencies, namely, Standard and Poor Global Ratings, and Fitch, put much pressure on the government and its citizens (Justin Brown, 2017; Hilary Joffe, 2017). At the time of writing this book, the ratings agency (Fitch) indicated that the reasons for the downgrade were the political events in the country, including the Cabinet reshuffle, which would lead to weakening standards of governance and public finances. The consequences of downgrading are a rise in government debt-servicing costs, which means that there will be less money for essential services such as housing, education, and sanitation. Also, the unintended consequences could be more protests about the quality of service delivery. As discussed in the previous section, Stats SA (June 2017) indicated that South Africa was in a state of recession because of a decrease in GDP in two quarters in a row. Currently, there is pressure on the government to change the trajectory of the economy, and there has been much talk about the National Development Plan 2030 which will continue to be pursued as government policy. The vision of the NDP is the elimination of poverty and inequality and specific targets have been set to achieve this vision by 2030 (NPC, 2012: 116). There are certainly synergies between the vision and goals of the NDP and that of the policy of social development as provided in the White Paper for Social Welfare (1997). The *Report of the Review of the Implementation of the White Paper for Social Welfare* has recommended that the White Paper be revised and that a National Social Development Act be introduced thereafter (RSA, 2016). However, it is clear that the integration of social and economic development will continue to feature as a fundamental premise for both current and future welfare policy in addition to social and economic justice, and the empowerment and participation of citizens. South African society has evolved to such an extent that all of these characteristics should be integral to welfare policy. As indicated in Chapter 1, an important feature of transformative social welfare policy is the focus on both the care of human beings and the integration of members of society into economic and political activity. As much as universalism would be an ideal principle to strive towards in welfare policy, this will largely be dependent on the 'availability of resources' which is articulated in the South African Constitution (1996).

Economic policies that focus solely on economic growth are unlikely to succeed on their own. They need to be complemented with social welfare policies that enable the poor to participate in economic growth. Midgley and Sherraden (2009: 283) observe that this requires the adoption of a people-centred, inclusive economic development process in which governments actively promote economic participation and adopt methods that will increase employment, income, and educational skills, and enhance standards of living. Policies to confront inequality in South Africa must therefore combine effective economic and social policies to:

1. generate high and sustained economic growth that is pro-poor;
2. provide effective social safety nets to protect the poor especially in the short-term; and very importantly
3. build human capital and other assets of those at the bottom of the inequality ladder.

Inequality is inimical to development, and thus impedes social and economic development.

The sixth and final Millennium Development Goals (MDGs) Country Report for 2015 provides an overview of the progress South Africa has made towards achieving the eight MDGs (MDG Report, 2015; Stats SA, 2017). As mentioned previously, the MDGs are:
1. To eradicate extreme poverty and hunger
2. To promote universal primary education
3. To promote gender equality and empower women
4. To reduce child mortality
5. To improve maternal health
6. To combat HIV/Aids, malaria and other diseases
7. To ensure environmental sustainability
8. To develop a global partnership for the development.

This report reflects the intense national effort, from a range of institutions, organisations, and individuals, to improve the lives of all South Africans, particularly the poor and marginalised.

According to one of the recommendations from the MDG Country Report (2015: 35, 36), government initiatives must focus on addressing key structural drivers of gender inequality, including patriarchal and harmful attitudes and practices. This could be advanced through enhancing female participation in public and private leadership positions, particularly at local government level, improved employment rates among women, and reducing the levels of gender-based discrimination.

South Africa's fiscal and social policies are widely acknowledged as being pro-poor and contributing to reduced poverty headcounts. South Africa's leveraging of its taxation system in the fight against poverty and inequality has enabled expansion of the social assistance system, increasing access to health care and education, and extending free basic services to large numbers of indigent households (MDG Report, 2015). Various interventions, including the MDGs, have shifted and changed approaches to social welfare policy and provision over the decades. Thus, social welfare has changed from being viewed as a charitable intervention to part of mainstream government and society-wide intervention to address structural poverty and inequalities.

South African policies have shifted in emphasis away from the decades of both pre-apartheid and apartheid welfare policy with fragmented, inappropriate services, and white people being favoured to benefit from the largesse of the government. Developmental social welfare policy was introduced in the post-apartheid era with a focus on inclusive services. This welfare policy is transformative since it is underpinned by the values of social justice and human rights. The trajectory and discourse of this current welfare policy is egalitarian and non-discriminatory, and is effective in dealing with mass poverty and inequality.

# CONCLUSION

- This chapter deals with theories and approaches of social welfare policy together with the characteristics of these theories and approaches. The approaches that are discussed include the residual, institutional, normative theory, developmental social welfare, and the feminist approaches. These approaches and theory are underpinned by ideological views which vary from conservative, liberal to radical perspectives.
- Government's involvement ranges from major involvement which may be construed as 'welfarist' or institutionalism or intervention with minimal involvement where the state believes that individuals take responsibility for their own well-being, that is, residualism.
- Extensive discussion is spent on the developmental social welfare approach and its five themes since it is fundamental to South African welfare policy. There are synergies between the developmental social welfare approach and South Africa's Constitution and National Development Plan because the concern with human rights and social justice lies at the core of each of these.
- The integration of social and economic development is a crucial feature of developmental social welfare. Emphasis on one aspect such as economic growth to the detriment of social or human development will result in distorted development. Harmonisation needs to be obtained between social and economic development in order to contribute to effective and just social welfare policies.

# QUESTIONS

1. What approaches are relevant to South African welfare policy and why? Motivate your answer.
2. Discuss Developmental Social Welfare which underpins the White Paper for Social Welfare (1997), and in particular the five themes which comprises this approach?
3. What are the differences between universalism and selectivity and how do civil, political and social rights link with each of these?
4. Read the case study below. What approaches, in your view, are relevant to this case study? Please motivate your answer.

---

**☑ Case Study**    **MRS NCUBE'S STORY**

The Ncube family lives in a shack located in Orange Farm. The family consists of the grandmother who receives a monthly social pension, Mrs Ncube, the mother of three teenage children (18, 16, and 14 years), and a 3-year old child, who is the niece of Mrs Ncube. Mrs Ncube had taken care of this child, Thembi, since she was a baby because Mrs Ncube's sister had died of HIV/Aids. Recently, Mrs Ncube had lost her job as a domestic worker because her employers had moved out of the country. She does not qualify for unemployment benefits because her employers had not contributed to the Unemployment Insurance Fund. Mrs Ncube is really worried since she has to take care of four children, and their grandmother's pension of R1600 per month does not go very far in paying for rent and groceries.

---

5. Given the social welfare policy in your country of birth in Africa, what benefits will the Ncube family qualify for and which approach will be applicable to this case?
6. In South Africa, do you think that poor families will be selected for universal or selective benefits for social security benefits?

# REFERENCES

BROWN, J (2017) SP cuts SA to junk status for the first time in 17 years. *City Press* [Online]. Available: City-press.news24.com/Business/sp-cuts-sa-to-junk-status-for-the-first-time-in-17-years-20170403 [16 November 2017].

DOLGOFF, R & FELDSTEIN, D (1980) *Understanding social welfare*. New York: Longman.

DOMINELLI, L (2010) *Social Work in a Globalizing World*. Cambridge, UK; Malden, MA, USA: Polity Press.

EDIGHEJI, O: 'Constructing a democratic developmental state in South Africa: potentials and challenges' in Edigheji, O (ed.) (2010) *Constructing a democratic developmental state in South Africa: potentials and challenges* at pp. 1–33. Cape Town: HSRC Press.

EDITORIAL: 'Protests show that nothing has changed'. *Mail and Guardian*: 12 May 2017.

ESPING-ANDERSEN, G (1999) *Social Foundations of Post-Industrial Economies*. Oxford: Oxford University Press.

FESTER, G (2015) *South African Women's Apartheid and Post-Apartheid Struggles: 1980 – 2014. Rhetoric and Realising Rights, Feminist Citizenship and Constitutional Imperatives: A Case of the Western Cape*. Germany: Scholars' Press.

GIDDENS, A (1998) *The Third Way: The Renewal of Social Democracy*. Cambridge: Polity Press.

GIDDENS, A (2002) *Runaway World. How Globalisation is Reshaping Our Lives*. London: Profile Books.

GIL, DG (1979) *Beyond the Jungle. Essays on Human Possibilities, Social Alternatives, and Radical Practice*. Cambridge, Mass: Schenkman Publishing Company.

GILBERT, N (2002) *Transformation of the Welfare State. The Silent Surrender of Public Responsibility*. New York: Oxford University Press.

GILBERT, N: 'Welfare Pluralism and Social Policy' in Midgley, J & Livermore, M (eds.) *The Handbook of Social Policy* (second edition) at pp. 236–246. Los Angeles, London, New Delhi, Singapore: Sage Publications Inc.

GRAY, M (2006) 'The progress of social development in South Africa' *International Journal of Social Welfare* 15 (Suppl 1), S53–S64.

HALL, N & MIDGLEY, J (2008) 'Social Policy for Development: Local, National and Global Dimensions' *Social Policy for Development* at pp. 1–43. Thousand Oaks, London, New Delhi, Singapore: Sage Publications Inc.

HARDIMAN, M & MIDGLEY, J (1982) *The Social Dimensions of Development*. London: John Wiley.

HASSIM, S (2014) 'Texts and Tests of Equality: The Women's Charter and the Demand for Equality in South African political history' *Agenda: Empowering women for gender equity* (28:2), pp. 7–18.

HYDE, C: 'Feminist Approaches to Social Policy' in Midgley, J & Livermore, M (eds.) (2009) *The Handbook of Social Policy* (second edition) at pp. 247–262. Los Angeles, London, New Delhi, Singapore: Sage Publications.

INTERNATIONAL LABOUR ORGANISATION (ILO) (2011). *Brazil: an Innovative Income-lad Strategy* (Geneva: ILO).

JANSSON, B (2005) *The reluctant welfare state. A history of American social welfare policies* (fifth edition). Pacifica Grove, CA: Brooks/Cole.

JOFFE, H (2017) Fitch downgrades South Africa to junk status. *Business Day* [Online]. Available: https://www.businesslive.co.za/bd/economy/2017-04-07-fitch-downgrades-south-africa/ [16 November 2017].

MARSHALL, TH (1950) *Citizenship and social class and other social essays*. Cambridge: Cambridge University Press.

MARSHALL, TH (1963) Sociology *at the crossroads*. London: Heinemann.

MATHEWS, M (2014) *The Trialogue CSI Handbook 2014*, 17th edition. Cape Town: Trialogue.

MIDGLEY, J & SHERRADEN, M: 'The Social Development Perspective in Social Policy' in Midgley, J & Livermore, M (eds.) (2009) *The Handbook of Social Policy* (second edition) at pp. 279-294. Los Angeles, London, New Delhi, Singapore: Sage Publications Inc.

MIDGLEY, J: 'The Institutional Approach to Social Policy' in Midgley, J & Livermore, M (eds.) (2009) *The Handbook of Social Policy* (second edition) at pp. 181-194. Los Angeles, London, New Delhi: Singapore:Sage Publications Inc.

MILLENNIUM DEVELOPMENT GOALS (MDG) REPORT (2015). Executive Summary MDG Country Report.

MISHRA, R (1999) *Globalization and the Welfare State*. Cheltenham, UK; Northampton, Mass., USA: Elgar Publishing.

MPEDI, LG & ROSS, F: 'The reception, accommodation and general protection of refugees in the Republic of South Africa' in Frey, C & Lutz, R (eds.) (2013) *Social Work of the South. Vol. IV. Sozialarbeit des Suedens. Band 4 - Flucht und Fluechtlingslager* at pp. 199 - 212. Erfurt University of Applied Sciences, Oldenburg: Paulo Freire Verlag.

NAIDOO, K: 'Operationalising South Africa's move from macroeconomic stability to microeconomic reform' in Padayachee, V (ed.) (2006) *The development decade? Economic and social change in South Africa 1994-2004* at pp. 108-125. Cape Town: HSRC Press.

OZAWA, M: 'Social Security' in Midgley, J & Livermore, M (2009) *The Handbook of Social Policy* at pp. 347-366. Los Angeles, London, New Delhi, Singapore: Sage Publications.

PATEL, L & HOCHFELD, T (2012) 'Developmental social work in South Africa: Translating policy into practice' *International Social Work* 56 (5) at pp. 690–704.

PATEL, L & TRIEGAARDT, J: 'South Africa: Social Security, Poverty Alleviation and Development' in Midgley, J and Tang, K-l (2008) *Social Security, the Economy and Development* at pp. 85-109. Basingstoke, Hampshire; New York, NY: Palgrave MacMillan.

PATEL, L (2015) *Social Welfare and Social Development*. Cape Town: Oxford University Press Southern Africa (Pty) Ltd.

PATEL, L: 'Globalisation and social welfare' in Patel, L (2005) *Social welfare and social development in South Africa* at pp. 10-37. Cape Town: Oxford University Press.

RAUTENBACH, J & CHIBA, J: 'Introduction' in Nicholas, L, Rautenbach, J and Maistry, M (eds.) (2010) *Introduction to Social Work* at pp. 1–39. Claremont: Juta and Company.

SEEKINGS, J & NATTRASS, N (2016) *Poverty, Politics & Policy on South Africa. Why has poverty persisted after Apartheid?* Johannesburg: Jacana Media (Pty) Ltd.

SEN, A (1999) *Development as Freedom*. New York: Knopf.

SOANES, C AND STEVENSON, A (eds.) (2008) *Concise Oxford English Dictionary* (11th edition revised). Oxford: Oxford University Press.

SOUTH AFRICA. (1996) *Constitution of the Republic of South Africa*. Pretoria: Government Printers.

SOUTH AFRICA. (1997) *The White Paper for Social Welfare*. General Notice 1108 of 1997. Pretoria: Government Printers.

SOUTH AFRICA. (2016) *Review of the Implementation of the White Paper for Social Welfare Report*. Pretoria: Government Printers.

SOUTH AFRICA. MINISTER OF FINANCE (2014) *Budget Speech*. Cape Town: Parliament.

SOUTH AFRICA. MINISTER OF SOCIAL DEVELOPMENT (2017) *Budget Speech*, 25 May. Cape Town: Parliament.

SOUTH AFRICA. NATIONAL PLANNING COMMISSION (NPC) (2012). *National Development Plan 2030: our future - make it work*. Pretoria: Department: The Presidency, National Planning Commission.

SOUTH AFRICA. NATIONAL TREASURY (2013). *2013 Budget Review*. Pretoria: National Treasury. RP 344/2012.

STATISTICS SA (2017) [Online]. Available: www.statssa.gov.za [19 April 2017].

STATISTICS SA (2017) [Online]. Available: www.statssa.gov.za [6 November 2017].

SWEETMAN, C: 'Editorial' in Sweetman, C (ed.) (2005) *Gender and the Millennium Development Goals* at pp. 2–8. Oxford, UK: Oxfam.

TAYLOR, V (2002) Report of the Committee of Inquiry into a Comprehensive System of Social Security for South Africa. *Transforming the Present – Protecting the Future*. RP/53/2002. Pretoria.

TITMUSS, RM (1968) *Commitment to Welfare*. London: Allen & Unwin.

TITMUSS, RM (1974) *Social Policy: An Introduction*. London: Allen and Unwin.

TRIEGAARDT, J (2005) 'The Child Support Grant in South Africa: A Social Policy for Policy Alleviation?' *International Journal of Social Welfare* 14 at pp. 249–255.

TRIEGAARDT, J (2009) *Challenges for Refugees/Migrants in South Africa: Social Policy Issues and Considerations for Social Work*. Unpublished paper. NASC Conference, Champagne Castle, Drakensberg, 14–16 October.

WEYERS, M (2013) 'Towards the Reconceptualisation of Social Welfare in South Africa: An Analysis of Recent Policy Trends' *Social Work/MaatskaplikeWerk* Vol. 49 (4) at pp. 433–455.

WILENSKY, H & LEBEAUX, C (1965) *Industrial Society and Social Welfare*. New York: Free Press.

ZASTROW, C (2014) *Introduction to social work and social welfare: empowering people* (11th edition). Belmont: Brooks/Cole.

# Glossary of terms

**developmental social welfare:** it is an approach that is characterised by extensive state intervention in welfare services and social security, being inclusive and non-discriminatory, and targets mass poverty and unemployment

**feminist approach:** it is characterised by the awareness of the political, economic and social well-being of women and their families, and the structural and collective processes that contribute to the oppression, exploitation and disempowerment of women.

**government and the state:** the government is an administrative arm of the state. From a social welfare policymaking point of view, parliaments, the judiciary, the military/police, etc. are all part of the state. Governments implement state social welfare policies. So the state and government both play a role.

**human capital:** it refers to the knowledge and skills that each individual retains. It may be measured by levels of education and skills.

**institutional approach:** this approach is characterised by comprehensive state involvement in the provision of welfare services and social security, and is universal in scope.

**normative theories:** these theories are used to provide a value framework for social welfare policy. They provide assistance in identifying desirable social policies or social welfare policies in relation to different sets of values, ideologies and political objectives (Hall and Midgley, 2008: 26).

**residual approach:** this approach to social welfare is characterised by minimal state intervention in the provision of social welfare services and social security.

**rights-based approach:** this approach is concerned with the rights of all citizens and meeting the needs of people, particularly those who are disadvantaged.

# Transforming social welfare policy and developmental social welfare services

*Viviene Taylor*

*'We live in a country where everybody feels free, yet bounded to others. ...The welfare of each of us is the welfare of all ...'* (NPC, 2011: 11 & 20)

The above quote from South Africa's National Development Plan is part of the vision that tells a new story of what South Africa could be in 2030. Yet, everyday, in South Africa and elsewhere on the continent, the experiences of the poorest people and those who are most vulnerable reveal gross human rights violations and personal tragedies. Violations of people's rights and denial of access to the most basic developmental welfare services as illustrated by the Life Esidemeni tragedy in South Africa (News24, 9 October 2017) are stark reminders of why we need to have a transformative social welfare policy approach to the provision of developmental social welfare services on the continent. Without such an approach that combines public social provision with care and responsibility towards the most vulnerable, at-risk, and poorest people, the outcomes are likely to remain tragic and lead to the death of hundreds of people with psychiatric illnesses, as in Esidemeni, or other social conditions. Such examples reinforce the importance of using a human rights approach to developmental social service provision in Africa.

Chapter 4 of this book looks at the links between social welfare policy, on the one hand, and specific policies and legislation for the implementation of developmental social welfare services for people, on the other. The objectives and outcomes for this chapter are listed below.

## Chapter objectives

✓ Deepening the understanding of transformative social welfare policy and its impacts on the provision of social welfare services in South Africa and more generally in Africa.

✓ Examining some of the main shifts in social welfare policy pre- and post-1994 and the implications of these shifts for the provision of social welfare services.

✓ Using South Africa as an example to analyse how social welfare policy and legislation can align with a country's constitution and other policy instruments and strategic plans – in this instance, the Constitution of the Republic of South Africa, 1996 (the Constitution) and the National Development Plan – to ensure a rights-based approach.

✓ Explaining how social service professionals can work within an approach that is transformative and protects individuals, families, households, and communities, and that empowers them to develop.

✓ Analysing critically existing social welfare policy frameworks in Africa and identifying what needs to be done to ensure compliance with African human rights frameworks.

## Chapter outcomes

✓ Understanding the links between transformative social welfare policy and the types of social provision available to people.

✓ Linking the functions of and approaches to transformative social welfare policy to the contexts in which they provide social services.

✓ Applying transformative social welfare policy and practice in line with constitutional and human rights values and principles.

✓ Promoting constitutional and human rights within social welfare and social service practice in countries in Africa and countries such as South Africa that should comply with such rights.

✓ Understanding the importance of the African Charter for Human and Peoples' Rights and the African Charter for the Rights and Welfare of the Child as normative policy frameworks for social service provision.

# 4.1 Introduction

Preceding chapters provide the background, politics, economic factors, and approaches that influence the development of social welfare policy and the provision of services in countries in Africa and especially South Africa. The purpose of this chapter is to provide social service practitioners, including social workers, with a more detailed understanding of the links between social welfare policy and specific policies and legislation for the implementation of developmental social welfare services for people. Social welfare policy provides guidelines for programme action, usually undertaken by governments, to address the needs of people in a society. The institution of social welfare is a response to the complexities of modern societies and the inability of families, religious, and community institutions (Gilbert and Specht, 1986) to provide the types and levels of mutual support required to enable people to function and cope with social disintegration and vulnerabilities. Social welfare policy and the provision of social welfare services come into effect when governments, and more broadly societies, recognise that the social needs of individuals, families, households, and communities are not being met. Unmet needs and other social conditions that affect people's functioning and their abilities to integrate into social and economic institutions require government and societal interventions. Social welfare policy and social welfare services are formal responses by governments to assist people to integrate into society and to build their psychosocial capabilities and resilience to function and overcome the problems they experience.

# 4.2 Shifting the social welfare policy agenda for services in Africa

Initiatives underway in Africa to advance a social welfare policy agenda reflect a shift away from an *ad hoc and incremental approach* towards an approach that places emphasis on social protection and social development. This shift was evident at a roundtable meeting of African countries, convened in Livingstone in Zambia in 2009, when policymakers and senior government officials met to discuss a number of priorities to promote a social policy and sustainable development agenda. The themes that cut across many of the high-level discussions at this meeting and others included the urgency of addressing poverty, inequalities, social disintegration, and exclusions of vulnerable and at-risk groups. Ten[1] countries were present at the Livingstone Roundtable Meeting in 2009. Among the seven objectives that these countries set for the Livingstone Roundtable Meeting, two are of particular relevance for social welfare policy and social welfare service provision in Africa. These two objectives are to:

- establish strategies for social development and social policy in the Southern African subregion; and
- make recommendations on how to effectively implement comprehensive and integrated social development interventions in the region (Department of Social Development – *Report of the Southern African Social Development and Social Affairs Ministries and Departments Regional Social Policy Roundtable*, 2009).

The above objectives show that there is a decisive policy shift towards a social development approach to the needs and welfare of citizens in countries in the Southern African region. It also reveals that the Southern African regions' understanding of a social development approach to social welfare services is one that is comprehensive in addressing the needs of people who are experiencing multiple deprivations and who are trapped in poverty. Such comprehensive services may be understood to include income support in the form of cash grants, therapeutic interventions in the form of counselling and community care and support, livelihood support strategies, assistance to people whose rights are violated, and a wider range of social and economic development strategies that promote inclusion of people who are vulnerable and at risk.

> **ad hoc and incremental approach:** This means the social welfare policy is founded on making decisions about whose social welfare needs should be addressed, how they should be addressed, and what resources should be allocated to address these needs or problems without using rational or reasoned arguments based on research evidence. Often the decisions made are dependent on political expedience and the views and voices that dominate rather than on policy, policy criteria, and established standards for social services.

Another significant aspect of these objectives is the emphasis on integrated social development interventions. This could be understood as a move away from seeing social welfare provision as a purely psychosocial and therapy-oriented approach to one that locates people within the social, political, and economic environments in which they live and work. The policy shift and social provision is therefore moving away from seeing individuals and households as the cause of social crises, and people as having pathologies, towards understanding that people experience social problems and have unmet needs because they are affected by political and social structures and economic systems that undermine their development. The Livingstone Roundtable Meeting and subsequent social policy initiatives led by the African Union provided the impetus for countries in the Southern African region to focus attention on how to address what they identified as the common issues and challenges that influence a sustainable social development agenda.

> *From a social development perspective it is these structures and systems that require change even as social service professionals enable individuals, families, and households to cope and overcome the impacts of structurally based poverty, unemployment, and social crises.*

Policymakers and government officials in Africa identified four central issues that require urgent attention for the region to address poverty and social development challenges. The first included macro-strategic issues of linking social and economic policies within national development plans, prioritising budget allocations for social protection and social development, and developing national social policy frameworks in each country.

The second common issue identified was that of creating awareness within countries and on the continent of Africa of the important foundational role of social protection and social development in facilitating economic development that is sustainable and inclusive. A third issue affecting countries in Southern Africa focuses on establishing and strengthening national institutions and organisations for the provision of social protection and social development benefits and services. A fourth common issue is the difficulty experienced in targeting the people who need benefits and services because of the lack of demographic data and comprehensive national data bases (*Report of the Southern African Social Development and Social Affairs Ministries and Departments Regional Social Policy Roundtable*, 2009).

Identifying social welfare policy issues and challenges to advance social protection and social development across the Africa region was a critical step in moving away from a Western model or approach to social welfare policy and provision (i.e. the residual and institutional approaches which are explained in detail in Chapter 3) as such approaches are acknowledged as inappropriate for countries in Africa in the twenty-first century. The impact of colonialism and its accompanying economic project of modernisation, industrialisation, and the resulting social, economic, cultural, and environmental dislocations continue to be experienced by Africa's people. The influence of colonial and postcolonial governance in social welfare policy and social welfare service provision is still evident in Africa today. In the next section, African theoretical perspectives on social welfare and social work are discussed.

## 4.3 Rethinking social welfare policy and social services in Africa

Attempts to craft a new and inclusive vision of social welfare services in African contexts onto existing social welfare processes and programmes have fallen short of the desired goals because of structural conditions that shape economic and social development underpinned by a history of imperialism, colonialism, and postcolonial regimes. Questioning the appropriateness, relevance, and effectiveness of Western models of social welfare service provision for contemporary African societies, some theorists acknowledge that the heterogeneity and diversity on the continent requires an approach that is developmental and responsive to the cultural, social, political, and economic diversity that exist in each country (Mwansa, 2012; Mupedziswa, 2001).

The types of social welfare services that exist in different parts of Africa (West, East, Central, and Southern Africa), representing the 54 countries that make up the continent, bear little resemblance to the features of social welfare services in advanced industrial contexts to which former colonial administrators belonged. Yet, theories and the design of social welfare services in Africa are influenced by Western industrial models and approaches to social service provision. The major function of social welfare under colonial regimes, as argued by Spitzer (2014) was consistent with the broader processes of imperialism and colonialism, and was to ensure compliance of the people in the colonies with the agendas of colonial administrators. The design of social welfare policies, institutions, and services reflected the thinking and aims of colonial administrations and had little respect for indigenous systems, cultural and social histories of the indigenous people, or the need to build inclusive and just social welfare systems.

A shift in thinking about the social well-being of people occurred when African countries came together under the ambit of the Organisation of African Unity (now renamed the African Union), after achieving political independence, to find alternatives to the dominant Western thinking that social work and social welfare as it applies in modern industrial societies should be the way to resolve Africa's social conditions. Such alternatives in the form of the African Charter on Human and Peoples' Rights (Organisation of African Unity –African Union, 1981) was a significant turning point in pushing an agenda for the advancement of the human needs and rights of people on the continent (refer to Chapter 1). Since then other charters such as the African Charter on the Rights and Welfare of the Child (Organisation of African Unity– African Union, 1991) provide guidelines that take into account the historical, economic, political, social, and cultural contexts of countries, and offer guidelines and protocols for the well-being of people.

The founding fathers of the Organisation of African Unity, including Emperor Haile Selassie of Ethiopia, President Kwame Nkrumah of Ghana, and President Jomo Kenyatta of Kenya

The emergence of African responses to recurring social and economic crises was an acknowledgement that the theories and models of the West were inappropriate and irrelevant to the historical contexts, and the social, cultural, political, and economic realities of post and neocolonial contexts in Africa. Along with other international human rights instruments to which countries become signatories, the establishment of specific African Charters and human rights-based policy frameworks, including that of the Social Policy Framework for Africa (African Union, 2008), provide normative guidelines for policy implementation in the delivery of social services. The next section provides more details on how normative frameworks can be used in countries on the continent of Africa.

## 4.4 Normative frameworks for social welfare policy and services in Africa

Normative policy frameworks provide guidelines on what standards and protocols should be upheld in the pursuit of human development, human rights, and human dignity. Such frameworks are consistent with internationally approved standards, and can take the form of international conventions and charters. They prescribe a set of measures with which state parties – who become signatories to them –have to comply. An example is the African Charter on Human and Peoples' Rights (ACHPR) that was adopted by the Organisation of African Unity (OAU, which later became the African Union) in Nairobi in June 1981. It emerged as a normative framework for African countries to ensure that the rights and basic freedoms of people are protected and promoted. The ACHPR came into force in 1986. It is characterised as an international human rights instrument with the aim to promote and protect the human rights and basic freedoms of all people on the African continent. In the absence of overarching social welfare policy frameworks and constitutional provisions for the social and economic rights of citizens in some countries on the continent it can provide a basis for social service professionals to advocate for the needs, social issues, vulnerabilities, and risks of people to be addressed. It is important to note that the ACHPR was written and affirmed with due regard to the promotion of the conventions of the United Nations and the Universal Declaration of Human Rights of 1948. The Charter (ACHPR) contains 63 Articles. The Charter distinguishes itself from other UN conventions in Article 2 which pledges to eradicate all forms of colonialism from Africa and to co-ordinate and intensify efforts to achieve a better life for the peoples of Africa. It recognises the historical tradition and values of African civilisation as a point of departure, which ought to characterise the concept of human and peoples' rights.

The OAU established the African Commission on Human and Peoples' Rights in Addis Ababa (Ethiopia) in November 1987 to oversee and implement the ACHPR; the Commission has since moved to Banjul (Gambia). There can be no doubt that the ACHPR is considered an important human rights instrument on the continent to guide the achievement of people's rights. This was evident when a protocol to the Charter was introduced in 1998 to create an African Court on Human and Peoples' Rights, which was put into effect in January 2004. By 2016, all 54 member states of the African Union ratified the Charter. Ratification of the Charter means that the African Commission on Human and Peoples' Rights can request member states to report on the status of achieving rights and can investigate violations of such rights through the African Court. As a normative framework for social welfare policy provision and services the Charter promotes and protects people's right to work (Article 15), the right to health (Article 16), and the right to education (Article 17). Other provisions on the right to life (Article 4), right to health (Article 16), and right to development (Article 22) are also contained in the Charter (Organisation of African Unity – African Union, 1981).

Overwhelming evidence of the extent and depth of the social crises experienced on the continent resulted in an additional human rights-based framework that social service professionals can use to ensure governments make adequate social welfare provision for people, especially children (Taylor, 2015). This is the African Charter on the Rights and Welfare of the Child (Organisation of African Unity – AU, 1990). There are 31 Articles in this Charter (refer to pp. 89 and 90 which highlights the Articles in Part 1 of the Charter). The rights, freedoms, duties, and responsibilities in the Charter on the Rights and Welfare of the Child make explicit the types of protection that all children under the age of 18 years should have to ensure their well-being. The Articles in the Charter are expected to take precedence over religious, customary, traditional, and cultural rights that are not consistent with the best interests of the child. Article 11 states that every child has the right to an education, to develop his or her personality, talents, and mental and physical abilities to their fullest potential, and Article 13 indicates that every child who is mentally or physically disabled has the right to special protection to ensure his or her dignity in conditions that promote the child's self-reliance and active participation in the community (Organisation of African Unity – AU, 1990).

This indicates that the Charter places strong emphasis on the human development of children on the continent and enjoins governments to ensure such rights are being achieved.

Noteworthy, in the Charter, is the duty placed on governments to take special measures in respect of female, gifted, and disadvantaged children, to ensure equal access to education for all sections of the community. Realising the rights in Article 14 would ensure that all children have access to safe drinking water, nutritious food, and adequate health care and yet the social and economic indicators in Chapters 5 and 6 of this book reveal the stark realities of malnutrition, stunting, infant mortality rates, deepening poverty, and increasing social inequalities on the continent. Article 15 places the duty on states to ensure that children are not exploited economically, and Article 16 requires states and all of society to ensure that children are not tortured or harmed in any way. Physical, mental, and emotional abuse is considered a violation of children's human rights.

A significant step was taken in Article 21 to ensure the protection of children from harmful social and cultural practices. This Article requires that governments take the necessary measures to eliminate practices that undermine the welfare, dignity, growth, and development of the child. Such practices that require government intervention include cultural practices that are harmful to a child's health; discriminate on the grounds of sex, especially against the girl child; and condone child marriage. Such discrimination and practices are to be prohibited by governments, and require that countries introduce legislation specifying the minimum age of marriage as 18 years. The rights and protections in this Charter provide an explicit normative policy framework for social service professionals in Africa to work to mobilise action for social service improvements that will ensure the welfare of children. The African Charter on the Rights and Welfare of the Child provides a useful policy framework and platform from which each country can put into place legislation and social services to ensure the protection, development, and human rights of children.

Since the adoption of the African Charter on Human and Peoples' Rights (in 1981) and the African Charter on the Rights and Welfare of the Child (in 1990), the African Union acknowledged that a more comprehensive and explicit social policy framework was necessary to guide countries in addressing persistent social and economic development crises on the

The United Nations declared 11th October as the International Day of the Girl Child to highlight the rights of girls and the challenges they face

continent. The Social Policy Framework (African Union, 2009) was approved at the First Session of the AU Conference of Ministers in charge of Social Development in Windhoek (Namibia) in October 2008. It is the first explicit social policy framework agreed by all member states. There are 18 thematic social development issues that are prioritised for implementation by governments in the region. These priorities provide the backdrop against which social welfare services and social provision in each country should be planned, designed, and implemented in accordance with the historical, demographic, social, and economic imperatives that influence the particular country and its people.

Among the priorities that are considered urgent and high on the African Union's agenda are:
- development;
- labour, and employment;
- social protection;
- health with particular emphasis on HIV/Aids,
- TB, malaria, and other infectious diseases;
- migration;
- education;
- agriculture, food, and nutrition;
- the family;
- children, adolescents, and youth;
- ageing;
- disability;
- gender equality; and
- women's empowerment.

Furthermore, the Social Policy Framework (SPF) makes specific reference to the need for governments on the continent to pay urgent attention to drug and substance abuse; crime prevention; sport; civil strife and conflict situations; and the foreign debt crisis (African Union, 2009). These priorities reinforce the need for social services to be designed and delivered in a systematic and integrated way in every country in the region. Importantly, there is strong commitment to a social development agenda that is integrated into the regions wider development agenda. According to the SPF, social development and social policies are not an afterthought or secondary but are part of an interdependent development process that ensures both human and economic development. It lays a firm basis for governments and social service providers in particular to ensure that national development planning processes within countries prioritise and include planning for developmental social welfare services, health and education, as well as social protection. South Africa is used as an example in this book to show how countries can use such processes to give effect to the progressive realisation of rights that ensure protection and empowerment.

At a conceptual level the African Union's social policy framework and programme for social development is consistent with a human development or people-centred approach with the aim to promote human rights and dignity. In this conception of social welfare or human development people are understood to be both the means and the beneficiaries of sustainable development (Sen, 1999). However, according to the Social Policy Framework, the needs and conditions of marginalised and disadvantaged groups and communities and those who are most vulnerable and at risk should be prioritised in the provision of social welfare and, more broadly, social development services.

The theoretical and conceptual frameworks of recent shifts in thinking in social policies and social welfare service provision fit well with a human rights and entitlement perspective that embeds people as the primary concern of development (Taylor, 2015). Clearly stated by the African Union Commission (2009: 10):

> 'The main purpose of this Social Policy framework for Africa (SPF) is to provide an overarching policy structure to assist AU Member States in the development of their national social policies to promote human empowerment and development in their ongoing quest to address the multiple social issues facing their societies. The SPF moves away from treating social development as subordinate to economic growth. Rather, the framework justifies social development as a goal in its own right. It acknowledges that while economic growth is a necessary condition of social development, it is not exclusively or sufficiently able to address the challenges posedby the multi-faceted socio-economic and political forces that together generate the continent's social development challenges.'

This statement moves countries away from seeing social welfare provision as interventions that are required when economic markets fail people towards an approach that is rights-based and places the needs and conditions of people at the centre. It also ensures that structural and cyclical crises are addressed through interventions that have a bearing on the root causes of social conditions. The changes in regional social policies create an integrated platform from which governments and civil society organisations can review existing social service provisions and advocate for a co-ordinated, developmental, and human rights-based approach.

Part 1 Chapter 1

## THE AFRICAN CHARTER ON THE RIGHTS AND WELFARE OF THE CHILD

**Article 1:** Member States of the Organization of African Unity Parties will recognize the rights, freedoms and duties in this Charter and will adopt laws these rights. Any custom, tradition, cultural or religious practice that is inconsistent with these rights are discouraged.

**Article 2:** A child means every human being below the age of 18 years.

**Article 3:** Every child should be allowed to enjoy the rights and freedoms in this Charter, regardless of his or her race, ethnic group, colour, sex, language, religion, political or other opinion, national and social origin, fortune, birth or other status. [Setter: Please align text as in my attempt above for the whole charter.]

**Article 4:** If children can voice their opinions, then those opinions should be heard and taken into consideration during legal and administrative proceedings.

**Article 5:** Every child has a right to live.

**Article 6:** Every child has the right to be named and registered at birth.

**Article 7:** Every child who is capable of communicating his or her own views should be allowed to express his or her opinions freely.

**Article 8:** Every child has the right to free association and freedom of peaceful assembly, in conformity with the law.

**Article 9:** Every child has the right to freedom of thought, conscience and religion.

**Article 10:** Children have a right to privacy.

**Article 11:** Every child has the right to an education, to develop his or her personality, talents and mental and physical abilities to their fullest potential. This education also includes the preservation and strengthening of positive African morals, traditional values and cultures.

**THE AFRICAN CHARTER ON THE RIGHTS AND WELFARE OF THE CHILD (continued)**

Governments should also take special measures in respect of female, gifted and disadvantaged children, to ensure equal access to education for all sections of the community.

**Article 12:** Children have a right to play and to participate fully in cultural and artistic life.

**Article 13:** Every child who is mentally or physically disabled has the right to special protection to ensure his or her dignity, promote his self-reliance and active participation in the community.

**Article 14:** Every child shall has the right to enjoy the best attainable state of physical, mental and spiritual health. This includes the provision of nutritious food and safe drinking water, as well as adequate health care.

**Article 15:** Children should be protected from all forms of economic exploitation and from performing any work that is likely to be hazardous or to interfere with their physical, mental, spiritual, moral, or social development.

**Article 16:** Children should be protected from all forms of torture, inhuman or degrading treatment and especially physical or mental injury or abuse, neglect or maltreatment including sexual abuse.

**Article 17:** Every child accused or found guilty of having broken the law should receive special treatment, and no child who is imprisoned or should be tortured or otherwise mistreated.

**Article 18:** Families are the natural unit and basis for society, and should enjoy special protection.

**Article 19:** Children should, whenever possible, have the right to live with their parents. No child should be separated from his or her parents against his or her will, except when authorities believe this would be in the child's best interest.

**Article 20:** Parents or other persons responsible for the child should always act in the best interest of the child.

**Article 21:** Governments should do what they can to stop harmful social and cultural practices, such as child marriage, that affect the welfare and dignity of children.

**Article 22:** Children should not be recruited as soldiers, nor should they take a direct part in fighting wars.

**Article 23:** Refugee Children should receive appropriate protection and humanitarian assistance.

**Article 25:** Children who are separated from their parents should get special protection and should be provided with alternative family care. States should also take all possible steps to trace and re-unite children with parents.

**Article 26:** States should address the special needs of children living under regimes practicing racial, ethnic, religious or other forms of discrimination.

**Article 27:** Children should be protected from all forms of sexual exploitation and sexual abuse.

**Article 28:** Children should be protected from the use of narcotics and illicit use of psychotropic substances.

**Article 29:** Governments should take appropriate measures to prevent the abduction, the sale of, or traffic of children for any purpose.

**Article 30:** States should provide special treatment to expectant mothers and to mothers of infants and young children who have been accused or found guilty of breaking the law.

**Article 31:** Children have responsibilities towards their families and societies, to respect their parents, superiors and elders, to preserve and strengthen African cultural values in their relation with other members of their communities.

Source: Adapted from the *African Charter on the Rights and Welfare of the Child,*
Organisation of African Unity (African Union), 1990

The next section provides a detailed analysis of the background and shifts in social welfare policy and social welfare service provision in South Africa.

# 4.5 Transforming social welfare policy and services: South Africa

Historically, four major pieces of legislation regulated social welfare services in pre-1994 apartheid South Africa. These are the National Welfare Act 100 of 1978, Social Work Act 110 of 1978, Fundraising Act 107 of 1978, and Social Assistance Act 59 of 1992 (refer to Table 4.1 below). These pieces of legislation determined the structure and organisation of social welfare services in South Africa. They also provided regulations for the education and training of social work professionals and for establishing the employment and professional practices of social workers. Funding sources for social welfare services were very tightly controlled through legislation as well as the type and amount of social assistance benefits that people could receive. All these pieces of legislation revealed the racial distribution of services and the racial design of social welfare services. Moreover, they reflected the inequities in the allocation of social welfare services to whites based on universal access compared to the benefits and a very residual and limited range of services provided to the majority of black people on a discriminatory basis.

The pieces of legislation that governed and regulated social welfare services in the past are no longer used, but it is important to note that these pieces of legislation set in place the social welfare system and delivery of social welfare services in the country, and transforming the system and services remains an on-going process.

Table 4.1 Four major Acts regulating social welfare services in South Africa before 1994

| Legislation | Objective | Issues |
|---|---|---|
| National Welfare Act 100 of 1978 | • Establish SA Welfare Council.<br>• Regional Welfare Boards, Welfare Committees.<br>• Direct policymaking.<br>• Registration and regulation of welfare organisations. | • Corrective, remedial, curative approach based on behaviour modification.<br>• Promoted (racial) separate development and unequal discriminatory implementation of welfare services.<br>• Excluded community organisations. |
| Social Work Act 110 of 1978 | • Establish SA Council of Social Work.<br>• Defines powers and functions.<br>• Regulates and controls social work education, training, qualification, registration). | • Promotes professional elitism and hierarchy antithetical to values and principles of egalitarian society.<br>• Promotes practice based on foreign (predominantly British and USA) models.<br>• Neglects development approach. |
| Fundraising Act 107 of 1978 | • Appoint Director of Fundraising.<br>• Establish Disaster Relief Fund, Defence Force Fund and Refugee Relief Fund.<br>• Declaration of certain disasters.<br>• To regulate, govern and control funds raised by public. | • State abdicates responsibility to provide necessary funds to address social problems.<br>• Charity/philanthropy approach does not address root causes.<br>• Unequal ability of different communities to raise funds in market.<br>• Was selectively applied; used to restrict funding of anti-apartheid organisations. |

| Social Assistance Act 59 of 1992 | • Provides social assistance to persons, national councils and welfare organisations.<br>• Determines the kind of social services available, administration and rendering of social services.<br>• Determines who are beneficiaries. | • Applied through means test.<br>• Limits access to services to needy persons.<br>• Does not address the needs of all those who are vulnerable, in poverty and at risk.<br>• Ignores root causes of structural inequalities and poverty.<br>• State assistance not a right; major onus is on individual, family and community.<br>• Residual approach – state assistance is a safety net.<br>• Does not integrate occupational (work related) and fiscal welfare benefits (contributions from the state through tax benefits).<br>• Major administrative problems. |

Source: Adapted from ANC, 1994:11

As mentioned above, before 1994, the organisation of social welfare policy and services was regulated by the National Welfare Act, Fundraising Act, Social Work Act, and Social Assistance Act. Apart from these, service providers also had to comply with other pieces of legislation which determined what types of services would be available, who could provide these services, and who would receive such services.

### 4.5.1 Background to shifts in South African social welfare policy and social welfare services

As noted in the previous section, the pre-1994 social welfare policy regime was tied very closely to the apartheid government's approach of 'divide and rule' (separate and racially segregated development) through the discriminatory and unequal provision of social welfare services. After 1994, with the formation of a new democratic government, the RDP (ANC, 1994) and the new Constitution of the Republic of South Africa (Act 108 of 1996) directly influenced shifts in social welfare policy, moving away from a discriminatory, paternalistic, and fragmented system to one based on the promotion of human rights. The White Paper for Social Welfare Policy of 1997 further reinforced this paradigm shift towards a developmental social welfare approach.

After 1999, the realisation that both social and economic development processes of the majority were undermined by structural inequalities and racial discrimination led to a substantive paradigm shift towards social development. This shift towards social development recognised that the roots of poverty, social inequalities, and related deprivations were structurally designed within a political and economic system which excluded the majority. Therefore, interventions to improve the lives of people require an approach that links social and economic policy goals at a macro level and integrates these goals in planning and programme processes that will ensure social welfare services to all those who need such services on an equitable basis. The shift towards social development reflects an intention to effect structural changes through macro policies, institutional systems of social welfare, capacity-building, and the resourcing of social service provision nationally.

Between 2002 and 2010, there was a further paradigm shift in the approach to social welfare policy and services. This shift arose from the growing recognition that, despite national efforts to improve the well-being of people and provide the means for them to live with dignity, African countries are part of the global economy and suffer as a result of global economic crises that are triggered elsewhere in the world. Thus, more comprehensive social welfare approaches to poverty and inequalities are necessary to prevent people who live in extreme poverty and deprivations from falling into deeper poverty. It was in 2002 that the concept of social protection emerged as a response to chronic structural conditions of poverty and the risks and vulnerabilities experienced by people throughout their life cycles (Taylor, 2002). By 2016, the integration of social protection and developmental social welfare became part of the NDP and transformation agenda for social welfare policy.

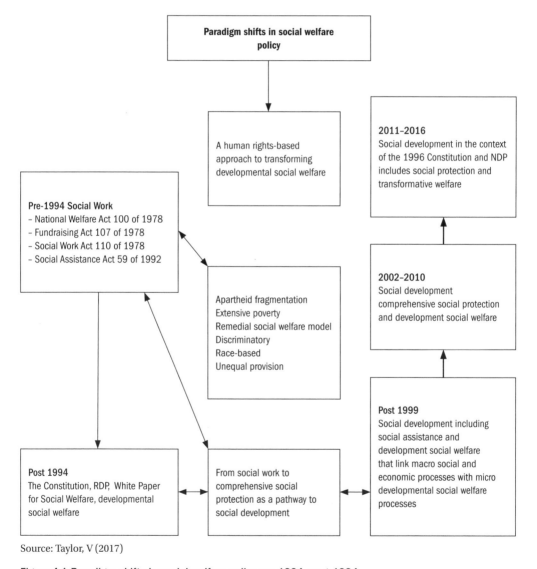

Source: Taylor, V (2017)

Figure 4.1 Paradigm shifts in social welfare policy pre 1994–post 1994

Prior to 1994, social welfare and social work systems were fragmented along racial lines, and were characterised by inequities and a low or nonexistent standard of services for black people, despite the fact that they were the majority of the population. Discriminatory practices and inequities existed in the provision of all social services including social work, education, health, basic services such as water and sanitation, housing, and income support through social grants and social security (Taylor, 2014).

The impetus for changes to social welfare policy and services can be traced to the period between 1992 and 1994 when the democratic movement under the leadership of the African National Congress (ANC) developed a wide range of policies as part of a programme of reconstruction and development for the country. Arising from consultations with social workers, communities, and progressive formations, the concept of social welfare was redefined within a National Social Welfare and Development Plan (ANC, 1994a). This document clarified the role of social welfare and social work in a democratic state and included the values and principles that would inform social service provision and the restructuring of the welfare system.

Attempts to move away from a race-based, fragmented, and inequitable system of social welfare services are evident in the aims of the National Social Welfare and Development Plan. These aims stated that within a future democratic society, a social welfare system would be developed that would be based on values and principles that include *'equity, social justice and the protection of human rights and fundamental freedoms'* of all South Africans (Taylor, 1994: ii cited in ANC, 1994a). The values and principles adopted by the democratic government that influenced changes in social welfare policy and services are also in the first State of the Nation address by the late President Nelson Mandela who said:

> *'My Government's commitment to create a people-centred society of liberty binds us to the pursuit of the goals of the freedom from want, freedom from hunger, freedom from deprivation, freedom from ignorance, freedom from suppression and freedom from fear. These freedoms are fundamental to the guarantee of human dignity. They will therefore constitute part of the centrepiece of what this government will seek to achieve, the focal point on which our attention will be continuously focused'* (Nelson Mandela, 1994: 10).

President Nelson Mandela delivering the state of the nation address in the first democratic parliament in South Africa

The necessity of changing from a narrow, fragmented system of social welfare to one which is comprehensive and applies universally to all those who need services is supported by the Constitution, the social and economic context of extreme hardship and deprivations of the majority, the changing demographic structure, and increasing levels of inequality. Importantly, the Constitution mandates the right of access to health care, food, water, and social security under the Bill of Rights, Chapter 2 of the Constitution. Specifically, Section 27(1)(c) states that everyone has the right of access to social security, including, if they are unable to support themselves and their dependents, 'appropriate social assistance'. Subsection 27(2) states that:

> *'The state must take reasonable legislative and other measures, within its available resources, to achieve the progressive realisation of each of these rights'* (RSA, Constitution of 1996: 13).

A major policy change in social welfare that seeks to align with the Constitution is contained in the White Paper for Social Welfare of 1997. The *White Paper for Social Welfare* of 1997 states that apartheid-era welfare policies, legislation and programmes were inequitable, inappropriate, and ineffective in addressing poverty, basic human needs, and the social development priorities of all in South Africa. It further highlights the sector and geographic (rural-urban) biases in access to and delivery of welfare services under the apartheid regime. At the time, systems for delivering welfare services were organised along specialist lines and fragmented with regard to different fields of service (for example, child and youth care, family therapy, mental health, disabilities, aging, and offender rehabilitation).

In addition to an overview of pre-1994 social welfare policy and services, the *White Paper for Social Welfare* (1997) included the concept of developmental social welfare that first emerged in policy documents of the ANC (ANC, 1994a). This was an important advance in shifting from a colonial approach to social welfare policy to a policy approach that situated the needs, issues, and problems of individuals and families within South Africa's unique socio-political context of institutional racism and socioeconomic inequality. The concept of developmental social welfare emphasises that the psychosocial trauma and social alienation caused by structural inequalities require an approach that protects and empowers people while working to change systems and structures that are oppressive and exploitative. Furthermore, social welfare policy has to be aligned with legislation and this is dealt with in the next subsection.

## 4.5.2 Aligning social welfare policy and legislation for services

While the Constitution is the overarching framework for all policies and legislation in South Africa, it is the *White Paper for Social Welfare* of 1997 that specifies the broad policy areas and goals for social welfare services, social security provision, and other types of services available to people in need. In each area of social welfare service provision, particular policies and pieces of legislation have been promulgated[2] since 1997. Existing legislation was amended or new legislation was drafted in various areas of welfare service to bring it into line with the Constitution (RSA, 1996) and *White Paper for Social Welfare* (RSA, 1997).

The national Department of Social Development is responsible for ensuring that policies and legislation include agreed standards and service delivery norms, and for implementing social welfare. Examples of social development policies that were established after 1997 include: the *White Paper on Families*; the National Drug Master Plan (which is reviewed every five years); the Anti-substance Abuse Policy; National Policy Guidelines for Victim Empowerment; the

South African Older Persons Policy; Policy on Services for People with Disability; Policy on Financial Awards; the Integrated Social Crime Prevention Strategy; and the Policy Framework for Accreditation of Diversion Services in South Africa. Some of the laws enacted since 1997 include: the Older Persons Act 13 of 2006; Prevention of and Treatment for Substance Abuse Act 70 of 2008; Social Service Professions Act 110 of 1978 as amended; Probation Services Act 116 of 1991; Child Justice Act 75 of 2008; and Children's Act 38 of 2005 as amended. Between 2015 and 2017, the national Department of Social Development has worked on amendments to the Children's Act, Non-profit Organisations Act, Victim Empowerment Services Bill, and developed a Draft Policy on Early Childhood Development. In addition, changes were made to the Older Persons Draft Amendment Bill, Policy Framework on Social Service Professions, and the Social Assistance Act (Department of Social Development, 2016).

Amendments to legislation and policy are usually made according to three criteria:

- aligning changes with the constitutional provisions;
- ensuring that the policy and legislation address the demographic changes in the population (aging, birth rates, mortality rates, and life expectancy); and
- considering the social conditions and problems that expose people to risk and make them vulnerable, such as poverty, violence, hunger, and unemployment.

Table 4.2 below shows how policies and legislation align with the Constitution (1996) and the *White Paper for Social Welfare* (1997) to provide care, treatment, and interventions to assist people who experience a variety of social conditions and problems.

Besides alignment with the Constitution, policies and legislation passed or amended since the White Paper for Social Welfare of 1997 are now aligned with international conventions and protocols that the South African government has signed and thereafter ratified[3]. For example, South Africa signed the International Covenant on Economic, Social and Cultural Rights in 1994, and ratified it in 2015. It also ratified the Convention on the Elimination of All Forms of Discrimination against Women (CEDAW) in 1998. The Convention on the Rights of the Child of 1993 was ratified in 1995. The government has also ratified the Optional Protocol to the Convention on the Rights of the Child on the involvement of children in armed conflict and the Optional Protocol on the Sale of Children, Child Prostitution and Child Pornography. It has also signed the Hague Convention on the Protection of Children and Co-operation in Respect of Intercountry Adoption, and the Hague Convention on the Civil Aspects of International Child Abduction. The Convention on the Rights of Persons with Disabilities of 2006 was signed and ratified in 2007, as was the related Optional Protocol. This means that the government is required to implement national policy and legislation as well as comply with the international agreements and protocols that it has ratified.

Table 4.2 Constitutional and legislative frameworks for social welfare services

| | |
|---|---|
| Constitution of the Republic of South Africa (Act 108 of 1996) | Chapter 2 – Bill of Rights, section 27 |
| Overarching policy framework | White Paper for Social Welfare (1997) |
| Older persons | • South African Policy for Older Persons<br>• Older Persons Act 13 of 2006 and Social Assistance Act 13 of 2004 |

| Persons with disabilities | • Chapter 1 – Bill of Rights, section 9(3)<br>• White Paper on the Rights of Persons with Disabilities (2015)<br>• Policy on Services for People with Disability |
|---|---|
| HIV and Aids | • Social Assistance Act 13 of 2004 and National Health Act 61 of 2003 |
| Children | • Chapter 2 – Bill of Rights, sections 27 and 28<br>• Children's Act 38 of 2005<br>• Child Justice Act 75 of 2008 |
| Families | • White Paper on Families (2013)<br>• Support documentation include the<br>  – Manual for Marriage Preparation and Marriage Enrichment (2007)<br>  – DSD Manual on Family Preservation Services (revised) (2010);<br>  – Guidelines on Reunification Services for Families (2012)<br>  – Norms and Standards for Services to Families (2012)<br>• Framework on Mediation for Social Service Professionals Mediating Family Matters (2012)<br>• Keeping Families Together Customised Manual on family preservation (2013)<br>• Services for emerging organisations including faith-based and emerging community-based organisations<br>• Fatherhood strategy (2013), as well as a Training Manual (undated)<br>• Families in Crisis and an Integrated Parenting Framework (undated) |
| Crime prevention and support | • Probation Services Act 116 of 1991<br>• Integrated Social Crime Prevention Strategy<br>• Policy Framework for Accreditation of Diversion Services in South Africa |
| Victim empowerment | • National Policy Guidelines for Victim Empowerment<br>• Policy Framework and Strategy for Shelters for Victim of Domestic Violence in South Africa (2003)<br>• National Policy Guidelines for Victim Empowerment<br>• Victim Empowerment Programme (VEP) Cluster and Technical Support<br>• Integrated Indicator Set for the National Victim Empowerment Program (2009)<br>• Social Development Guidelines on Services for Victims of Domestic Violence (2010)<br>• Shelter Strategy for Victims of Crime and Violence in South Africa (2010)<br>• Working with Victims of Human Trafficking: Training manual on Restoration and Healing Programme (2011)<br>• Manual on the Establishment of a Khuseleka One Stop Centre Model (2011)<br>• Mentoring and coaching model for emerging CSOs (2013) |
| Substance abuse care | • National Drug Master Plan (which is reviewed every five years)<br>• Anti-substance Abuse Policy<br>• Prevention of and Treatment for Substance Abuse Act 70 of 2008 |
| Refugees care and interventions | • Refugee Act 130 of 1998, section 24<br>• UN Convention relating to the Status of Refugees (1951)<br>• OAU Convention Governing The Specific Aspects of Refugee Problems in Africa (1969) and Protocol relating to the Status of Refugees (1967)<br>• Basic Agreement between the Government of South Africa and the UNHCR (1993)<br>• Immigration Act 13 of 2002 |

Sources: Compiled from RSA, Department of Social Development (2016), Constitution (1996), Department of Home Affairs (2017)

Other influences on social welfare policies in countries in Africa include the African Charter on the Rights and Welfare of the Child and the African Charter on Human and Peoples' Rights.

The information below indicates some of the changes in policy and legislation that came into effect in South Africa in the post-democratic era. It also shows that implementing social welfare services to achieve a transformative agenda that improves the well-being of the most deprived remains an on-going project.

---

**Transforming social welfare**    **SOME HIGHLIGHTS AND CHALLENGES**

- A number of new social welfare policies have been developed since 1997 to advance a transformative agenda as part of a social development process.
- In addition to policies, new legislation and amendments to existing legislation and secondary legislation in the form of regulations, norms and standards, and protocols were developed.
- New and amended legislation is aligned with the Constitution, National Development Plan Vision 2030, and international and regional instruments.
- Transformative and developmental social welfare with social protection are understood as pathways to social development which will ensure that basic social welfare rights are accessible to all.
- The distribution of and access to both public and private social welfare services remains skewed along racial and/or income lines, with the wealthy having access to relatively effective private services.
- Challenges exist in how to translate developmental social welfare and social protection into programmes and services that reach all those in need.

---

The provision of social welfare services and benefits is dealt with in the next subsection.

## 4.5.3 Provision of social welfare services and benefits

Policies and legislation are important steps in ensuring that a framework exists to guide the implementation and delivery of social welfare services. Together they provide guidance on what services should be provided, through which organisations, and to whom such services should be made available. Social welfare policies and legislation also provide clarity on the roles and responsibilities of the national and provincial spheres of government and on how services are delivered, monitored, and evaluated. In addition to providing social welfare services, the government works in partnership with the non-profit organisations (NPOs) and voluntary welfare organisations (VPOs) to procure essential social welfare services. The government has the responsibility to ensure that funds or subsidies are provided, especially for the provision of statutory social welfare services provided by NPOs and other agencies. However, the funding of NPOs and VPOs for the provision of social welfare services is uneven and inadequate and limits the equitable distribution of social welfare services to those who need them.

Figure 4.2 summarises the political economy of social welfare service provision by the different sectors.

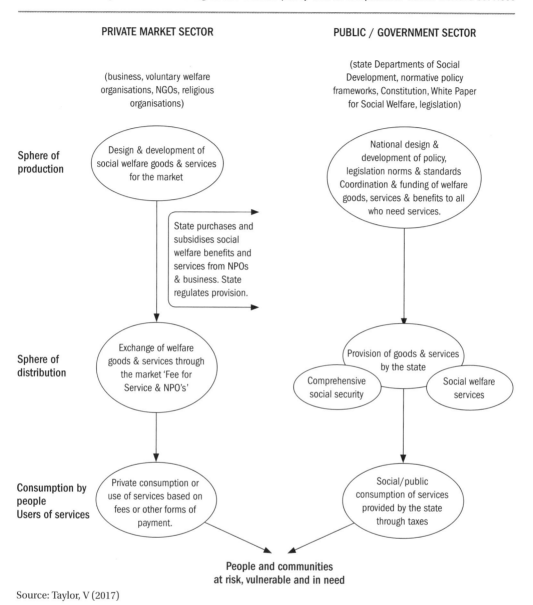

**Figure 4.2 The political economy of social welfare services within a mixed economy of social welfare**

Source: Taylor, V (2017)

The government provides social security benefits, for example, through social grants for people who are income poor and unable to provide for their own needs. The administration of social grants has been centralised through the South African Social Security Agency (SASSA). The combination of government and non-profit as well as services for which people pay through the private sector are reflected in Figure 4.2.

The next subsection provides an understanding and analysis of how transformative social welfare links to social protection and social development.

### 4.5.4 Transforming social welfare methods

The social welfare service delivery process is an outcome of the policy in the White Paper for Social Welfare of 1997 and individual pieces of legislation that focus on needs and social problems/conditions that affect people through their lifecycle. Social welfare services as provided by social workers draw on models of treatment that evolved over time. Social welfare methods of service shifted from psychodynamic casework to social group work, family therapy, community organisation, and cognitive behaviour therapy (Goldstein, 1973). More recently, an ecological systems approach to problem solving became prominent as progressive social service professionals began to link individuals, families, and groups with broader and interconnecting systems of society.

African countries – and especially South Africa because of the systemic violation of human rights of the majority of black people before 1994 –grappled with a range of interventions to address social problems. Challenges experienced by social service practitioners in the care and treatment process in South Africa include the lack of sufficient resources to follow a rational process from assessment to intervention to evaluation, while upholding the rights of people in the process. In the next section, developmental social welfare policy is discussed including the element of social protection.

# 4.6 Transformative developmental social welfare policy

Chapter 1 of this book explains the links between social protection and developmental social welfare as pathways to social development. It is important to realise that the different concepts used in social welfare policy and in planning social services are not in conflict with one another but rather complement one another. Chapters 5 and 6 of this book provide evidence to show the extent of social deprivations, poverty, and inequalities on the African continent. Given these complex challenges, it is not possible for a single path to achieve the transformation required to lift people out of poverty and the deprivations they experience on a daily basis. The NDP thus broadens the process and ends of social development to include social protection (this includes social assistance in the form of social grants, social insurance, and in-kind measures such as health care and education), developmental social welfare services to eliminate poverty, reduce inequalities, and provide therapeutic services where these are needed (NPC, 2011). People need a secure foundation from which they can expand their capabilities and improve their lives. This foundation can be understood as the basis of social protection. The NPC (2011) states that, by 2030, South Africa must achieve a defined social protection floor with social welfare as an explicit element, providing social assistance for households that have not achieved the basic standard of living. A combination of public and private services will be needed to attain a vision of universal and inclusive systems of social protection with an agreed social floor being the central platform (refer to Figure 4.1). Non-governmental welfare organisations cannot be expected to respond alone to the scale and complexities of South Africa's poverty, social fragmentation, and lack of social support systems. The NGO-state partnership model of social welfare service provision does not relieve the state of its responsibilities to ensure that children, people with disabilities, women, and families are well served and that funds are effectively spent.

## 4.6.1 Pathways to social development

This subsection provides a detailed analysis and understanding of social protection and developmental social welfare as pathways to achieve social development and the goals in the NDP.

### 4.6.1.1 Social protection as a pathway to social development and transformation

Chapter 11 of the National Development Plan (NDP) in (National Planning Commission, 2011) positions social protection as a critical part of public policy and focuses on providing support that reduces vulnerability, alleviates and ultimately prevents poverty, and empowers individuals, families, and communities through a range of social development services. It articulates the goal of creating a caring state and nation that has a defined social minimum or social floor that prescribes a standard of living below which no one should fall. The NDP specifies that such a goal should include access to social protection and basic social welfare services. Social protection as a concept and approach to social welfare and development is more appropriate in Africa to address issues of poverty, inequalities, and vulnerabilities as a result of shocks and downturns during the life cycle. It enables transformative social welfare policy to prioritise the needs and conditions that affect people who are most vulnerable and at risk of falling into deeper poverty while also creating a platform from which people can address structural conditions that trap them in poverty (Taylor, 2008; 2014). Social protection measures cover the entire life cycle of an individual from conception (by ensuring that a pregnant mother has adequate nutrition) up to old age.

Questions about what forms or types of social provision benefits and services should be part of the social minimum or social floor are dependent on the social and economic context and the revenue base in a country. Social benefits in South Africa, for example, include both cash and in-kind provisions such as social grant income (social assistance), social insurance such as pensions and related benefits to which workers contribute during their working lives, social welfare services such as trauma counselling, mental health services, family and child care services, and wider developmental strategies. These benefits are designed to assist people who experience hardship and various crises during various stages of their lives.

Transformative social welfare policy and developmental welfare services are dimensions of a comprehensive social protection package of benefits and services. These dimensions include a specified *minimum guaranteed level of entitlements to social benefits including income support (social grants); basic social welfare services (psychosocial interventions); basic services (such as water, electricity, transport, housing, sanitation); primary education; primary health care; and food.* Minimum guarantees (or standards) of social welfare benefits and services are usually determined by governments in consultation with experts who provide a policy evaluation and analysis of the availability, distribution, adequacy, and sustainability of the services and benefits that should be provided to those who need such services. The process of establishing such a minimum is referred to as standard setting and is a normative approach to social policy. This means that a norm or standard is set that determines the types of benefits and services that are available to respond to people's needs and problems.

Countries in Africa are working towards determining a set of norms, standards, and specific criteria for basic levels and types of social protection and social development services that ought to be provided for people who need such services. Setting a social minimum for social benefits is also affected by other factors that require broader social development interventions. Social workers and social service practitioners are required to understand the types of benefits and welfare services available so that they can ensure that the people they serve have access to these services, especially those who are vulnerable and at risk and require protection. Interventions that social service practitioners may use to assist people include psychosocial therapeutic counselling and prevention strategies that enable households and communities to understand the root causes of social problems and conditions such as poverty, illiteracy, and deprivations in health care among many others.

The next subsection provides a more detailed analysis of how the functions of social protection and those of developmental social welfare relate to social development to produce transformation.

### 4.6.1.2 Functions of transformative developmental social welfare and of social protection

Transformative social welfare policy builds people's resilience and empowers them to take control of their lives and their choices to bring about the social change that is necessary, which ought to comply with the provision for the *progressive realisation of social and economic rights* in the South African Constitution (Act 108 of 1996). The functions of social protection are a response to people's expectations for both a change in the policy environment and in the structures through which they receive help or psychosocial support. Such changes enable people to regain their human dignity and reflect a commitment to social justice. The functions of social protection give practical effect to transformative social welfare policy as reflected below.

#### Protective function

Social protection and transformative social welfare policy provide measures and services to save lives and reduce levels of deprivation. These measures and services could include food; social assistance; social insurance; social welfare services; protection from violence, discrimination and abuse; education; health care; and basic services such as water and sanitation. A number of protective services are provided for children, people with mental health conditions, and others who have disabilities. Usually protective functions involve a range of therapeutic interventions that include methods of social work such as trauma counselling, group counselling, and community humanitarian interventions that are responsive to wide-scale human devastation, conflict, and starvation.

#### Preventive functions

Achieving functions that prevent people from falling into deeper poverty or being unable to cope throughout the different stages of their lives requires specific measures to ensure protection in good times and in bad times. Such measures can act as a safeguard against poverty during unemployment or during financial crises, or death, disabilities, or during disasters such as droughts, floods, and other environmental conditions. Savings, insurance schemes, and guaranteed social minimums provide such safeguards and prevent people and a country from social and economic collapse.

#### Promotion

Both transformative social welfare services and social protection services function in ways that create formal spaces and processes to build individual, household, community, and institutional capabilities. Social service professionals achieve this function when specific groups, communities, and members of broader society are given the information and knowledge that help them to mobilise for social change that reduces poverty, inequalities, and social alienation. Social protection and transformative developmental social welfare protect and promote the social and economic rights of those who are excluded, at risk, and vulnerable. Achieving this function requires social service professionals to use adult education techniques and knowledge and community development strategies that include conscientisation as a method of raising awareness and mobilising citizens to address the root causes of their problems).

REFLECTION **CHARACTER OF SOCIAL DEVELOPMENT**

Paulo Freire (1970), in his book called *Pedagogy of the Oppressed*, refers to the process of problem-posing education as education that raises the awareness of individuals in their real world contexts so that they can become involved as change agents to resolve conditions that affect them. Conventional educational methods are based on a process through which the student is seen as not having knowledge and experience and the educator deposits knowledge in the minds of students and anaesthetizes and inhibits creative power. Problem-posing education, on the other hand, involves a constant unveiling of reality that leads to the emergence of consciousness and critical intervention in reality. This process is understood as the practice of freedom as opposed to the practice of domination.

The significance of Freire's contribution to social development is in the methods of problem-posing education that he developed. This method enables people to develop their power to understand critically how they live in the world and how they relate to the people and conditions in which they find themselves. People are empowered to see themselves as actors in the process of transforming the world in which they live.

## *Developmental and generative*

Social protection and transformative social welfare functions focus on increasing the consumption patterns of the poor, promoting local economic development, and enabling poor people to access economic and social opportunities. This is achieved through social transfers and by integrating people into productivity generating initiatives including community development and social enterprise activities. Providing skills, seed (or start-up) funding, grants, and other infrastructure as incentives for poor people to develop their capabilities is a developmental and generative function that increases the ability of people to improve their purchasing power and reduce their poverty (Taylor, 2008).

### 4.6.1.3 Developmental social welfare

Developmental social welfare services are transformative when they are part of a broader macro policy framework that introduces measures (through governments, the private sector, and NPOs) that build the capabilities of individuals, families, and communities to overcome conditions that are oppressive, discriminatory, and exploitative. Transformative outcomes include changes in policies, laws, budgetary allocations, taxation, and other redistributive measures that establish the framework for the progressive and developmental achievement of social welfare services (NPC, 2011).

Social welfare at individual, family, and community levels is a critical component of social development and social inclusion. Social development is an overarching process to create a more equitable distribution of social welfare services and benefits to achieve human development. While transformative developmental social welfare services and social protection provide the means to enable people to cope with risks and to overcome vulnerabilities, social development addresses the structural conditions that keep people trapped in poverty. The United Nations' declaration on social development elaborates on this:

*'Social development is inseparable from the cultural, ecological, economic, political and spiritual environment in which it takes place. It cannot be pursued as a sectoral initiative. Social development is also clearly linked to the development of peace, freedom, stability and security, both nationally and internationally'* (United Nations, 1995:30).

## CONCLUSION

- This chapter provided an understanding of social welfare policy and its impact on the provision of social welfare services in South Africa and more generally in Africa. It went beyond focusing on understandings of social welfare services to examine some of the main shifts in social welfare policy in South Africa before and after 1994 and the implications of these shifts for the provision of social welfare services in the country.
- The chapter also highlighted the social welfare policy journey towards an approach that is transformative and that protects and empowers individuals, families, households, and communities to develop with dignity.
- The alignment of post-1994 social welfare policy and legislation with the Constitution (1996) and the National Development Plan (NPC, 2011) were examined.
- Moreover, the chapter deepened the understanding of the links among transformative and developmental social welfare, social protection, and social development. It clarified the role of government, the private sector, and the not-for-profit sector in the design and distribution of developmental social welfare services.
- Shifts in thinking and the formulation of normative policy frameworks for Africa through the African Union create the possibilities for better co-ordinated, integrated, and more comprehensive social welfare service provision on the continent. At country level, social welfare service providers can use the policy, legislation, and constitutions of their countries to ensure that social welfare services are responsive to the needs of people.
- In the absence of national policy and constitutions, countries and social welfare policy advocates now also have regional social policy frameworks and human rights instruments to guide them towards progressively achieving a human rights agenda for social welfare services in Africa.

## QUESTIONS

1. Discuss the paradigm shifts that took place in social welfare policy and social welfare services during different periods.
2. Using the African Charter of People's Human Rights and the African Charter on the Rights and Welfare of the Child as normative policy guidelines critique policy and legislation designed to protect children in your country.
3. Discuss your understanding of pathways to social development and how these pathways could include services and programmes at micro and macro levels to achieve transformation.

## REFERENCES

AFRICAN NATIONAL CONGRESS (1994a) *National Social Welfare and Development Plan.* Cape Town, Bellville: SADEP, University of the Western Cape.

AFRICAN NATIONAL CONGRESS (1994b) *The Reconstruction and Development Programme (RDP).* Johannesburg: Umanyano Publications (for the African National Congress).

AFRICAN UNION (2009) 'Social Policy Framework for Africa' [Online]. African Union Commission, Addis Ababa. Available: www.africa-union.orgpdf.

FREIRE, P (1970) *Pedagogy of the oppressed*. New York: Herder and Herder.

GILBERT, N & SPECHT, H (1986) *Dimensions of Social Welfare Policy* (second edition). USA: Prentice-Hall.

GOLDSTEIN, H (1973) *Social work practice: a unitary approach*. Columbia, South Carolina: University of South Carolina Press.

MANDELA, NR (1994, May 24) 'State of the Nation Address' (Parliament of the Republic of South Africa) [Online]. Available: http://www.gov.za/node/538197.

MUPEDZISWA, R (2001) 'The Quest for Relevance: Towards a Conceptual Model of Developmental Social Work Education and Training in Africa' *International Social Work* 44(3), pp. 285–300.

MWANSA, LK: 'Social Work in Africa' in Healy, LM and Link, RJ (eds.) (2012) Handbook of International Social Work. Human Rights, Development and the Global Profession at pp. 365–371. Oxford: Oxford University Press.

NEWS24. 9 October 2017. *Life Esidimeni: The greatest cause of human right violations since democracy* [Online]. Available: https://www.news24.com/SouthAfrica/News/life-esidimeni-the-greatest-cause-of-human-right-violations-since-democracy-20171009.

ORGANISATION OF AFRICAN UNITY (African Union). African (Banjul) Charter on Human and Peoples' Rights [Online]. Adopted by the Eighteenth Assembly of Heads of State and Government June 1981 – Nairobi, Kenya. Available: http://www.achpr.org/instruments/achpr/.

ORGANISATION OF AFRICAN UNITY (African Union). African Charter on the Rights and Welfare of the Child [Online]. Adopted by the Organisation of African Unity Assembly on 11 July 1990. Available: http://www.achpr.org/instruments/child/.

SEN, A (1999) *Development as Freedom*. Oxford: Oxford University Press.

SOUTH AFRICA (1996) *Constitution of the Republic of South Africa Act 108 of 1996*. Pretoria: Government Printer. [Laws.]

SOUTH AFRICA. Department of Home Affairs (2017) [Online]. Available: http://www.dha.gov.za.

SOUTH AFRICA. Department of Social Development (2009) 'Report of the Southern African Departments and Ministries of Social Development and Social Affairs Regional Social Policy Roundtable 22– 25 NOVEMBER, 2009' [Online]. Available: http://www.dsd.gov.za/index2.php?option=com_docman&task=doc_view&gid=131&Itemid=3 [February 2017].

SOUTH AFRICA. Department of Social Development (2016)'Comprehensive Report on the Review of the White Paper for Social Welfare, 1997' [Online]. Available: www.dsd.gov.za [January 2017].

SOUTH AFRICA. National Planning Commission (2011) The National Development Plan, Vision for 2030. Pretoria: Government Printer. Available: http://www.gov.za/sites/www.gov.za/files/devplan_2.pdf.

SPITZER, H: 'Social Work in African Contexts: A Cross-cultural Reflection on Theory and Practice' in Spitzer, H, Twikirize, JM & Wairire, GG (eds.) (2014) *Professional Social Work in East Africa*. Kampala: Fountain Publishers.

TAYLOR, V (2008) *Social Protection in Africa: An Overview of the Challenges*. (Research Report prepared for the African Union). Available: www.eprionline.com/wpcontent/uploads/2011/03/Taylor2008AUSocialProtectionOverview.pdf.

TAYLOR, V: 'Achieving food security through social policies: Comprehensive social protection for development' in Fukuda-Parr, S & Taylor, V (eds.) (2015) *Food Security in South Africa: human rights and entitlement perspectives* at pp. 145–166. Cape Town: University of Cape Town Press.

TAYLOR, V: 'Human Rights, Social Welfare, and Questions of Social Justice in South African Social Work Curricula' in Libal, K, Berthold, SM, Thomas, RL and Healy, LM (eds.) (2014) *Advancing Human Rights in Social Work Education* at pp. 247-272. United States of America: Council on Social Work Education.

TAYLOR,V (2002) *Consolidated Report of the Committee of Inquiry into a Comprehensive System of Social Security for South Africa, Transforming the Present - Protecting the Future, 2002* (Taylor Report). Pretoria: Government of the Republic of South Africa.

UNITED NATIONS (1995) The Copenhagen Declaration and Program of Action: World Summit for Social Development, 6-12 March 1995. New York: UN Department of Publications.

## Endnotes

1   The 10 countries at the Livingstone Roundtable Meeting in 2009 were Democratic Republic of the Congo, Malawi, Mauritius, Seychelles, South Africa, Swaziland, Tanzania, Zambia, and Zimbabwe.
2   After policies and legislation have been debated and amended, they are approved by Parliament and then gazetted. The term used to indicate that they are finally approved for implementation is 'promulgated'. This means they are ready to be shared with the public and adopted for implementation.
3   When governments ratify an international convention, document or agreement they are giving the convention and agreement formal recognition within their country and making it official. This means that legislation and policies need to also align with such agreements.

# Using evidence to shape transformative social welfare policy

# Demographic contexts and social and economic challenges in social welfare policy

*Viviene Taylor*

Across Africa there is a growing focus on the relevance and appropriateness of social welfare responses to the structural and systemic crises confronting countries. Often ineffective responses are the result of inadequate information on which to formulate appropriate responses. Chapter 5 of this book deals with these types of information such as demographic, social, and economic data and indicators that are needed to transform social welfare policy and services. The outcomes and objectives for this chapter are listed below.

## Objectives

✓ Providing an understanding of the uses of demographic, social, and economic data and evidence in transforming social welfare policy.

✓ Explaining the links among social and economic indicators and their significance in understanding whose needs and conditions ought to be prioritised in social welfare policy.

✓ Expanding on how policymakers and social service professionals interpret and use data and evidence to assess the distribution of social welfare services and target interventions at those who require such services.

✓ Assessing the adequacy, access, and quality of social welfare policy goals against objective evidence-based data and social and economic trends.

✓ Illustrating how to use demographic and social and economic data to advocate for changes in social welfare policy and social service provision.

✓ Analysing inequalities in the South African context with particular reference to discrimination, poverty, and deprivations experienced by women.

## Outcomes

✓ Understanding the importance of using demography data to transform and analyse social welfare policy.

✓ Using evidence from social and economic conditions and professional social service practice to make policy recommendations.

✓ Reviewing professional social welfare practice and assessing responses to needs and challenges.

✓ Understanding how to use evidence-based practice to transform social welfare policy and practice.

✓ Analysing critically information and knowledge from professional practice to influence policy agendas.

## 5.1 Introduction

Social welfare responses to the structural and systemic crises confronting countries are assumed to be based on evidence and indicators that reflect the needs, issues, and conditions of people who require social welfare services. Lack of information and data on the range and quality of social welfare services being delivered can prevent the transformation process and undermine principles of fairness in the distribution, access, adequacy and quality of services. For example, a recent review to assess progress on the implementation of the White Paper for Social Welfare Policy of 1997 (RSA, 1997) finds that social service professionals in both government and the NPO sector are unable to motivate for policy changes and additional resources because they do not provide supporting evidence (Department of Social Development, 2016). Figure 5.1 below illustrates the relationships among evidence-based knowledge, professional social service practice, and the demographic and social and economic conditions in which people live. Evidence used to provide services for people ought to be based on the actual circumstances in which people live and not just on quantitative measures that mask or obscure the quality of people's experiences.

It is not that policymakers and social service professionals do not want to make changes to policy but rather that they lack the capacity and resources to collate, analyse, and use evidence-based knowledge to influence policy changes in the design and distribution of social welfare services. Professionals use therapeutic (treatment-oriented services), preventive (community development), and developmental (poverty reducing) interventions to respond to social conditions and needs of people. When professionals provide services, they usually record who is receiving services for different types of needs and the geographical and economic locations of people who need services. Such information and data is available in 'case records' but are seldom converted into aggregate (put together) data that can be used to reflect a growing or declining trend in the demand for particular services over a period of time.

Developing the capacity and making time available to collate and make sense of the numbers of people who require certain types of services enable professionals to reflect on how they can use this evidence when making policy arguments on the distribution of services and the resources required to provide such services (refer to Figure 5.1). Differing understandings and experiences in practice settings among social service professionals lead to competing claims about what services are provided and to whom these are provided, and, at times, there is reluctance to document the process and keep records. Yet, this information is vital because it is experiential.

Evidence-based knowledge is factual and can be described either through people's experiences, through observations made by professionals over a period of time, and through surveys, census data, and other methods of research that social service professionals use. A critical factor in transformative social welfare policy is that of ensuring policy is responsive to people's needs and conditions or the context in which people live. Being responsive means that social service practitioners and policymakers should be aware of the demographic changes as well as social and economic trends in a country so that services can reach those who need them. A country or an organisation can have a very good social welfare policy on paper but if it does not relate to the actual circumstances in which people live and to the social conditions that affect people then the policy becomes irrelevant.

Policymaking is a dynamic and continuous process that should take account of demographic changes and the social, economic, environmental, and political contexts. When policies remain the same over a long period of time and these policies are used as frameworks within which legislation is made to regulate social service professionals, there can be a gap between the policy, legislation, and the realities within which professionals serve people. This gap between policy intentions and legislation and regulations that govern professional practice means that the feedback loop from practice through to the policymaking process is not working as it should. Determining whose needs, conditions, and social problems are addressed, when they will be addressed and how is influenced by processes of evidence-based and responsive policymaking and social service practice. Understanding how to develop and collate evidence from professional practice to change policies is an important way through which social service professionals can become agents of transformation (refer to Figure 5.1).

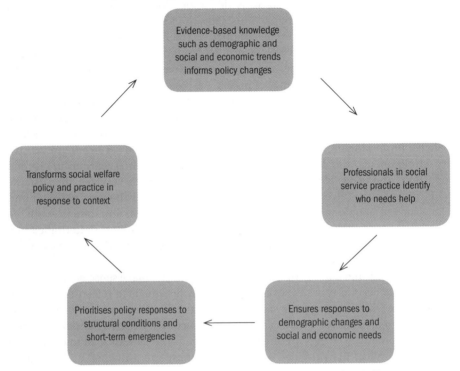

Figure 5.1 Building evidence-based knowledge to transform social welfare policy

**Evidence-based policymaking** is increasingly gaining ground as an approach that yields better results when making changes to social welfare policy in many African countries. It denotes a shift from making policy as an ad hoc, incremental[1] approach that is based on political expediency[2] and the strength of advocacy of interest groups[3] towards a more reasoned or rational basis for changes to policy and legislation. This is because it is assumed that evidence is factual, accurate, and has an empirical[4] basis but this is not always the case. The type of evidence that is available and that informs social service professional practice and policy-making depends on a number of factors. The distribution and quality of social services are also influenced by normative and evaluative assessments of individuals, families, households, communities, and countries' policymakers and providers of such services. The ways in which evidence and data are also often shaped by the class, race, and gendered experiences and frames of reference of policymakers and service providers are also important. As some writers caution:

> *'Evidence means proven or undisputed facts. Still when considering the notion of evidence, it is wise to bear in mind that it has something to do with determining the facts or deciding what counts as truth'*
> (Gray, Plath and Webb, 2009: 4).

Despite these cautionary references, evidence such as demographic data and social and economic indicators provides knowledge that helps policy makers and decision-makers understand how changes in the contexts in which people live and work affect their well-being. Amendments to existing policy and legislation or the introduction of new policies to address identified social conditions and priorities are less likely to be contested if they have their basis in evidence-based knowledge and are supported by what happens in professional practice settings. Countries in Africa, especially South Africa, use evidence-based knowledge to inform government audits and performance evaluations as well as to test the efficacy of policy implementation (refer to Chapter 14 of this book). It is important to note, however, that the process of acquiring evidence-based knowledge is also contested. This is because when constructing evidence-based policy knowledge, often such knowledge is also shaped by how those who are powerful in an organisation, and who are the dominant professionals, often use their values and philosophies about the contexts in which people live to shape evidence and information. The use of demographic data that can be verified, of social, economic and environmental trends that are research based together with expert information on standards and norms for social welfare provision do nevertheless provide ways of using evidence-based knowledge to transform social welfare policy through practice.

The next section explains the importance of South Africa's and the region's demography and social and economic trends for transforming social welfare policy and service delivery. Subsequent sections also highlight how to use changes in the growth of populations and in the structure of populations when it comes to gender, race, age, and other features in making social welfare policy. Economic, social, and environmental trends are also important factors that influence the range of social welfare conditions and needs that are put on the policy agenda. Changes in the proportion of young people, in the numbers of females, in the different types of families and households, and in the number of people in rural and urban areas influence social welfare policy and outcomes directly. Exclusions from social welfare benefits on the basis of race, gender, age, and spatial features in countries often means that social welfare policy does not address the social rights of people who are in dire need.

## 5.2 Transforming social welfare policy as a response to changing demographic contexts

Reference to the demography of a country or region means a focus on the population size, the structure of the population including the various age cohorts, characteristics such as race, ethnicity, gender, and language, and the spatial location of people. There can be gradual or accelerated population changes in countries depending on the age structure, birth rate, fertility rate, life expectancy at birth, and infant and adult mortality rates. These demographic changes inform policy decisions on which parts of the population require urgent attention, and they should determine how services and benefits are distributed as well as the potential for development and progress in each country. Demographic features such as the size and structure of populations – broken down according to age categories, gender, and population density in rural/urban areas – are thus important considerations when reviewing social welfare policy or making new policies to respond to people's needs and conditions.

There are three main reasons why social service professionals and policymakers should use demographic data to build an evidence base for more responsive and transformative social welfare policy and professional practice. These reasons are discussed below.

### 5.2.1 Demographic trends

Demographic trends provides explanations and analyses of population categories (children, youth, women, men, and elder persons) and an understanding of how the population will grow or decrease in the future, and what social services would be required to meet the needs of each category of people.

### 5.2.2 Demographic structure

The demographic structure explains how any changes in a population can put pressure on social welfare services. If, for example, a country has a rapidly aging population because life expectancy is increasing as a result of good health care, food and nutrition, and related social development programmes, then social welfare policies will need to focus on the provision of care for those who are aging, especially focusing on elder persons who may not have any access to family or community support. In such instances, issues of institutional care for frail elder persons and for community level support may be a policy option for consideration.

### 5.2.3 Census data

Governments usually undertake a national census on a regular basis (for example, South Africa undertakes a national census every 10 years) and such census data provides useful indicators that provide a picture of the country. The data collected through the census includes surveys with household members and provides important information on the population. It provides demographic profiles of where people are living, migration patterns, and also who is vulnerable and exposed to risk. This knowledge can be used by policymakers and social service practitioners to plan and implement social welfare strategies to respond appropriately to people who are vulnerable and at risk.

Using demographic data of some countries in Africa, the next section provides an analysis of how such data can be used to tell a social welfare policy story about the current and future social welfare needs of people. It is possible to use demographic data to explain which parts of a population require help and what the impacts would be if social welfare policy and provision does not reach them. The next section also shows how demographic data can be used by social service professionals to build a demographic map of the structure of populations in each country to enable appropriate responses to people's needs according to each age category over the life cycle.

## 5.3 Using demographic indicators for social welfare policy in Africa

A country's ability to care for those who are vulnerable and exposed to risk and living in multidimensional poverty is dependent on the reliability of its demographic data acquired through either census or surveys. Using such data-based knowledge for social welfare policy decisions and social service provision ensures that those who need services are identified using available evidence. Governments do not always have the resources to make adequate provision for all those who need social development services and they rely on demographic data and profiles to guide their decisions on which parts of the population require social welfare services so that the needs of these people can be addressed. A key demographic feature in each country is the size and structure of the population. According to the Africa Development Bank (2017), Africa as a region has a total population size of 1214 428 with an average growth rate (between the period 2000 to 2015) of 2,58%, with male population growth at 2,61% which is slightly higher than that of females at 2,56% (African Development Bank, 2017). Specific country and regional data is in Table 5.1 below.

Disaggregating or breaking down these population trends according to countries and regions reflects a slightly different picture. For example, in Table 5.1 we note that at least five countries have an average population growth rate of over 3%. These countries are Angola, Democratic Republic of Congo, Malawi, Tanzania, and Zambia (African Development Bank, 2017).

**Table 5.1 Population estimates for countries in Africa**

| | Mid-year population estimates | | | | | | | | |
| | Total population (thousands) | | | Female population (as % of total) | | | Average growth rate, 2000–2015 (%) | | |
| Countries | 2000 | 2010 | 2016 | 2000 | 2010 | 2016 | Total | Female | Male |
|---|---|---|---|---|---|---|---|---|---|
| Angola | 15 059 | 21 220 | 25 831 | 50,7 | 50,5 | 50,4 | 3,34 | 3,31 | 3,38 |
| Botswana | 1 737 | 2 048 | 2 304 | 50,2 | 50,0 | 50,0 | 1,99 | 1,98 | 1,99 |
| Burkina Faso | 11 608 | 15 632 | 18 634 | 50,9 | 50,5 | 50,4 | 2,99 | 2,93 | 3,04 |
| Cameroon | 15 928 | 20 591 | 23 924 | 50,2 | 50,0 | 50,0 | 2,54 | 2,52 | 2,55 |
| Democratic Republic of Congo | 48 049 | 65 939 | 79 723 | 50,4 | 50,2 | 50,1 | 3,22 | 3,19 | 3,26 |
| Ghana | 18 825 | 24 318 | 28 033 | 49,5 | 50,5 | 50,2 | 2,42 | 2,34 | 2,50 |
| Lesotho | 1 856 | 2 011 | 2 160 | 51,5 | 50,9 | 50,4 | 1,18 | 1,03 | 1,33 |
| Madagascar | 15 745 | 21 080 | 24 916 | 50,2 | 50,2 | 50,1 | 2,83 | 2,81 | 2,85 |
| Malawi | 11 193 | 14 770 | 17 750 | 50,4 | 50,2 | 50,1 | 3,11 | 3,06 | 3,15 |
| Mauritius | 1 185 | 1 248 | 1 277 | 50,4 | 50,4 | 50,6 | 0,39 | 0,46 | 0,33 |
| Mozambique | 18 265 | 24 321 | 28 751 | 52,0 | 51,4 | 51,1 | 2,83 | 2,73 | 2,93 |
| Namibia | 1 898 | 2 194 | 2 514 | 50,9 | 51,2 | 51,3 | 2,24 | 2,20 | 2,29 |
| Nigeria | 122 877 | 159 425 | 186 988 | 49,4 | 49,2 | 49,1 | 2,70 | 2,66 | 2,73 |
| Seychelles | 81 | 93 | 97 | 50,2 | 49,0 | 49,4 | 0,71 | 0,80 | 0,62 |
| South Africa | 44 897 | 51 622 | 54 979 | 50,8 | 50,9 | 50,8 | 1,08 | 1,04 | 1,13 |
| Swaziland | 1 064 | 1 193 | 1 304 | 51,6 | 50,8 | 50,5 | 1,52 | 1,40 | 1,64 |
| Tanzania | 33 992 | 45 649 | 55 155 | 50,2 | 50,3 | 50,3 | 3,21 | 3,19 | 3,23 |
| Zambia | 10 585 | 13 917 | 16 717 | 50,3 | 50,1 | 50,1 | 3,09 | 3,08 | 3,11 |
| Zimbabwe | 12 500 | 13 974 | 15 967 | 50,2 | 50,6 | 50,7 | 2,19 | 2,24 | 2,14 |
| **Region** | | | | | | | | | |
| Africa | 812 865 | 1042 551 | 1 214 428 | 50,1 | 50,0 | 50,0 | 2,58 | 2,56 | 2,61 |
| Central Africa | 81 055 | 109 378 | 130 710 | 50,3 | 50,1 | 50,1 | 3,02 | 3,00 | 3,05 |
| East Africa | 217 092 | 288 508 | 340 162 | 50,2 | 50,2 | 50,1 | 2,80 | 2,78 | 2,81 |
| North Africa | 146 217 | 170 681 | 190 448 | 49,7 | 49,8 | 49,8 | 1,83 | 1,82 | 1,84 |
| Southern Africa | 135 983 | 169 597 | 194 471 | 50,8 | 50,7 | 50,6 | 2,31 | 2,27 | 2,36 |
| West Africa | 232 519 | 304 387 | 358 637 | 49,7 | 49,6 | 49,5 | 2,78 | 2,74 | 2,81 |
| SADC | 218 104 | 281 277 | 329 446 | 50,6 | 50,5 | 50,4 | 2,68 | 2,64 | 2,71 |

Source: Compiled from African Development Bank Report (2017: 22)

This population growth rate of over 3% can be compared against the economic growth projections of these countries to determine whether population growth is outpacing economic growth. If this is the case, then the social welfare policy implications will be that these countries are likely to have higher incidences of income poverty, unemployment, and vulnerability compared to other countries in Africa (refer to Table 5.2 to compare population growth against poverty trends).

Table 5.2 reflects poverty trends for the years in which reliable data was available and recorded, and some countries measures of poverty may have changed since this data was recorded. National and international income poverty measures such as poverty lines and inequality measures based on differences in income (such as the Gini coefficient)[5] are standards that are set according to accepted criteria to enable policymakers and social service professionals to base decisions on whose needs to prioritise. Such measures in social welfare policy are called normative measures because they set the standard or norms according to criteria, determined by experts using a basic needs approach, for what people need in order to live. For example, the poverty line of U$1,9 per day per person tells us that this amount will purchase a basic basket of food for an individual at today's prices. The proportion of population living below a certain poverty measure tells us the extent of income poverty in a particular country and provides policymakers with information on whose needs to prioritise when it comes to the provision of social grants and public services.

**Table 5.2 Poverty trends for countries in Africa**

| Countries | Population in poverty (%) | | | | International lines | | | Gini coefficient | |
|---|---|---|---|---|---|---|---|---|---|
| | Population below poverty line | | | | % Population living | | | | |
| | Survey year | Rural | Urban | National | Year | Below $1,9/day | Below $3,1/day | Year | Index |
| Angola | 2008 | 58,3 | 18,7 | 36,6 | 2008 | 30,1 | 54,5 | 2008 | 42,7 |
| Botswana | 2009 | 24,3 | 11,0 | 19,3 | 2009 | 18,2 | 35,7 | 2009 | 60,5 |
| Burkina Faso | 2014 | 47,5 | 13,7 | 40,1 | 2014 | 43,7 | 74,7 | 2014 | 35,3 |
| Cameroon | 2014 | 56,8 | 8,9 | 37,5 | 2014 | 24,0 | 43,5 | 2014 | 46,5 |
| Democratic Republic of Congo | 2012 | 64,9 | 61,6 | 63,6 | 2012 | 77,1 | 90,7 | 2012 | 42,1 |
| Ghana | 2012 | 37.9 | 10,6 | 24,2 | 2005 | 25,2 | 49,0 | 2005 | 42,8 |
| Lesotho | 2010 | 61,2 | 39,6 | 57,1 | 2010 | 59,7 | 77,3 | 2010 | 54,2 |
| Madagascar | 2010 | 81,5 | 51,1 | 75,3 | 2012 | 77,8 | 90,5 | 2012 | 42,7 |
| Malawi | 2010 | 56,6 | 17,3 | 50,7 | 2010 | 70,9 | 87,6 | 2010 | 46,1 |
| Mauritius | - | - | - | - | 2012 | 0,5 | 3,0 | 2012 | 35,8 |
| Mozambique | 2008 | 56,9 | 49,6 | 54,7 | 2008 | 68,7 | 87,5 | 2008 | 45,6 |
| Namibia | 2009 | 37,4 | 14,6 | 28,7 | 2009 | 22,6 | 45,7 | 2009 | 61,0 |
| Nigeria | 2009 | 52,8 | 34,1 | 46,0 | 2009 | 53,5 | 76,5 | 2009 | 43,0 |
| Seychelles | 2013 | 37,2 | 39,0 | 39,3 | 2013 | 1,1 | 2,5 | 2013 | 46,8 |
| South Africa | 2010 | 77,0 | 39,2 | 53,8 | 2011 | 16,6 | 34,7 | 2011 | 63,4 |
| Swaziland | 2009 | 73,1 | 31,1 | 63,0 | 2009 | 42,0 | 63,1 | 2009 | 51,5 |
| Tanzania | 2011 | 33,3 | 15,5 | 28,2 | 2011 | 46,6 | 76,1 | 2011 | 37,8 |
| Zambia | 2010 | 77,9 | 27,5 | 60,5 | 2010 | 64,4 | 78,9 | 2010 | 55,6 |
| Zimbabwe | 2011 | 84,3 | 46,5 | 72,3 | 2011 | 21,4 | 45,5 | 2011 | 43,2 |

Source: Compiled from African Development Bank Report (2017: 37)

A further look at Table 5.2 tells us that, using a lower bound international income poverty line set at U\$1,9 per person per day, the Democratic Republic of Congo has an exceptionally high poverty rate at over 77% with similar trends evident for Madagascar at 77,8%. It is notable that Lesotho, Malawi, Mozambique, and Tanzania also have high incidences of poverty compared to other countries in the region. Interestingly, Seychelles has a poverty rate of 1,1% in 2013 and Mauritius has a poverty rate of 0,5% in 2012 (African Development Bank, 2017). These countries have the lowest poverty rates on the continent.

Taking account of the total population of each country in Table 5.1 and comparing it against the poverty and inequality (Gini coefficient) measures in Table 5.2, it is possible to determine what proportion of the population is likely to require social welfare services because the poverty and inequality trends provide this information. Thus, when designing social welfare policy responses to conditions of poverty and inequality, it will be important to focus on people who fall below a national or international lower bound poverty line because they would be most at risk and vulnerable to hunger, malnutrition, and other deprivations. While narratives and anecdotes[6] based on peoples' lived experiences also tell policymakers and social service professionals about the conditions under which people live, they do not provide a full and reliable picture of the entire population that is experiencing a particular condition (Taylor, 2015). This is why it is important to support narratives of peoples' experiences with demographic data.

Cassava is a key food crop in sub-Saharan Africa and makes up almost 50% of people's diet

In the subsection that follows, the significance of changes in population for social welfare policy is explained using data from some country examples in Tables 5.1, 5.2, and 5.3.

### 5.3.1 Significance of changes in population structure for transforming social welfare policy

Social service professionals and policymakers respond to the needs of people in particular contexts, whether these contexts are rural, peri-urban or urban. As populations grow and develop, policy and legislation should also take account of such changes to ensure that people's needs are addressed. It is particularly important for governments and non-governmental organisations to keep abreast of demographic trends so that they can promote transformative social welfare policy responses that are backed by statistical evidence. The following are examples of how to understand and introduce changes based on such evidence.

**Gender breakdown of population:** Men and women and girls and boys have very specific biological needs and the design of policies to address people's social welfare needs should take account of these different needs. A review of the gender profiles of countries in Africa, using the population statistics in Table 5.1, indicates that there is not much difference between the numbers of men and women in these countries. Indeed, across Africa the average male-female population breakdown was at 50% by 2016, showing a gender balance in the population structure (African Development Bank, 2017). In 2016, the proportion of men and women of the total population – for example, in Angola, Botswana, Cameroon, Democratic Republic of Congo, Ghana, Lesotho, South Africa, Zambia, and Zimbabwe – is relatively even. This could imply that there are little differences between the birth rate of male and female infants or that preference for male children is no longer as strong in the twenty-first century as it was in past decades. It could also show that as access to education and health care expands prejudice and discrimination against girl children is reduced.

Equal gender proportions in the population do not tell us much about the quality of life of girls and boys or women and men in any country. Social service professionals as well as policymakers will have to rely on other evidence to find out whether girls and women have equal access to social welfare rights and benefits and the extent to which there is discrimination against girls and women because of entrenched systems of patriarchy.[7] Anti-discriminatory social welfare policy responses ensure that gender disparities are addressed so that both girls and boys and women and men have their gender-specific needs met. For example, in Africa, girls who live in poverty struggle to attend school during their menstrual cycles because they do not have access to sanitary towels, adequate protection, and medical care. Unless such gender differences are understood and addressed through social welfare provision, girls' attendance at school and participation in related activities will be undermined. The social welfare policy responses in a country's social development programme should take account of the specific needs of women and girls and protect them from particular forms of discrimination and violations.

**Age structure of populations:** In Table 5.3 some demographic data is provided for 2016 for selected countries according to the age structure of populations or, as sometimes referred to, age cohorts. Such a breakdown of the population according to age tells us about the proportion of the population in each age category. This data is important if a government or non-governmental organisation wishes to take a life cycle approach to social welfare policy and provision. For example, in each age category the developmental needs of people will differ and this means that the social welfare policy responses should also take account of such age differences. Africa's population structure shows a high concentration of people between the ages 0 to 14 years and 15 to 49 years. This makes Africa's population relatively young as can be seen in Table 5.3. In 2016, for example, the age structure of some African countries reflects the high population percentages in the 0–14 age category. These countries are: Angola (47,52%); Botswana (31,89%); Cameroon (42,33%); Democratic Republic of Congo (45,86%), Ghana (38,78%); Zambia (45,72%); and Zimbabwe (41,54%) (African Development Bank, 2017).

Using a social welfare policy lens to make sense of this data, it is important to assess if social welfare services for children in this age category in these countries take account of their developmental needs. Such developmental social welfare needs could include early childhood development (ECD) facilities, nutrition schemes for children, health education and parenting programmes in communities, access to schooling, health care, and essential basic services including clean water and sanitation (Taylor, 2008). The other factor that policymakers will need to pay attention to is the type of social service professionals that are required to provide services to children and the education and support that these professionals need to ensure that they are capable to render quality services.

A review of Table 5.3 also shows that, in 2016, there is a high proportion of people in the age category 15–49 years in countries such as Botswana (55,89%), Cameroon (48,17%), DRC (44,83%), Ghana (50%), Lesotho (53,42%), South Africa (54,98%), Zambia (46,48%), and Zimbabwe (50,42%). Although young people between 15 and 18 years are expected to be in secondary school in some countries, they begin working as early as 15 years and are considered to be part of the active workforce. Age-related social welfare policy responses for the 15–49 age group could include work-related skills training, programmes designed to enhance their health and educational development, youth inclusion policies and programmes, and substance prevention and treatment interventions as well as others.

**Table 5.3 Population and age structure of select countries in Africa**

| Countries | 2016 Total population ('000) | 2016 Proportion of population from Age 0–14 (%)* | 2016 Proportion of population from Age 15–49 (%)* | 2016 Proportion of population from Age 50–64 (%)* | 2016 Proportion of population from Age 65+ (%)* |
|---|---|---|---|---|---|
| Angola | 25 831 | 47,52% | 44,23% | 5,88% | 2,33% |
| Botswana | 2 304 | 31,89% | 55,89% | 8,49% | 3,68% |
| Cameroon | 23 924 | 42,33% | 48,17% | 6,26% | 3,19% |
| DRC | 79 723 | 45,86% | 44,83% | 6,32% | 2,96% |
| Ghana | 28 033 | 38,78% | 50,01% | 7,16% | 3,39% |
| Lesotho | 2 160 | 36,01% | 53,42% | 6,43% | 4,16% |
| Namibia | 2 514 | 36,58% | 51,98% | 7,87% | 3,53% |
| South Africa | 54 979 | 28,92% | 54,98% | 10,95% | 5,11% |
| Zambia | 16 717 | 45,72% | 46,48% | 4,89% | 2,88% |
| Zimbabwe | 15 967 | 41,54% | 50,42% | 5,06% | 2,94% |

*Note: Percentages may not add up to 100 because of rounding to the nearest decimal.*

Source: Compiled from the African Development Bank (2017)

**Life expectancy:** Countries in which the life expectancy of people has increased because of improvements in health care and education have higher percentages of people in the 50–64 year age group. Looking at Table 5.3 we can see that, in 2016, Botswana (8,49%), Ghana (7,16%), Lesotho (6,43%), Namibia (7,87%), and South Africa (10,95%)  had relatively higher numbers of people in this category than other countries in the region (African Development Bank, 2017). This is also evident in the 65+ age bracket. While most countries reflect that on average less than 4% of their total populations reach 65 years and above, South Africa at 5,11% and Lesotho at 4,16% exceeds the average (African Development Bank, 2017). As populations show increasing numbers of aging, social welfare policies and provisions will also have to cater for the specific needs of elder persons. Such policy provision will be required to address issues of vulnerability and poverty of elder persons, especially those who are unable to work or do not have access to income support.

**Age-related dependency ratios:** Another important feature for policymakers and social service professionals to consider is that, based on these numbers, Africa has a high youth (0–14 years) dependency ratio and a growing elderly population (over 60 years) dependency ratio. According to the African Union (2008), in the period from 1995 to 2000 the 0–14 years dependency ratio was 78,6 and over 60 years dependency ratio was 22,9. Such exceptionally high youth dependency ratios, because youth under the age of 14 are not yet working, place pressure on these countries to provide adequately for health, education and other social infrastructure needs.

Governments introduce social welfare policies to provide a range of social protection measures including social grants, residential care for frail and elder persons, day care facilities, support to families, and community centres. Providing care and services for specific age groups or categories over their life cycles requires social service professionals and policymakers to understand the proportion of people in each category. It also requires an analysis of who among these categories are living in poverty and are at risk and vulnerable so that social welfare policies and services can be designed to address their needs.

**Mortality[8] rates of populations:** Indicators such as infant mortality rates also reflect a country's development and a government's ability to care for its people. Estimates showed in 2005 that Africa's mortality rates were among the highest in the world. The African Union (2008) indicated that in 2005 the crude death rate was 13,2 deaths per 1000 persons and the infant mortality rate in 2006 was 95 deaths per 1000 live births. Maternal mortality rates are also high as a result of a lack of reproductive health care and rights for women. Mothers who die during childbirth or because of HIV and Aids are also an important factor in social welfare policy responses. Projections show increasing numbers of child-headed households and orphans as a result of HIV/Aids-related deaths, and this has a direct impact on the care and custodial arrangements that families and governments are required to make in such circumstances (Taylor, 2008). More recent evidence by the African Development Bank (2017) shows that by 2015 infant mortality rates have dropped to 52,2 deaths per 1000 live births. This is a significant reduction reflecting improvements in health care in countries on the continent. Social welfare policy responses to address increased access to health and social care for mothers and infants are important in reducing mortality rates of females and infants.

**Other demographic features:** The numbers of people who have different forms of **disabilities** (either physical or mental) are important in providing knowledge for policymakers and practitioners on who requires social welfare services and the type of services that they require. It is also important to consider where people live. For example, if there are more people who are over 60 years living in **rural areas** and more young people living in urban areas, social service providers will need to consider what services should be available and where these should be located. **Migration patterns** are also significant and should be considered in social welfare policy and legislation as **are household compositions** and the numbers of working adults as well as dependents in each. In Chapter 6 of this book issues related to households and families are dealt with in greater detail as factors that shape household and family life are very important for the well- being of all people in a country.

In the next subsection, a more in-depth analysis is provided of South Africa as an example to illustrate clearly how social service professionals and policymakers can use demographic data and knowledge to change and improve social welfare policy responses.

## 5.3.2 South Africa's demographic context

Postcolonial and post-1994 features of South Africa's population continue to reflect the race, class, and gender-based inequalities of decades of apartheid style development and governance. Some of these features are discussed below.

**Population features:** Black South Africans are more likely to be poor and unemployed, and to experience an accumulation of social and economic deprivations that trap them in intergenerational cycles of poverty. According to the African Development Bank (2017), South Africa's population reached 54,979,000 in 2016. There are three features that are similar to other countries in Southern Africa. First, population growth has slowed as a result of the impacts of HIV/Aids and increasing levels of education and health care. Second, it is already evident (refer to Table 5.3) that the size of the economically active population (15–49 years) is growing, constituting 54,98% of the population in 2016. Third, the gender balance of the population is almost equal yet there are a number of gender disparities experienced by women and girls in all spheres of life.

> **intergenerational cycles of poverty:** This is where people are born into families and households whose great grandparents and grandparents as well as parents lived in income poverty and experienced deprivations in health and education capabilities. As a result they do not have access to resources to move out of poverty and remain trapped in such conditions.

**Population age structure:** Combining the active workforce to include people aged 15–64 years accounts for approximately 65,9% of the total population. As evident in Table 5.3 South Africa's population age structure mirrors other countries in the region. There is a significant youth bulge which has the potential to contribute to a positive outcome or demographic dividend if the economy is able to absorb these new young entrants into the workforce. Social welfare policies in the context of a youthful population should be responsive to the needs of youth in the next decade. However, declining economic growth, alongside long-term unemployment, limits the availability of jobs which means the employed workforce is reduced. This has an impact on young people and those who have been unemployed for many years. The psychosocial impacts of being excluded from the productive workforce are many as well as the economic impacts that are evident in increasing levels of poverty (for a more detailed analysis of poverty refer to Chapter 6 in this book).

**Aged-based dependency:** Despite the lack of employment opportunities for young people, it is interesting to note that the age-based dependency ratio in South Africa dropped from 56,0 to 51,7 between 2007 and 2014 with young people (0–14 years old) and those over 60 years included as dependents. This is largely because of social protection measures that were changed through social assistance legislation since 2002 to provide Child Support Grants (CSG) to caregivers of poor children up to the age of 18 years and Social Old Age Pensions (SOAP) for all poor elder persons over 60 years. Such social welfare policy responses have made a huge difference to poor households and act as lifelines that reduce destitution and hunger (Taylor, 2015).

**Race-based trends:** When we break down the population according to race, we find stark differences in the features of each group with regard to fertility rates, mortality, and migration. For example, black South Africans have shorter life expectancy and higher fertility rates than white South Africans. Immigration is predominantly from other African countries, while emigration is mainly by white South Africans (National Planning Commission, 2011). Tables 5.1 and 5.3 show that South Africa's population growth rate is slowing because of a declining birth rate, but, compared to other countries in the region, increasing numbers of people live longer as their access to treatment for HIV and Aids as well as access to social protection measures in the form of social grants improves.

**Life expectancy and HIV/Aids:** Comparing and contrasting differences in life expectancy for black and white South Africans provides stark evidence of how black citizens are affected by HIV/Aids as a result of disparities and deprivations in living conditions. According to the National Development Plan (NPC, 2011), the life expectancy of black African women will reach on average just over 60 years by 2030 while that of white women will remain at 76. The inequities between the development of black African men and white men also reveal a similar story. Black African men, for example, have a life expectancy that will reach just under 56 years by 2030 and that of white men increases slightly from over 72 to over 73 in the same period. Social welfare policy responses for elderly people will thus need to prioritise the needs of black African elder persons until such disparities are addressed.

# World
## Elder Abuse Awareness
## Day
### • June 15 •

The South African Older Persons Act 13 of 2006 is aimed at protecting the well-being and rights of older persons

As in other middle-income countries such as Botswana, HIV and Aids has led to drastic decreases in average life expectancy and a rise in mortality figures (Taylor, 2008).

**Fertility rates:** The African Development Bank Report (2017) shows that South Africa's fertility levels are among the lowest in sub-Saharan Africa since the 1960s. Note that this drop in fertility rates is gradual with decreases from an average of 6,7 children per woman during the late 1960s to 2,92 in 2001, 2,8 in 2006, and 2,35 in 2011 (Stats SA, 2010). Yet, if we look at fertility patterns in relation to other characteristics such as race, province, geographical location in terms of rural or urban residence, and educational levels, a very different picture emerges. For example, the 2007 Community Survey (Stats SA, 2010) indicates that fertility rates are lower in metropolitan areas and higher in rural areas.

Using data from the 2007 Community Survey, the above report estimates that the O R Tambo district in the Eastern Cape has the highest fertility rate at 4,1 followed by the Greater Sekhukhune district in Limpopo Province with a rate of 3,7, and the Uthukela district in KwaZulu-Natal with a fertility rate of 3,6. The metropolitan areas of Gauteng and the Western Cape had the lowest fertility rates (Stats SA, 2010). Such evidence tells us that women living in rural areas without access to education, health care, and employment are more likely to have more children and to live in poverty. As access to education, health care, and wage income improves, there are likely to be more planned families and a decrease in fertility rates. This is also the case with infant and maternal mortality rates. As access to health, nutrition, and education improves, the evidence shows that there is a drop in infant and maternal mortality rates (NPC, 2011).

**Migration:** South Africa's population growth rate on average is at 1,4% in the period from 2000–2015 and is among the lowest on the continent yet the size of the population has increased by approximately 10 million and this is attributed largely to migration (NPC, 2011). Migrant flows into South Africa from neighbouring countries in the region are an outcome of social, economic, and political factors. People from other parts of Africa migrate to South Africa for a number of reasons. Some of the reasons include political and economic instability in their countries, and the need to find paid work and other opportunities. Estimates are that border crossings in the region rose from 5,1 million people in 1996 to 7,5 million by 2010 (Stats SA, 2010). Distinctions must also be made between migrants who are in the country legally and those who are illegal or have refugee status (for more details on migrants and refugees refer to Chapter 8 in this book). Social welfare policy and programmes are designed to afford all those who live in the country, especially children, social development services and protection under the law.

**Urbanisation** is a feature of the demographic and social and economic landscape in South Africa. Internal migration patterns within South Africa show that more people move from rural areas to cities and large metropolitan areas in search of work opportunities and improvements in the quality of their lives. Gauteng and the Western Cape attract an inflow of migrants from other parts of South Africa such as the Eastern Cape, Northern Cape, Limpopo, and the Free State. The impacts of forced removals and migration under the apartheid regime also had a devastating impact especially on black family life as working-age adults migrated to centres where employment opportunities were more available (for more details on families and risk and vulnerabilities refer to Chapter 7 in this book). Urbanisation levels in South Africa increased to 60% by 2007 (NPC – Diagnostic Report 2010). Evidence reflects that approximately 44% of South Africa's population are in the four largest metropolitan areas – Johannesburg, Pretoria, eThekwini, and Cape Town. The provinces that have the largest share of South Africa's population are KwaZulu-Natal with 10,8 million or 21,4% of the total population and Gauteng with 11,3 million or 22,4% of the total population (Stats SA, 2011). Poor migrants usually live in peri-urban informal settlements with little access to social welfare facilities and under extremely difficult conditions.

Demographic data and national household survey data provide social policymakers and social service practitioners with valuable statistical information they can use to develop analyses of trends so that policies and plans can be adjusted according to projected increases or declines in demographic and household indicators in different parts of a country. However, such data only provides part of the narrative or profile of what happens in a country. A full understanding or picture of the conditions experienced by people in a country is provided through the use of both statistical trends and qualitative data sources. Qualitative data on people's lived experiences and the social and economic impacts of structural conditions on their lives is usually obtained from social and community surveys conducted by research institutes, universities, professional social service practitioners and researchers working either in the non-profit sector or the government sector as well as independent research agencies. Social and economic research on conditions such as poverty, inequality, and people's experiences can also be found on official government websites, and can be obtained from Human Science Research Councils and United Nations organisations such as UNICEF, UNDP, and UFPA.

In the next section, some contemporary social and economic conditions that affect the well-being of people in Africa are discussed briefly.

## 5.4 Contemporary social and economic challenges in Africa and transformative social welfare policy responses

Postcolonial, independent African countries reflect a mixed picture of social and economic achievements with the largest share of the world's poor of whom many still live in situations of intolerable cruelty and multiple deprivations. Transformative social welfare policy provides measures to address these deprivations and prioritises interventions in economic, social, political, and environmental factors to create conditions that prioritise the needs of people trapped in intergenerational systems of poverty and inequality. African countries, especially in the Southern African region, are introducing social welfare policy and programme interventions to address some of the most pressing problems related to income poverty, unemployment, vulnerabilities through the life cycle and other conditions. However, these policy interventions do not always reach people who need such services and assistance in the ways that are required and at the service delivery points that are accessible to people.

In East Africa, for example, a study undertaken by the Akiba Uhaki Foundation (2007) found that for many people their everyday realities are far removed from the human rights and social justice pronouncements made through policies and political rhetoric. This study points out that in Burundi, Kenya, Rwanda, Tanzania, and Uganda issues that undermine people's access to human rights and justice include poverty, ignorance of rights and entitlements, inaccessible systems of justice, deprivations in socioeconomic conditions, widespread insecurity, and, in some areas, armed conflict. Alongside these issues are the persistent neglect of children and women and the violations of people's most widely accepted social, economic, civil, and political rights (Taylor, 2013). For example, estimates of poverty in Uganda show increases from 34% in 2000 to 38% in more recent studies (Akiba Uhaki Foundation, 2007). According to the Commission on the Review of the Constitution of Kenya, 56% of households in Kenya were estimated to live below the poverty line, and if the household is assumed to have an average of two children, there are at least 7,516,859 children living below the poverty line. Average life expectancy is 49,3 years with a slight variation from province to province in Kenya. The death rate is about 4,7 deaths per 1000 people while the infant mortality rate is estimated at 59,07 deaths per 1000 live births (Akiba Uhaki Foundation, 2007). Such social and economic indicators provide a picture of the welfare and development of people in these countries.

Other indicators of countries' social, economic, and political stability are also reflected in the numbers of internally displaced persons (IDPs), refugees, and migrants. Trends in East Africa reveal disturbing levels of internally displaced people and refugees. At the heart of such trends are experiences of victimisation, exclusions, discrimination, and other injustices (Taylor, 2013). The United Nations Office for the Coordination of Humanitarian Affairs (OCHA) in East Africa revealed in its 2012 displaced populations report that, at the beginning of April 2012, there were 5,715,096 refugees and IDPs in the region. There was an overall increase of 291,882 people (5,4%) between 30 September 2011 and the end of March 2012. The Democratic Republic of the Congo (DRC) and Somalia continue to host more than one million IDPs each, while Kenya, Ethiopia, and Tanzania host more than 250,000 refugees each (UN-OCHA, 2012 cited in Taylor, 2013).

Ignorance of rights, social welfare policies, and laws that afford basic protections is a direct result of deprivations in access to education and health care, and of other forms of poverty. East African human rights and social justice networks indicate that these conditions and problems will continue to be a concern for some time despite the political changes that have taken place (Akiba Uhaki Foundation 2007). Political changes include those in Kenya and Tanzania, where at least three democratic presidential elections have been held. Uganda and Rwanda have had transitions from military regimes to democratically elected civilian governments. On 23 February 2006, Ugandans took part in general elections under a multiparty dispensation after 25 years of single party rule. Yet, despite these moves towards democratic participation and civilian rule, the narrative of social exclusion and deprivation for the poor majority continues (Taylor, 2013). To be sure, this narrative is not new and has its roots in many internal and external political and economic factors but the significance lies in how such economic and political processes undermines social welfare policy transformation in the region.

The importance of health, education, and related social and economic aspects of human development together with inclusive economic development can change such conditions. However, to do this policymakers require evidence-based research and reliable demographic indicators to be able to focus social welfare policy and service provision on the needs of people trapped in poverty and excluded from mainstream society. These indicators and trends highlight the social and economic impacts of a variety of challenges in Africa. They also reflect the need for social welfare policies to focus on both long-term structural conditions that trap people in poverty through income support, social welfare services, access to education and health care and on the need for humanitarian assistance that responds to violence, armed conflict and internally displaced peoples as well as migrants.

A more detailed discussion on social and economic conditions in South Africa follows as an example to illustrate how social and economic conditions influence social welfare policy responses.

## 5.4.1 South Africa's demography and social and economic contexts as influences in social welfare policy

This section uses South Africa as an example and illustrates how to apply a demographic and social and economic analysis using data and evidence to understand the lived experiences of individuals, families, households, and communities in other countries on the continent. Although it is more than two decades since South Africa gained independence, demographic trends and human development indicators continue to reveal significant levels of social fragmentation, unacceptable levels of social alienation, and the breakdown of social institutions in South Africa (National Planning Commission (NPC), 2010). The demography and social and economic contexts highlight an absence of fully functioning families, households, communities, and neighbourhoods with an inability on the part of social welfare institutions to provide adequate services that will improve social functioning of members of society and enhance social integration because the scale and scope of the conditions are enormous. Comparing demographic and social and economic data explains the extent of the social crises facing the country as well as the people who are living in extreme deprivation.

**Demographic features:** The age structure and other related features of South Africa's population provide indicators that enable the country to develop and prioritise the needs and well-being of people living in desperate circumstances. Demographic projections highlight that by 2018 young people under 15 years will fall below 30% due to declining birth and fertility rates and that the proportion of people over 65 years will increase to 6% in 10 years' time. Alongside these demographic changes the working-age population is projected to increase to 67% by 2030 (NPC, 2011). Such an increase in the working-age population together with high levels of unemployment and low levels of job creation place more people at risk of poverty or falling into deeper levels of poverty (refer to Chapter 6 in this book).

**Unemployment and employment:** The Quarterly Labour Force Survey (Stats SA, 2014), using a narrow[9] definition of unemployment, found that 25,2% of the population was unemployed and that when using a broad[10] definition of unemployment the proportion was higher at close to 37%. An interesting picture emerges when we analyse employment trends in South Africa. For example, 70% of employed individuals are in the non-agricultural formal sector, 16% work in the non-agricultural informal sector, 6% in agriculture, and 8% in private households. A further breakdown of those who work in private households reveals that they generally are low-waged domestic workers who constitute 15% of all employed women and 3% of all employed men. Analysing employment figures according to race, we find that 90% of employed white people are in the formal sector compared to 65% of employed Africans. Inequalities in employment opportunities are particularly evident when we put these figures differently. For instance, one in every ten African employed people work in private households earning very low wages (Department of Social Development, 2016).

When a population has such high levels of unemployment due to low and declining economic growth rates, the impacts on social welfare policies are many. Most importantly, it affects employment and the ability of working-age adults to secure decent waged work in the formal sector. The lack of waged employment opportunities pushes people into deeper income poverty and often households without income from wages require government social grants to eke out an existence. They are social welfare policy responses that ensure social protection measures such as social grants are available and food and nutrition programmes are accessible for children and elderly people to prevent malnutrition and related deprivations.

**Poverty and inequality:** Other important social and economic features that shape social welfare policy responses are the levels of poverty and inequality in a country. More than two decades after democracy the evidence shows that South Africa's poverty and inequality indicators reflect shocking race, gender, age, and spatial disparities. Stats SA found in 2011 that the country had an overall headcount poverty[11] rate of 46% but racial differences in experiences of poverty indicate that the rate among Africans was 67% when compared to less than 1% for white people (Stats SA, 2014).

**Gender inequalities** with regard to poverty are revealed when comparing the male rate of poverty which is at 55% to female poverty rates which are 59%. **Child poverty** including all children under the age of 18 years was 56%. Poverty in rural areas was 81% compared to 41% in urban areas, which explains why people migrate from rural to urban areas (Stats SA, 2014).

Another indicator that tells us more about poverty and inequality dynamics in South Africa is the source of **income for heads of households**. For example, 11% of female heads of households' source of income was from social pensions, social insurance, and family allowances and only 3% of 'male-headed' households received income from similar sources. Income received from work also differs in female and male-headed households with women receiving 63% and men 76% (Department of Social Development, 2016). A more detailed analysis on poverty, inequality, and vulnerability, and social welfare responses to such conditions is provided in Chapter 6 of this book.

Further analysis of the role of women in poor communities highlights that care work also includes housework, care of children and persons in frail health, and community-based work. The social impacts from the burden of care work imposed on women restrict them from using their time and resources for their own development and keep them out of opportunities for engaging in decent waged labour. The Review Report cites Stats SA's Time Use Survey of 2010 as evidence to show that women spend an average of 229 minutes per day on unpaid care work, compared to the 97 minutes per day spent by men on this work (Department of Social Development, 2016: 59–60). Using such evidence, social service professionals can expose gender inequities in the provision of social care work and the assumptions that such roles ought to be undertaken by women. In many countries it is in the social and economic spheres that patriarchy and structural inequalities are deeply ingrained and reproduced. Transforming social welfare policy requires using data and various forms of evidence to make visible such inequities so that girls and women are able to meet their human development needs and escape from poverty traps.

**Health and Education:** Health and education indicators provide evidence of the efficacy of a country's social welfare policy responses. These indicators provide evidence of those who are accessing health care, nutrition, and education. Importantly, health and education are instruments that enable individuals and members of households to improve their capabilities so that they can find decent waged work. Black people's access to health and education remains a challenge in South Africa, because of past racial inequities in the distribution of health and education services and the poor quality of education, health care and social welfare services that the majority received (Taylor, 2015). The links among health, education and earning capacities of people are aptly illustrated by the impacts of the HIV/Aids pandemic across Africa with the highest incidence in South Africa (NPC, 2011).

Education statistics tell us that South Africa's schooling system caters for just over 14 million learners and that, by 2007, the gross enrolment ratio was 98% for learners from grades 1 to 7, which is very close to full enrolment figures. The links between what happens in the home, school environment, and in communities also need to be understood to provide an explanation for enrolment numbers dropping to 85% for grades 8 and 12. The issues that affect how learners experience the school system, the quality of education and teaching, and the resources that learners have access to influence drop-out rates and pass rates. Statistical analysis shows that of those learners who continue up to matriculation only 15% achieved an average mark of 40% or more (NPC, 2010). Transformative social welfare policies are designed to address both inequities in the educational and health processes as well as the outcomes.

# CONCLUSION

- This chapter has highlighted how the effects of social, economic, and environmental crises can be better addressed using demographic and statistical data to determine who are likely to suffer the worst impacts of such crises.
- Social welfare policies and programmes need to take account of demographic, social, economic, and environmental contexts and use evidence to analyse the conditions affecting the most at risk and vulnerable.
- The chapter explained the importance of using evidence-based knowledge to transform social welfare policy so that services reach those who need them most.
- Among the tools that can be used to advance a rights-based agenda for social welfare policy transformation is that of evidence that links peoples' experiences with the structural conditions that influence their lives.
- Professional practice without critical consciousness of people's life experiences and analysis of the root causes will not lead to a qualitative improvement in human development of those most at risk, vulnerable, and excluded from the benefits of development.

# QUESTIONS

1. Explain why social service professionals and policymakers need to use demographic data and social and economic indicators to transform social welfare policy and respond to people's needs.
2. Using Tables 5.1, 5.2 and 5.3, select a specific country and analyse the demographic data for that country to build a profile of the population structure, the mortality and other rates, and poverty indicators. You can use the South African example in the chapter as a guide to analyse the specific country you select.
3. Discuss how you would use demographic and social and economic indicators to address unequal social service provision in a country.
4. Use demographic and other social and economic data to identify who are excluded and explain how you would change or transform existing social welfare policy to address their needs.

# REFERENCES

AFRICAN DEVELOPMENT BANK (2017). *Indicators on Gender, Poverty, the Environment and Progress toward the Sustainable Development Goals in African Countries, Volume XVIII* [Online]. Côte d'Ivoire: Economic and Social Statistics Division. Available: https://www.afdb.org/en/documents/publications/gender-poverty-and-environmental-indicators-on-african-countries/.

AFRICAN UNION (2009) *Social Policy Framework for Africa*. Addis Ababa: African Union.

AKIBA UHAKI FOUNDATION (2007) *Study Report on Mapping of Human Rights and Social Justice Organizations in the Eastern Africa Region [Kenya, Uganda, Tanzania, Rwanda and Burundi]*. Nairobi, Akiba Uhaki Foundation, prepared by Projects and Allied Consultants. Available: http://akibauhaki.org/index.php?option=com_docman&task=doc_download&gid=13&Itemid=.

FUKUDA-PARR, S & TAYLOR, V (2015) *Food Security in South Africa: A Human Rights & Entitlement Perspective*. Cape Town: University of Cape Town (UCT) Press.

GRAY, M, PLATH, D & WEBB, SA (2009) *Evidence-Based Social Work: A Critical Stance*. Abingdon: Routledge.

ORGANIZATION OF AFRICAN UNITY (OAU) (1981) African Charter on Human and Peoples' Rights (Banjul Charter), 27 June 1981, CAB/LEG/67/3 rev. 5,21 I.L.M. 58 (1982). Available: http://www.refworld.org/docid/3ae6b3630.html [13 October 2017].

SOUTH AFRICA. Department of Social Development (2009) *Report of the Southern African Departments and Ministries of Social Development and Social Affairs Regional Social Policy Roundtable 22 – 25 November, 2009.* Available: http://www.dsd.gov.za/index2. php?option=com_docman&task=doc_view&gid=131&Itemid=3.

SOUTH AFRICA. Department of Social Development (2016) *Comprehensive Report on the Review of the White Paper for Social Welfare of 1997* [Online]. Available: www.dsd.gov.za.

SOUTH AFRICA. National Planning Commission (2011) *National Development Plan: Vision for 2030* [Online]. Available: http://www.gov.za/sites/www.gov.za/files/devplan_2.pdf.

SOUTH AFRICA. National Planning Commission (NPC) (2010) *Human Conditions Diagnostic Report* [Online]. Available: http://www.gov.za/sites/www.gov.za/files/diagnostic report_2.pdf.

STATISTICS SOUTH AFRICA (2007) 'General Household Survey'. Pretoria: Statistics SA.

STATISTICS SOUTH AFRICA (2010) *Estimation of fertility from 2007 Community Survey of South Africa.* Report No.-03-00-04. Pretoria: Statistics South Africa.

STATISTICS SOUTH AFRICA (2012) *Social Profile of Vulnerable Groups in South Africa, 2002 to 2012*, Report No. 03-19-00. Pretoria: Statistics South Africa.

STATISTICS SOUTH AFRICA (2014*) Poverty Trends in South Africa: An examination of absolute poverty between 2006 and 2011.* Report No. 03-10-06. Pretoria: Statistics South Africa.

TAYLOR, V (2008) *Social Protection in Africa: An Overview of the Challenges* (Research Report prepared for the African Union). Available: www.eprionline.com/wpcontent/ uploads/2011/03/Taylor2008AUSocialProtectionOverview.pdf.

TAYLOR, V: 'Achieving food security through social policies: Comprehensive social protection for development' in Fukuda-Parr, S & Taylor, V (eds.) (2015) *Food Security in South Africa: A Human Rights & Entitlement Perspective.* Cape Town: University of Cape Town (UCT) Press.

TAYLOR, V: 'Social Justice: Reframing the "Social" in Critical Discourses in Africa' inTangen, S (ed.) (2013) *African Perspectives on Social Justice.* Kampala: Friedrich-Ebert-Stiftung.

## Endnotes

1  Ad hoc and incremental approaches to policymaking are based on policymakers or decision-makers not wanting to create major disruptions to existing social development processes. They therefore make slight changes to existing policies and legislation without engaging in wide-scale transformation.

2  Political expediency in this sense means that policymakers and other decision-makers make choices on changes according to what is in their best interests or the best interests of those they know rather than the best interests of the public they serve.

3  Interest groups can include women's groups, children's rights groups, resident associations, civic movements, non-profit social welfare organisations, and many other organised groups that have the capacity to represent their views and make their voices heard.

4  An empirical basis means that the evidence is an outcome of research that can be tested and verified using similar or the same factors or conditions.

5  The Gini coefficient is used to calculate the difference in income of people living in a country. The Gini coefficient, as a normative measure, ranges between 0 and 1, where 0 means perfect equality (all individuals earn the same) and 1 refers to maximum inequality (1 person earns all income) and others nothing.

6  Narratives and anecdotes refer to stories or descriptions of people's experiences as expressed by them or others such as social service professionals who observe how people live. These narratives and anecdotal stories are usually about individuals or particular households and do not reflect whether the descriptions fit a whole population or part of a population.

7  A system of patriarchy is one which is embedded in the social structures of society and is understood as a system in which men have power and are in authority over women in all spheres of life. African countries that uphold human rights of people generally do not support patriarchal attitudes that undermine girls and women's development.

8  Mortality rates mean death rates. For example, when reference is made to infant mortality rates it means the numbers of children who die at birth. These rates are usually measured as the numbers who die per every 1000 people in the population.

9  A narrow definition of unemployment only counts those working-age adults who have been actively seeking work in the last two weeks before being surveyed.

10 The broad definition includes people who are not in employment, who feel discouraged, and who have been experiencing long-term structural unemployment.

11 Headcount poverty shows the actual number of people who fall below a given poverty line. The poverty line is one that is set by a government based on an amount of money it would take a person to purchase a basket of basic food and essential items to survive.

## CHAPTER 06

# Poverty, inequalities, risk and vulnerability and social welfare policy responses

*Viviene Taylor*

'*Poverty is pain. Poor people suffer physical pain that comes with too little food and long hours of work; emotional pain stemming from the daily humiliations of dependency and lack of power; and the moral pain from being forced to make choices – such as whether to use limited funds to save the life of an ill family member, or to use those same funds to feed their children*' (Narayan et al., 2000: 3).

## Chapter objectives

✓ Deepening professionals and policymakers understanding of the theories and concepts of poverty, inequalities, risk and vulnerability.

✓ Explaining the linkages among poverty, inequalities, risk, and vulnerabilities.

✓ Providing an understanding of measures used to identify those who are experiencing poverty, inequalities, risk, and vulnerabilities

✓ Providing a framework to analyse poverty and deprivations and to understand some responses to poverty.

## Chapter outcomes

✓ Understanding the concepts of poverty, inequalities, risk, and vulnerability.

✓ Analysing the differences and links among these concepts.

✓ Identifying the different types of poverty and deprivations that people experience.

✓ Utilising indicators to analyse whose needs and conditions to prioritise when addressing poverty through social welfare policy.

✓ Determining the social welfare policy responses to poverty, vulnerability, and risk in different local contexts.

# 6.1 Introduction

Responses to poverty, inequalities, and risks and vulnerabilities require an understanding of the root causes that give rise to these conditions, problems, and challenges. There are differing understandings and explanations for these causes and for experiences of vulnerability, risk, poverty, and inequalities. These understandings and explanations influence the types of policies that are designed to address poverty, inequalities, and vulnerabilities. They also influence the approaches taken in policies and the policy interventions necessary to respond to the needs of individuals, families, households, and groups who are vulnerable during the life cycle, and who live in conditions of chronic poverty that expose them to extreme risk and hardship. Policymakers and social service professionals are required to respond to the immediate impacts of social and economic crises and simultaneously address the underlying causes that contribute to poverty and social inequalities which expose people to risk and make them vulnerable.

Contemporary societies in postcolonial and post-independent Africa experience complex social and economic challenges that expose people to risks and make them vulnerable. The twenty-first century has also brought with it tremendous technological and environmental changes. These changes result in new and different risks and vulnerabilities that are evident in environmental disasters, health pandemics such as HIV and Aids, forced migration, and changing work patterns (Taylor, 2008). These new risks and vulnerabilities together with pre-existing conditions of chronic poverty and increasing inequalities provide the impetus for transforming conventional social welfare policy and programme responses to address both structural and systemic conditions. Such responses can either be short-term interventions in the form of emergency relief measures, charitable and humanitarian aid, or they can include long-term preventive and developmental measures that deal with the root causes of conditions which expose people to risk and make them vulnerable (Taylor, 2013). Social service professionals, policymakers, and students of social welfare policy tend to work within predetermined policy, legislative, and programme frameworks. Their professional roles are often determined by the regulations that are in place or by the resources available for them to provide the services that people need in specific contexts. Enabling people to cope, to survive extreme deprivation, and to overcome the persistent conditions that keep them trapped in intergenerational cycles of poverty[1] require knowledge of causes and impacts of these conditions and the policy responses to them.

Conditions that reproduce poverty and inequalities, and make people vulnerable and insecure are not new and, over many centuries, policymakers and professionals have tried to introduce measures to reduce and eliminate these conditions. The persistence of such conditions and the increasing scope, levels and depth of poverty in countries in Africa reveal that little has changed for people in many of these countries. For example, countries such as Angola with 36,6% of its population living below the national poverty line in 2008, Burkina Faso with just over 40% of the population in poverty in 2014, the Democratic Republic of Congo with 63% of the population in poverty in 2012, Madagascar with 75% in 2012, and Nigeria with an estimated 46% in 2009, struggle to address poverty and its multiple effects. Malawi, Mozambique, South Africa, Swaziland, Zambia, and Zimbabwe are countries in the African region in which over 50% of the population live below the international poverty line of US$ 1,9 per day (African Development Bank, 2017: 37). These poverty indicators when combined with other indicators such as infant and maternal mortality rates, education levels, life expectancy at birth, and employment trends provide a picture of the desperate and intolerable living conditions of people.

In every country in the African region the combination of poverty, lack of waged work and insecure livelihoods, and lack of health care and education keeps people trapped in conditions that make them vulnerable and expose them to risk. Individuals, families, and communities living in such conditions of poverty are usually referred to social workers and other social service professionals for social welfare services. The typical social welfare responses available to such professionals are limited to the provision of coping strategies such as psychosocial therapeutic interventions and referrals for short-term emergency relief in the form of cash grants, food aid, and health care. These measures make a huge difference to the survival of people but they do not deal with the structural conditions that give rise to poverty, inequalities, and risk. Such structural conditions are outcomes of policy choices regarding the distribution of wealth, work opportunities, education and health care services, and social infrastructure (such as schools, transport networks, clinics, water, and housing settlements).

Policy choices on how to address poverty, inequalities, and vulnerabilities are made through parliamentary processes in the political sphere, and such choices influence the types of interventions introduced in the economic and social spheres. For example, some countries may decide that the best way to address poverty is through job creation and interventions that may be introduced could include public employment programmes or subsidies made to businesses to provide jobs. Other countries may decide that the situation is so dire that urgent interventions are required through social provision in the form of grants, food aid, and other forms of assistance. Bad and inappropriate policy choices and decisions and maladministration through incompetence and corruption are among the many reasons for the persistence of poverty, inequalities, and vulnerabilities on the continent. The stubborn features of poverty and inequalities across the world led to the United Nations and its agencies promoting global action to address these features. This action took the form of global commitments made by countries to work towards achieving the Millennium Development Goals (MDGs) and, more recently, the Sustainable Development Goals (SDGs) (www.un.org).

Despite such commitments, the experiences for millions of people living in chronic structural poverty remain hazardous and life threatening. These are some of the reasons for an alternative policy approach to social welfare on the continent. Transformative social welfare policy responses and measures provide the basis for alternatives and can enable people to move out of intergenerational cycles of poverty, and reduce inequalities, risk, and vulnerability. A transformative approach to conditions of poverty, inequalities, and vulnerabilities addresses both the root causes of these conditions as well as the symptoms. Such an approach places emphasis on helping people to cope and survive in dire circumstances, and most importantly, provides people with the means and tools to overcome the roots of poverty, inequalities, and vulnerabilities (Taylor, 2013). Transformative social welfare policy responses can promote individual and collective or community coping strategies that enable people to build their resilience to respond to poverty, risk, and vulnerability. Later in this chapter, some policy responses in South Africa show the effects of interventions in reducing poverty and inequalities as well as preventing people, who are at risk and vulnerable, from falling into deeper poverty or from becoming socially excluded.

The next section provides the theoretical underpinnings of concepts of poverty, inequality, risk, and vulnerability and the links among these conditions.

# 6.2 Theoretical and conceptual understandings of poverty and inequalities

Two aspects influence how policymakers deal with poverty. The first is the understanding of poverty and its relationships with other social development concerns such as the vulnerabilities and risks people experience during different stages of their lives, and the second is the relationship between poverty and the ownership of assets, the distribution of assets as well as the type of exchange transactions one can make in a market economy. These two aspects are discussed in this chapter. Poverty as a concept and as a structural condition that requires social welfare policy responses is complex. It is often understood as people having low income or not having the ability to purchase basic goods and services to meet the requirements for human survival. This is indeed an aspect of poverty but not the only one. Having insufficient income to purchase the daily necessities to sustain life and improve one's development and that of one's family or household shows that income (whether this is income from wages or from social transfers such as grants) is part of the chain in trade or exchange relations and is instrumental to human well-being. However, poverty is not only the lack of income which in turn leads to deprivations but it is also a lack of access to public facilities and programmes (such as social welfare services, health, education, and transport).

Theories on poverty and its causes as well as attempts to understand poverty in all its dimensions have evolved over many years. Over a century ago, Seebohm Rowntree conducted one of the first poverty studies in York, England. Rowntree examined poverty at household level and then defined a minimum level of material subsistence (food and basic requirements) below which a family would be categorised as 'poor' – this idea of the poverty line is still used today to measure poverty (Rowntree, 1901). Since Rowntree's influential study, the concept of poverty has continued to evolve to include other dimensions. At first, it expanded beyond income poverty to include deprivations resulting from low levels of education and health through the work of the United Nations Development Programme reported in Human Development Reports (UNDP – Human Development Reports, http://hdr.undp.org/). Recently, the poverty concept has included another dimension – that of vulnerability and 'voicelessness' – as expressed by poor people themselves. This dimension of poverty emerges strongly from a review of 81 Participatory Poverty Assessment reports that were based on discussions held with more than 40,000 poor women and men in 50 countries in the 1990s. Arising from the review, this study defines poverty from the perspective of poor people as:

> *'Poverty is pain. Poor people suffer physical pain that comes with too little food and long hours of work; emotional pain stemming from the daily humiliations of dependency and lack of power; and the moral pain from being forced to make choices – such as whether to use limited funds to save the life of an ill family member, or to use those same funds to feed their children'* (Narayan et al., 2000: 3).

Such a multidimensional view of poverty – lack of income, hunger, deprivations in health care, and lack of power and voice – provides policymakers and professionals with a deeper understanding of what poverty means and how to respond.

In contemporary societies in Africa there are increasing recognition that responses to poverty must go beyond addressing deprivations in basic material needs and include responses to other dimensions. For example, the powerlessness people experience in their daily lives as a result of their systemic exclusions from social and economic processes of development also requires urgent attention (World Development Report, 2001: 15). Besides the many aspects of their lives which are affected by poverty, the chronically poor (people living in households who are experiencing intergenerational poverty over decades) share a history of deprivation which may be transmitted across generations through economic, political, social, and cultural isolation.

Other studies on poverty and vulnerability conclude that:

> *'Any reasonable definition of poverty implies that significant numbers of people are living in intolerable circumstances in which starvation is a constant threat, sickness is a familiar companion, and oppression is a fact of life'* (Kanbur and Squire, 2001: 183).

The African Development Bank Report (2017) provides compelling statistical evidence indicating that many people on the continent live in poverty and in households that remain outside of mainstream economic and social processes of development. It is their experiences of exclusion because of conditions of poverty that contribute to their inability to find and maintain secure livelihoods through decent work with predictable income (Taylor, 2013). The lack of waged work and sustainable livelihoods also means they are unable to access health care, education, and welfare services. Since the 1980s, the influence of the shifts in thinking about poverty and the realities that the poorest people face every day as they struggle to survive at the most basic level is evident in policy responses.

Deprivations in basic health care and education limit the possibilities for people to move out of income poor households. Millions of people on the continent of Africa are unemployed or underemployed while millions more do not earn enough to meet the most basic of human needs. They are unable to cope with shocks ranging from catastrophic injury to uncontrolled inflation (monetary inflation is when currency is overvalued to the extent it loses its actual market value and food price inflation is when food prices are increased beyond its market value) and disasters resulting from fires, floods or drought. Bad economic and social policies, ineffective implementation by governments, lack of public institutions and administrative capacity, and corruption are contributors to structurally based poverty (Taylor, 2013). Put differently, if people are excluded from mainstream economic, political, and social institutions and experience isolation and deprivations as a result of these exclusions, then policy changes must be made in the economic, political, and social institutions to ensure that the needs of people are met and that processes for inclusion and human development are integrated within a human rights framework.

## 6.2.1 A framework to respond to poverty and inequalities from a transformative social welfare policy perspective

Advances in how to achieve such processes of social and economic inclusion were expressed in the pioneering work of Amartya Sen (1982; 1999). According to Sen (1999), poverty, in its broadest sense, is concerned with restricted capabilities – the inability to exercise humanity's most basic freedoms (Sen, 1999). It is this inclusive definition of poverty that demonstrates why a comprehensive approach to poverty, inequality, risk, and vulnerability is needed. The many understandings and theories on poverty can appear complex and can make it difficult to know what approach and framework should be used to design social welfare policies that are capable of making a difference in poor people's lives. However, Sen, writing on poverty and famines (Sen, 1982), provides a very useful framework that includes a human rights approach and helps to identify what people should be entitled and have access to social welfare in order to lead lives that are free from poverty, hunger, and deprivations in health and education.

A framework is simply a way of organising the issues and aspects of a condition or problem so that policymakers and professionals are able to undertake an analysis of the condition or problem to address parts of the problem or all aspects related to it. A transformative and rights-based approach to social welfare policy responses requires a framework that provides entry points to address the structural causes of poverty and an understanding of the political and economic choices made that underpin these causes. A transformative approach to poverty, inequalities, and vulnerabilities also requires an understanding of how historical processes, reinforced by political, social and economic institutions, determine the ability of a person to be free from poverty, hunger and other deprivations.

Sen explains his theoretical understanding of poverty and entitlement relations by making the links with the structure of ownership patterns in a country. In his view, when people are denied ownership of land and of assets to enhance their capabilities and allow them to engage in trade and exchange relations, they become trapped in poverty. Sen's analysis of people's experiences of starvation and poverty is linked to the structure of ownership relations (1982). His framework focuses on ownership relations as providing people with entitlements (refer to Box 6.1 for an explanation of entitlements that are achieved through ownership relations in a market economy). Sen's theories and framework on entitlement and capabilities are aligned with a human rights and transformative social welfare policy approach (1999).

## 6.2.2 Amartya Sen's theory of poverty and entitlements

**Transformative Framework**  **AMARTYA SEN'S THEORY OF POVERTY AND ENTITLEMENTS**

According to Sen:
'An entitlement relation applied to ownership connects one set of ownerships to another through certain rules of legitimacy. It is a recursive relation and the process of connecting can be repeated. Consider a private ownership market economy. I own this loaf of bread. Why is this ownership accepted? Because I got it by exchange through paying some money I owned. Why is my ownership of that money accepted? Because I got it by selling a bamboo umbrella owned by me. Why is my ownership of the bamboo umbrella accepted? Because I made it with my own labour using some bamboo from my land. Why is my ownership of the land accepted? Because I inherited it from my father. Why is his ownership of that land accepted? Each link in this chain of entitlement relations 'legitimises' one set of ownership by reference to another, or to some basic entitlement in the form of enjoying the fruits of one's own labour' (Sen, 1982: 1–2).

Amartya Sen (right) and Viviene Taylor (left). Photo taken at Trinity College, Cambridge University (2001).

The significance of Sen's theory and framework on poverty and entitlement relations is that it analyses the structural relations that either enable people to engage in exchange in a market economy or to build their capabilities to use opportunities to function in a society. Box 6.1 demystifies the causal relationships or, as Sen (1982: 2) refers to it, the 'chain of entitlement relations' that exclude people from engaging in market transactions and exchanging their labour or products for commodities or items that they need to live. During the colonial era, countries in Africa were deeply affected by dispossession from their land, exploitation of mineral and raw materials and people's labour. These patterns of ownership and monopolies over resources were carried through in the postcolonial and post-independence period. Ownership and entitlement relations became the monopoly of those in power or those who inherited wealth because of either race (as in the case of South Africa) or because of elite expropriation of resources. The demographic features of countries in Africa, and their social and economic indicators (refer to Chapter 5), reflect the extent of poverty and vulnerabilities in the majority of countries.

Sen's framework provides a way of analysing the root causes of poverty and inequalities as well as the symptoms. His framework (Sen, 1982: 2–8) analyses entitlement relations that influences people's abilities to develop and engage in economic and social relations in a market-based society and includes the following four entitlement dimensions:

1. **Trade-based entitlement**: This entitlement is achieved by people owning something either through an exchange by trading with a willing party or parties. In this process of acquiring resources or assets through trade the issue to note is that the process is not based on force or coercion but the willingness of all parties to engage in trade to procure a commodity at a value that is set by the market and regulated by the state in the interests of all.

2. **Production-based entitlement**: In this form of entitlement, Sen argues that there are certain prerequisites that determine a person's ability to engage in exchanges within a market economy. If a person does not have these prerequisites, this leads to poverty and starvation. The factors that determine a person's entitlement through production depend on the availability of employment for the set of skills that the person has as well as the length of employment and the wages that is earned for the exchange of labour.

3. **Own-labour entitlement**: This entitlement is achieved by using one's own labour to engage in trade and in the production of goods or services. The money earned through this process gives one an entitlement to engage in other forms of exchanges. The process of using one's own labour is dependent on what a person can earn by selling what is produced and how much it costs to produce the goods and services using one's own labour and other assets.

4. **Inheritance and transfer entitlement**: When something is inherited or given to one by someone who legitimately owns it, usually after the latter's death, then that inheritance becomes an entitlement. In some countries, inherited wealth can take the form of assets such as land, housing, money, and any asset that, if sold or exchanged through the market, acquires a value (Sen, 1982: 2–8).

Exchange entitlements are influenced by a number of other factors. These include the ability to enter the market economy and exchange one's labour for waged employment, the assets and wealth that one is able to accumulate either through own labour production or employment, inheritance, and the rules that govern how social and economic systems work in modern market or capitalist systems. When market economic systems do not function effectively or fail, governments put into place social security or social protection measures to assist those who require help. Social protection systems include social transfers in the form of social grants for the poor children, older people living with disabilities, and other benefits such as unemployment insurance, medical care, and education. A combination of the four entitlements together with social protection measures should enable poor households to improve their capabilities and lead meaningful lives.

A political economy perspective conceptualises poverty as an accumulation of deprivations that people experience as a result of factors that deny them ownership or entitlements to income and wealth, including the denial of political, civil and economic rights. This theoretical understanding identifies the root causes of poverty as unequal access to entitlements such as land, power, wages, and economic and social transfers. This understanding fits well with the evidence in countries such as South Africa and other postcolonial and post-development contexts (discussed in Chapter 5 of this book) in which decades of exclusions of the majority, with a concurrent accumulation of privilege and entitlements by a minority, lead to extreme poverty and inequalities experienced by the majority.

The next section discusses the links among poverty, inequality, risk, and vulnerability in greater detail. It shows how these aspects are connected to each other and how responding to poverty and inequalities may lead to different outcomes in terms of risk and vulnerability.

## 6.3 The links among poverty, inequality, risk, and vulnerability

Conditions that keep people trapped in poverty, expose them to risk, and make them vulnerable through the life cycle are interrelated. Poverty and inequality limit the ability of individuals, households, and governments to finance the enhancement of skills, education, and training.[2] In this way, poverty reinforces a trap that keeps living standards of people in conditions of extreme deprivation and prospects for their human welfare dim. Vulnerability and insecurity as a result of chronic poverty prevent individuals and families from assuming their basic responsibilities and enjoying their fundamental rights. Chronic poverty and deprivation are systemic in nature and require multidimensional responses. Besides the many aspects of their lives affected by poverty, people who are chronically poor share a history of accumulated deprivations which may be transmitted across generations through economic, political, social, and cultural isolation. While deprivations in basic health care and education are being addressed to some extent in countries in Africa, there is a lack of social welfare responses to the psychosocial effects of chronic income poverty. At household level this reduces the resilience of poor people to cope with vulnerability and risks.

Income poverty is a direct cause of people's inability to secure employment, or even when they do obtain employment, they do not earn enough to meet the most basic of human needs, much less cope with shocks ranging from catastrophic injury to uncontrolled inflation and disasters, resulting from fires, floods or drought. It is these conditions that expose people living in chronic conditions of poverty, making them vulnerable to deeper poverty and compromising their well-being and human development. In contemporary Africa, the most acute expression of chronic structurally based poverty is hunger, malnutrition, food insecurity, and other markers of deprivation such as low life expectancy and unemployment. Daily risks and vulnerabilities arise in other ways as well. When people remain severely deprived because of a persistent lack of – or neglect of – social and economic institutions (such as schools, hospitals, water, electricity, roads, and transport), their daily experiences of insecurities and loss of human dignity expose them to risks and can be directly linked to a failure of clear and effective social welfare policy responses (Taylor, 2005).

Both absolute poverty and relative poverty incorporate the concept of risk. When individuals, households, and communities are at risk of falling into poverty or of experiencing even deeper levels of poverty, their well-being and human development become compromised.

While there is a degree of mutual vulnerability resulting from the downside risks of economic globalisation and resultant lack of work-based income, some people have a higher exposure to risk and a reduced ability to cope with adverse effects (United Nations Division for Economic and Social Affairs, 2001). For example, vulnerability and exposure to risk varies through people's life cycles, situations, and economic circumstances.

**absolute poverty:** Absolute poverty means that individuals and households live in extreme or severe deprivation without the most basic essentials for survival – such as food, drinking water, clothing, and essential services – and without income to purchase the minimum requirements.

**relative poverty:** Relative poverty is a concept that refers to all those who fall below a minimum standard of living set by a society and measured in relation to income or a basket of goods and services, which individuals and households lack. As a result, they cannot achieve an average or acceptable quality of life.

Some risks such as natural disasters (for example, floods and droughts) and economic and financial declines have the potential to affect everyone. The impacts of these risks are not evenly distributed and everyone is not equally vulnerable because countries in Africa are not homogeneous.

Certain categories of individuals or groups, due to their position in society or other characteristics such as age, race, or gender, may be more vulnerable than others to the negative consequences of economic, political, and social instability (Taylor, 2013). Among these categories are poor women, children, people with disabilities, the unemployed, and households and communities with limited or no assets or exchange entitlements who become vulnerable and are least able to cope with the effects of, for example, cutbacks in basic social services and reduced public transfers in the form of cash or kind benefits (Taylor, 2013).

> **vulnerable:** People are vulnerable when they are at greater risk of victimisation because of gender, race, ethnicity, language, and social status, or because they are afraid of being victimised. Others are vulnerable and at risk because they do not have access to food or resources to meet the most basic of nutritious requirements.

Within the poverty framework, risk is embodied in 'vulnerability' which is primarily defined as 'the risk that a household or individual will experience an episode of income or health poverty over time' (Taylor, 2002: 19). Risk can also be understood in terms of future threats that people anticipate which are beyond the control of individuals and communities. Examples of this in Africa would include the threat of conflict, civil wars, resource-based wars (over land, natural resources and minerals), violence, severe illness or disability, crime, environmental degradation, and natural disaster.

In light of their links, the prescriptions for addressing the core elements of poverty, inequality, risk, and vulnerability are surprisingly different. While the World Bank's description of poverty has expanded to include nonmaterial elements, its remedy is still focused on addressing income poverty through increasing economic growth. Economic growth through international trade is touted as the key to eliminating the other dimensions of poverty. By focusing narrowly on economic growth, other aspects of poverty that are also fundamental to ensuring human well-being are perceived as less important than economic growth (Taylor, 2005). The psychological and social effects of intergenerational cycles of poverty, and of exposure to risk and vulnerabilities, are usually ignored when the solutions narrowly focus only on income poverty without including other social welfare policy interventions to respond to such long-term deprivations.

But understanding the effects of poverty, inequalities, vulnerability, and risk is not enough. At local levels social service professionals must be able to identify and prioritise those who are experiencing the worst effects and who are at greatest risk. But how do we identify, in ways that are based on objective criteria, those whose needs should be prioritised through social welfare policy responses? The next section provides an analysis of some of the main features of poverty, inequalities, vulnerability, and risk and some policy responses to these.

# 6.4 Poverty, inequalities vulnerability and risk factors and policy responses

## 6.4.1 Impacts of HIV and Aids

Over the past two decades, countries in Africa, especially in the Southern African region, have been experiencing the devastating impacts of the HIV/Aids pandemic. HIV infections and Aids have made large parts of the poorest sections of the population vulnerable, and while entire populations have been exposed to risks, poor women and children have been particularly hard hit by the disease. Some countries such as South Africa provide free anti-retroviral (ARV) treatment programmes for people infected with the disease, but many other governments on the continent cannot afford to provide such treatment. The effects of the HIV/Aids pandemic are many. These include high mortality rates, declines in life expectancy (Chapter 5 of this book provides details of these indicators), impacts on the local and national economies due to loss of productive years of people living with the disease, and the enormous social and economic costs that households and communities have to carry because of the long-term care required.

The effects of HIV and Aids have made it very difficult for existing social welfare policies and programmes to respond appropriately and for social service professionals to provide essential services. Although HIV infection levels among adults in South Africa remain high, progress was made in reducing mother-to-child transmission of HIV because of increasing access to free ARV treatment and other prevention measures (Department of Social Development, 2016: 59–60). Besides free ARV treatment, South Africa also introduced para-professional, home-based care workers to assist in the treatment and care of people living with Aids. These home-based carers are now part of the team together with social workers or social service professionals who provide essential services.

Among the many challenges social service professionals experience are the large numbers of children who have lost parents and are orphaned. The reality for countries in the Southern African region is that the burden of care, of members living with the disease and of children orphaned, falls on extended family members, on community members, and on the social services provided by the state. The high incidence of orphans has led to changes in social welfare policies related to children, especially with regard to the placement of children in foster care or in households with kinship arrangements. Orphaned children live in households that experience extreme income poverty. The South African government has had to introduce social grants to provide income support for children who are orphaned as a result of HIV and Aids (Department of Social Development, 2016: 59–60).

The scale of the problems linked to the HIV/Aids pandemic requires interventions that typical social welfare policies and programmes are not designed to offer. One way of doing this is by establishing a socially acceptable and agreed minimum floor based on normative measures, which in South Africa's case would include the Constitution.

## 6.4.2 Vulnerability and risk factors and children

There are many social conditions affecting children on the continent. Children and youth under the age of 18 years are reliant either on their parents or their extended family for their emotional and physical development. Demographic indicators in Chapter 5 of this book indicate that children and youth constitute a significant proportion of the total population in countries in Africa and a large proportion of them live in poverty. Poverty and social inequalities exposes them to a disproportionate level of risk and vulnerability. During different stages they are reliant on adults and their home and educational environments for their development. When living conditions within their households and in their communities are unsuitable, make them vulnerable and expose them to risk, their development is seriously compromised.

The extent of the social crisis as a result of the impact of HIV and Aids, for example, in South Africa is evident when one reviews the estimates of children in need of care and those placed in foster care and who received foster care child grants. South Africa's National Department of Social Development estimates that there were 537 150 children in foster care and receiving foster child grants by the end of June 2014 (Department of Social Development, 2016). This is a huge growth in numbers and is more than ten times the number of children placed in foster care in 1996/97. The need for changes in social welfare policy and social provision in the form of child grants is mainly attributed to the impacts of HIV and Aids that left children in the poorest households without parents or adults to care for them.

Evidence shows that exposure to risk and vulnerability is linked to economic status and in South Africa especially to race inequalities. Households that are exposed to risk and most vulnerable are black African. Stats SA's *General Household Survey of 2014* (Stats SA, 2014) provides an analysis of children receiving foster care grants and indicates that of the child beneficiaries 93% are African, 5% coloured, 2% white, and less than 1% Indian. Such trends of children in need of foster care and foster care grants show that in postcolonial and post-democratic South Africa exposure to risk and vulnerability continues to have similar race, class, and gender dimensions as existed under the apartheid regime. However, because children's constitutional rights are entrenched in Chapter 2 of the Constitution (RSA, 1996), the South African government is able to make changes to existing legislation to ensure essential social protection measures for children in need of care.

Many children in South Africa live in child-headed families

Children also experience violations and abuse because they are unable to protect themselves. Social workers and the police are usually the first respondents in dealing with children who are either vulnerable, at risk, neglected or abused. In many parts of Africa there is under reporting of child abuse, violence against children, and child neglect and thus the actual extent of child abuse and neglect is not known and not documented. In South Africa, the Children's Act 38 of 2005 and the Children's Amendment Act 41 of 2007 and regulations to these Acts provide a comprehensive and progressive policy and legislative framework to ensure the protection of children including those who are neglected and abused (Department of Social Development, 2016). Children who live in precarious and dangerous conditions because of poverty and neglect move out of their communities and increasingly live 'on' or 'off' the streets in urban areas. In these situations they are exposed to sexual and other forms of exploitation and their exposure to risks increases. Most often children who run away from home and are forced to engage in activities that place them at risk are unlikely to report such activities. The numbers of children in these situations are unknown but indications are that there are growing numbers of children who end up living 'on' or 'off' the streets in urban areas in many countries in Africa.

Other conditions that expose children to risk and make them vulnerable include using children for labour on farms, as domestic workers in households, in other exploitative illicit activities such as sex trafficking, trafficking in drugs, and many other dangerous activities.

### 6.4.3 Households, families and exposure to vulnerability and risk

In many countries in Africa, the use of the term 'household' is a more precise way of identifying the members who share the home than the family. This is because members who live together in a house are not always closely related but may also include relatives, people from the same village or geographic area, or people who have some common experience. A study by Aliber (2001) shows that increases in household size and dependency ratios place an extra burden on poor household's asset base and contribute to chronic poverty and hunger. In other words, dependency ratios increase (numbers of non-wage earning members who depend on income from a member or members in the household) when the numbers of children and the presence of a third generation in a household increase (Fukuda-Parr & Taylor, 2015). The resulting effects on poor people's access to food and other necessities are disastrous and their exposure to vulnerabilities and risk increases.

### 6.4.4 Gender and poverty

There is also a gender dimension to experiences of poverty and vulnerability in households. Aliber (2001) provides evidence to show that single parent-headed households were twice as likely to be in long-term poverty, especially if headed by females. The gender of household members and the structure of households tell us who is likely to experience poverty, and more likely to be vulnerable. Vulnerability is more pronounced and evident in families and households that are chronically poor (chronic poverty is a term used to refer to people who have lived below any acceptable standard for many generations and have been trapped in poverty).

### 6.4.5 Children, older people, people with disabilities and poverty and vulnerabilities

Children, older people, women, people who suffer from serious ill health, people living with disabilities, and those in peri-urban and remote areas are more likely to be vulnerable and exposed to further risks. For example, a survey undertaken by Stats SA and published in a *Social Profile of Vulnerable Groups* (Stats SA, 2013) finds that vulnerability affects a significant proportion of the population despite the country's level of development and wealth. Stats SA's (2013) survey finds that children in poor communities are particularly vulnerable. A revealing finding when it comes to household and family composition is that, in South Africa, 4% of children are double orphans, 10,6% are paternal orphans and 3,2% are maternal orphans, with only 34% of children living with both parents. These children are not only living in conditions of extreme poverty but are vulnerable and exposed to numerous risks and exploitation. In addition, close to 7,8% live in skip generation households (children living with a grandparent).

Females constitute 41,2% of all heads of households and older females (especially social grant recipients) are more likely to live in extended households because members of families tend to live with those who receive a predictable income from social grants.

## 6.4.6 Social inequalities

South Africa's postcolonial apartheid history continues to be a determining influence in the type of inequalities that people experience.

Race-based inequalities in access to benefits and services are notable between black and white children. Stats SA (2013) reveals that 70,5% of black African children live in low-income households while only 4,4% of white children live in low-income households. Gender inequalities are being reproduced, despite changes to policies and legislation, because more than half of female-headed households (57%) are poor compared to only 36% of male-headed households. Poverty and vulnerability are linked and therefore the 64,5% of South Africa's children who live in households in the bottom two income quintiles with a per capita income of less than R765 per month find it very difficult to move out of the poverty and vulnerability that are a part of their lives. Families and households that do not have a reliable, predictable source of income because of unemployment, casual work, and no social grant income from the government move in and out of extreme poverty and live in a state of persistent insecurity.

> **social inequalities:** The concept of social inequalities is broader than income inequalities because it includes race-based inequalities, gender disparities, spatial differences, age-related differences, differences in the treatment of people living with disabilities, and people who are treated unequally because they belong to minority groups.

## 6.4.7 Income inequalities

In this subsection the focus is on income inequalities that link to race-based inequalities to show how these inequalities are reproduced over time and have long-term structural effects on people's abilities to move out of poverty and to reduce their vulnerability. South Africa provides a particular example of how the combination of race, gender and income-based inequalities deprives people of opportunities to improve their lives and keeps them trapped in intergenerational cycles of poverty.

Statistical evidence shows that inequalities in income remain skewed along race and gender lines. For example, the median earnings for a white man were six times as high as that for an African woman. It is interesting to note that such income inequalities are not due to unequal pay for the same kinds of work, but instead are a result of the fact that African women and men are usually employed in unskilled and low-skilled work which results in very low-waged income earnings (RSA – The Presidency, 2014 cited in Fukuda-Parr and Taylor, 2015). Deprivations in health and education also lead to inequalities in access to decent work and wages. The accumulation of deprivations that black people experience has a direct link to the type of employment opportunities they are able to access and to the incomes they are able to earn.

> The **relationships among social policies and economic policies**, as well as the enactment of legislation to ensure equity in access to services, benefits, and opportunities, are crucial to reducing inequality and removing people from poverty.

However, because people have both subjective and objective experiences of poverty, it is extremely difficult to measure and assess whose conditions should be prioritised. This is why the next section focuses attention on recent attempts to measure poverty, inequalities, and vulnerabilities using indicators.

## 6.5 Measuring poverty, inequalities, risk and vulnerabilities for social welfare policy

Since Rowntree's attempts at measuring poverty (Rowntree, 1901) there have been many other studies on the extent, incidence and dynamics of poverty and inequality (Sen, 1982; 1999; Carter, 1999; Kanbur and Squire, 2001; Stats SA, 2012). Policymakers and social service professionals can use both the methods and results of these studies to determine the multidimensional aspects of poverty and its interactions with inequalities, vulnerabilities, and risk.

In contemporary African countries, there is **increasing and reliable evidence** that is both quantitative in the form of statistics and qualitative in the form of people's lived experiences of poverty and inequalities to help policy interventions reach those who need them most.

Quantitative methods of measuring poverty rely mainly on what is called a money-metric measure that determines a persons' lack of income against an agreed national poverty line or an international poverty line. Multidimensional poverty is measured using an index (Multiple Poverty Index – MPI) that includes the lack of basic services, education, health, sanitation, and other essential aspects such as electricity and importantly people's subjective experiences of poverty (self-perceived).

A study undertaken by May (2001) finds that the measurement of poverty varies across countries and can differ from locality to locality. The United Nations Development Programme (UNDP) led the work in developing the Human Development Index (HDI) to measure human well-being using longevity (how long a person is expected to live), educational attainment (the number of years of schooling to achieve the ability to read and write), and standard of living (per capita income) (May, 2001). Most countries, such as those in Africa, do not have reliable data and statistical records to establish a HDI. Other countries find that the HDI is too general as a measure to enable effective policy interventions that reach the poorest and most vulnerable people. Countries, including South Africa, have designed an index called the Multiple Poverty Index to better prioritise the needs of those who are in extreme poverty and vulnerable. South Africa also included both statistical and subjective experiences in its measures of poverty and human development (UNDP-HDR, 2000). Lesotho has introduced poverty measures that go beyond material needs and include the effects of social isolation and lack of voice (May, 2001: 41).

Kanbur and Squire (2001) reinforce the view that poverty requires understanding of the local social context. Some countries set upper and lower poverty lines using material and nonmaterial items as criteria for people's human well-being. When people fall below a poverty line, this is an indication of a poverty gap (Poverty Gap Index) and reflects the intensity of poverty experienced by them. Studies in South Africa show that, irrespective of the type of poverty or deprivation which is measured, those people who are vulnerable remain vulnerable under every indicator of poverty (Aliber, 2001; Carter, 1999; May, 2001). There is growing consensus in Africa that measures used to determine poverty and its interactions should be socially and culturally sensitive as well as reliable to provide useful evidence for policymaking.

Income inequality is usually calculated using a measure known as the Gini coefficient. A country's Gini coefficient can range between 0 and 1, where 0 means perfect equality (all individuals earn the same or have the same level of wealth) and 1 refers to maximum inequality (where 1 person earns all income or has all the wealth). The Gini coefficient is useful because it is an indication of the distribution of income in a country. For example, in 2011, South Africa's Gini coefficient was estimated at 0.69 which was higher than Brazil's at the time (Stats SA, 2014). Such high levels of inequality combined with chronic poverty can undermine the social and economic development of the country.

Another measure that can be used to measure inequalities is one that calculates the share of national consumption between the richest and poorest quintiles in the country. In South Africa, the richest 20% of the population accounted for over 61% of national consumption and the bottom 20% of the population had a share of national consumption at below 4,5% (Stats SA, 2014). These measures reveal the extreme inequalities in the country. A social welfare policy response to such high levels of inequality and concentrations of wealth among a few would need to focus on both structural change in the form of policies to address issues of distribution of resources and services and programme changes to respond to the conditions of people living in poverty.

The next section provides an overview of some social welfare policy responses that governments and countries use or could use to address poverty, inequalities, vulnerability and risk.

## 6.6 Social welfare policy responses

There are complex interactions among the various dimensions of poverty. For example, social welfare policy responses designed to improve educational attainment of poor people also increase their ability to be aware of the impacts of Aids, improves economic livelihoods, and empowers people to participate and develop their political voice. These dynamic interactions reinforce health outcomes which in turn improve livelihoods through increased productivity, and also increase school attendance (for teachers and students). Evidence of the linkages among different dimensions of poverty and heightened experiences of vulnerability and risk enhance the abilities of professionals to eradicate poverty, reduce risk, and ensure better social welfare policy outcomes.

The most important criterion in responses to poverty, inequalities, risk, and vulnerability is to identify who is or should be the focus of the policy. A country that sets a poverty line or a level of consumption below which no one should fall may find it easier to use such normative standards to identify who should be the focus (Sen, 1982). The importance of a comprehensive response to poverty and deprivations was reinforced in the *Report of the Committee of inquiry into Comprehensive Social Security* (Taylor Report, 2002). This report states that:

> 'Providing the basic means for all people living in the country to effectively participate and advance in social and economic life, and in turn to contribute to social and economic development is essential to eradicating poverty. Such an approach must incorporate developmental strategies and programmes designed to ensure, collectively, at least a minimum acceptable living standard for all citizens' (Taylor Report, 2002: 15).

A developmental, transformative and capability-focused policy response to poverty, inequalities, vulnerabilities, and risk can be achieved through the implementation of a prioritised integrated package of measures focused on addressing essential or core social and economic deficiencies or deprivations and can include responses identified in Table 6.1 below. Policy responses to eradicating poverty and reducing inequalities can be located within approaches that are protective, that prevent people from falling into deeper poverty and, that promote human development while transforming ownership patterns and power-relations through developmental strategies. Importantly, these approaches should include measures to address income poverty, asset poverty, and capability poverty. Countries experiencing intergenerational cycles of poverty and low economic growth also need to determine the social welfare policy requirements for a comprehensive social protection package to address issues of risk and vulnerabilities and to achieve human welfare.

Table 6.1 Social welfare policy and programme responses to poverty, vulnerability and risk

| Policy approach | Objective | Some social welfare policy and development examples |
|---|---|---|
| Protective | Aims to protect the most vulnerable and at-risk individuals and households from further exposure to poverty and deprivation and to provide prompt assistance when exposure has happened. | • Residential facilities for care of older people, people with physical and mental disabilities, neglected and abused children, people with addictions, youth in trouble with the law and a range of others<br>• Food parcels<br>• Social grants in the form of income support.<br>• Safe houses for survivors of violence<br>• Substance abuse treatment & care. |
| Preventive | Aims to prevent people from falling into (deeper) poverty and vulnerability by promotional activities in communities, schools and employment spaces in which formal and informal sector workers receive income. | • Education programmes<br>• Health care<br>• Social grants<br>• Food gardens<br>• Developmental programmes for people during the various life stages.<br>• Teenagers Against Drug Abuse<br>• Comprehensive social security (including social insurance measures).<br>• Public Employment programmes. |
| Promotive | Aims to enhance the capabilities of individuals, communities and institutions to participate in all spheres of activity through developmental, rehabilitative and therapeutic services. | • Protective workshops<br>• Early childhood development programmes<br>• Skills training for prisoners<br>• Aftercare services. |
| Transformative | Aims to reduce inequities and vulnerabilities through systemic and redistributive changes that provide an enabling environment for broadening access and quality of social development services. | • Changes in policy, in legislation and in resource allocations to address root causes and symptoms of poverty, inequalities, vulnerabilities and risk.<br>• National minimum wage<br>• Redistribution through taxes and through social transfers. |
| Developmental and generative | Aims to promote local economic and social development to enable poor and vulnerable people to access economic and social opportunities. | • Social grants<br>• Education and skills training<br>• Public employment programmes<br>• Community development programmes<br>• Expansion of services to under-served rural and peri-urban areas. |

## CONCLUSION

- This chapter has examined the conceptual and theoretical understandings of poverty and discussed how the concept and theories that underpin it have changed over time. A framework for analysing both the root causes of poverty and some of the impacts was provided drawing on Sen's work (1982).
- The links among poverty, income inequality and social inequalities as well as vulnerabilities and risk were analysed. Significantly, the chapter identified those who are most likely to be categorised as people living in conditions of poverty and who are at risk and vulnerable.
- Using country examples from Africa, some policy responses to poverty and vulnerabilities were also described. Poverty and inequality are historically crafted, politically designed, structural features of most countries in Africa. Besides the many aspects of their lives affected by poverty, the chronically poor share a history of deprivation which may be transmitted across generations through economic, political, social and cultural isolation.
- Millions of people are unemployed or underemployed while millions more do not earn enough to meet the most basic of human needs, much less cope with shocks ranging from catastrophic injury to uncontrolled inflation and disasters resulting from fires, floods, or drought. The scale and the depth of both render state intervention in the form of transformative social welfare policies essential.

## QUESTIONS

1. Define the concept of poverty and discuss how understandings of poverty have changed over time.
2. Explain the linkages among poverty, inequalities, vulnerabilities and risk using evidence from your country to identify the people affected by these conditions.
3. Use one exchange entitlement from Sen's Entitlement Framework to analyse the causes and impacts of poverty in your country.
4. Critique the current social welfare policy responses to poverty, inequalities, vulnerabilities, and risk in your country.

## REFERENCES

AFRICAN DEVELOPMENT BANK (2017*) Indicators on Gender, Poverty, the Environment and Progress toward the Sustainable Development Goals in African Countries* Volume XVIII. Côte d'Ivoire: Economic and Social Statistics Division. Available: https://www.afdb.org/en/documents/publications/gender-poverty-and-environmental-indicators-on-african-countries/.

ALIBER, M (2001) 'An Overview of the Incidence and Nature of Chronic Poverty in

CARTER, M (1999) 'Getting Ahead or Falling Behind? The Dynamics of Poverty in

FUKUDA-PARR, S & TAYLOR, V (2015) *Food security in South Africa: A human rights and entitlement perspective.* Cape Town, UCT Press.

KANBUR, R & SQUIRE, L: 'The evolution of thinking about poverty: exploring the interactions' in Meier, GM & Stiglitsz, JE (eds.) (2001) *Frontiers of Development Economics.* New York: Oxford University Press.

MAY, J (2001) 'Policy Choices for the Poor' (Chapter 1). UNDP, March 2001. Available: http://www.undp.org/dpa/publications/choicesforpoor/ENGLISH.

MCKAY, A & LAWSON, D (2002) 'Chronic Poverty: A Review of Current Quantitative Evidence' *CPRC Working Paper No 15*, Chronic Poverty Research Centre. Nottingham: School of Economics, University of Nottingham.

NARAYAN, D, PATEL, R, SCHAFFT, K, RADEMACHER, A & KOCH-SCHULTE, S (2000) *Voices of the Poor: Can Anyone Hear Us?* Washington, D.C.: Oxford University Press.

Post-Apartheid South Africa', mimeograph. Madison: University of Wisconsin.

ROWNTREE, S (1901) *Poverty: A Study of Town Life.* London: Macmillan.

SEN, A (1982) *Poverty and Famines: An Essay on Entitlement and Deprivation.* Oxford: Oxford University Press.

SEN, A (1999) *Development as Freedom.* Oxford: Oxford University Press.

SOUTH AFRICA. *Chronic Poverty Research Centre Background Paper No. 3, May.*

SOUTH AFRICA. Department of Social Development (2016) *Comprehensive Report on the Review of the White Paper for Social Welfare of 1997.* Pretoria: Department of Social Development. Available: www.dsd.gov.za.

SOUTH AFRICA. The Presidency, Republic of South Africa (2014) *Twenty Year Review – South Africa: 1994 – 2014.* Pretoria: The Presidency.

STATISTICS SOUTH AFRICA (2012) *Social Profile of Vulnerable Groups in South Africa, 2002 to 2012* Report No 03-19-00. Pretoria: Statistics South Africa.

STATISTICS SOUTH AFRICA (2014) *Poverty Trends in South Africa: An examination of absolute poverty between 2006 and 2011* Report No. 03-10-06. Pretoria: Statistics South Africa.

STATISTICS SOUTH AFRICA (2017) *Poverty Trends in South Africa: An examination of absolute poverty between 2006 and 2015.* Pretoria: Statistics South Africa.

TAYLOR, V (2002) *Consolidated Report of the Committee of Inquiry into a Comprehensive System of Social Security for South Africa, Transforming the Present – Protecting the Future, 2002* (Taylor Report). Pretoria: Government Printer.

TAYLOR, V (2005) *A Comprehensive Approach to Poverty* (Unpublished) Paper presented to a mini conference on Poverty in the Cape Winelands. Cape Town, 27 May 2005.

TAYLOR, V (2008) *Social Protection in Africa: An Overview of the Challenges.* (Research Report prepared for the African Union) [Online]. Available: www.eprionline.com/wpcontent/uploads/2011/03/Taylor2008AUSocialProtectionOverview.pdf.

TAYLOR, V: 'Social Justice: Reframing the "Social" in Critical Discourses in Africa' in Tangen, S (ed.) (2013) *African Perspectives on Social Justice.* Kampala: Friedrich-Ebert-Stiftung.

UNITED NATIONS (UN) *The Millenium Development Goals and The Sustainable Development Goals [Online].* Available at: www.un.org [2017].

UNITED NATIONS DEVELOPMENT PROGRAMME (UNDP) *Human Development Reports* [Online]. Available: http://hdr.undp.org/ [2017].

UNITED NATIONS DIVISION FOR ECONOMIC AND SOCIAL AFFAIRS (UNDESA) (2001) *Report on the World Social Situation 2001.* New York: UNDESA.

WORLD BANK (2001) *The World Development Report 2000/2001.* Washington, D.C.: World Bank.

## CHAPTER 07

# Social welfare policy as a response to risks and vulnerabilities of families in South Africa

*Ndangwa Noyoo*

As intimated by other authors in preceding chapters, social welfare policy in this book is examined from a political economy lens. Chapter 7 of this book discusses the family as a fundamental component of society and the need for social welfare policies to protect vulnerable and at-risk families in South Africa. It also looks at the erosion of the African family in a post-apartheid era, for example, in the case of the mining industry which led to the Marikana tragedy. The chapter objectives and outcomes for Chapter 7 are listed below.

## Chapter objectives

✓ Explaining how historical and structural forces have determined the outcomes of South African families for centuries.

✓ Discussing how social welfare policy is able to bring together various mechanisms and tools to protect families from adversities in a society such as South Africa.

✓ Explaining how social workers and other social service professionals help to meet the needs of families that are vulnerable and at risk.

## Chapter outcomes

✓ Understanding how social welfare policy responds to the risks and vulnerabilities of families in South Africa.

✓ Understanding how macro and structural forces impact on families in South Africa.

✓ Demonstrating a deeper conceptual and theoretical understanding of social welfare policy and vulnerable and at-risk families in the context of South Africa.

## 7.1 Introduction

In approaching social welfare policy from a political economy perspective, we acknowledge that social welfare policy is inextricably bound up with the politics and economy of a particular country. In essence, the social welfare system and social welfare policy are anchored in the socio-political and economic context of a country. In the case of South Africa, the politics and economy of the country have a bearing on the way social welfare policy responds to the plight of families in general and to their risks and vulnerabilities in particular. Essentially, social welfare policy would be given effect by mainly social workers and other social service professionals who understand that social welfare policy impacts individuals and families who do not receive benefits, services, resources, and rights to which they are entitled (Jansson, 2016). Hence, when discussing risks and vulnerabilities, we take it that anyone who is vulnerable is synonymous with a person who is in need of services of the state (Herring, 2016). Conversely, vulnerable families or those families who are enfeebled by risks and vulnerabilities require state intervention, through different social welfare services. In the next section, we will pay attention to the conceptual and theoretical underpinnings of the chapter.

## 7.2 Conceptual and theoretical premise

The family takes centre stage in the discussions and analyses of this chapter. What is worth mentioning at the outset is that the concept of family is malleable and quite difficult to define. There are many definitions that are proffered when it comes to the family, and since it is such a familiar concept, almost everybody thinks that they know what a family is. It is due to this dilemma that when it comes to families, ideological and conservative positions creep into family discourses all over the world. This may lead to policy obfuscation and legislation that is out of touch with reality. To begin with, it is important to state that the family is a fundamental and complex component of all human societies. It is concerned with the organisation of sexual relations and the reproduction of the human species through the process of (legitimate) mating, and procreation, but its functions also extend to the organisation of economic production, the social division of labour, the (re)distribution of property, the transfer of culture, the training (or socialisation) of children, and the provision of personal services such as the care of the elderly (Turner, 1999: 232). Moreover, the institution of the family is essentially multidimensional in nature in that it affects and is affected by the various social, economic, cultural, and political institutions which together form the social structure of any society. Thus, changes in the structure and functions of the family are fundamentally occasioned by changes in other institutions in the family's environment (Amoateng and Richter, 2007).

The foregoing descriptions can be taken as features or characteristics of a family. In this chapter, South African families are regarded as similar to African families on the African continent. For generations, the Western definition of the family was popularised around the world by European scholars. In this respect, the notion of the nuclear family (a father, mother and children) as universal to humanity became popular. However, this idea of family did not resonate with most parts of the world, especially the developing world. In Africa, the concept of a family took and continues to take on different forms to the ones in the West. There is a broader conceptualisation of the family in Africa, which includes father, mother, grandparents, uncles, aunts, cousins, and other relatives. The family was (and still is) based on the kinship system where roles, responsibilities, and people's obligations to one another are defined within a particular cultural setting. Families were also defined along clan lines. In some cultures, polygamy was permissible and practised, and this is still existing in most part parts of modern Africa. The family, as mentioned in the first part of the book, is a support system that acts as a social security measure against want and deprivation for its members or when they experience shocks due to lack of income or illness. Given the foregoing, for purposes of this chapter, families will refer to social groups that are related by blood (kinship), marriage, adoption, or affiliation with close emotional attachments to one another that endure over time and go beyond a particular residence. Family groups also share the following features: they are intimate and interdependent; they are relatively stable over time; and they are set off from other groups by boundaries related to the family group such that one family is separate from another in a variety of ways (Amoateng and Richter, 2007: 14–15).

South African families are a little different to those in most of sub-Saharan Africa as they are composed of other races apart from the indigenous ethnic groups which make up the South African society. These are namely the white, coloured (mixed), and Indian population groups. Due to this, South African families are multiracial and multi-ethnic. However, the majority African population's families resemble those found across sub-Saharan Africa. Makiwane et al. (2016) point out that the composition of the family in South Africa is a complex pattern of nuclear, multigenerational, extended, and reconstituted families. They note that the family in South Africa reveals significant changes over the years brought about by the impact of colonisation and apartheid on traditional African family systems. There are also new and different family types that have emerged in the country such as those of the same sex, which are protected by South Africa's legal system. Also, single parent families are on the rise as well as child-headed families. These new family types have posed some challenges to social welfare service provision as sometimes their needs have overtaken the content of services. Therefore, innovative approaches to social welfare services are needed to respond to the needs of such families as opposed to the traditional ones.

In examining risks and vulnerabilities of families, we first take the view that risks are themselves part of human society. However, the way they are now perceived and tackled by societies or governments, for example, is very different from the way they were approached in past epochs. Therefore, the thinking around risks in human society has evolved. Green (2007: 396) asserts that one of the defining beliefs that emerged from the industrial era was that we could predict, manage, and control our exposure to dangers and hazards. As a consequence, dangers were reclassified as risks, thus removing them from the arena of uncertainty and contingency and relocating them within the boundaries of science, research, and expertise. Herring (2016: 6) states that **vulnerability** has its origins in the Latin word '*vulnerare*', meaning to 'wound'. This can either be physically or emotionally. **Risk** has been defined as any influence that increases the probability of onset, digression to a more serious state, or the maintenance of the problem condition (Fraser, 1997 in Malucio et al., 2002). Therefore, a risk or vulnerability represents a heightened probability of a negative outcome based on the presence of one or more factors such as genetic, biological, behavioural, socio-cultural and demographic conditions, characteristics, or attributes (Kirby and Fraser, 1997 in Malucio et al., 2002). The risks that families face can be regarded as triggers of unfavourable conditions within families which will more than likely worsen the already precarious standing of families. **Risk factors** 'involve stressful life events or adverse environmental conditions that increase the vulnerability (defencelessness or helplessness) of individuals or other systems' (Ashman and Hull, 2006: 21), such as families.

What flows from the above definitions is an understanding that all human beings are susceptible to vulnerabilities. Also, there are specific forces and conditions that give birth to vulnerabilities in society. Some members of society may be insulated from vulnerabilities to larger degrees than others due to a multiplicity of factors, for instance, family setting, socioeconomic status, level of education, class, and many others. A critical point of departure here is that all human beings (and by extension, families) have needs and these have to be met in society by various systems. Furthermore, meeting people's needs results in them functioning optimally. For Noyoo (2015) it is all about the state creating an enabling environment for people (families included) to meet their needs and flourish. If people are unable to meet their needs, then they become dysfunctional. Hence, the meeting of people's needs, by the state, will enable them to function effectively in society. Social welfare policy will then become the main vehicle that will provide well-being to individuals and families who cannot meet their needs. Maluccio et al. (2002: 31) assert that the greatest of all threats to families is poverty. Many risks that families face are more likely to be associated with, or derived from, a family's economic status. Some of these risks are: unemployment; inadequate housing or homelessness; divorce and family disintegration; family and community violence; school failure; inadequate health care; teenage pregnancy; and a wide range of other health risks and vulnerabilities from HIV/Aids and poor nutrition. Hence, it becomes imperative to place families in a political economy context when responding to their needs.

| FAMILIES | SOCIAL WELFARE SHOULD MEET PEOPLE'S NEEDS |

- It can be argued that risks and vulnerabilities of families are increased when their needs are not met. This understanding is of crucial importance because human needs are those resources people require to survive as individuals and to function appropriately in their society.
- Needs vary, depending on the specific individual and the situation, and include the following: sufficient food, clothing and shelter for physical survival; a safe environment and adequate health care for treatment, protection from illness and accidents; and relationships with other people that provide a sense of being cared for (Johnson et al., 1997: 4).
- In addition, needs would also include opportunities for emotional, intellectual, and spiritual growth and development, including opportunities for individuals to make use of their innate talents and interests. Also, opportunities for participation in making decisions about the common life of one's own society, including the ability to make appropriate contributions to the maintenance of life, are important factors in the meeting of needs (Johnson et al., 1997: 4).
- Families need to be nourished and supported in society if they are to play their requisite roles. If they cannot meet their needs, then their functioning will be impaired. This is where the social welfare system intervenes in order to meet the needs of families. This would necessitate, for example, social welfare policies and programmes which provide for cash transfers, social relief, and enabling and developmental services that ensure that people have adequate economic and social protection during times of unemployment, ill health, maternity, child-rearing, widowhood, disability, old age and so on (Ministry for Welfare and Population Development, 1997).
- Therefore, social welfare policy and social work practice respond to risks in general and specifically family risks in ways that they can be subjected to actuarial processes, so as to enable probabilities to be assigned in a stable fashion to event alternatives (Green, 2007).

The meeting of people's needs is not something that is straightforward as it is also linked to principles governing access to welfare. The next section explains how social welfare systems help to strengthen family well-being.

## 7.3 The social welfare system and family well-being

When moving from a normative premise, as this book is doing, social welfare is conceived in its most progressive and inclusive form. Therefore, a definition of social welfare befitting this perspective places emphasis on the idea of social welfare being a state or condition of human well-being. It denotes a state of being or doing well (Midgley, 1997; Burch, 1999). This approach to social welfare would apply to families in the way that social welfare programmes endeavour to develop their well-being. According to Segal (2016: 2), in the term social welfare, 'social' speaks to the collective nature of society of citizens as being part of many systems, and thus systems combine to form the larger society. Furthermore, Zastrow (2010: 2) observes that the goal of social welfare is to fulfil the social, financial, health, and recreational requirements of all individuals in a society. Social welfare seeks to enhance the social functioning of all age groups, both rich and poor. Thus, social welfare mobilises financial resources needed for social workers and social service professionals to intervene on behalf of vulnerable groups. In this way, social welfare is a discretionary spending choice that provides basic necessities for the poor through taxes (Burch, 1999). Social welfare policy thus gives effect to social welfare programmes, and, in this light, it is an essential part of any social worker's or social service professional's work. This is because it defines and shapes social welfare programmes such as social security; education and training; housing, health and community care services; work and training services; criminal justice services and policy; and personal services (Walsh, Stephens and Moore, 2000: 19).

Social workers and social service professionals give meaning to the policy intent that is expressed by a particular country's social welfare policy. Hence, family-centred social work practice which is concerned with safeguarding and promoting the well-being of families and children plays a crucial role here. In their work with families and children, social work practitioners and social service professionals are guided by knowledge on resilience, coping and adaptation as key constructs in understanding human beings and human behaviour (Maluccio et al., 2002). Therefore, a social welfare system that is informed by a political economy approach fits with the approach to social welfare that is *rights-based* and which is founded on *social citizenship*. In this formulation, the principle of need is counterposed to that of the market. The principle of social citizenship overrides (at least in theory, even if not always in practice) that of the market, in that it is argued that every member of society has a right to be able to participate fully in that society (Lister, 2008). Globally, social welfare provision has moved from exclusivity to inclusivity and at times swung back to exclusion. It is never fixed at a particular historical point because the politics of the day and the type of economy in any specific country will fundamentally influence who are able to access social welfare services and how they will do that. Ideologies and other considerations will often come into play to define and determine access to welfare services. The next section focuses on social welfare policy and social welfare service provision in the context of South Africa.

# 7.4 **Background and context**

Just like in other parts of Africa, the African people had their own forms of indigenous welfare systems which were underpinned by African value systems of the various ethnic groups of South Africa. Therefore, the development of social welfare policy in South Africa is deeply rooted in the history of colonial conquest and occupation, on the one hand, and apartheid, on the other. It is also embedded in the traditional social fabric of the indigenous African populations of this country. In this sense, the beginnings of social welfare and, later, social welfare policy in South Africa are directly linked to the initial annexation of the Cape peninsula and eventual subjugation of indigenous peoples by a white settler population.

Colonial conquest, industrial development, and the institutionalisation of racism that culminated in the creation of an apartheid state in 1948 are all important milestones that shaped the social welfare system and social welfare policy in the country. Earlier sections of this book discussed the background to colonial occupation and apartheid as well as the development of social welfare in South Africa in detail. In this chapter, it is important to mention that the foregoing issues had a bearing on indigenous families' existence and continue to influence them in present times. Colonial rule led to the annexation of the land of the indigenous people and displaced their

Krotoa, the niece of the Khoi Chief Autshumao, worked as a domestic worker and interpreter in Jan van Riebeeck's household in the 1650s when the Dutch colonised the Cape

families. The discovery of diamonds and gold in the late nineteenth century and subsequent industrialisation, dismantled the African peasantry, which would become the chief source of cheap unskilled labour (Marais, 2001).

The *Green Paper on the Family* observes that the sole purpose of Africans in the colonial and apartheid era was that of labourers (i.e. labour inputs) for the capitalist economy. With time, other laws were passed in order to keep Africans in impoverished and economically unviable geographic locations with little or no employment opportunities (Department of Social Development, 2011). Furthermore:

> 'Colonial conquest and exploitation weakened the African family on two key fronts. Firstly, enforced labour migration compelled families to live apart. Secondly, the policies, laws and practices were aimed at impoverishing African families, which also had dire long-term consequences for them' (Department of Social Development, 2011: 25).

The mining industry was heavily dependent on the migrant labour system which effectively uprooted African men from their villages and brought them to the urban areas and mining enclaves in different parts of South Africa. This type of labour recruitment was facilitated by the hut tax which Africans had to pay to the colonial authorities. This also coincided with the integration of the African traditional sector into the European capitalist system and the money economy. In order to have a guaranteed supply of labour for the expanding mining industry, Africans were compelled to pay the hut tax. It was based on the logic that any African male who owned a hut had to pay a hut tax to the colonial authorities. In order to make the payments, these men had to trek to urban centres or mines to work and earn a wage or otherwise they would be jailed by the colonialists for non-payment of the hut tax.

In 1948, the Afrikaner-led National Party came into power on the platform of 'separate development'. This policy was bizarrely rationalised as aiming to fulfil the various ethnic groups' aspirations to separate nationhood and development. By granting to each group political institution, the argument went, the country would avoid endemic conflicts (Thompson and Prior, 1982). After apartheid was formally adopted as a national ideology by the National Party in the late 1940s, it was concretised through policies and legislation in the 1950s and afterwards. Apartheid laws had directly and negatively affected African families in significant ways. Some of them were:

- Prohibition of Mixed Marriages Act 55 of 1949
- Immorality Amendment Act 21 of 1950
- Population Registration Act 30 of 1950
- Prevention of Illegal Squatting Act 52 of 1951
- Group Areas Act 41 of 1950
- Bantu Education Act 47 of 1953
- Reservation of Separate Amenities Act 49 of 1953
- Natives Abolition of Passes and Co-ordination of Documents Act 67 of 1952.

Patel (2005) asserts that African welfare needs were neglected during the apartheid era. She argues that the principle of racial differentiation in social welfare was tied to the political and economic objectives of the ruling elite. Racial differentiation also operated through the wide network of separate structures and institutions created for the different population groups. In many respects, social welfare policy was influenced by Eurocentric models of intervention (Noyoo, 2003) which had disadvantaged African families.

# 7.5 Post-apartheid South African social welfare policy and families

In South Africa, social welfare policy is given expression by the *White Paper for Social Welfare* (1997). After South African became democratic, efforts were made by the government and other roles players in the welfare sector to transform it. These culminated in the promulgation of a new social welfare policy that espoused a developmental approach to social welfare or social development. Therefore, the mission of the country's social welfare policy is to serve and build a self-reliant nation in partnership with all stakeholders through an integrated social welfare system which maximises its existing potential, and which is equitable, sustainable, accessible, people-centred, and developmental (Ministry of Welfare and Population Development, 1997). Among other goals, the social welfare policy aims to facilitate the provision of appropriate developmental social welfare services to all South Africans, especially those living in poverty, those who are vulnerable, and those who have special needs. These services include rehabilitative, preventative, developmental and protective services and facilities, as well as social security, including social relief programmes, social care programmes, and the enhancement of social functioning (Ministry of Welfare and Population Development, 1997). In addition, South Africa's welfare policy is rights-based, integrates family-centred and community-based services, follows a generalist approach to service delivery, and delivers community development and developmental welfare services. It seeks to harmonise social and economic policies, enhance participation of citizens and democracy; is informed by welfare pluralism or collaborative partnership, and attempts to bridge the macro and micro divide (Patel, 2005). Patel (2005: 98) asserts that the developmental perspective to social welfare's goals include achieving social justice, a minimum standard of living, equitable access and equal opportunity to services and benefits, and a commitment to meeting the needs of all South Africans with special emphasis on the needs of the most disadvantaged in the society. She further informs us that these ideals are firmly embedded in the Constitution of the Republic of South Africa (1996), which guarantees to all citizens the right to dignity as one of its central values.

Furthermore, the Bill of Rights and other sections of the Constitution make provision for legally enforceable economic and social rights such as the right to housing (section 26), the right to health care, food, water and social security (section 27), and the right to education (section 29) (Patel, 2005). In section 27(1)(*c*) and section 27(2) of the Constitution it is stated that everyone has the right to have access to social security, including, if they are unable to support themselves and their dependants, appropriate social assistance. However, these rights are bound by certain limitations as the state has to take reasonable legislative and other measures, within its available resources, to achieve the progressive realisation of each of these rights (Republic of South Africa, 1996). Social welfare policy in South Africa acknowledges the centrality of the family in human functioning. According to the *White Paper for Social Welfare*, the family is the basic unit of society. It seeks to strengthen and promote family life through family-oriented policies and programmes (Ministry for Welfare and Population Development, 1997). According to Patel (2006: 167–168), social welfare policy is based on the following major thrust to services:

- **Family as the basic unit of society** – This recognises that the family is the basic unit of society and plays a key role in the survival, protection and development of children under 18 years of age.

- **Continuum of services** – Families require a range of supportive services to promote family survival and development.
- **Multiple service strategies** – A range of methods of service delivery are possible – from counselling and peer counselling; to mutual aid and self-help; to family-centred, home and community-based care; to support and community development interventions.
- **Balance of intervention strategies** – This refers to an approach to service delivery that balances rehabilitative, preventative and developmental interventions.
- **Shifting focus to redress** – Services should be accessible and relevant to the basic needs of children and families within the context of the family and community.
- **Diversity and gender sensitive social work** – Social services which are rendered to families should mirror this.
- **Rights and advocacy** – This entails the protection, promotion, facilitation of access to rights and advocacy.

It was indicated earlier that poverty is one of the major risks confronting families. Poverty in South Africa indeed poses major risks to families. It also translates into other societal ills. Compounding this situation is the high levels of inequality in the country. South Africa has one of the highest levels of inequality in the world with a Gini coefficient of 0.69 in 2011 (Stats SA, 2014). In 2006, more than half (57,2%) of the population of South Africa were living in poverty. While there was a marginal decline in 2009 to 56,8% by 2011, less than half (45,5%) of all South Africans were living below the poverty line (Stats SA, 2014). With an unemployment rate of about 34,2%, most families in South Africa remain vulnerable. Unemployment negatively impacts on the mental health of the unemployed and makes them have less say over their lives. It further leads to poor health, a reduction in decision-making, loss of prestige, and social exclusion and diminishes family and community ties (Stranglemand and Warren, 2008). Some of the direct impacts of poverty on families are, *inter alia,* hunger, disease, homelessness, illiteracy, social dislocation, and crime. There are also indirect outcomes of poverty, for instance, substance abuse, child abuse, domestic violence and so forth.

## SOUTH AFRICA'S RESPONSE — SOCIAL GRANTS AND THE SOCIAL WAGE

The South African government has responded to the risks and vulnerabilities of families broadly through social policy and social welfare policy interventions. Social assistance is the government's major Anti-poverty Programme. It encompasses the following social grants: Social Relief of Distress; Grant-in-aid; Foster Care Grant; Disability Grant; War Veterans' Grant; Old Age Grant; and Child Support Grant. Furthermore, what is referred to as the social wage plays a significant role in helping to reduce the risks and vulnerabilities of families in South Africa. Close to 60% of government spending is allocated to the social wage (National Treasury, 2013). The social wage includes the provision of the following: free primary health care; no-fee paying schools; Reconstruction and Development Programme (RDP) housing and low-income housing subsidies. It also includes the provision of basic services to households, namely: sanitation and free water and electricity; school-feeding schemes; public employment schemes; minimum wage levels for low-paid workers such as agricultural and domestic workers; and support for households engaged in subsistence and small-scale farming activities (Stats SA, 2014).

The Department of Social Development in 2012 arrived at a draft *White Paper on Families* which has now been finalised. This policy on the family is regarded as another way of remedying the shortfall in the social welfare services to families. This is because services designated as those for the family were tailored in such a way that they focused on individual members of the family such as children, youth or the aged, and not on the family unit. Therefore, the *White Paper on the Family* is supposed to holistically respond to the needs of the family, as a unit, and not as individuals. This policy views the family as a key development imperative and seeks to mainstream family issues into government-wide, policymaking initiatives in order to foster positive family well-being and overall socioeconomic development in the country (Department of Social Development, 2012). Its objectives are to:

- Enhance the socialising, caring, nurturing and supporting capabilities of families so that their members are able to contribute effectively to the overall development of the country.
- Empower families and their members by enabling them to identify, negotiate around, and maximise economic, labour market, and other opportunities available in the country.
- Improve the capacities of families and their members to establish social interactions which make a meaningful contribution towards a sense of community, social cohesion and national solidarity (Department of Social Development, 2012: 9).

The Department of Social Development (2013) takes the family as the central unit in communities whilst providing the following services:
- Family preservation
- Family therapy
- Family and marriage enrichment.

Lastly, both the White Paper for Social Welfare (1997) and the *White Paper on Families* (2012) are informed by the developmental approach which 'incorporates social welfare service delivery at a personal, interpersonal and community level'. This approach according to the Department of Social Development also provides a 'framework where social security, development and social welfare services are integrated for the benefit of marginalised, poorest of the poor and most vulnerable groups' (Department of Social Development, 2013).

Despite the proclaimed paradigm shift to developmental social welfare services, there are still many continuities with the past dispensation and these militate against social welfare policy's ability to effectively respond to risk and vulnerabilities of South African families in a developmental way. The notion or meaning of 'developmental' seems to have been misconstrued as the state abdicating its responsibility of providing social welfare services to families and other groups. This discussion concurs with the following observation which was made by the National Development Plan which seriously questions the abilities of both the welfare system and social welfare policy to meet the needs of South Africa's vulnerable populations:

> *'South Africa needs to confront the reality that social services are critical for improving social integration and human development. The current model of shifting the burden of care, treatment and rehabilitation to the non-governmental sector and the poorest communities is not working. The scale of social fragmentation and loss of purpose requires more systematic engagement with both governmental and non-governmental social service providers. Statutory services for children, young offenders, the elderly, people with mental health problems and people living with disabilities need well-conceived state and community interventions. Complex social problems require professional interventions to deal with the symptoms and underlying causes of social pressures, most evident in*

*schools, workplaces and neighbourhoods that are plagued by gang warfare and households afflicted by violence, including the abuse of women and children. Urgent and systematic attention is required to deal with these issues'* (National Planning Commission, 2011: 338).

The above approach has deficits which were sharply brought to the fore in the aftermath of what has come to be known as the Marikana tragedy. The next section provides a case study of Marikana and pays a closer attention to the foregoing issues.

## 7.6 Risks and vulnerabilities of families in South Africa: Any lessons from the Marikana tragedy?

A case in point relating to the illuminated issues is what has now come to be referred to as the 'Marikana Massacre' in South Africa. On 16 August 2012, the South African police shot and killed 34 mineworkers who were striking for higher wages and better working conditions at the Lonmin Platinum Mine in the North West Province of South Africa. This was an unprotected strike which was declared illegal by the mining company and thus negotiations were marred by violence and intimidation. In the ensuing chaos, about 780 miners were wounded and close to 250 people were arrested. Subsequently, a commission of enquiry was established by the former President Jacob Zuma, on 23 August 2012, to investigate the incidents that led to the shooting of the miners. Even though this was not stated, at the heart of the protracted strike was the essence of the mining industry itself in a post-apartheid South Africa and how it continues to replicate apartheid labour patterns. Also in question was the ANC government's inability to abolish this colonial migrant labour system so many years after democracy. Curiously, when it came to counting the dead miners and establishing where they originated, it was ascertained that most of them were from the Eastern Cape Province, which is one of the poorer provinces of South Africa. They were migrant labourers who were recruited by a mining company that was mining platinum, one of the most expensive minerals in the world, which it sold on the international market. Despite this, the miners' wages were very low.

The findings from a research study which was conducted by the Bench Marks Foundation, and which briefed the Mining Portfolio Committee responsible for the oversight of the Department of Mining as well as several statutory bodies, paint a grim picture in regard to the living conditions of the miners. The Foundation had conducted research in six of the twenty mining areas in the Rustenburg region and unearthed several problems. For starters, it found that unemployment was rife in the informal settlements where the miners resided, particularly amongst young people. Secondly, the mines tended to employ migrant male workers and local females. This led to various social problems including various forms of sexual abuse. Other problems in the area were illiteracy (Parliamentary Monitoring Group, 2012). Thirdly, mushrooming informal settlements were overtaxing the sewage systems and the water supply was insufficient. This was because miners had resorted to informal housing in a bid to save costs. Fourthly, social and labour plans were not made public. Fifthly, extensive damage was caused to the environment. Sixthly, there was a high prevalence of HIV/Aids. In addition, the Foundation reported that there were no recreational facilities. Also, there was excessive abuse of alcohol, by the miners and this had affected productivity (Parliamentary Monitoring Group, 2012). These were just some of the key pressing problems which confronted the miners in Marikana and the people in the surrounding communities.

Thirty-four mineworkers died during the Marikana Massacre on 16 August 2012

What the Marikana tragedy sharply brought to the fore was that the mining industry was still contributing to the erosion of the African family in a post-apartheid era. The other critical issue was that this incident exposed some of the shortcomings of social welfare policy's responses which showed that they are still mainly reactive or predisposed to 'mopping up' the ravages of capitalism, especially when it comes to social issues that emanate from an inequitable and untransformed political economy. In the case of Marikana, the evidence from the above research, subsequent research, and a commission of enquiry all showed that the migrant labour system reflects the inability of the mining industry to humanise itself and allow miners to have their families living with them on a permanent basis. This issue has not even been interrogated by the government, mining industry, and relevant stakeholders from the premise of sustainable mining and development. Hence, major reforms are needed in the mining sector and should be undertaken from the point of view of bolstering the business side of the mining sector. Comparatively, in the region, it is ironic that the stabilisation of labour was undertaken during the peak of colonial rule in the then Belgian Congo (now the Democratic Republic of the Congo – DRC) and Northern Rhodesia (now Zambia) from a purely profit motive. Mining companies had recognised that the migrant labour system was archaic and unprofitable and thus made bold undertakings and allowed the settlements of Africans to be permanent in urban areas. Due to this, the mining sectors in the Belgian and British colonies instituted reforms in the 1940s that led to the abolishing of the migrant labour system. In colonial Zambia, it was concluded that, on the one hand, social policy and social welfare policy had to accommodate and facilitate such permanence, especially for the potential and existing African working class and, on the other hand, it meant that a class of Africans not directly involved in formal employment and their families would also be residing in the urban environment and would be needing services (Mhone, 2004).

| REFLECTION | ABOLISHING THE MIGRANT LABOUR SYSTEM |

In the Belgian Congo (DRC), a pro-industry though pernicious form of social engineering was pursued by the colonial authorities in order to create permanent urban settlements for the African population. Firstly, the labourers were selected by physicians according to strict medical criteria. Secondly, the Belgian social scientists and authorities decreed that all labourers had to marry. They argued that married men had a better morale and higher morality than single men. As a consequence, their ratios for sickness, mortality, desertion, and absenteeism were lower and their productivity was much higher, according to the colonial authorities (Belien, 2005). After the mining companies forced African employees to marry and even paid for their bride price, they built houses for them which were semi-detached. The workers were also fed by the company with a protein-rich diet while much attention was paid to hygiene. Health care was free, as was the education of the children, who had to be sent to kindergarten and to primary school, where they learned basic skills, including French (Belien, 2005). What should be taken from these examples is that the mining industry and the colonial businesses in general had come to a conclusion, which made business sense, that the migrant labour system was not profitable. After this, they had taken steps to abolish this labour practice and had made African settlements permanent in urban areas. Thus, family units were built for miners in both colonial DRC and Zambia in the sprawling mining townships. Schools and health care centres were also erected by the colonial mining establishments for the African miners and their families. This legacy endures in Zambia where the mining industry still plays a patronage role to the workers and surrounding communities although in a muted form. The question that then arises is:

*Why does South Africa, after 23 years of democracy, continue to adhere to the migrant labour system that has helped to disintegrate the African family and does not make any business sense to the mining industry in the long run?*

As can be seen from the examples above, social policy and social welfare policy were taken as both economic and political imperatives even though from the narrow and selfish vantage points of the colonial mining industries and, by extension, the colonial governments. Due to this, Africans had some semblance of well-being when these measures were introduced by the colonial business sector, not based on altruistic grounds, but purely on profit motives. In the latter case, in regard to social welfare's shortcomings *vis-à-vis* the Marikana tragedy, it can be argued that South Africa's social welfare policy and even social policy are not in the main shaping economic and political discourses and approaches in the country but seem to be reactive. Most probably this is because they do not have a political economy anchoring. After the miners were shot dead by the police, the National Department of Social Development (DSD) helped with the repatriation of the corpses to their places of origin which were mainly in the Eastern Cape Province. Also, more than 50 social workers were deployed by the DSD to counsel grieving family members and offer psychosocial services to them. The DSD also distributed blankets to the families of the deceased miners. As important as such interventions were, it should be recognised that social welfare responses were not supposed to have *only* been located at this level. They should have also been raised at the macro level where the labour policies and the role of the mining sector in post-apartheid South Africa should have been effectively interrogated by the DSD. The role played by the mining industry in the continued erosion of the African family should have been raised sharply at the national policy level and located in present-day realities of family disintegration. This would not have been something novel as some thinking in this area had begun to crystallise a while back, although it seems like it was not followed through:

*'Despite the progress made by Government and other role-players in raising the livelihood of many South Africans, families still live in extremely perilous conditions. In many respects, the history of South Africa and the country's political economy continue to mould the quality of life of most families in significant ways, for example, the industrialisation of South Africa in the late 19th century, after the discovery of diamonds and gold, and the resultant urbanisation are inextricably bound to the past and contemporary erosion of the family. The migrant labour system, based on the carving up of 'African reserves' which, in turn, guaranteed a steady supply of cheap labour to the emerging industrial and capitalist enclave, was a direct product of industrialisation. This form of labour was regarded as temporary and connected to the reserves'*
(Department of Social Development, 2011: 6).

One serious conclusion that can be made from the Marikana example is that there are many mining areas spread across South Africa with similar social outcomes. The only exception is that there was no tragedy of this nature in such places. At the centre of the negative social outcomes is the family. Apart from the cited challenges of HIV/Aids and sexual exploitation of women residing in the informal settlements of Marikana (and other mining areas) by the miners, there is the phenomenon of dual family systems emerging in these places. This is because miners have established new family forms in the mining areas – away from their 'real' families in the rural areas. These family types are not part of the conventional family systems as they seem to be temporal and seem to have no guidelines of building relationships and nurturing. Therefore, social workers and social service professionals have to be innovative to readily respond to the needs of these new family forms. The duality of families and the increase of social ills, such as commercial sex work in the villages and townships near the mines, also contribute to the dysfunctionality of the family in South Africa.

## CONCLUSION

- This chapter's main objective was to bring to light the manner in which social welfare policy responds to the risks and vulnerabilities of families. To this end, it unpacked the concepts that informed its discussions and also provided the theoretical bedrock for its analysis. In examining the role of social welfare policy in responding to families' risks and vulnerabilities, the chapter also shed some light on human needs and how social welfare services were supposed to meet them.
- The chapter then observed that the non-fulfilment of needs results in risks and vulnerabilities to families. Hence, social welfare policy has to respond to these needs in order for families to function in an effective manner. The chapter's main argument was that social welfare policy is the product of a specific socio-political and historical context. In this regard, the current social welfare policy emerged out of South Africa's past of colonialism and apartheid. Therefore, this past and the birth of the country's social welfare system were examined.
- Social welfare policy was discussed in the post-apartheid era and some of its shortcomings were highlighted. It can be concluded that even though there has been a shift in the philosophy and thinking as regards social welfare in general and social policy in particular, what obtains in practice is still in most cases not in line with the purported shift to a

developmental welfare perspective. There seems to be a disjuncture between the policy intent and the services that are provided to the citizens and particularly families. Continuities from the apartheid era are still discernible in social welfare responses to families.

- Even though the *White Paper on Families* was developed to address some of these shortcomings, it also falls short of addressing the root causes of the various risks and vulnerabilities confronting families. Many of these, such as structural poverty, high unemployment levels, and the migrant labour system are derived from South Africa colonial-apartheid past. Therefore, the past is still enduring in many ways and there is still more work to be done in this area.

## QUESTIONS

1. How was the African family negatively impacted by colonialism and apartheid?
2. Can you describe the forces that still continue to shape family life in the post-apartheid era?
3. How do social workers and social service professionals respond to the needs of families in South Africa today?

## REFERENCES

AMAOTENG, AY & RICHTER, LM: 'Introduction' in Amaoteng, AY & Heaton, TB (2007) *Families and Households in post-apartheid South Africa* at pp. 1–26. Pretoria: Human Sciences Research Council (HSRC),.

ASHMAN, KK & HULL, GH, Jr. (2006) *Understanding Generalist Practice* (fourth edition). Belmont, CA: Thomson Brooks/Cole.

BELIEN, P (2005) 'A Social Model in Africa: The Congo, 1908–1960' [Online]. Available: www.brusselsjournal.com/node/41 [15 November 2011].

GREEN, D (2007) 'Risk and social work' *Australian Social Work* 60(4), pp. 395–409.

HERRING, J (2016) *Vulnerable Adults and the Law*. Oxford: Oxford University Press.

JANSSON, BS (2016) *Social Welfare Policy and Advocacy: Advancing Social Justice through 8 Policy Sectors*. Thousand Oaks, CA: SAGE Publications.

JOHNSON, LC, SCHWARTZ, CL & TATE, DS (1997) *Social Welfare: A Response to Human Need* (fourth edition). Boston, MA: Allyn and Bacon.

LESTER, A (1996) *From Colonisation to Democracy: A new historical geography of South Africa*. London: Tauris Academic Studies.

LISTER, R: 'Citizenship and Access to Welfare' in Alcock, P, May, M & Rowlingson, K (2008) *The Student's Companion to Social Policy* (third edition) at pp. 233–240. Malden, MA: Blackwell Publishing.

MAKIWANE, M, KHALEMA, NE, GUMEDE, NA & MZIKAZI, N 'Introduction' in Makiwane, M, Nduna, M & Khalema, NE (2016) *Children in South African Families: Lives and times* at pp. xiv–xxi. Newcastle upon Tyne: Cambridge Scholar Publishing.

MALUCCIO, AN, PINE, BA & TRACY, M (2002) *Social work practice with families and children*. New York, NY: Columbia University Press.

MARAIS, H (2001) *South Africa – Limits to Change: The Political Economy of Transition*. London: Zed Books.

MHONE, G: 'Historical trajectories of social policy in post-colonial Africa' in Mkandawire, T (2004) *Social policy in a development context at* pp. 308–338. Houndsmill: Palgrave Macmillan.

MIDGLEY, J (1997) *Social Welfare in Global Context*. Thousand Oaks, CA: SAGE Publication.

NOYOO, N (2003) *Social Welfare Policy, Social Work Practice, and Professional Education in a Transforming Society: South Africa*. Johannesburg: University of the Witwatersrand (PhD-thesis).

NOYOO, N (2015) *Social Policy and Human Development in Zambia* (third edition). Pretoria: Kwarts.

NOYOO, N: 'Social Development in Southern Africa' in Calvelo, L, Lutz, R & Ross, F (2015) *Development and Social Work: Social Work of the South* Volume VI at pp. 167–185. Oldenburg: Paulo Freire Verlag.

PARLIAMENTARY MONITORING GROUP (2012) 'Living conditions at Marikana and other platinum mines: research by Bench Marks Foundation' [Online]. Available: https://pmg. org.za/committee-meeting/14901/ [6 June 2017].

PATEL, L. 2005. *Social welfare and Social Development in South Africa*. Cape Town: Oxford University Press.

SOUTH AFRICA. 1996. *Constitution of the Republic of South Africa Act No. 108 of 1996*. Pretoria: Government Printer. [Laws.]

SOUTH AFRICA. Department of Social Development (DSD) (2011) *Green Paper on Families: Promoting Family Life and Strengthening Families in South Africa* in GG 34657 of 3 October 2011. Pretoria: Government Printer.

SOUTH AFRICA. Department of Social Development (DSD) (2012) *White Paper on Families* (Draft). Pretoria: DSD.

SOUTH AFRICA. Department of Social Development (DSD) (2013) *Framework for Social Welfare Services*. Pretoria: DSD.

SOUTH AFRICA. Ministry of Welfare and Population Development (1997) *White Paper for Social Welfare*. in GG 18166 of 8 August 1997. Pretoria: Government Printer.

SOUTH AFRICA. National Planning Commission (NPC) (2011) *National Development Plan: Vision for 2030*. Pretoria: NPC.

SOUTH AFRICA. National Treasury (2013) Budget Review. Pretoria: National Treasury.

SOUTH AFRICA. Statistics South Africa (Stats SA) (2014) *Poverty trends in South Africa: An examination of absolute poverty between 2006 and 2011*. Pretoria: Stats SA.

STRANGLEMAND, T & WARREN, T (2008) *Work and Society: Sociological approaches, themes and methods*. Abingdon: Routledge.

THOMPSON, L & PRIOR, A (1982) *South African Politics*. Cape Town: David Philips.

TURNER, BS (1999) *Classical Sociology*. London: SAGE Publications.

WALSH, M, STEPHEN, P & MOORE, S (2000) *Social Policy & Welfare*. Cheltenham: Stanley Thorne.

ZASTROW, C (2010) *Introduction to Social Work and Social Welfare: Empowering People (tenth edition)*. Belmont, CA: Brooks Cole.

# CHAPTER 08

# Transformational policies and social justice for migrants, refugees and displaced people

*Rinie Schenck and Jean D Triegaardt*

*'In the midst of migrants in search of a better life there are people in need of protection: refugees and asylum-seekers, women and children victims of trafficking...Many move simply to avoid dying of hunger. When leaving is not an option but a necessity, this is more than poverty'* (Antonio Guterres, U.N. High Commissioner for Refugees).

Chapter 8 provides an overview of migration globally, and to and within South Africa, and discusses the vulnerabilities and risks to which migrants and refugees are exposed. Using South Africa as an example, it critically analyses how policies and legislation apply to migrants, refugees, and displaced people in the country. The chapter's objectives and outcomes are listed below.

## Objectives

✓ Defining the concepts migrants, asylum seekers, refugees, displaced, and stateless people.

✓ Providing an overview of migration globally and locally.

✓ Describing and explaining the vulnerabilities experienced by migrants, refugees, and displaced and stateless people.

✓ Describing the developmental social welfare, human rights, and capability approaches as theoretical frameworks to understand the development of policies related to migrants, refugees, and displaced people.

✓ Explaining the criteria for and application of transformative social welfare policies towards migrants, refugees, and displaced people.

## Outcomes

✓ Explaining the concepts migrants, refugees, stateless and displaced people,

✓ Understanding global and local perspectives on migrants, refugees, and stateless and displaced people.

✓ Explaining and describing the vulnerabilities to which migrants, refugees, and stateless and displaced people are exposed.

✓ Analysing critically transformative social welfare policies in relation to the developmental social welfare, human rights, and capability approaches as theoretical frameworks.

✓ Reflecting critically on the transformative social welfare policies for migrants, refugees, and displaced people in South Africa.

## 8.1 Introduction

The chapter discusses the theories which underpin people's actions and what and how transformative social policies should be crafted and applied to support migrants, refugees, and displaced people. It also looks critically at some of the international instruments, and current policies and legislation in place in South Africa in relation to refugees and migrants. As social service professionals these policy responses will guide one's actions towards migrants and refugees. The chapter further reflects on some social services rendered to migrants and refugees and services that should be rendered.

> In this book the concept migrant is sometimes used to include refugees, displaced, and stateless people.

It is relevant for social service professionals to note that the White Paper for Social Welfare was formulated in 1997 (RSA 1997), based on the then newly formulated Constitution of 1996, to change welfare services in South Africa towards a more equitable welfare system, eradicate poverty, and reduce inequalities. The White Paper (1997), however, does not make reference to services for migrants, refugees, and displaced people. This gap existed despite the fact that sections 27, 28 and 29 of the Bill of Rights of the Constitution of the Republic of South Africa Act 108 of 1996 provide that all who live in South Africa *should* have access to welfare, education, housing, and health. It is only the *Comprehensive Report on the Review of the White Paper for Social Welfare, 1997*, accepted in 2016 (DSD, 2016), that stipulates that migrants should have equal access to health and social services compared to South African citizens. The SASSA (2013) guide also indicates that refugees have access to social security provided that their documentation is in order. Therefore, this does not apply to undocumented economic migrants.

Furthermore, the *National Development Plan 2030* (NPC, 2012) emphasises the creation of an enabling environment for all people in South Africa, including migrants and refugees. It aims to develop their capabilities, create social cohesion, resilience, and a caring community (DSD, 2016).

## 8.2 Theoretical and conceptual framework underpinning social welfare policy for refugees, displaced persons, and migrants

There are two policy approaches that countries can adopt when they respond to the needs and human rights of refugees, migrants, and displaced people. Firstly, there is the developmental social welfare approach that seeks to integrate people into social development processes in the host or receiving country. Secondly, there is the humanitarian policy approach that responds to the safety, care, and protection of people in dire or life threatening situations through emergency aid or relief. In both contexts, countries and governments need to ensure that social welfare policies include provision for social welfare services, fiscal welfare, and occupational welfare services.

## 8.2.1 Developmental social welfare approach

Developmental social welfare is underpinned by values such as respect, equality, social justice, and human rights. It must be noted that, unlike most countries, South Africa did not undertake to place refugees into camps, but instead allowed refugees to be integrated into local communities. This step is an indication that as an integral aspect of the protection of refugees, South Africa accepts that refugees need to be self-reliant and integrated into the community. Refugees can only lead a productive life by becoming self-sufficient. This method resonates with developmental social welfare since this approach acknowledges the integration of social development with economic development. This approach is concerned with enhancing individuals' capacities to participate in the productive economy. Thus, one of the principles of the developmental social welfare approach is the harmonisation of economic and social development. If more emphasis is paid to economic development, this will lead to distorted development. The second principle is that economic development be people-centred and inclusive in order to promote the well-being of the population. And, thirdly, social welfare programmes are investment oriented and contribute to economic development (Midgley and Sherraden, 2009: 283).A more detailed discussion on developmental social welfare is provided in Chapter 3.

A particular emphasis of developmental social welfare is the protection of refugees, displaced people, and migrants. Therefore, the policy and legislative framework is crucial in the protection of refugees, displaced persons, and migrants. Thus, the discussion that follows laterin this chapter provides a detailed analysis on this topic.

Before discussing the transformational policy options regarding migrants, we need to create a conceptual framework to guide our thinking regarding policy and service options for migrants.

| ACTIVITY 1 | THEORETICAL FRAMEWORKS FOR SOCIAL WELFARE POLICY IN SOUTH AFRICA |
|---|---|

Refer to Chapters 1 and 3 to refresh your mind regarding theoretical frameworks for policy. Take note of the current frameworks relevant for the social welfare policy in South Africa such as human rights, social development, and socioeconomic development. Write a short paragraph motivating the relevancy for the South African and your own country's context. Motivate your answer.

According to South Africa's Constitution (1996) and the NDP 2030 (NPC, 2012), all policies need to:

1. promote human rights;
2. promote social justice;
3. reduce inequalities and vulnerabilities;
4. create an enabling environment to broaden capabilities and access to services; and
5. create a socially cohesive and resilient country.

**APPROACHES TO SOCIAL WELFARE POLICY**

Complete the following activities:
1. What should a policy entail to facilitate the promotion of the above five aspects? Think of a policy or Act that you have learnt about that is enabling and a policy or aspects of the Acts that are restrictive. Discuss what the enabling/restrictive factors are.
2. For an overview of different policies in Southern Africa, read the 2009 publication New trends and responses by the Forced Migration Studies Programme, available at http://www.migration.org.za/wp-content/uploads/2017/08/Zimbabwean-migration-into-Southern-Africa-new-trends-and-responses.pdf.
3. Make a comparison between the responses of the different countries discussed in the publication above and compare this with South African policies and responses. In what way do these policies and application of policies comply with the above framework?

## 8.2.2 Human rights approach

Note that it is important to elaborate on the human rights perspective as South Africa's Constitution (1996) and all other policies are or should be based on the human rights perspective.

For policies and services to be transformational, all actions and decisions should be based on the five human rights principles illustrated in Figure 8.1.

Source: Adapted from Androff (2015)

Figure 8.1 The five principles of human rights

As social service practitioners, we have to ensure that the dignity of migrants is always protected. There should be no discrimination against migrants, and all decisions and actions should be participatory, inclusive, and transparent. We should also take responsibility and accountability for our decisions and actions with regard to migrants and should hold people like employers and officials accountable for their actions. A human rights perspective is first and foremost a self-reflexive process as we have to begin by evaluating our actions against the human rights principles. For example, we need to ask ourselves questions such as: 'What do I do when a migrant or refugee tells me that they have been bribed by an official at the Department of Home Affairs or SAPS?' or 'what do I do if I know that people are exploited by their employers and landlords or services being refused?'

---

**✅ Case Study**   **IMPLICATIONS OF A HUMAN RIGHTS PERSPECTIVE**

A human rights perspective implies responsibilities for the social service practitioner. Write a short paragraph on the implications for practice regarding migrants in the following case study:

*Mr A is an economic migrant in Durban from a rural area of KwaZulu-Natal. I met Mr A on the streets of Durban when he was collecting waste to sell to earn a living. He was pushing a trolley. In the trolley, in addition to the waste he collected, he had two children under the age of five with him. According to him, the mother of the children died and he, the father, was now responsible for the children. Previously, the children's mother had received a child support grant (CSG) for the children but since her death that income lapsed as he did not have an ID to enable him to apply for the CSG. He said he did not have the time or money to apply for an ID and he did not have anywhere where he could leave the children. He was scared the Department of Social Development would remove his children and he, therefore, avoided it. Without his ID he could not access a clinic or school and he struggled to get support from social services, clinics, and the Department of Home Affairs.*

According to our Constitution and the human rights perspective, what should our responsibilities as social service practitioners and citizens be?

---

## 8.2.3 The Capability Approach (CA)

Amartya Sen's Capability Approach (CA) (1999) appears to be implicitly the theoretical framework guiding the NDP 2030 and will also be used to guide our thinking around policy options for migrants and refugees.

Amartya Sen's CA (1999) focuses on increasing the well-being of the person and communities and provides a holistic and multifaceted theoretical framework. The CA includes five kinds of basic freedoms which facilitate people's well-being and contribute to the capabilities of individuals to live the life they value. According to Sen (1999), the five freedoms are:

1. **Economic facilities** which are the opportunities people have to utilise economic resources to be able to work, produce, buy, and exchange.
2. **Social opportunities** which refer to the measures society takes to ensure the provision and accessibility to quality essential services like education, health care, psychosocial support services, etc.
3. **Transparency guarantees** deals with social interactions and how individuals relate to one another. The focus here is on creating an open transparent society (as described within a human rights perspective).

4. **Protective security** is referring to creating safety nets for vulnerable people such as the poor and unemployed, refugees, and migrants to prevent them from falling below a basic standard of living.
5. **Political freedoms** refer to people's need to have a voice and to be heard. It includes having systems in place for people to vote, participate, and determine the life they value.

In summary, the aim of the CA is to equalise and increase opportunities, capabilities, and freedoms for every person. Well-being will be promoted with the expansion of their increasing capabilities and freedoms (Sen, 1999; Neff, 2007). Policies should be drafted and services rendered so that they facilitate these freedoms outlined by Sen (1999).

| ACTIVITY 3 | CA AND TRANSFORMING SOCIAL WELFARE POLICY |
|---|---|

1. Write a short essay on how you think the CA can contribute to the policy on migrants.
2. Revisit Chapter 1 and define social welfare policy from a transformative human rights approach.

In summary, approaches guide social welfare policy in relation to migrants. When people's human rights are violated in their countries of birth or origin, they then seek refuge, migrate or are displaced. In particular, the discussion above on the developmental social welfare and humanitarian approaches will be helpful when responding to the needs and human rights of refugees, migrants, and displaced people.

The next section provides a discussion on a refugee protection system which is underpinned by international instruments and protocols, and national provisions.

# 8.3 Applying international human rights approaches in social welfare policy

Policies and legislation were introduced by the South African government to protect and safeguard the human rights of all its citizens, refugees, and displaced persons. As a consequence of these policies and legislation, a refugee protection system was formulated congruent with values enshrined in the Constitution, and international norms and protocols. The protection of refugees and asylum seekers in South Africa is illustrated by three elements. International instruments such as the Convention Relating to the Status of Refugees have a profound influence on the protection of refugees and asylum seekers in South Africa. These rights are further reinforced by the Bill of Rights contained in the Constitution of the Republic of South Africa (RSA, 1996). The Constitution is the cornerstone of human rights and ensures that all citizens and people within its borders are assured of respect and human dignity. These rights include the right to equality and the right to access social security, including social assistance (see Chapter 1 for a discussion on transformative and human rights approach). A second feature is that South Africa's policy and regulatory framework is characterised by the principle of self-sufficiency and local integration of refugees and asylum seekers (Mpedi and Ross, 2013: 211). Some of this discussion takes place in the previous section of this chapter. South Africa as a host country has opted not to encamp refugees. A third feature is that, in spite of South Africa being an emerging economy with economic challenges such as unemployment, poverty and inequality, it still undertakes to respect the rights of refugees and asylum seekers.

Refugees and permanent residents qualify for social grants. SASSA's booklet (2013) titled *Social assistance for refugees* indicates that social grants are available to all South African citizens, permanent residents, and refugees. Care dependency grants were the first type of social grant to be made available to refugees as a result of court action brought against the Department of Social Development. This court case which was settled out of court resulted in an amendment to the 2008 Regulations for refugees to gain access to the care dependency grant (DSD, 2016: 72).

Refugees in principle are covered by welfare, social assistance and social insurance. They are entitled to the same basic health services (for example, free basic health care to children under six years and pregnant women) and basic education (free basic education) to which the citizens of South Africa are entitled (section 27(*g*) of the Refugees Act 130 of 1998). Refugees with inadequate means may apply for immediate temporary relief such as social relief of distress (section 13 of the Social Assistance Act 13 of 2004).

With respect to social insurance, refugees may engage in formal employment and qualify for the various social insurance schemes, for example, unemployment insurance and occupational injuries and diseases scheme ((Mpedi and Ross, 2013: 207). A more recent development is that refugees and asylum seekers will be covered by the National Health Insurance scheme which is in its pilot stages. This scheme will be extended in accordance with the provisions of the Refugees Act and international human rights instruments that have been ratified by South Africa (Department of Health, 2011: 23).

Before discussing the policy options for migrants, refugees, and displaced people, it is important to clarify some of the relevant concepts.

## 8.4 Migration

*'A small Sudanese boy is carried into Panyido refugee camp, Ethiopia, on the shoulders of his uncle. He doesn't know where his parents are. He doesn't know if he will ever see his family again. So begins AherAropBol's story – an epic quest of survival, education, family and meaning – and the journey that will see him flee Sudan as a young child, and return many years later via Kenya, Tanzania, Malawi, Mozambique, Zimbabwe, and South Africa'* (Bol, 2009 back cover).

*Migrants* are people who live and work outside of the areas or countries from which they originate. *Migration* – the movement of these people – is a global phenomenon. Since 2000, the global map of migration has changed to such an extent that in 2009 the United Nations Development Programme (UNDP) stated that migration had replaced fertility and mortality that brings demographic changes. It was estimated in 2015 that approximately 244 million persons globally are international migrants (UN DESA, 2015). This was an increase of more than 40% since 2000 (IOM, 2010). The main reasons for migration are seen as seeking economic opportunities, and escaping from armed conflict, political turmoil, and persecution. At the same time, rural to urban migration within countries is also happening, mostly due to economic reasons (avoiding poverty and moving because of the possibility of work) (IOM, 2015). People migrate across borders and within borders. South Africa is no different. In South Africa there are three sets of major migrations:

- migrants from other countries exiting and entering South Africa's borders (for example, to and from Zimbabwe, Mozambique, and Malawi);
- migrants moving across provincial borders within South Africa (for example, from the Eastern Cape to the Western Cape and from Limpopo to Gauteng); and
- migrants within South Africa moving from rural to urban areas within provinces (for example, from rural Lusikisiki in the Eastern Cape to Mthata in the Eastern Cape), or across provinces (for example, from the rural Nsikazi District in Mpumalanga to Pretoria in Gauteng).

The start of the twenty-first century has seen major refugee crises in African countries, such as the Democratic Republic of the Congo, Somalia, Sudan, and Zimbabwe. Until today, most of the migrants and refugees moving to South Africa come from these countries.

| ACTIVITY 4 | **RESEARCH PROJECT** |
| --- | --- |

Do some research about migrants and refugees by reading newspapers, or visiting the website of the United Nations High Commissioner for Refugees (UNHCR) – the UN's Refugee Agency: (www.unhcr.org. Sketch a map of the world and indicate the following:
1. The countries from which most migrants originate (migrant producers).
2. The countries hosting the largest numbers of migrants (migration destinations).
3. Try and obtain numbers of people moving between the countries indicated in questions 1 and 2.
4. Reflect on the activity: Write down your impressions about migrants and migrations before and after doing the activity; think about how your perceptions changed and developed by doing the activity.

If you have completed Activity 1, you will be aware of the human migration and suffering that are happening globally and locally on a daily basis due to, for example, poverty, wars, famines, natural disasters, and political unrest. For the destination or migrants accepting countries, migrations are challenging social cohesion and social bonds, resource allocations, and create new multicultural communities. The magnitude of this human suffering is a tragedy, and social welfare policies, social work, and social service professions need to respond to these issues. This chapter will mainly focus on migrants, refugees, and displaced people in the South African context.

In the following subsection, the different concepts are discussed.

## 8.4.1 The concept of migration

Migration refers to the movement of people from one place to another. The reasons for migration are varied, and may include wars, political or ethnic persecution, climate changes and disasters, lack of job opportunities, and poverty. Broadly, reference is made of two types of migration (Posel, 2004 and UNDP, 2010):
- **Forced migration** is when people do not have a choice but to migrate. In this case, migration can be a matter of survival.
- **Voluntary migration** is when people migrate to a different country or province simply because they want to enjoy a better standard of living. It is a matter of choice.

In the Table 8.1 we provide some push and pull factors that may lead to people migrating nationally and internationally. It is a 'working table' and you can add to the table.

Table 8.1 Push and pull factors stimulating migration

| Push factors for migration | Pull factors for migration |
| --- | --- |
| Unemployment | Employment opportunities |
| Lack of services | Low crime rates/safety |
| High crime | Good food supply |
| War | Political security and safety |
| Poverty | Attractive climate |
| Drought | Quality of life |
| Flooding | |

When you look closely at these push and pull factors, you will find that the reasons for migration are either forced or voluntarily.

The rest of the chapter will focus on forced migration and forced migrants. Figure 8.2 illustrates the categories of migrants and forced migrants which are discussed in more detail below.

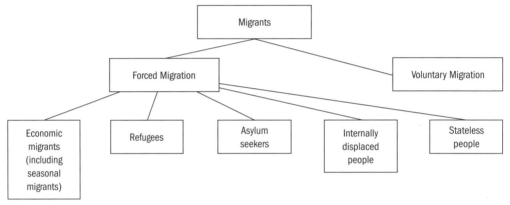

Figure 8.2 Categories of migrants

### 8.4.1.1 Migrant workers/economic migrants

In a poetry book titled *I am a Migrant Too!*, launched by the City of Johannesburg and the UNHCR to celebrate International Migrants Day, Kabelo Mazibuko wrote:

> '*I am a migrant to a city no one calls home (Johannesburg)*
> *A traveller from the deepest villages of Mpumalanga ...*' (IOM, 2012: 13A).

*I am a migrant too* can be downloaded for free at: https://southafrica.iom.int/system/files/drupal-private/Poetry_Book_WEB_v3.pdf.

As shown in Figure 8.2 above, economic migration is regarded as forced migration due to poverty and because people do not have other means to make a living. The majority of migrants globally are those that migrate because of poverty and unemployment. According to the International Labour Organisation (ILO), economic globalisation has created more migrant workers than ever before. Unemployment and increasing poverty have prompted many workers in developing countries to seek work elsewhere, while developed countries have increased their demand for labour, especially unskilled labour. As a result, millions of workers and their families travel to countries other than their own to search for work. Africa and Asia are regarded as the biggest exporters of labour, particularly youth labour (ILO,

2016). Economic migrants are regarded as important because migrant workers contribute to the economies of their host countries. In turn, the remittances they send home help to boost the economies of their countries or provinces of origin. It is estimated that developing countries are benefiting by billions of US dollars each year (Crush, Chikanda and Skinner, 2015). The volume of remittances sent by migrant workers back to the developing countries, from which they originate, has been growing significantly to the extent that remittances have become the second largest source of external funding after direct foreign investment (Maphosa, 2005). According to The Africa Report (2014), the remittances sent from all Zimbabweans in the diaspora over the world were estimated at 1,8 billion US Din 2013. The existence of economic migrants can therefore be economically beneficial for host countries and destination countries.

Crush et al. (2015) conducted intensive and extensive studies on informal businesses created by foreigner nationals in South Africa. The authors demonstrate that some of the most dedicated and resourceful entrepreneurs in South Africa's informal economy are immigrants and that they create jobs, which include jobs for unemployed South Africans.

## 8.4.1.2 Refugees, asylum seekers, internally displaced people (IDP) and stateless people

### Refugees
According to the UNHCR a refugee is a person who:
- is **outside** his or her country of origin
- has a **well-founded fear** of persecution because of his or her race, religion, nationality, membership in a particular social group or political opinion
- is **unable** or unwilling to avail him or herself of the protection of that country, or to return there for fear of persecution (UNHCR, 1999:16).

### Asylum seekers
The South African Refugees Act 130 of 1998 distinguishes between a refugee and an asylum seeker. According to this Act, a person who is in the process of seeking recognition as a refugee in the Republic of South Africa is known as an 'asylum seeker'. A refugee is a person who has been granted asylum in terms of the Refugees Act. In order to be recognised as a refugee, an asylum seeker must comply with the above definition of a refugee.

It is important to understand that, legally speaking, a person who flees for safety to another country and then applies for refugee status is an asylum seeker. That person remains an asylum seeker until he or she is officially recognised as a refugee. This process may take years and in so doing leaves the person in an undesirable and vulnerable state as will be discussed later in this chapter.

### Internally displaced people (IDP)
According to the *Guiding Principles on Internal Displacement* (UNHCR, 1998), internally displaced persons are:

> 'Persons or groups of persons who have been forced or obliged to flee or to leave their homes or places of habitual residence, in particular as a result of or in order to avoid the effects of armed conflict, situations of generalized violence, violations of human rights or natural or human-made disasters, and who have not crossed an internationally recognized State border.'

During the 1980s there were many IDP's in South Africa and Zimbabwe due to civil wars, massacres or genocides, and internal fighting between ethnic groups (e.g. the Gukuhurandi massacre in Zimbabwe). People who flee their homes but stay within the borders of their country are referred to as people 'who are on the run in their own country' (UNHCR, 1999).

IDPs are regarded as among the world's most vulnerable people. Unlike refugees, IDPs have not crossed an international border to find sanctuary but have remained inside their home countries with little or no protection. Even if they have fled for similar reasons as refugees (armed conflict, violence, genocides, human rights violations), IDPs legally remain under the protection or exploitation of their own government – even though that government might be the cause of their flight.

Regrettably, some of the world's largest internal displacement situations continue to take place in Africa. With 4,9 million people displaced, Sudan has the largest reported IDP population (UNHCR, 2015). There is an estimated 2 million IDPs in the Democratic Republic of the Congo and some 1,3 million people have been forced to flee their homes in Somalia. In total, 19 African countries confront problems of forced displacement resulting from conflict, violence, and human rights abuses (UNHCR, 2015).

In addition, millions of other people have become homeless and fled their countries of origin due to natural disasters such as droughts and floods. These people are also considered as IDPs. According to Greenpeace (2017), out of the 27,8 million people being displaced in 2015, 19,2 million people became internally displaced due to natural disasters in 113 countries, while 8,6 million people were displaced due to conflict. It is expected that climate change will increase the number of displaced people due to natural disasters (Greenpeace, 2017).

## Stateless people

A stateless person is, what it says, a person without a state. Globally there are around 10 million stateless people (UNHCR, 2017). The UNHCR (2017) regards stateless people as a major problem. A stateless person has no documentation from any government proving that he or she is part of any state. They are people who are marginalised and are not recognised by any government. Imagine if you did not have an identity document or any form of permit to be in South Africa? You would not be able to access health services or education; you would not be able to open a bank account, not to mention obtain credit facilities. You would not be able to get married officially and you would not be able to enrol at a school or university. In principle, you would not legally exist, despite the fact that you existed in person. Just think how often you are required to show some form of identity documentation. According to the Lawyers for Human Rights (LHR) (2015), before 2013, children born from stateless people were not recognised as citizens and also regarded as stateless. Currently, the South African government does recognise the child when born in South Africa and still living in South Africa at the age of 18 years, and the government will provide such a child with a birth certificate and an identity document (ID).

**Case Study** **CHALLENGES OF BEING STATELESS**

Read the following case study and recommend the policies that could be used to solve this kind of problem.

*Eve was born in Ghana to a Lebanese mother. Her father was a South African citizen; however, he died in Ghana before her birth was registered in South Africa and her South African citizenship confirmed. Her mother was unstable and gave up guardianship to Eve's South African grandparents in South Africa where she came to live. The South Africa government has refused to register her birth and recognise her as a South African, because the Birth and Death Registration Act (BDRA) does not allow legal guardians to register children unless the parents have passed away. It also requires the father to sign for paternity at registration. Eve's mother is unavailable and her father is deceased. Eve's grandparents are unable to financially support her and are unable to apply for a social grant to look after her. She has been placed in foster care. Eve is stateless.*

Section 9 of the BDRA does not allow guardians to register children unless both biological parents are dead. Regulation 12 requires the father to sign for paternity in order to be recorded as the father of the child and to pass nationality to his child (Lawyers for Human Rights, 2015).

**ACTIVITY 5** **PERCEPTIONS ABOUT MIGRANTS AND REFUGEES**

Before describing the migration context in South Africa, you need to do some self-reflection.
• What is your perception of migrants and refugees living in South Africa or your own country, if not from South Africa?
• Think about any experiences you have had with migrants and/or refugees and jot them down. If you are a migrant yourself, what are your experiences of moving away from your country and your reception in the host country?

# 8.5 The South African context and migrants

In South Africa there are two major migration patterns: internal migration within South Africa; and external migration to and from South Africa. Migration has deep historical roots in South Africa (Lurie and Williams, 2014). Under the apartheid government, migration from the surrounding countries such as Zimbabwe, Lesotho, Swaziland, Malawi, and Botswana was common practice in particular to provide labour for the mining industry. Internal migration also took place from rural to urban areas, and from areas known as the 'independent homelands' at the time in order to work and earn money on the mines. The apartheid Group Areas Act 41 of 1950 and Aliens Control Act 96 of 1991 ensured that these migrants could not stay within South Africa or in urban areas for any purpose other than work. The movement of people was tightly monitored and controlled. The migrants, therefore, became what is referred to as 'circular migrants'. They always had to return home after a period of time to visit their families and take remittances home. They were not permitted to migrate with their families permanently to the cities to be close to their work environment.

During the 1970s and 1980s, the migrant phenomenon and the patterns of migration and its impact on families were well researched (Posel, 2004). As a result, the main characteristics of migration during this period can be summarised as follows:

1. As mentioned, migration patterns were mostly circular. The government of the time had bilateral agreements with neighbouring countries to enable people to work on the mines. The people were very tightly regulated and monitored once they had been recruited.

2. The apartheid policies promoted permanent white migration while black migration (for work) was only on a temporary basis. Black migrants could not settle in areas close to the mines or their places of work. It was also during this time that many men's hostels were built in the townships. Family units could not relocate.

3. The third major characteristic of apartheid-era's migration was that it was predominantly males who migrated to the work on the mines while the women had no choice but to remain and run their households without their partner (Posel, 2004). Women were restricted not only by the apartheid policies, but also by tradition, as their husbands, fathers and leaders did not allow them to leave the rural areas (See Chapter 3 of this book for further discussion on patriarchy and apartheid's impact on women).

# 8.6 Current characteristics of migration in South Africa

After 1994, it was expected that internal migration would decrease, or that if and when people migrated, it would be permanent in nature. To the surprise of the researchers and policymakers, internal migration did not decrease as expected. Instead migration increased and took on totally new dimensions. Foreign born migrants increased due to the political unrest and economic crises that African countries experienced, particularly Zimbabwe. South Africa became and is still currently regarded as one of the main destinations for African refugees and migrants. There is no clear figure on how many documented and undocumented migrants and refugees are living in South Africa (Landau and Segetti, 2009; Triegaardt, 2013). The South African government is criticised (Landau and Segetti, 2009) for failing to collect adequate data to enable it to determine the number of migrants and refugees in South Africa. There is no indication of when migrants arrive, how long they stay, or what they do while they are living in South Africa. The current speculative numbers range from between 1,2 million to over 8 million migrants being in South Africa (Landau and Segetti, 2009) or 3,4 million according to the Department of Social Development (DSD, 2016).

Since 1994, the following migration dimensions have been noted (Landau and Segetti, 2009; McDonald, Mashike and Golden, 1999; Posel, 2009):

1. Post-apartheid migration is characterised by a mix of circular, permanent and transit migration, but the majority of migrants are still circular and economic migrants. Authors like Landau and Segetti (2009) are critical of the current policies and practices of the post-apartheid government. They are of the opinion that, similarly to the apartheid government, the current government supports the impermanence of migrants in South Africa.

2. The second characteristic of post-apartheid migration is somewhat different in the sense that women and children are now also migrating. Coupled with the increase in female migrants, it was found that fewer people, women in particular, are getting married, the number of young unemployed men increased, and the household structures changed (Posel, 2004). Collinson, Tollman and Kahn (2003) found that most remittances to households were provided by unmarried males and females. The unmarried females

had to move to urban areas to earn an income to be able to look after their families and children. The children were left with the grandparents or other household members (Landau and Segetti, 2009).

3. The third characteristic of the post-apartheid migration patterns is that the migrators keep in touch with their homes in rural areas or their countries of origin and still carry the responsibility for supporting their families. They still go and visit when they have money and pay remittances to the families or households at home.

4. A fourth feature of the migration pattern after 1994 is that while the apartheid government allowed predominantly skilled and qualified Europeans into South Africa, the greater component of migrants in current times are unskilled, unqualified and youth (Landau and Segetti, 2009; Mkwananzi, 2017). However, McDonald et al. (1999) and Crush et al. (2015) found that migrants in post-apartheid South Africa are motivated, educated, skilled, and enterprising.

5. In addition, there is a growing concern that children as young as seven years are migrating from neighbouring states due to the death of their parents and lack of money (Mkwananzi, 2017).

Posel (2009) and Landau (2006) further mention that internal migrant parents seldom bring their children to the new destination. The children are left with the grandparents or other members of the household. This is because destination households maybe crowded, unsafe, insecure, and the children may be left without proper care. The same does not apply to political refugees, who usually bring their children with them.

It is interesting to note that there is some evidence that African migrants are of the opinion that South Africa has the moral obligation to open its doors and socioeconomic rights to African countries as they were accommodating to South Africans during apartheid when some South Africans had to go into exile (McDonald et al., 1999; Mkwanazi, 2017).

---

**ACTIVITY 6**     **CHALLENGES OF BEING A MIGRANT**

Have a discussion with a person who is/was a migrant. Ask the person to share with you some of the difficulties she or he experienced while moving to or within South Africa or the host country and the challenges of settling in South Africa or the new destination.

---

Now that you have a better understanding of migrants and refugees in the South African context, in the next section we discuss the vulnerabilities experienced by migrants.

# 8.7 Understanding the vulnerabilities of migrants

This section describes some of the general vulnerabilities to which migrants are exposed. It is important to understand these vulnerabilities in order to consider policies, structures and services that will be required to address them.

## 8.7.1 Traumatic experiences and losses

In the case of forced migration people often have to leave behind their homes, their families and everything they own. These experiences of loss are traumatic. In the country/place they migrate from and on the way to the host country they are often exposed to horrific and traumatic experiences.

For example, during the 1980s there was intense violence in what is now KwaZulu-Natal and as a result there were many displaced people. A person described the following incident when fleeing which remained vivid in his mind:

> '... we found about twenty-three people hacked to death along the road of about two kilometres. We found them along the entire road about a few metres apart. They were sort of chopped in layers. The last person was a child. She was about a year. Although she was dead, her eyes were open. I can still see her looking at me' (Wade and Schenck, 2012: 355).

The following scenario may assist you to comprehend the depth of human tragedy experienced.

 **Case Study    INTERVIEW WITH A WOMAN IN A REFUGEE CAMP IN BOTSWANA**

This experience was noted by Okello-Wengi (2004: 158) who interviewed a woman from Uganda in a refugee camp in Botswana.

'Amina was interrogated many times on the whereabouts of her husband, who had fled to Kenya. She was beaten, humiliated and tortured by burning her thighs with hot iron, which left large scars. Together with other women, she was repeatedly raped several times every day. The rapes were performed by a group of young and old militias. She was also present when other women were raped. Once she witnessed the death of an 11 year-old girl after multiple rapes and torture.'

In the hope for a better life en route to a country of refuge, migrants are vulnerable. Refugees reported witnessing and/or experiencing physical violence. There are reports of women resorting to 'survival sex' in return for resources such as food and water, or in exchange for being guided through the bush. Many participants reported experiences of and witnessed assaults, rape, and murders.

The experience related in the case study above give some insight into the situations migrants endure in their home countries and on their way to their new countries.

## 8.7.2 Exploitation and human rights violations

Migrants (internal and external) are vulnerable, dependent, and at times desperate, and can be exploited by people such as officials, employers, home owners, and human traffickers (FMSP, 2009) as they fall easy prey to these abusers/predators. They are easily bribed, exploited to work for long hours for little payment, or asked to pay exorbitant prices for their accommodation. Migrants, particularly those without documents, can be exploited as they cannot rely on any form of protection. McDonald et al. (1999) found that most of the migrants who were part of their study were underpaid for the work they had been doing. The theme of exploitation will emerge in the other vulnerabilities discussed in this chapter.

### 8.7.3 Accommodation/shelter

One of the major vulnerabilities for migrants is finding accommodation if they do not have friends or family who can host them temporarily (Masendu, 2011). They often have to stay in overcrowded accommodation, sleep in the veld, or are exploited in paying higher rent than locals. This was confirmed in a study by Blaauw and Schenck (survey data, National Day Labour Study 2017) which revealed that foreign day labourers paid much more for renting a room than local day labourers. 'This is how we get back what they take from us' (Blaauw and Schenck, survey data) was a comment from one the of the local day labourers when the researchers tried to understand the reasons for the difference in what locals and foreigners pay for accommodation.

Below is an extract from Miworc (2015: 44) explaining some of the experiences of migrants.

> 'When someone wants to come [to South Africa], they can speak to a relative or friend whom they are close to, who can send them money, first to apply for a passport, if they don't have one and then transport money. On arrival one normally stays with a relative or friends. Even though it's normal to share accommodation there are often disagreements about buying food, rentals and so forth.'

### 8.7.4 Unwelcoming host

When South Africa drafted its Refugees Act in 1998, it had to decide whether to host refugees in camps, or expect refugees to be self-sufficient. Instead of encamping refugees, the government opted for the principle of self-sufficiency and local integration of the refugees (Mpedi and Ross, 2013). This decision recognised that refugees can lead a productive life, contribute to the host country, and become self-sufficient. Only in the case of mass migration or where refugees need to be kept safe will camps be considered. The downside of this is that refugees do not necessarily arrive in welcoming environments. Instead they may experience unhelpful, hostile, bribing officials, and xenophobic, hostile and even violent host communities. Furthermore, they need to find and network and negotiate their own accommodation and work as mentioned above (Mwkananzi, 2017 and Mpedi and Ross, 2013).

Some of these challenges also apply to local migrants moving from rural to urban areas and having to find accommodation and work, particularly in the current context where work is scarce.

### 8.7.5 The fear of being arrested, detained and deported

In the study by Mkwananzi (2017), the fear of being arrested, detained and deported was clearly expressed. Refugees risk being randomly arrested, detained, deported or stripped of their assets. Mkwananzi (2017) highlights the example of the Mozambican immigrant taxi driver, Mido Macia, who died in police custody after he was handcuffed to the back of a police van and dragged in the township of Daveyton in Benoni, Gauteng. The police alleged that he was obstructing the traffic. Many more stories have been told of municipal police confiscating the assets of migrants and refugees living and working on the streets. Being vulnerable they are easy targets for corrupt police and security staff.

## 8.7.6 Accessing work

To be able to access work in South Africa is a human right for refugees and asylum seekers (Kavuro, 2015). Employment for refugees and asylum seekers is, however, challenging due to a range of difficulties such as high unemployment in South Africa, ill sentiments of citizens towards noncitizens as well as legal and procedural barriers (Kavuro, 2015). The South African unemployment figure stood at 27,7% in 2017 (the narrow definition of unemployment) (Stats SA, 2017). The Forced Migration Studies Programme (FMSP) (2009) emphasised that the position is worse for economic migrants who cannot apply for refugee or asylum status and are undocumented. It is, therefore, difficult and highly competitive for migrants to find work in the formal or informal sectors. Masendu (2011) found that it took at least three months for a person to find or create formal or informal work if they did not have a contact who could introduce them to work or employ them. Yet migrants have to find a way to survive until they find employment. The UNHCR, in this respect, offers some support to refugees. A refugee who comes into the country and registers with the UNHCR on entry and claims refugee status because of persecution, for example, receives a stipend from the UNHCR until the person manages to find work.

It was also found that most migrants, despite the fact that they maybe skilled, will do unskilled work until they are able to access work for which they are trained.

The quotes below illustrate that migrants may be willing to work for any payment, even if they are underpaid.

 **Case Study**     **MIGRANTS SHARE THEIR EXPERIENCES**

**Experience 1:**
*'Almost two weeks you don't find a job (informal day labour) because we are so many and you see what happens whenever you stop your car there? Everyone asks for a job. So it's hard to find a job'* (Smith: survey data).

**Experience 2:**
*'I came to South Africa [but] I never got a real job. I only got [work] ... where I was paid R200–R250 per week, so it wasn't much. I could not afford to pay rent; I used to stay at Methodist (church in Johannesburg) before it was shut down'* (Mwkananzi, 2017: 146).

The last quote clearly illustrates the exploitation which migrants may experience. If they are undocumented and not formally employed, there are a few structures such as NGOs like Lawyers for Human Rights or systems in place where they can access protection from exploitation as they cannot request protection from the police or other formal government institutions.

## 8.7.7 Language complications

When migrating from countries where English is not spoken, such as Mozambique (Portuguese) or the DRC (French), or from rural areas to urban areas, where migrants cannot understand or converse in the language of the host destination, it adds to their difficulty to negotiate entry into the host community. Blaauw (2010) found that day labourers functioning in the informal sector who were proficient in Afrikaans or English accessed work more easily than those who could not speak either language. Employers prefer not to employ a person with whom they cannot converse.

## 8.7.8 Accessing services

Access to health, education, and social services are basic human rights in the South African Bill of Rights (1996) which are critical to migrants and refugees. According to the Refugees Act of 1998 and the Immigration Act of 2000 as well as the *Comprehensive Review of the Welfare Policy of 1997* (DSD, 2016), refugees and asylum seekers have the right to access to these services. It needs to be further emphasised that all children who live in South Africa –no matter who are their parents (migrants, refugees, displaced people, etc.) – are constitutionally entitled to access education, health care, and any other protective services that they require. There is no ambiguity about these provisions for children in the law or in policy. From a policy and legislative perspective, the grey area is ensuring compliance at the point of delivery of such services so that children and refugees receive the services to which they are entitled. Noncompliance mainly results from provincial and local government officials' lack of understanding of how to implement the policies or their reluctance to do so because of their own bias. On the other hand, NPOs are unable to provide the necessary assistance because they lack the necessary resources.

However, not having documents prevents access to these services. Access to health, education, and social services and social protection are seen by the United Nations' Sustainable Development Goals (UN, 2015) as important for reducing inequalities, especially for the youth, migrants and vulnerable communities, yet numerous cases continue to be reported of people struggling to access services. Policies such as the *White Paper for Social Welfare* (1997) were not originally clear and specific about services to migrants.

Lurie and Williams (2014) emphasised that migration has major health implications for migrants and their host countries. Migration has contributed to the spread of diseases such as HIV and tuberculosis in South Africa. The reason for this is that it led to the concentration of large numbers of high-risk people, who were susceptible to diseases for various reasons, in confined spaces. It is important for health services to be accessible for all in order to prevent spreading illnesses.

## 8.7.9 Xenophobia

Despite the fact that South Africa has a progressive outlook on economic migrants from neighbouring countries, xenophobic outbreaks often occur. Migrants are blamed for 'stealing' work resources and opportunities, and for crime and sexual attacks. During xenophobic attacks the migrants' properties are often destroyed, they experience physical attacks, isolation, and belittling. As its title suggests, the book *Mean streets: Migration, Xenophobia and informality in South Africa* by Crush et al. (2015) illustrates how vulnerable migrants in South Africa are and the dangers to which they are exposed. Xenophobic attacks emphasise the urgent need to develop strategies for the political, social, and economic integration of migrants into host societies, so that the strength of national identities and democratic citizenship can be enhanced.

Refugees in South Africa have been the victims of xenophobia

 Case Study — **THE LIFE OF A REFUGEE**

Experience 1:
*'The life of a refugee is really hard. You are manipulated by greedy politicians. You are abused, disempowered and mocked by citizens who do not recognise your humanity' (Bol, 2009: 108).*

Experience 2:
*'...I have run [from] my country for protection and humanity*
*And have been welcomed by hatred and xenophobia*
*That looted, killed innocents and burned people alive*
*And "Kwerekwere" will I be called ever, as I am a migrant too.*

*I thought of finding a space to survive and enjoy the same rights*
*But come to live and beg on the streets of Johannesburg*
*Undermined, facing theft, crime and bad weathers*
*And could not raise my voice, cause I'm a migrant too...'*
Excerpt from a poem by Godel Sefu (IOM, 2012: 12)

## 8.7.10 Identity and belonging

Migration results in vulnerabilities regarding identity and belonging. Good integration into a new country or new community can assist migrants with the development of new identities and experiences of belonging and becoming a citizen. There is a stark contrast between the experiences of hostility, xenophobia, and harassment described in the extract from the poem above and the vision of securing a new identity and sense of belonging and social cohesion (Mkwananzi, 2017).

# 8.8 Criticisms of the current policies for migrants and refugees

Turning our attention to the past, the Aliens Control Act 96 of 1991 under apartheid could be considered the cornerstone of the immigration policy in the 1990s. According to Crush (2008), the Aliens Control Act was used as a weapon of racial control. No recognition was given to refugees and asylum seekers in the policies and Acts during the apartheid era.

After apartheid ended, the Aliens Control Act was declared unconstitutional and discriminatory. Under the new democratic government the Refugees Act 130 of 1998 and the Immigration Act 13 of 2002 came into effect. The latter Act was amended and the Immigration Amendment Act 19 of 2004 is still in use today. Unlike the Aliens Control Act, these Acts were based on the Constitution of the Republic of South Africa (Act 108 of 1996). In principle, they promote migration in a way that migrants are responsible for negotiating their own settlement and self-sufficiency (instead of encampment).

---

**ACTIVITY 7**  **ENCAMPMENT OF REFUGEES**

For some insight into the encampment of refugees, search the internet for Botswana's Dukwi Refugee Camp and Namibia's Osire Refugee Camp.
1. Make a summary of your perspectives of refugee self-sufficiency (as in South Africa) vs encampment (as in Namibia and Botswana).
2. What are the implications of the minimisation process of refugees from 20 000 to less than 4 000 in the Osire Refugee Camp in Namibia?

---

The NDP 2030 states:

> *'We have welcomed people from distant lands*
> *Who have chosen to live among us ...'* (RSA, 2012: 20)

The post-apartheid Acts allow refugees and asylum seekers to apply for employment and to access public education, health care, social services, and social protection. In principle, the Acts provide immigrants and refugees with the freedom and/or difficulty to find their way around the country (Crush, 2008). However, despite our policies, in practice, these policies have been criticised for not assisting in integrating migrants and foreign nationals or refugees into South African society as they are still experiencing difficulties in accessing documentation and services (Crush, 2008; Crush et al., 2015; Landau and Segetti, 2009; Mkwananzi, 2017). The repeated outbreaks of xenophobic attacks are evidence of this. They highlight the fact that, despite the improved policy responses, reform is hindered mainly by the lack of capacity (such as providing the necessary documentation), inefficiency and misinformation, and anti-migrant sentiments within and outside government (Landau and Segetti, 2009; Kavuro, 2015). According to Landau and Segetti (2009), government has an inefficient system to address the needs of locals and migrants in South Africa, which increases competition for scarce resources and therefore intensifies xenophobia. In a nutshell, government's inefficiency prevents social cohesion in South Africa. MiWorc (2015) confirm this sentiment in their research, finding that migrants and refugees mostly rely on informal relationships and protection to assist them when migrating and settling in South Africa.

Triegaardt (2013) has expressed criticism by saying that the above Acts are silent on how migrants can access health and social services. There are also still restrictive stipulations in the Refugees Act (1998) which do not permit refugees to work while waiting on the outcome of their applications for asylum. However, they may start working if the application takes longer than six months. This raises the question as to how refugees are expected to survive while waiting to be granted asylum. They still have to find a way of surviving even though it is only for the first six months. The law is further silent on whether they can access services such as health care and housing while waiting for asylum (Triegaardt, 2013).

In summary, despite the fact that the South African government opened its borders for migrants to enter South Africa, it still does not embrace immigration and the migrants. The major challenges regarding policy implementation can be summarised as a lack of political will, human capacity, service delivery, and resources. Given that sufficient resources are not available for local South Africans, making provision for the millions of migrants is putting more pressure on the resources and relationships.

While the above section provides a critique of the current policies and legislation relating to migrants and refugees, the next section provides some guidelines for transformative policies. The understanding of transformative social welfare policy aligns with a normative and developmental commitment to meeting human needs as a right of citizenship (see Chapter 1 of this book).

## 8.9 Guidelines for transformative policies

According to the DSD (2016), transformative policies facilitate first and foremost the reduction of inequalities and vulnerabilities through systemic and redistributive changes, enabling environments, and the broadening of access to services.

If we take into consideration the developmental social welfare approach, human rights perspective, and the CA approach (creating freedoms and opportunities), the following facilitative aspects should be taken into consideration for drafting policies regarding migrants and refugees:

1. **Changing perceptions towards viewing migrants and refugees as opportunities:** Crush et al. (2015) said we should move away from the notion of policies as control and deportation and instead see policies as being facilitative. The government should see migrants and refugees as opportunities (Kavuro, 2015). Instead of controlling them, government should focus on increasing capabilities and opportunities by capitalising on and valuing the skills, knowledge and innovation they bring to the country or area.

2. **Changing perceptions of local citizens**: This process includes changing the perceptions and behaviour of local citizens by providing information, raising awareness, and encouraging appreciation. This is relevant to migrants and refugees, for example, the great influx of people from the Eastern Cape to the Western Cape creates animosity towards the 'inkommers' (that is, those coming in from other parts of the country) and the same applies to the '(ma)*kwerekweres*' (a generally derogatory slang word meaning foreigners) from Zimbabwe. As long as these negative perceptions prevail, no social integration and social cohesion will be possible.

3. **Focusing on the root causes of forced migration:** It is also the responsibility of government to invest in attending to the root causes of economic and political migrations such as the political instabilities in the countries of origin, and the poverty, corruption, and lack of service delivery in provinces such as the Eastern Cape.

4. **Investing in and valuing people:** Changing perceptions and valuing citizens, migrants, and refugees will result in governments investing in health care, shelter, education, food security, social protection, decent working conditions, and access to social services not only for citizens but for all. This will assist in reducing inequalities, helping people to contribute to the socioeconomic growth of the country. Facilitating people's entering into the job market (formal or informal) is central to enabling them to earn a living, be self-sufficient, and to integrate into the local community. Preventing asylum seekers from accessing work is therefore unlawful, as is barring them from collecting waste to sell or from making a living in the informal sector. Rather, governments should create facilitating policies to increase political, economic and social opportunities for all.

5. **Updating and aligning policies:** The South African government should constantly update policies to align with international standards set by organisations such as the UNHCR (refugees and asylum seekers), ILO (decent work), and the World Health Organisation (WHO).

6. **Strengthening government's implementation and enforcement of policies:** According to the NDP 2030 (RSA, 2012: 408), a 'plan is only as credible as its delivery mechanism is viable. There is a real risk that South Africa's development agenda could fail because the state is incapable of implementing it'. South Africa is known for good policies and poor implementation. Good policies are of no use when officials are ineffective and corrupt, and resort to harassing and bribing people who have nowhere to go and are in need of support. Such conduct indicate a need to train and raise the awareness of staff, streamline processes, put monitoring and evaluation measures in place, and provide adequate funding of services. Refugees should be protected from harassment and corrupt officials. In fact, citizens should take responsibility to ensure oversight of services to all vulnerable populations including migrants and refugees.

7. **Bringing services closer to people:** When policies are drafted for poor and vulnerable people, they should also take into consideration how services should be accessed. They need to take into account the cost involved in obtaining documentation, distances to travel, and time spent at offices such as Home Affairs and SASSA.

8. **Creating safety nets:** Transformational policies create safety nets through ensuring social protection and social insurance (in the workplace) to prevent people from falling below 'the poverty line'. Originally the Refugees Act of 1998 did not make provision for foreign nationals to access social protection. In 2003, however, the Constitutional Court found that the law should change to allow permanent residents to access social assistance, which was then changed in the Social Assistance Act 13 of 2004. SASSA's

2013 booklet (SASSA, 2013) indicates that 'all grants are available to South African citizens, permanent residents and refugees'. Although social security is now available to locals and refugees, access to documentation is still a major barrier in this process. Social security includes access to work and an income. Without access to work or social protection, no migrant or refugee can be self-sufficient. Given the fact that we have an unemployment rate of 27,7% (Stats SA, 2017), we should be more open-minded about the informal sector and facilitating processes so that people can make a living. There is currently a process facilitated by the United Nations Development Programme and the Department of Planning, Monitoring and Evaluation to search for opportunities and options to provide social protection to informal workers in South Africa, which will cover the informal economic migrants. A document on this process can be accessed at: http://www.za.undp.org/content/dam/south africa/docs/POLICY%20OPTIONS%20FOR%20EXTENDING%20SOCIAL%20PROTECTION.pdf.

9. **Protecting unaccompanied minors and refugees with disabilities:** Women, children, and refugees and migrants with disabilities are exceptionally vulnerable as we have seen in the vignettes described in this chapter. The Refugees Act (1998) makes provision for unaccompanied children to be brought before the Children's Court and be granted asylum status. It also provides for refugees with disabilities to be assisted with obtaining asylum status. Children and refugees with disabilities are then to be dealt with under the Children's Act 38 of 2005 and the Mental Health Care Act 17 of 2002, respectively.

10. **Valuing the role of all role players:** Assisting migrants and refugees is not the responsibility of government alone, but an interplay among international organisations such as the UNHCR, ILO, government as well as non-governmental organisations (NGOs) in particular. The South African government signed a memorandum of understanding with the UNHCR in 1993 which allowed refugees to enter South Africa and aligned government's actions with those of the UNHCR. Furthermore, the ILO plays an important role in the development of decent work and minimum wage standards and minimum wages. It is the role of the NGOs and faith-based organisations which should be strengthened and supported as they are the organisations at the coalface that respond to the physical, legal, psychosocial, health, and economic needs of the migrants and refugees. These NGOs should be funded and supported. The Department of Home Affairs and other state departments are responsible for migration management, and therefore policies should make provision for institutional interaction and partnerships (Triegaardt, 2013). This will be discussed in the next section.

# 8.10 Reflecting on social services for migrants and refugees

In this section we will briefly provide a framework for services rendered by social service professionals, NGO's, faith-based organisations, and government to people in general and to migrants and refugees in particular. In this regard, the framework provided by David Korten (1991) is useful to guide our thinking when reflecting on and planning services.

Korten (1991) refers to four 'generations' of service delivery or development work. Table 8.2 below provides a summary of Korten's service delivery 'generations'.

Table 8.2  Korten's generation services and development initiatives

| First generation strategies | Second generation strategies | Third generation strategies | Fourth generation strategies |
|---|---|---|---|
| Direct service delivery – provision of food, health care, shelter and social security/protection. Counselling and support services. | Develop the capacities and capabilities of people towards self-reliance and self-sufficiency. (Developmental social welfare) | Facilitate and advocate changing of policies and institutions. | The core objective of the fourth generation is people's movements to address the root causes of the problem. |

Source: Table created by the author based on Swart and Venter (2000) and Korten (1991)

Reflecting on the vulnerabilities experienced by the migrants and refugees as explained in this chapter, most services currently delivered to migrants and refugees are *first generation strategies*. This includes assistance with documentation, food, health, shelter, trauma counselling, psychosocial support, and access to social security/protection and insurance. In addition, this may include services such as the protection of women and children. Agencies such as the UNHRC, government, NGOs, faith-based organisations, UCT Refugee Rights Clinic, and churches play a major role in providing these services.

Although these services are critical and important services, the recipients on this level are passive and the services offer temporary alleviation.

*Second generation strategies* are regarded by Korten (1991) and Swart and Venter (2000) as those which are developmental in nature and include capacitating towards self-sufficiency. Migrants and refugees can be offered training such as literacy and/ or language classes to be able to function in the new home country, they can be re-skilled to access existing work opportunities, and they can be provided with human rights information to capacitate them to act against injustices. Applying services on the second generation level implies more participation and collaboration between the service providers and the migrants. A growing self-sufficiency is important.

---

**ACTIVITY 8** | **DATA BASE OF SERVICES**

Compile a data base of the agencies and institutions in your area that provide first and second generation services to migrants and refugees.
Reflect on the results of your search.

---

For social workers, these levels of services are of critical importance in terms of preparing migrants and refugees for the labour market and integrating them into society, and for cohesion. Organisations capacitating refugees and migrants need to be accessible and affordable.

The *third generation strategy* refers to attempts to change and/or introduce local, national, and international policies and institutions. Civil society and NGOs usually play a critical role at these levels since they advocate for the changing and improvement of processes, policies, institutions, and practices that may inhibit the freedom and growth of people. Typical organisations which come to mind are the Lawyers for Human Rights (LHR) and the Socio-economic Rights Institute of South Africa (SERI). One such example of advocacy by civil society contributed to the change in the *White Paper for Social Welfare* (1997) for the inclusion of refugees in accessing social welfare service delivery, which has not been the case previously.

This strategy points mainly towards social workers being aware of human rights and social justice violations in areas such as:

- Social welfare service delivery – social, health and education services being refused or not being accessible or available.
- Occupational welfare – this refers to workplace violations, health and safety issues in the workplace, a lack of access to fair and decent work, and a lack of equal employment opportunities and practices. Typical questions to ask include: Are services and opportunities available and accessible to employees where they can complain about violations and unfair practices? Do employers treat migrants and refugees equal to other employees who are citizens?

---

**ACTIVITY 9  MIGRANTS IN THE INFORMAL ECONOMY**

**Read the paragraph and answer the questions below.**

As indicated, many unemployed documented and undocumented refugees and migrants often seek employment in the informal economy. Informality is unregulated and therefore create opportunities for exploitation by employers such as non-payment or underpayment and unhealthy and unsafe working conditions. People in the informal economy are often marginalised since there are few organisations who can advocate on their behalf. Existing organisations that are able to assist in some instances include organisations such as *Women on Farms*, the *Farm Workers Association*, the *South African Waste Pickers Association*, and the *Casual Workers Association*. It is, however, the responsibility of social workers to assist the workers to reach out to these organisations or for the organisations to reach out to the workers. It was found by Theodore et al. (2017) that worker centres in the USA made a tremendous difference to the lives of the documented and undocumented casual, domestic, and day labourers regarding skills training, improvement of health and safety, addressing wage theft, the setting of wage rates, and the introduction of job allocation systems.

1. Can an undocumented migrant get access to the CCMA?
2. What will you as social service practitioner do in such a case of unfair labour practice where the worker cannot access the CCMA for protection?

---

- Fiscal welfare –the third generation strategy also includes fiscal welfare. The question to be asked is whether provincial and national budgets include specific services, resources, and assistance to refugees and migrants.

The development and implementation of policies and practices which deliberately focus on and include migrants and refugees will assist in the transformation of their lives.

*Fourth generation strategies* are implemented by civil society, NGOs, and the media and address the root causes of the migration problem. Questions to be asked here include: Are we addressing the factors that push people to migrate such as poverty, a lack of service delivery, violence, political instability, and gross human rights violations?

| ACTIVITY 10 | ORGANISATIONS AND AGENCIES PROVIDING SOCIAL WELFARE SERVICES |
|---|---|

- Complete Table 8.3 below. Visit the websites of the listed agencies and determine which 'generation' of services, as outlined by Korten (1991), they deliver to migrants and refugees.
- Make an inquiry in your area about which organisations are active in supporting migrants and refugees and add them to the list in Table 8.3.

**Table 8.3 Complete the services for refugees and migrants**

| Institution | Services | Generation 1,2,3, or 4 Just add the number |
|---|---|---|
| UNHCR | | |
| Jesuit Refugee Centre (JRC) | | |
| Lawyers for Human Rights (LHR) | | |
| DSD | | |
| SASSA | | |
| Central Methodist Church in Johannesburg | | |
| Consortium for Refugees and Migrants in South Africa (CORMSA) | | |
| Foundation for Human Rights | | |
| Section 27 | | |
| Department of Home Affairs | | |
| SERI | | |
| Women on Farms | | |
| | | |

- Choose a migrant/refugee producing province (such as the Eastern Cape) or a country (such as the DRC, Sudan or Zimbabwe) and consider what possible interventions should happen to change the circumstances (if possible). Extensive reading will be required to understand what is happening in those provinces or countries.

# CONCLUSION

- Social protection for migrant workers is a key emerging policy area in Africa. Migration increases the vulnerability of workers and their families, particularly as they are not covered by any form of protection when they travel for work or return home. Fortunately, policies and legislation protect refugees in South Africa, but this protection is not necessarily guaranteed in South Africa and in the rest of Africa. Eligibility to social assistance schemes may often be restricted to citizens or permanent residents, and the portability of social insurance rights and benefits remains extremely limited (ILO, 2017: 119).

- Taking into consideration all the comments made by the migrants and the literature, South Africa has sound policies but faces great challenges regarding their implementation. Currently, the country fails to facilitate social integration and social cohesion between local citizens and foreign nationals.
- According to Holscher and Bozalek (2012), transformable, durable or sustainable change can only be brought about if we focus our policies and efforts on promoting respectful co-existence between foreign nationals and host communities. Respectful co-existence covers many aspects, which include the relationship between foreign nationals and the people amongst whom they live as well as the institutions with which they have to interact. These processes need to be facilitated and social service professions should take the responsibility for doing so. This is social justice – 'to reflexively engage with our own position in relation to structures and dynamics of injustice of which we may not be aware ... as discourse about justice arises from listening' (Holscher and Bozalek, 2012: 1110).
- Taking into consideration the Constitution, the human rights perspective, the developmental social welfare approach, and the CA, policies should be framed in a respectful and just way of thinking to create contexts that are safe and secure, and in which freedoms can be facilitated.

## QUESTIONS

1. Define the concepts migrants, asylum seekers, refugees, displaced, and stateless people. Are you clear about the differences?
2. Provide a brief overview of the reasons for push and pull factors that lead to migration.
3. Describe the vulnerabilities experienced by migrants, refugees, displaced, and stateless people.
4. Critically discuss the human rights, developmental social welfare, and capability approaches as theoretical frameworks to understand the development of policies related to migrants, refugees, and displaced people.
5. Explain the criteria for transformative social welfare policies and how it can address the many needs of migrants in the South African context.
6. Choose an aspect such as education, health, social welfare, or social protection and explore the current status of service delivery to migrants.

## REFERENCES

ANDROFF, D (2015) *Practicing Rights: Human Rights based approaches to Social Work practice.* New York: Routledge New York.

BENNET, R, HOSEGOOD, V, NEWELL, ML & MCGRATH, N (2015) 'Understanding family migration in rural South Africa: Exploring children's inclusion in the destination households of migrant parents' *Population, space and place* 21(4): 310–321.

BLAAUW, P, PRETORIUS, A, SCHOEMAN, C & SCHENCK, R (2012) 'Explaining migrant wages: The case of Zimbabwean Day Labourers in South Africa' *International Business and Economics Research Journal* 11(12): 1333-1346.

BLAAUW, PF, SCHENCK, CJ, PRETORIUS, AM & SCHOEMAN, CH (2017) 'All quiet on the social work front: The social construct of Zimbabwean day labourers in South Africa' *International Social Work* 60(2): 351–365.

BLOCH, A (2008) *Gaps in protection: Undocumented Zimbabwean Migrants in South Africa.* Migration studies working paper series #38. Johannesburg: Forced Migration Studies Programme, University of the Witwatersrand.

BOL, AA (2009) *The Lost Boy*. Cape Town: Kwela Books.

CASALE, D & POSEL, D (2006) *Migration and Remittances in South Africa. Background document on migration*. Durban: University of KwaZulu-Natal.

COLLINSON, MA & KAHN, K (2006) *Highly prevalent circular migration: Households, mobility and economic status in rural South Africa*. Paper prepared for conference on African Migration in comparative perspective. Johannesburg, 4-7 June.

COLLINSON, MA, TOLLMAN, SM & KAHN, K (2007) 'Migration, settlement change and health in post apartheid South Africa: triangulating health and demographic surveillance with national census data' *Scandinavian Journal of Public Health* 35(69): 77-84.

CRUSH, J & WILLIAMS, V (2010) *Labour Migration Trends and Policies in Southern Africa* Policy Brief No. 23. Cape Town: Southern African Migration Programme.

CRUSH, J, CHIKANDA, A & SKINNER, C (eds.) (2015) *Mean Sreets: Migration, Xenophobia and Informality in South Africa*. Cape Town: Southern African Migration Programme (SAMP), African Centre for Cities, and International Development Research Centre.

DE BRAUW, A, MUELLER, V & LEE, HL (2014) *The role of rural-urban migration in the structural transformation of sub Saharan Africa*. World Development DOI:10.1016/J.worlddev.2013.10.013.

DEACON, B, OLIVIER, M & BEREMAURO, R (2015) 'Social Security and Social protection of migrants in South Africa and SADC' MIWORC [Online]. Available: http://www.miworc.org.za/docs/MiWORC-Report-8.pdf [3 July 2018].

FORCED MIGRATION STUDIES PROGRAMME (FMSP) (2009) *Zimbabwean migration to Southern Africa: New trends and responses*. Johannesburg: University of the Witwatersrand.

GREENPEACE (2017) 'Climate Change, migration and displacement: The underestimated disaster' [Online]. Greenpeace Hamburg, Germany. Available: https://www.greenpeace.de/sites/www.greenpeace.de/files/20170524-greenpeace-studie-climate-change-migration-displacement-engl.pdf [1 September 2017].

HOLSCHER D (2016) 'Subjectivities of survival: conceptualising just responses to displacement, cross border migration and structural violence in South Africa' *Social Work/MaatskaplikeWerk* 52(1): 54–72.

HOLSCHER, D & BOZALEK, VG (2012) 'Encountering the other across the divides: Re-grounding social justice as a guiding principle for social work with refugees and other vulnerable groups' *British Journal of Social Work* 42 at pp. 1093-1112.

IDEMUDIA, ES, WILLIAMS, JK & WYATT, GE (2013) 'Migration challenges among Zimbabwean refugees before, during and post arrival in South Africa' *Journal of injury and violence research* 5(1): 17-27.

INTERNATIONAL LABOUR ORGANISATION (ILO) (2016) 'World development social outlook: Trends for youth 2016' [Online]. Geneva. Available:http://www.ilo.org/global/research/global-reports/weso/2016/lang--ja/index.htm [31 August 2017].

INTERNATIONAL LABOUR ORGANISATION (ILO) (2017) 'World Social Protection report 2017–2019: Universal Social Protection to Achieve the Sustainable Development Goals' [Online]. Geneva. Available: http://www.ilo.org/wcmsp5/groups/public/---dgreports/---dcomm/---publ/documents/publication/wcms_604882.pdf [9 April 2018].

INTERNATIONAL ORGANISATION FOR MIGRATION (IOM) (2008) 'Migrants; need and vulnerabilities in the Limpopo province, Republic of South Africa' [Online]. Available: file:///C:/Users/Admin/Downloads/IOM%20Migrant%20Needs%20and%20Vulnerability%20Assessment_Phase%201.pdf [6 June 2017].

IOM (2009) 'Data assessment of labour migration statistics in the SADC region: South Africa, Zambia and Zimbabwe' [Online]. Available: file:///C:/Users/Admin/Downloads/LabourMigrationpublication.pdf [31 August 2017].

IOM (2012) *I am a Migrant too! Poetry book* [Online]. Available: file:///C:/Users/Admin/Downloads/Poetry_Book_WEB_v3.pdf [31 August 2017].

IOM (2013) (for South Africa) 'Migration for the benefit of all' [Online]. Available: file:///C:/Users/Admin/Downloads/IOM%20SA%20brochure%202013.pdf [31 August 2017].

IOM (2014) 'Regional strategy for Southern Africa 2014-2016' [Online]. Available: http://southafrica.iom.int/wp-content/uploads/2014/06/IOM-Regional-Strategy-for-Southern-Africa.pdf [5 October 2015].

KAVURO, C (2015) 'Refugees and Asylum seekers: Barriers to access South Africa's Labour Market' *Law, Democracy and Development* 19: 232–260.

KIWANUKA, M & MONSON, T (2009) *Zimbabwean immigration into Southern Africa: New trends and responses Report*. Johannesburg: Forced Migration Studies Programme, University of the Witwatersrand.

KORTEN, D (1990) *Getting into the 21st Century: Voluntary action and the global agenda*. West Hartford, Connecticut: Kumarian.

LANDAU, LB & SEGATTI, AWK (2009) *Human development impacts of migration: South Africa Case study*. Human development Research Paper 2009/5. Johannesburg: Forced Migration Studies Programme, University of Witwatersrand.

LANDAU, LB (2006) 'Protection and dignity in Johannesburg: Shortcomings of South Africa's Urban Refugee Policy' *Journal of Refugee Studies* 19(3): 308–327.

LAWYERS FOR HUMAN RIGHTS (LHR) (2015) 'Childhood statelessness in South Africa' [Online]. Available: http://www.lhr.org.za/sites/lhr.org.za/files/childhood_statelessness_in_south_africa.pdf [2 September 2017].

LURIE, MN & WILLIAMS, BG (2014) 'Migration and Health in Southern Africa: 100 years and still circulating' *Health Psychology and Behavioural Medicine* 2(1): 34-40.

MAKINA, D (2007) *Survey of profile of migrant Zimbabweans in South Africa: A pilot study*. Research report. Pretoria: University of South Africa.

MAKINA, D (2012) 'Migration and characteristics of remittance senders in South Africa' *International Migration*. DOI: 10.1111/j.1468-2435.2012.00746.x.

MAPHOSA, F (2005) *The impact of remittances from Zimbabweans working in South Africa on rural livelihoods in the Southern districts of Zimbabwe*. Forced migration studies working paper series #14. Johannesburg: Forced Migration Studies Programme, University of the Witwatersrand.

MASENDU, TV (2011) *An exploration of the social and economic experiences of Zimbabwean youth immigrants in Cape Town*. Cape Town: University of Cape Town (MA-thesis in Social Development).

MCDONALD, DA, MASHIKE, L & GOLDEN, C (1999) *The Lives and Times of African Migrants and Immigrants in Post-apartheid South Africa*. Migration Policy Series No. 13. Cape Town: Southern African Migration Project (SAMP).

MCDONALD, DA, ZINYAMA, L, GAY, J, DE VLETTER, F & MATTES, R (2000) 'Guess who is coming to dinner? Migration from Lesotho, Mozambique and Zimbabwe to South Africa' *International Migration Review* 34(3): 813-841.

MIDGLEY, J & SHERRADEN, M: 'The Social Development Perspective in Social Policy' in Midgley, J & Livermore, M (eds.) (2009) *The Handbook of Social Policy* at pp. 279–294. Thousand Oaks, California; London, UK; New Delhi; Singapore: Sage Publications Inc.

MKWANANZI, WF (2017) *Exploring the lives and educational aspirations of marginalised migrant youth: A case study in Johannesburg South Africa*. Johannesburg: University of Johannesburg (PhD-thesis in Development studies).

MPEDI, LG & ROSS, F: 'The reception, accommodation and general protection of refugees in the Republic of South Africa' in Frey, C & Lutz, R (eds.) (213) *Social Work of the South* Vol. IV *Sozialarbeit des Suedens. Band 4 – Flucht und Fluechtlingslager* at pp. 201–213. Erfurt University of Applied Sciences, Oldenburg: Paulo Freire Verlag.

NEFF, DF (2007) 'Subjective well-being, poverty and ethnicity in South Africa: Insights from an exploratory analysis' *Social Indicators Research* Vol. 80: 313–341.

OKELLO-WENGI, S (2004) *Analysing the support systems in Southern Africa: The case of Botswana*. Pretoria: University of South Africa (Unpublished DPhil-thesis).

PERTSOVSKY, N (2017) 'Asylum seekers will have to live near borders if Home Affairs has its way' [Online]. Available: https://www.dailymaverick.co.za/article/2017-07-25-groundup-asylum-seekers-will-have-to-live-near-borders-if-home-affairs-has-its-way/ [25 July 2017].

POSEL, D (2001) 'How do households work? Migration, the household and remittance behaviour in South Africa' *Social Dynamics* 27(1): 165-189.

POSEL, D (2004) 'Have migration patterns in post-apartheid South Africa changed?' *Journal of Interdisciplinary Economics* 15(3-4): 277-292.

POSEL, D, FAIRBURN, JA & LUND, F (2004) *Labour migration and households: A reconsideration of the effects of the social pension on labour supply in South Africa*. African Development and Poverty Reduction: The Macro-Micro linkage Forum Paper at pp. 13-15.

ROESTENBURG, W: 'The life circumstances of refugees at the Central Methodist Church (CMC) in Johannesburg' in Frey, C & Lutz, R (eds.) (2013) *Social Work of the South* Vol. IV *Sozialarbeit des Suedens. Band 4 – Flucht und Fluechtlingslager* at pp. 252–270. Erfurt University of Applied Sciences, Oldenburg: Paulo Freire Verlag.

SCHIER, ML, ENGSTROM, S & GRAHAM, JR (2011) 'International migration and social work: A review of literature' *Journal of immigration and refugee studies* 9: 38-56.

SEN, A (1999) *Development as freedom*. Oxford: Oxford University Press.

SMITH, M (in process) *Social Justice vulnerabilities and marginalised communities: A case study of Day Labourers in Mbekweni*. Survey data.

SOUTH AFRICA. 1950. *Group areas Act No 41 of 1950*. Pretoria: Government Printer. [Laws.]

SOUTH AFRICA. 1991. *Aliens Control Act No 96 of 1991*. Pretoria: Government Printer. [Laws.]

SOUTH AFRICA. 1996. *Constitution of the Republic of South Africa Act No 108 of 1996*. Pretoria: Government Printer. [Laws.]

SOUTH AFRICA. 1997. *White Paper for Social Welfare 1997*. Pretoria: Government Printer.

SOUTH AFRICA. 1998. *Refugees Act No 130 of 1998*. Pretoria: Government Printer. [Laws.]

SOUTH AFRICA. 2002. *Immigration Act No 13 of 2002*. Pretoria: Government Printer. [Laws.]

SOUTH AFRICA. 2004. Social Assistance Act 13 of 2004. Pretoria: Government Printer [Laws}

SOUTH AFRICA. 2005. *Children's Act No 38 of 2005*. Pretoria: Government Printer. [Laws.]

SOUTH AFRICA. Department of Health (2011) *National Health Insurance in South Africa*. Policy Paper. Pretoria: Department of Health.

SOUTH AFRICA. Department of Planning, Monitoring and Evaluation (2017) *Policy options for extending social protection to informal workers in South Africa: An issue paper for the National Planning Commission*. Pretoria: United Nations Development Programme.

SOUTH AFRICA. Department of Social Development (DSD) (2016) 'Comprehensive Report on the Review of the White Paper for Social Welfare, 1997' [Online]. Available: http://www.gov.za/sites/www.gov.za/files/Comprehensive%20Report%20White%20Paper_.pdf.

SOUTH AFRICA. Department of the Presidency. National Planning Commission (2012) *National Development Plan 2030 Our Future-make it work* [Online]. Available: https://www.brandsouthafrica.com/wp_download_viewer.php?file=wp-content/uploads/brandsa/2015/05/02_NDP_in_full.pdf [15 August 2017].

SOUTH AFRICA. South African Social Security Agency (SASSA) (2013) *Social assistance for refugees*. Pretoria: SASSA.

STATISTICS SOUTH AFRICA (Stats SA) 2018 [Online]. Available: http://www.statssa.gov.za/?s=unemployment+rate&sitem=content.

SWART, I & VENTER, D (2000) 'Challenge of fourth generation people centred development strategies' *Scriptura* 75: 449–464.

THEODORE, N, BLAAUW, D & SCHENCK, C (2017) *Migrant day labourers in South Africa: Worker centres and the regulation of informality.* Conference paper prepared for Migrating out of poverty conference. London, March 2017.

THEODORE, N, PRETORIUS, A, BLAAUW, D & SCHENCK, C (2017) 'Informality and the context of reception in South Africa's new Immigrant Destination' *Population, Place and Society* DOI:10.1002/psp2119.

TRIEGAARDT, JD: 'Policies and Institutional responses to refugees and migrants in South Africa' in Frey, C & Lutz, R (eds.) (2013) *Social Work of the South* Vol. IV *Sozialarbeit des Suedens. Band 4 - Flucht und Fluechtlingslager* at pp. 323-334. Erfurt University of Applied Sciences, Oldenburg: Paulo Freire Verlag.

UNITED NATIONS HIGH COMMISSIONER FOR REFUGEES (UNHCR) (2003) 'Ending statelessness' [Online]. Available: http://www.unhcr.org/stateless-people.html [31 August 2017].

UNITED NATIONS HIGH COMMISSIONER FOR REFUGEES (UNHCR) 'Guiding Principles on Internal Displacement', 22 July 1998, ADM 1.1, PRL 12.1, PR00/98/109 [Online]. Available: http://www.refworld.org/docid/3c3da07f7.html [14 August 2017].

WADE, B & SCHENCK, CJ (2012) 'Trauma is the "stealing of my sense of being me": A person-centred perspective on trauma' *Social Work/MaatskaplikeWerk* 48(3): 340-355.

# Glossary

**asylum seekers:** persons seeking protection as refugees, who have applied for such protection and are awaiting the official decision of their status.

**internally displaced persons (IDPs):** they have not crossed an international border to find sanctuary but have remained inside their home countries with little or no protection.

**migrants:** people who live and work outside of the areas or countries from which they originate.

**refugees:** defined as people who have fled their country of residence and crossed an international border because their lives, safety or freedom have been threatened by generalised violence, foreign aggression, internal conflicts, massive violation of human rights, or other circumstances which have seriously disturbed public order (Article III (3) of the Cartagena Declaration).

# PART 03

# Making social welfare policy

## CHAPTER 09

# Policy analysis and formulation: using a human rights approach

*Viviene Taylor and Jean D Triegaardt*

Policy formulation and analysis as part of the professional discipline of social policy has gained increasing attention in Africa in the last two decades. By 2008, the African Union (AU) had formalised a Social Policy Framework for Africa (www.au.int) that was agreed to by more than 50 member states. Chapter 9 of this book provides some insight into policy analysis and policy formulation within a human rights approach. The objectives and outcomes for this chapter are listed below.

## Objectives

✓ Equipping students of social welfare policy and policymakers within and outside of the state to better understand the processes of social welfare policy and law-making.

✓ Providing students with the knowledge of how to use a human rights approach in analysing and formulating social welfare policy.

✓ Providing an understanding of how an issue, need, right, or social problem is identified, researched, and analysed.

✓ Provide an understanding of the state-civil society relationship.

## Outcomes

✓ Understanding the processes of social welfare policy and law-making.

✓ Acquiring the knowledge of utilising a human rights approach in the analysis and formulation of social welfare policy.

✓ Understanding how to identify, research, and analyse an issue, right or social problem.

✓ Gaining knowledge of the state-civil society relationship.

## 9.1 Introduction

Analysing and formulating policies and laws as guidelines for government and non-governmental action and delivery of services are now part of an accepted tradition in administrations. It has also become an important process through which state and non-state actors can be held accountable for delivering or not delivering on the social and economic rights and needs of people. Contemporary processes highlight that social welfare policy is determined by political and economic agendas in the real world. For example, the impetus to focus on the formulation and analysis of social policies in Africa was reinforced by the social and economic context of increasing poverty, unemployment and growing inequalities. The Social Policy Framework for Africa, developed by the AU, together with other national and international policy guidelines accelerated the move towards a professional disciplinary approach to social welfare policy analysis and formulation.

The next section provides an overview of the conceptual and theoretical issues that inform frameworks for social welfare policy analysis and formulation.

## 9.2 Conceptual and theoretical issues in policy analysis and formulation

Social policy, and particularly social welfare policy, is not just a technical process. Policy choices and decisions about what needs, rights and issues should be addressed and how these should be addressed are based on value judgements and normative standards that policymakers and professionals use to guide them. As noted in Chapter 3, values, norms and standards have their basis in ideological and theoretical perspectives that people have about societies and the roles and responsibilities of individuals, families, states, and non-state actors (such as the private business sector and religious institutions) in ensuring the well-being of all members of society.

The assumption made by social policy professionals is that social welfare policy analysis and formulation are undertaken to ensure that public interests (which means the well-being and interests of all citizens in a country are taken into consideration by decision makers so that collectively their interests and needs are addressed) are protected. Such assumptions can be a point of contestation since the formulation of policies and analysis of such policies reflect a number of different publics (men and women, older persons, people with disabilities, business interests, religious institutions, traditional sectors, etc.) and the values and beliefs they have vary. Take, for example, policies and legislation on abortion and reproductive health and rights. Theorising from a progressive and rights-based approach promotes the rights of women to have control over their bodies and their rights to bodily integrity and protection. Theorising from a conservative value base one could argue that the right to make choices related to an unborn foetus links with the right to life and that it is morally wrong to sanction abortion as a policy and law. Opposing value judgements on what would be in the best interests of society as a whole in such contexts requires an understanding of how theories, values and judgements of people, especially policymakers, influence policy analysis and formulation.

Theories and conceptual values that influence policy analysis are as varied as the ideologies they represent and are derived from philosophical, sociological, political science, and social administration disciplines. In the real world context policy analysis and formulation are complex, and the factors that influence how existing policies are analysed or new policies are formulated include beliefs, values, theories, class location, gender, race, ethnicity, religious and political affiliation, and subjective experiences. According to Gil (1992: xix), 'policy analysis is not expected to provide definite answers to moral and value dilemmas'. It can be confusing for students and policymakers to know how to proceed to determine what to do when there are multiple issues and needs to be addressed, and there are as many theories and value judgements about these issues and needs. Gil clarifies how to engage in policy analysis within such contexts and asserts that:

> 'An effective analytic approach should, however, enable analysts to identify aspects of social policy issues which require moral and value choices, and to distinguish these from other aspects which can be decided on the basis of factual information' (Gil, 1992: xix).

This statement highlights why value judgements based on morality should be distinct from factual data and why policy analysts need to use demographic and social indicators to analyse issues, needs, and rights.

Theoretical influences in social welfare policy analysis are evident in the principles that inform and guide the processes of analysis and formulation. The principles of social equality and of equity are considered central in addressing social justice and issues of redistribution when it comes to poverty, inequalities, and multiple deprivations. Analysing contributions of other theorists, Gil (1992) sees social equality as an organising principle in policy analysis and argues strongly that it ought to shape the quality of life and circumstances of individuals and groups and ought to be the basis for structuring human relations in society. Social equality as a principle for social welfare policy analysis implies that 'all individuals should have the right to freely actualise their inherent human potential' and 'be free of exploitation, alienation and oppression' as long as individual and group rights do not undermine the identical rights of other individuals and groups (Gil, 1992: xxi). When existing policies and legislation serve to subordinate the needs and interests of a majority of people or a group of people and privilege a minority over the majority, it can be argued that such policies are based on value judgements that are unequal and unjust.

The fulfilment of human needs to ensure that there are improvements in the quality of life of all people – not just those born into inherited wealth and assets or who benefit from an accumulation of privilege through unjust policies and laws (Sen, 1982) – has been emphasised in theories and conceptual frameworks for policy analysis (Gil, 1992; Sen, 1982; Taylor-Gooby, 1991). Theories on the interrelatedness of basic human needs and other essential aspects of human well-being also influence how policies are analysed and formulated. Policies can be analysed from a very narrow perspective by only focusing on whether the goals and impact achieve the fulfilment of basic needs. Alternatively, policy analysis can examine whether the basic human needs that are being achieved include those that are biological and material, social and psychological, productive (work) and creative, and spiritual, as well as the need for self-actualisation (Gil, 1992: 16–17). Analysis of social welfare policies from this perspective provides a more comprehensive lens of human well-being and focuses on how policies include the full range of human needs to ensure the preservation of human life, the security of people, and the harmonisation of human beings with the environment. This view of the fulfilment of all human needs integrates social and economic needs with environmental concerns.

Theoretical influences in how social welfare policies can be analysed and formulated from a perspective that integrates the fulfilment of social and economic needs are evident in discourses on human development and human rights (Sen, 1999). These discourses recognise that unmet needs are not outcomes of individual weakness or failure but rather reflect failures of existing social policies and institutions that do not recognise how people's human rights are being violated. South Africa's pre-1994 social welfare policy regime under the undemocratic apartheid government illustrates how social welfare policies can be used to discriminate and undermine the human development of people. This example lends credence to Gil's (1992) compelling theoretical argument that formulating new social policies to solve perceived social problems should be preceded by thorough analysis of existing policies and the institutional processes because the roots of such problems could be with existing policies.

Critical analysis of existing and past policies and formulation of new policies based on such analysis can help to eliminate and prevent violations of rights. Policy analysis can contribute to transformation when policy professionals take a comprehensive view of the politics, the economics, and the social context within which people live to understand the conditions that prevent them from meeting the people's needs. Such critical analysis of existing policies and institutions can lead to the formulation of new policies to overcome inequalities in control over resources, access to decent waged work, access to education and health care, social welfare services, and human rights. Chapter 1 of this book provides, in Figure 1.2, a way of bringing all aspects that influence people's well-being together so that a critical and transformative approach can be taken to policy analysis and formulation.

The next section provides a more detailed discussion of how a human rights approach to policy analysis and formulation influence transformation and draw on South Africa as an example.

## 9.3 A human rights approach to analysing and formulating social welfare policy

Approaches to analysis and formulation of policy can be narrow by focusing only on a particular condition or need without linking this to other areas of life. Usually this approach is termed 'welfarist' because the analysis that leads to reforming and amending the policy and actions are ameliorative. A comprehensive and integrative approach taken to analysing and formulating social welfare policy has its basis in human rights and aligns with international conventions that set standards for social and economic rights. Such an approach to policy analysis and formulation is more likely to achieve change in social relations and the redistribution of resources so that the principles of equality and equity are achieved. Policy analysis using a human rights approach would assess existing policies and establish new policies within a developmental and preventive approach to human well-being. According to Gabel, a rights-based approach is based on a vision of what our society should be and orients our actions toward reaching normative standards. Whereas a needs-based approach focuses on securing additional resources for groups deemed vulnerable, a rights-based approach incorporates the needs-based approach and calls for existing resources to be shared more equally by placing values and participation at the very heart of the approach (Gabel, 2014: 293–294). Importantly, this point clarifies the links between human needs and human rights. Addressing human needs through social welfare policy is thus not inconsistent with a human rights approach as long as addressing such needs do not violate the rights and entitlements of others (refer to Figure 1.2 in Chapter 1).

In Africa, especially in countries that are constitutional democracies, it is possible and necessary to analyse and formulate social welfare laws and policy using a human rights approach, and to assess such policies against normative standards for the achievement of socially just and equitable outcomes within the national context and in accordance with international human rights instruments. A rights-based approach to social welfare policy is thus **normatively** based on international human rights and standards and **operationally** directed to promoting and protecting the human rights of people. When a human rights approach is used to formulate social welfare policy, the norms, standards and principles of the international human rights system are used to set the standard to be achieved and integrated into policies, pieces of legislation and processes of development.

The Universal Declaration of Human Rights (United Nations, 1948) and the specific articles relevant to social and economic rights (such as Articles 22, 23 and 25) provide a sound basis from which policy professionals can engage with multiple stakeholders or interest groups to discuss how to assess existing policies and formulate new policies. These articles are spelt out in the section below to provide a clear understanding of the norms and guidelines they establish for the social welfare and development of people.

Article 22 states that:

> 'Everyone , as a member of society, has the right to social security and is entitled to its' realization, through national effort and international cooperation and in accordance with the organisation and resources of each State, of the economic, social and cultural rights indispensable for his (sic) dignity and the free development of his (sic) personality.'

Article 23 states that:

> '1. Everyone has the right to work, to free choice of employment, to just and favourable conditions of work and to protection against unemployment.
> 2. Everyone, without any discrimination, has the right to equal pay for equal work.
> 3. Everyone who works has the right to just and favourable remuneration ensuring for himself and his family an existence worthy of human dignity & supplemented, if necessary by other means of social protection.
> 4. Everyone has the right to form and to join trade unions for the protection of his (sic) interests.'

Article 25 states that:

> 'Everyone has the right to a standard of living adequate for the health and well-being of himself and of his family, including food, clothing, housing and medical care and necessary social services and the right to security in the event of unemployment, sickness, disability, widowhood, old age or other lack of livelihood in circumstances beyond his control' (United Nations, 1948, General Assembly, 10 (12)).

Using such articles, it is possible for policy professionals to assess whether national social welfare policies:

- Provide an express linkage to people's rights and entitlements in the standards set for meeting a human a need or to prevent the violation of a right.
- Ensures attention to the needs and rights of vulnerable groups and prevents their exposure to risk.
- Focus on who is accountable and responsible for providing the needs and protecting and promoting access to the rights specified in the policy.
- Address the redistribution of resources to those whose rights were violated and who were discriminated against.
- Establish institutional arrangements for the empowerment and participation of citizens in monitoring the implementation and review of the specific policy.
- Links the achievement of social and economic needs and rights in implementing the provisions and rights.

Rights-based approaches are comprehensive in considering the full range of indivisible, interdependent and interrelated rights: civil; cultural; economic; political; and social. Social welfare policies that are framed within a rights-based approach should mirror internationally guaranteed rights and cover, for example, health care, education, social protection (including social welfare services), and social insurance. The objectives of social welfare policy provision in terms of particular rights should thus be legally enforceable. When analysing or formulating social welfare policy from a human rights perspective, it is necessary to examine the duties and obligations on states, citizens and non-state institutions and actors in realising and implementing the policy. If social welfare policies and laws do not include expressions of normative links to international, regional and national human rights instruments where these exist, then policy professionals identify the gaps and address these in their analysis and formulation of new policies. A rights-based approach to social welfare is not compatible with policies, projects or activities that violate people's rights and that trade off human rights against economic development.

South Africa's Constitution (RSA, 1996), for example, is framed within a human rights approach and gives special protection to certain fundamental rights. The Constitution contains a Bill of Rights that addresses both civil and political rights as well as socioeconomic rights. No reference is made in the Bill of Rights to the traditional division between first, second and third generation rights. Social and economic rights have exactly the same status as civil and political rights in South Africa. Traditionally, a distinction has been made between first (civil and political), second (socioeconomic) and third generation rights. The United Nations (1948), for example, made a distinction between first, second and third generation rights by introducing two separate Covenants. The first Covenant contains only first-generation rights and the second Covenant contains second and third generation rights. Underlying the decision to draft two separate Covenants was the assumption that second and third generation rights imply legal obligations and enforcement that differs substantially from first generation rights. However, South Africa's Constitution (RSA, Act 108 of 1996) gives the same constitutional status to social and economic rights as civil and political rights and places emphasis on the fact that these rights are interrelated, interdependent and indivisible.

The interrelatedness of social and economic rights was emphasised by the Constitutional Court (CC) in South Africa. The Constitutional Court has made it clear that realising a particular socioeconomic right, such as the right to access housing, would require that other elements which do at times form the basis of other socioeconomic rights, such as access to land, must be in place as well (*Government of the Republic of South Africa and Others v Grootboom and Others* 2000 11 BCLR 1169 (CC)). In the *Grootboom* judgement, South Africa's Constitutional Court not only identified which rights of the community were being violated in relation to the Constitution but also showed how the particular right to housing was affected by the right to access to land. The recognition by the Court that these rights are mutually supportive and have a significant impact on the dignity of people and their quality of life was ground breaking in delivering social justice for poor communities. However, recognising that the South African government does not have the resources to deliver the rights immediately, the Court ruled that the government had to develop a programme to ensure the progressive realisation of the right to housing within a reasonable time frame and within its resources. These examples are vitally important because it provides policy professionals with actual rulings that can influence future policy direction for example on other rights and needs.

Another example of how rights and entitlements in constitutions framed within human rights can be used for policy analysis and formulation is in the area of social security or, as is recently conceptualised, social protection policies. Policies on social security or social protection are a socioeconomic right both in international conventions and the Universal Declaration of Human Rights (UN, 1948). The constitutional entrenchment of social security rights has significantly strengthened the mandate of the state to provide comprehensive social protection. The South African Constitution introduces in Chapter 2, which is The Bill of Rights, a constitutional imperative whereby the government is compelled to ensure the 'progressive realisation' of the right to access social security. The Constitutional Court has the power to ensure that these rights are given effect in a way that does not undermine the well-being of the people they are intended to help. Any analysis or formulation of policies and legislation with regard to social welfare provision should determine the content of each of the rights contained in the Constitution and assess whether these are given effect to through the policy or legislation.

It is thus important for policy professionals to understand the implications of judgements made in the Constitutional Court to better analyse the content of policies and legislation and whether they are interpreted to give effect to the access to rights. Further, policy analysts learn from international human rights instruments and national constitutional judgements how to assess and ensure the institutional arrangements are in place and conditions under which these rights are expected to be enforced do not undermine the dignity of people. In the area of social protection (social grants and social benefits) the Constitutional Court in South Africa is playing a strong role in holding the government to account for the delivery and administration of social grants. When analysing or drafting social welfare policy, therefore, it is imperative to reflect on these trends and developments, as they undoubtedly influence the future direction of social welfare policymaking, regulation, and practice.

Applying a human rights approach in the analysis and formulation of social welfare policies should be guided by principles such as equality, equity, redistribution, social solidarity, access, adequacy, responsiveness, transparency, and accountability. Analysing social welfare policies to assess the principles of equality means that one is looking at whether the benefits and services to address need and rights apply equally to all who, according to the demographic and other data, qualify for such services and benefits. Equity, as a principle, recognises that not all citizens have the same starting points and their needs and rights are not equally guaranteed or accessed because of this. For example, persons with disabilities are not able to access the benefits that people without disabilities can access. Similarly, people living in chronic poverty, who are deprived of education and health care as well as waged work, may be unable to access services and benefits from the state. Applying the principle of equity in these instances would require that a policy analyst identify and specify the requirements that would address the particular disadvantage or deprivation.

The principle of redistribution is particularly significant in situations of great social inequalities and in situations that seek to address disparities related to income, race, gender, age, geographic location, and others. Assessing how this principle is reflected in a policy or could be introduced in a new policy would require one to have an understanding of how existing resources and ownership of goods and services are distributed and to identify who is left out of this distribution. It would then be necessary to analyse the means through which redistribution can be effected and the processes that would be used to do this. Applying redistribution as a principle also implies that a country and government accepts, either through its constitution or other forms of agreements (social contracts), the principle of social solidarity or *Ubuntu* (people are people through their relations with and in service of other people). Social solidarity as a principle in policies means that governments seek to ensure the interests of all people are secured through distributive measures that result in benefits (social, economic, political, and cultural) for all. The direct benefits may not be the same for all but the outcomes lead to social cohesion and nation-building by ensuring fairness, for example, in tax systems, in social services, and in other areas.

Principles of access, adequacy, responsiveness, transparency, and accountability are usually analysed against the actual provisions in the social welfare policies. They relate to who has access to the benefit or service and under what conditions, whether the arrangements for access are appropriate and fair, and whether the actual provision is adequate to meet the needs and ensure the rights of those for whom the service and benefit is designed. Principles of transparency and accountability relate to the duties and responsibilities of those who are delivering the benefits, rights, and needs, and also to those who are receiving them. Analysis of social welfare policies against these principles will ensure that existing policies and newly formulated policies are transformed in the interests of all in a particular country.

It is very difficult to analyse and formulate policies in a country without understanding the formal institutional spaces within which these policies are approved and adopted, and the government departments that are mandated to implement them. A policy is formal when it has usually been approved through a parliamentary process. As part of the analysis and formulation of policies, policy professionals should know how to engage in parliamentary processes by using evidence and research analysis to influence policymakers regarding the changes that should be made.The next section therefore provides a discussion on the role of parliament in the process of making policy and legislation and uses the South African parliamentary processes as an example.

## 9.4 The role of parliament in making policy and legislation

South Africa is a constitutional democracy in which the national Parliament and its committees play a central role in making and influencing policy and legislation. This section therefore focuses on the formal institutional space of Parliament and the role of civil society formations in making policy and influencing legislation in social welfare. The two Houses of Parliament – the National Assembly (NA) and the National Council of Provinces (NCOP) – have distinct functions. The role of the National Assembly is to ensure direct representation of the people in the country in parliamentary processes, especially those related to policy and legislative processes and monitoring of the implementation of policies and legislation. This is achieved through the national legislative process and by providing a national forum for raising issues and exercising oversight of the executive arm of government (Cabinet and officials in government). The NCOP's role is limited to representing provincial interests at national level. It does this by participating in the national legislative process and providing a national forum for public consideration of issues affecting provinces.

The Constitution gives parliamentary committees considerable powers. National Assembly committees may initiate and prepare legislation. They must also maintain political oversight of the national executive. This includes monitoring the implementation of legislation and ensuring that all executive organs of state are accountable to Parliament for their actions. The 9th edition of the Rules of the National Assembly contains comprehensively revised rules of the National Assembly (Parliament of RSA, 2016) that provide additional powers to its committees. These include the ability to:

> *'monitor, investigate, enquire into, and make recommendations relating*
> *to any aspect of the legislative programme, budget, rationalisation,*
> *restructuring, functioning, organisation, structure, personnel, policy*

*formulation or any other matter it may consider relevant, [to] government
department or departments falling within the category of affairs consigned
to the committee.'*

It is clear that parliamentarians do have the power to review and amend policy based on
investigations. This implies that parliamentarians are required to take a rational approach
to policy and legislative analysis and formulation. Investigation and analysis of legislation
and policy requires knowledge of demographic data, trend analysis of development and
poverty indicators, and related research (refer to Chapters 5 and 6).

### 9.4.1 The parliamentary committee system: representing multiple publics in policymaking

Prior to 1994, the majority of people (especially black) were not aware of how the apartheid
state functioned and the role of parliament in policymaking. Access to information and
participation in policymaking and legislative processes by the majority were not allowed
because the apartheid state did not allow any questioning by black people of the policy
choices made and how these were to be implemented. Parliament and its committees, at
the time, simply endorsed the Executive (Cabinet) decisions of the apartheid regime. The
new democratic dispensation post 1994, and the adoption of the final Constitution in 1996,
transformed the role of Parliament through a system of committees. It expanded the role of
committees and clearly articulated and established committees and the rules according to
which they would operate.

Parliamentary committees are considered as the formal institutional spaces within which
the executive (Ministers and officials) report on the implementation of policies and account
for the delivery or lack of delivery of services. This is the space within which members of the
public can also hold the Executive to account and can make representation on any changes to
policies, legislation, and programmes that would be in the public interest. The Constitution
ensures that parliamentary committees have considerable powers. National Assembly
committees may initiate and prepare legislation. They must also maintain political oversight
of the national Executive. This includes monitoring the implementation of legislation and
ensuring that all executive organs of state are accountable to Parliament for their actions.
NCOP committees may initiate or prepare certain types of legislation affecting provinces but
the NCOP has no oversight function. However, committees of both Houses have the power
to summon people to give evidence or to produce documents. They may ask any person or
institution to report to them on specific matters and receive petitions, representations or
submissions from any interested people or institutions. Party political representation on the
committees is proportional to the number of seats each party has in Parliament.

Many committees (Health, Education, Housing, Labour, etc.) interact in the social welfare
arena and their work overlaps with one another when it comes to social and economic
conditions affecting people's human development. However, it is the Portfolio Committee on
Social Development that is the main committee in the National Assembly and in the NCOP; it
is the Social Services Select Committee that has the responsibility for policies and legislation
related to social welfare and for oversight of its implementation. The Portfolio Committee on
Social Development's mandate is to approve and monitor the implementation of policy and
legislation related to social welfare, social security, and social protection measures. South
Africans – who were formerly denied the political and economic power to make decisions
affecting their lives – are now given the formal space provided through these committees

to contribute to policy and lawmaking on critical issues, rights, and needs affecting their human development.

Using democratically established institutional policy spaces to promote wider participation in crafting policy and legislation is important. The next section focuses on civil society's roles in making representation to or being summoned by parliamentary committees of both Houses on matters relevant to the policy.

## 9.4.2 The influence of civil society formations on policymaking and legislation

Post 1994, members of organised civil society formations have taken a keen interest in social welfare policy issues and the decisions which directly advance the interests of the members or communities they serve. During the apartheid era progressive organisations of civil society mobilised against the undemocratic apartheid government, which are discussed in greater detail in Chapter 10. Chapter 11 also discusses how the professional roles of social workers increasingly require them to implement policies and advocate for changes to existing policies. South Africa's experiences as well as evidence from elsewhere highlight the significance of civil society in contributing to an effective and democratic system of governance and ensuring links between policy intentions and outcomes. Carroll and Carroll (2004: 338) highlight the following four ways in which civil society adds value to policymaking and processes of democracy:

- First, it personifies the value of civility, allowing for political debate and disagreement without resorting to coercion or violence.
- Second, it provides the space for partial autonomy from the state within which individuals and groups can pursue personal and collective interests.
- Third, it assists in making the state accountable to the people.
- And lastly, it provides a forum for input into policy issues by the public.

These four points illustrate that the state-civil society relationship provides a forum and/or space for negotiation and reciprocity, which means that accountability becomes a key ingredient or requisite for the analysis and evaluation of policies. In the early days of democratic governance in South Africa, organisations involved in resisting the former apartheid state wrestled with their raison d'être, and sought to find a political identity and space free of party politics. As Seekings (2006: 323) noted, organisations that sought to redefine their political roles from the position of representing civil society included civic organisations, trade unions, the non-governmental development sector, and the media. Chapters 1, 4, 10 and 11 provide insights on the role of civil society during the apartheid era.

Two other countries on the continent developed a vibrant civil society. Both Botswana and Mauritius developed an active civil society in the 90s. Various civil society organisations in Mauritius meet regularly with the representatives of the state, both individually and in broad consultative meetings. Therefore, collectively, they ensure that the government is informed regularly about the concerns of most sectors of the society (Carroll and Carroll, 2004: 336). Government policy changes from time to time to accommodate the concerns raised by civil society organisations.

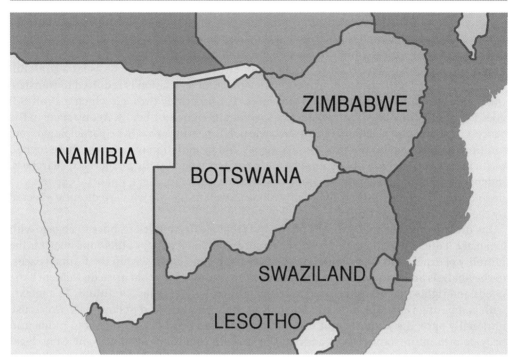

NGOs, for example, the Botswana Centre for Human Rights, are involved in raising public awareness and campaigning for changes in legislation and policies

In Botswana, towards the late 1990s, the general feeling was that there were hundreds of indigenous non-governmental organisations (NGOs). These NGOs had either indirect or direct contact with the state. Business groups, women's organisations, environmental groups, and developmental agencies were among the NGOs that had become particularly influential (Carroll and Carroll, 2004: 334). Business organisations assisted to lead the way in involving civil society in the policy process in Botswana. The government contracted with external organisations to draft policies in various fields, and the official policies that followed reflected much of the outside organisation's input. By the late 1990s, there was a feeling that interaction between the state and civil society was becoming an effective and integral part of the Botswana system of governance. The National Democratic Plan which was published in 2003, makes reference to the roles of NGOs or civil society in making and implementing policies, and acknowledges that NGOs and the private sector are key players in the development process (Botswana, 2003: 266).

Policymakers and legislators interact with representatives from civil society within and outside of Parliament. Drawing on experiences within the South African Parliament, Figure 9.1 below spells out the key steps in the policymaking and legislative process in South Africa. The process involves different stages through which data and evidence are used to identify policy issues that should be addressed before being drafted into discussion documents for the attention of Portfolio Committees. Initially discussion documents are called Green Papers and it is during the Green Paper stage that Parliament engages with civil society organisations, with researchers, policy analysts, and other interest groups for policy analysis and inputs. Parliamentary committees can convene public hearings on Green Papers to assess whether there is agreement on the issue, need or right that is the focus of the Green Paper.

Thereafter a White Paper is drafted and this is also subject to debate and discussion within Parliament before it is published in the *Government Gazette* for final inputs from the public at large. At various points in the process, public participation is required as shown in Figure 9.1. A White Paper becomes a policy framework and can be the basis for a Draft Bill and legislation if Parliament and government agree that legislation is required to translate the policy into practical programme measures. The processes through which a Draft Bill goes before it is translated into an Act are spelt out in Figure 9.1 below. At any stage in the process, parliamentary committees can convene public hearings and invite participation from multiple stakeholders in the process of analysis and formulation of policies. These invited participants can include policy analysts, economists, social policy experts, researchers, independent think tanks, practitioners, statisticians, demographers, financial experts and people from business, non-profit organisations as well as people who are directly affected by the condition, need or right.

The diverse range of policy views and analysis that parliamentarians have to engage with can make it difficult for them to develop coherent and rational policy options and choices. The plurality of expert and experiential perspectives that contribute, within the formal spaces, to the analysis and formulation of policies and the contestations that arise do influence the needs and rights that are prioritised, who benefits and under what conditions. In contexts with competing value judgements and analysis, policymakers and policy analysts can use nationally agreed standards and international human rights instruments to guide and provide minimum standards to address the specific condition, need or right. State legal advisors assist in translating the policy intentions in White Papers and Draft Bills into Acts and in this process some of the intentions of the policy can become diffused or lost in administrative and regulatory processes. Policy analysts monitor and evaluate and provide feedback to policymakers on amendments that can improve legislation to transform social welfare processes and outcomes.

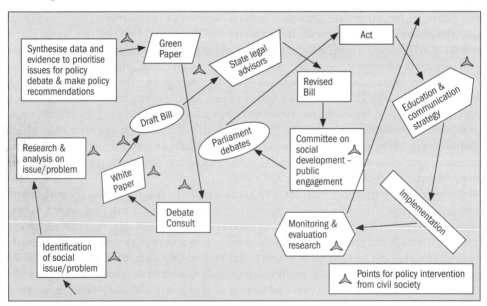

Source: Adapted from Friedman 1996 as cited by Taylor, 1997: 219

Figure 9.1 Key steps in the policymaking and legislative process in South Africa

The next section provides a framework (Taylor, 2002) that can be used by policy professionals to analyse and formulate social welfare policies using a transformative approach.

# 9.5 A framework for social welfare policy analysis and formulation

Social welfare policies are framed within particular contexts and these sociopolitical and economic contexts are reciprocal. Many frameworks for policy analysis and formulation are available and have been designed by social policy experts over the years (Hogwood and Gunn, 1984; Gilbert and Specht, 1986; Gil, 1992; Taylor, 2002). Frameworks can be very detailed and technical and, at times, require a level of interdisciplinary knowledge that is not easily available when policy recommendations are required. Generally, all frameworks include a set of core policy activities that should take place as part of analysis and formulation of policies. Frameworks provide a set of guidelines on what activities should be undertaken at different stages in the policy analysis process. Drawing on experience from policy analysis processes in South Africa and on the continent of Africa, Taylor (2002) provides a framework that maps the key activities and stages involved in policy analysis and formulation. This framework in Figure 9.2 below is an abbreviated version of Figure 1.2 in Chapter 1 that also provides a guideline for transformative policy change aligned to constitutional and human rights instruments. This section provides some practical guidelines on how to apply the framework in Figure 9.2.

## 9.5.1 Analysing the context and using evidence

Firstly, a policy analyst, using a political economy perspective and a human rights approach, would provide a critical analysis of the historical, political and economic context in which the condition, issue or right has developed (as shown in the first box on the left of Figure 9.2).

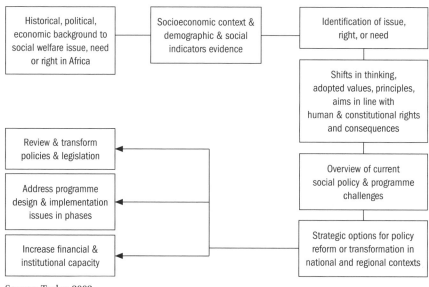

Source: Taylor, 2002

**Figure 9.2 Conceptual framework for the analysis and formulation of policy**

After mapping the history, the politics and the economic contexts that caused or influenced the condition, need, or right, a descriptive analysis should be written on the linkages among the political and economic contexts and the politics that influenced decisions and choices related to the condition, need or right.

Secondly, the social and economic context that influences the need, the condition and right should be analysed. Drawing on demographic data and relevant research (refer to Chapters 5 and 6 of this book), the policy analyst builds up an analysis on what needs to be addressed, whose needs should be prioritised, and under what conditions (refer to the middle box in Figure 9. 2). A set of questions is indicated below to assist policy analysts in building a comprehensive picture based on research evidence for the attention of policymakers and legislative drafters – for discussion, debate, approval and adoption before it becomes a policy or a law of the country (the set of questions are included under 9.5.2 below.

## 9.5.2 The social welfare need/social condition/right

The questions below should help to focus comprehensive rather than narrow and limited attention on the social need, condition or right. Questions also allow focused investigation and analysis on the core aspects that policymakers should be aware of when they make policy choices.

1.  What are the specific social needs/social conditions or rights which the policy aims to meet/address?
2.  What is the demographic and socioeconomic context of the country, region or group?
3.  What is the history of these conditions/needs or rights?
4.  Is there widespread agreement about the conditions, needs or rights?
5.  Identify and discuss the key people/organisations/stakeholders involved in lobbying for or against resolution of the unmet needs or social conditions.
6.  What are **the views** of stakeholders on the condition/need and what/whose interests are represented in these views?
7.  What is **your analysis** of the root causes of this condition/need and does any research evidence back up your analysis? Use appropriate data/evidence to do this.
8.  Discuss the scope/extent and severity of the condition and need to be addressed.
9.  How would you characterise the state's approach to the condition, need or right – e.g. neoliberal and residual, social democratic and institutional, developmental and transformative (refer to Chapters 3 and 4 of this book)?

## 9.5.3 Shifts in policy thinking and adopted values: constitutional and human rights

In the next stage of policy analysis and formulation of a new policy it is essential to assess the need, the condition or right against the requirements and principles and values of the Constitution and international human rights instruments. It is useful to highlight whether there have been any shifts in thinking about how to apply the principles and values that are consistent with a human rights approach in this stage so that recommended options can be framed using such principles.

## 9.5.4 Overview of the current social welfare policy and challenges

Before proposing alternatives to existing social welfare policies or legislation addressing the condition or need, it is necessary to analyse the efficacy of current social welfare policy responses, whether these are by the state or non-state actors (refer to Chapter 4). Policies may be analysed or formulated using the set of questions provided below.

### The current social welfare policy response

1. What are the goals, aims and objectives of the policy? Discuss the stated and implied objectives and what are likely to be the social, economic and political consequences of the policy. How do these aims align with the principles of constitutional and human rights?
2. Who is the social policy aimed at (who benefits directly and indirectly and in what ways) and how do such benefits influence the distribution of resources, power and human development of the poorest?
3. What theories and policy approaches (residual, institutional and normative) underpin the policy that you are analysing or that you are formulating?
4. Indicate what values and principles (universal, selective, equity, equality, adequacy, participation, individualistic, collective, anti-discriminatory, etc.) these theories represent. Discuss the appropriateness of the theories and approach taken by the policy. Clearly indicate how they affect policy choices made about what is allocated, to whom, and what provisions are made.
5. Discuss how such provisions are delivered and how they are financed.
6. Are there any groups or people who will be negatively affected as a result of the policy? Are the overall effects less harmful than the condition/need the policy is designed to resolve?
7. What social provision (cash or in kind services such as social grants or food, education, health care, counselling, housing, water, residential care, etc.) does the policy make?
8. Does the policy establish a minimum standard? Does it develop a benefit schedule (sequencing or phasing in of provision)? Is the population/category of people to receive the benefit clearly identified and are the criteria for receiving it explicit and unambiguous?

## 9.5.5 Options for strategic reform or transformation

Before deciding on the options for reform or transformation of existing social welfare policies on a specific issue or need, it is also necessary for policy analysts to consider the existing or potential side effects of such policies. Some questions that could guide strategic decision-making on the choices policymakers should consider are indicated below.

### Side effects of introducing a policy within a country

1. Are there likely to be any side effects on other parts of society? For example, the market/business sector, civil society organisations, religious organisations, etc.?
2. How will economic policies/economic development (national budget, taxation and other fiscal aspects) be affected?
3. How will political processes/development (such as building political unity, nationhood, promoting inclusion or reinforcing divisions) be affected?
4. How will the policy link to other social policies and social interest groups?
5. What will be the likely response from interest groups such as employers, the financial sector, property developers, voluntary welfare organisations, non- governmental organisations, churches?

### Side effects of existing and or new policy outside the country

1. Are there likely to be any side effects beyond the society? For example, how do you think the International Monetary Fund, the World Bank or Regional Development Banks will react to the policy?
2. How will other countries in the region be affected by the policy?
3. Will the policy result in new international benchmarks for social development or will it help to achieve any existing international commitments?

After considering all the possible effects of the current policy and or the new proposed policy the next step would be to discuss and explain the possible options for reform or transformation. In considering the alternative options and designing policy and programme choices for review by policymakers one could address the questions below under alternative approaches.

### Possible alternative approaches

1. Are there any alternative policies that could meet the same social need or condition?
2. If so, could these alternative social policies be in any way more effective? Provide any supporting evidence to justify your answer – evidence that indicates whether such policies have worked in other countries with similar socioeconomic and political conditions.

## 9.5.6 Implementation, monitoring and evaluation of the policy

Implementation, monitoring and evaluation of the use of policy inputs, the processes through which delivery takes place, and the impacts of the policy are dependent on how these aspects are included in the policy. The list of questions identified below can help with these activities.

1. What are the ways through which the policy will be implemented? Will it be implemented through a centralised or decentralised delivery system?
2. How and who will inform the public about the policy?
3. Will there be a partnership between the public and private sector and or the voluntary/ NGO sectors in the delivery of the service or benefit?
4. Will the social provision require professional staff and are these human resources readily available?
5. How will the client/community or beneficiary population be involved in decision-making?
6. Who will monitor the process, the policy objectives, and impacts?
7. Does the policy indicate clear evaluation criteria? If not, what do you suggest?

This section has provided a detailed framework to guide policy analysis and formulation. It has used a human rights approach as a basis and has provided a sequence of policy analysis activities drawing on Taylor (2002).

An example of an actual Family Policy is used as a basis for further discussion and analysis. The crafting of social welfare policies to address needs and rights of families is a contemporary issue in South Africa, and in other countries on the continent, and this example could provide practical insights on how policies are developed in real world contexts.

## 9.6 Family Policy in South Africa

Families are viewed as an enduring unit throughout the ages, and are thus a primary intervention tool for social work. The function of families includes biological and social reproduction, and they tend to undertake the task of restoration of emotional stability of individuals who experience psychological strains in formal settings of everyday life (Gil, 1979: 63).

Family Policy is addressed in Chapter 7 and the author does indicate that there was a shift in context from colonial rule to the apartheid era of racial capitalism and exploitation of black Africans, and particularly for the mining industry. These contexts had a particular impact and consequence for families whose lives were splintered because the males left home to work on the mines and would only see their families perhaps once a year. Migrant labourers for the mines came from the rural areas in South Africa, and countries such as Lesotho, Zambia, Mozambique, and Zimbabwe. Many of these families lived in impoverished conditions and the remittances sent home by the mineworkers were crucial for the survival of these families.

1. **Policy goals and objectives of Family Policy**: In broad terms, social welfare policy aims to facilitate the provision of appropriate developmental social welfare services to all South Africans, especially people living in poverty, those who are vulnerable, and those who are at risk and have special needs. In particular, family policy has the following objectives:
   - Enhance the socialising, caring, nurturing and supporting capabilities of families so that their members are able to contribute effectively to the overall development of the country.
   - Empower families and their members by enabling them to identify, negotiate around, and maximise economic, labour market, and other opportunities available in the country.
   - Improve the capacities of families and their members to establish social interactions which make a meaningful contribution towards a sense of community, social cohesion and national solidarity (Department of Social Development, 2012: 9).

2. **Target group for Family Policy**: The target group is definitely families as a unit, and not individuals. This fits in with the social development approach of making provision for cohesive, integrated structures to facilitate an inclusive and responsible engaged citizenry. This policy took into account the range of family forms since the Eurocentric notion of a nuclear family was not appropriate for the conditions in Africa, and particularly in the case of the Family Policy in South Africa. About one third of households are nuclear families which will consist of parents and children. There are a range of family forms, and these may include the extended family, reconstituted families, intergenerational families, single parent families and child-headed households. The latter family form is certainly unknown in many Western countries. About a fifth of households have three or more generations present (intergenerational households) (DSD, 2016: 145). Chapter 7 deals more in depth with these family forms.

3. **Theories and policy approaches which underpin Family Policy**: The theories and/or approaches which underpin Family Policy can be viewed from differing perspectives depending on one's ideological position. The *White Paper for Families* (2013) is underpinned by the developmental social welfare approach which implies that economic development should be integrated with social development (see Chapter 3 for the details of this approach). This approach is the foundational policy for the *White Paper for Social Welfare* (1997) and the more recent *Comprehensive Report on the Review of the White Paper for Social Welfare*

*1997* (Department of Welfare, 1997; DSD, 2016). Another perspective which may be mooted is that of conflict theory which is at the core of Marxism. This view holds that conflict is endemic to any group, community or interpersonal relationships, particularly since it is about people's relationships and transactions. Tensions and conflict are inevitable in any family as this is part of human nature. There is the systems approach which assumes that individuals will be served within the context of their families, and a change or impact on one individual will affect the other family members and the family as a whole. Therefore, a child may present with a problem, and as a result the family system will be targeted for intervention with welfare services.

4. **Values and principles at the core of Family Policy**: Human rights are embedded in the South African Constitution and Bill of Rights. Much of this discussion has taken place in previous chapters and in the above section. Clearly, the Constitution has been heralded as a landmark in terms of an inclusive approach to the fundamental rights and respect for the citizens of the country. Therefore, the values which are espoused in the Constitution will be reflected in the formation of policies and legislation, and in this example, Family Policy. The values and principles to which Family Policy subscribes are social justice, democracy, equality, the right to dignity, respect, and *Ubuntu*. *Ubuntu* means 'I am because you are' which is at the core of African philosophy of social justice. The notion of *Ubuntu* is further explained in Chapter 11 and in the above discussion.

5. **Financing of Family Policy**: Any policy that is formulated and mooted by government has to demonstrate how the funds will be provided. The funds for the Family Policy form an integral aspect of the Social Development budget which has subprogrammes, such as families and children. The Social Development budget for 2015/2016 comprised funds that were allocated for social security (88%), welfare services (10%), and administration (2%) (DSD, 2016: 76).

6. **Groups affected by Family Policy**: Since this policy is directed at impoverished families who are vulnerable, it is possible that many families who are considered middle class or even wealthy may not benefit from the funding of this welfare policy. The policy takes into account welfare services for family preservation, family therapy, and family and marriage enrichment (Department of Social Development, 2013).

7. **Social provision**: The social wage, that is, social protection provision plays a significant role in helping to reduce the risks and vulnerabilities of families in South Africa. In assessing the funds for 2015/2016 that were apportioned for developmental welfare services, 62% were allocated for children and families, 11% for older persons, 8% for HIV and Aids, 6% for disabilities and substance abuse, respectively, 4% for social crime prevention and victim empowerment, and 3% for youth development (DSD, 2016: 77). However, in spite of the gains made in providing services to the poor, there are still challenges for the poorest sections of society in gaining access to basic services.

8. **Minimum standards of Family Policy**: The pursuit of the developmental perspective to social welfare's goals means embracing social justice, the quest for a minimum standard of living for families, the provision of equitable access and equal opportunity to welfare services and social grants, and the commitment to meet the needs of all South Africans, with a particular emphasis on the needs of populations at risk and the most vulnerable. Thus, it is clear which groups will be targeted since they are the vulnerable and at-risk families. Policy documents by the Department of Social Development strongly advocate family preservation in order to prevent the statutory removal of children from families. Family preservation services focuses on the preventative and therapeutic services provided by social workers at family welfare organisations with a view to preserving

the family, and to prevent the removal of children by improving the family's coping skills, strengthening family bonds as well as empowering the family to utilise formal and informal resources (Strydom, 2012: 435).

## 9.6.1 Discussion on family policy

It should be noted that South Africa's welfare policy is rights-based, inclusive, integrates family-centred and community-based services, pursues a generalist approach to service delivery, and delivers community development and developmental welfare services. The *White Paper on Family Policy* went through various drafts as a result of inputs by various stakeholders such as NGOs. The current Family Policy (2013) was formulated in contrast to the previous draft (DSD, 2006) which was viewed as conservative since it failed to acknowledge the variety of family forms and the limitations of the discourse around what families looked like and how family functions (Hochfeld, 2007: 82). Single parent families were acknowledged in the draft policy but there was no recognition of the importance, effectiveness and impact of this form in the South African context. As a consequence of all these drafts and changes, Family Policy (2013) was required to be transformative since it needed to acknowledge the various forms of the family, focus on inequities and vulnerabilities of families, and provide redistributive measures in terms of the Social Development budgetary allocations.

Families exist in many forms

The budget for social protection for the financial year 2015/2016 amounted to R206,4 billion which is the equivalent of 15,3% of consolidated government expenditure, and 4,9% of GDP (National Treasury, 2015 in DSD, 2016). Concern has been expressed by NGOs that the social security portion of the budget is crowding out the budget for welfare services. However, the recommendations of the *Comprehensive Review of the White Paper* suggest that in keeping with the National Development Plan (NDP) that social welfare services must be expanded.

Given that there is still a gap regarding the provision of care for impoverished families, one's analysis is that South Africa and many African countries face structural violence. This structural violence is an unintended consequence of the fissures in the net of social protection. As much as the South African Constitution is progressive on social and economic rights, and provides for fundamental human rights, the social protection net is not all encompassing. Taylor (2015: 157) observes that South Africa's social grants are having an impact on the depth of poverty within households, but there are fracture points that leave millions of poor households food insecure. Gil (1979: 62) refers to conditions and acts obstructing development which originates on institutional and societal levels as 'structural violence'. At the societal level, institutional patterns and dynamics may be established and legitimated which result in phenomena such as poverty, discrimination, unemployment, inequality, and illness which inevitably limit the development of individuals and groups.

The benefits of the provision of resources for Family Policy are that poverty will be reduced amongst families. There should be gradual improvements in the quality of family life and this will have an impact on improving the physical, intellectual, educational, social, and emotional aspects of children's lives. This would promote more harmonious relationships amongst the family and should provide positive effects on the overall functioning of family members in and outside the home (Gil, 1992: 331).

The family systems approach discussed above under 'Theories and approaches which underpin Family Policy' indicates the rationale for providing family therapy as one of the welfare services provided by the Department of Social Development. Briar-Lawson, Naccarato, and Drews (2009: 317) observe that many policies and programmes draw from a hybrid of theories and strategies and undergo constant revision in trial and error improvements that may or may not be linked to evidence. Their concern is that many of these theories and strategies may not be tailored to the unique needs of families and children, their cultures, and economic challenges. This is a reminder that an important aspect of social welfare policy and practice is that research, monitoring, and evaluation should form an integral aspect of intervention. This contributes to evidence-based policies and practice.

One of the services conducted by Department of Social Development is family preservation. In research conducted in 2012, there is uncertainty among social workers regarding the actual content of family preservation services, with regards to the purpose and nature of service delivery, as well as the types of services that should be rendered (Strydom, 2012: 450). Therefore, it becomes apparent that social workers at family welfare organisations require thorough in-service training on the nature and extent of family preservation services. Families South Africa (FAMSA) was known before for its services on marital counselling which is another service required by the Department of Social Development. FAMSA's services have changed to include a wide range of activities, which includes trauma debriefing and home-based care for HIV and AIDS for families (DSD, 2016: 148).

The finalisation of the Family Policy was identified as an achievement on several occasions by the various stakeholders (for example, NGOs and CBOs) during the Committee's engagements of the Review process of the White Paper for Social Welfare 1997 (DSD, 2016: 148).

## CONCLUSION

- This chapter has provided a critical perspective of the conceptual and theoretical issues in social welfare policy analysis and formulation. It has also discussed the significance of using a human rights approach in analysing and formulating policies.
- A framework for analysing and formulating policies was discussed and questions to guide the technical process were also explained.
- This chapter focused on both descriptive processes explaining how policies are made and prescriptive processes that explain what ought to go into policies to ensure the vision of transformation is attained are essential for policy analysis and formulation.

- It also reinforces the view that policy analysis is socially relevant, multidisciplinary, integrative and problem solving with regard to dealing with social needs, conditions and rights, especially of the most marginalised.

## QUESTIONS

1. How would you analyse and formulate a social welfare policy of your choice utilising a transformative approach?
2. Using an example of an issue or problem that you have identified, how would you go about researching and analysing this issue or problem to formulate a social welfare policy?

## REFERENCES

BOTSWANA. Ministry of Finance and Development Planning (2003) *National Development Plan 9* at p. 266. Gaberone, Botswana: Government Printer.

BRIAR-LAWSON, K, NACCARATO, T & DREWS, J: 'Child and Family Welfare Policies and Services' in Midgley, J & Livermore, M (eds.) (2009) *The Handbook of Social Policy* (second edition) at pp. 315–332. Los Angeles, London, New Delhi, Singapore: Sage Publications.

CARROLL, T & CARROLL, B (2004) 'The Rapid Emergence of Civil Society in Botswana' *Journal of Commonwealth & Comparative Politics* Vol. 42 (3) (November) at pp. 333–355.

GABEL, SG: 'Analyzing Social Policies From A Rights-Based Approach' in Libal, KR, Berthold, SM, Thomas, RL & Healy, LM (eds.) (2014) *Advancing Human Rights in Social Work Education at pp. 293–310*. Virginia: Council for Social Work Education.

GIL, DG (1979) *Beyond the jungle. Essays on Human Possibilities, Social Alternatives, and Radical Practice*. Cambridge, Massachusetts: Schenman Publishing Company.

GIL, DG (1992) *Unravelling Social Policy*. Rochester, Vermont: Schenkman Books, Inc.

GILBERT, N & SPECHT, H (1986) *Dimensions of Social Welfare Policy*. Englewood Cliffs, New Jersey: Prentice-Hall.

HOCHFELD, T (2007) ‚Missed opportunities. Conservative discourses in the draft National Family Policy of South Africa' *International Social Work* Vol. 50(1): 79–91.

HOGWOOD, BH & GUNN, LA (1984) *Policy Analysis for the Real World*. New York, United States of America: Oxford University Press.

SEEKINGS, J (2006) *The UDF. A History of the United Democratic Front in South Africa 1983–1991*. Cape Town: David Philip Publishers.

SEN, A (1982) *Poverty and Famines: An Essay on Entitlement and Deprivation*. Oxford: Oxford University Press.

SOUTH AFRICA. 1996. *Constitution of the Republic of South Africa Act 108 of 1996*. Pretoria: Government Printer. [Laws.]

SOUTH AFRICA. Department of Social Development (2006) National Family Policy. Final draft. Pretoria: Department of Social Development.

SOUTH AFRICA. Department of Social Development (2011) *Green Paper on Families: Promoting Family Life and Strengthening Families in South Africa* in GG Vol. 4 No. 34657 (3 October). Pretoria: Government Printer.

SOUTH AFRICA. Department of Social Development (2012) *White Paper on Families* (Draft). Pretoria: Government Printer.

SOUTH AFRICA. Department of Social Development (2013) *Framework for Social Welfare Services*. Pretoria: Government Printer.

SOUTH AFRICA. Department of Social Development (2016) *Comprehensive Report on the Review of the White Paper for Social Welfare 1997*. Pretoria: Government Printer.

SOUTH AFRICA. Department of Welfare (1997) *White Paper for Social Welfare*. Pretoria: Government Printer.

SOUTH AFRICA. *Government of the Republic of South Africa and Others v Grootboom and Others* 2000 11 BCLR 1169 (CC).

SOUTH AFRICA. Parliament of the Republic of South Africa (2016) *Rules of the National Assembly* (ninth edition) Rule 227 [Online]. Available: https://www.parliament.gov.za/storage/app/media/Rules/NA/2016-09-28_NA_RULES.pdf [date accessed?].

STRYDOM, M (2012) 'Family Preservation Services: Types of Services Rendered by Social Workers to Families at Risk' *Social Work/MaatskaplikeWerk* 48(4): 435–455.

TAYLOR, V (1997) *Social Mobilisation: Lessons from the Mass Democratic Movement*. Bellville: Southern African Development and Education Policy Research Unit (SADEP), University of the Western Cape.

TAYLOR, V (2002) *A Conceptual Framework for Social Policy Analysis in Comparative Social Policy for Africa*. Cape Town: University of Cape Town (Unpublished lecture notes).

TAYLOR, V: 'Achieving food security through social policies: Comprehensive social protection for development' in Fukuda-Parr, S & Taylor, V (eds.) (2015) *Food Security in South Africa: Human rights and entitlement perspectives at pp.* 145–166. Lansdowne, Cape Town: UCT Press.

TAYLOR-GOOBY, P (1991) *Social Change, Social Welfare and Social Science*. Great Britain: Harvester Wheatsheaf.

UNITED NATIONS (1948) *Universal Declaration of Human Rights* General Assembly Resolution 217A adopted by the General Assembly on 10 December 1948. France: Paris.

# Glossary of Terms

**civil society:** this refers to a wide range of organisations which have a vested interest in welfare policy matters that directly affects them, and they engage in advocacy on these concerns.

# Social welfare policy and transformational participatory processes in South Africa

*Mimie Sesoko*

As outlined in Chapter 1 of this book, South Africa adopted a developmental approach to social welfare. This means that alongside the provision of the safety net (social assistance) which is aimed at alleviating the immediate suffering of the poor and vulnerable, the social development policy was developed with the purpose of empowering people to lift them out of poverty.

## Objectives

✓ Describing and outlining the concept participation with the purpose of reflecting on the different levels that public participation takes place when and in developing social welfare policy.

✓ Explaining the participation process with clear examples of the different steps and phases followed in policy formulation.

✓ Elaborating on the historical processes that South Africa followed in policy formulation and the transformative process including the strength and weakness in these processes.

✓ Describing the role of communities and the different stakeholders who participated in developing implementation strategies and follow-ups.

## Outcomes

✓ Defining the concepts participation, public participation, and democratic participation.

✓ Describing and outlining the different role players in policymaking phases.

✓ Analysing critically the evolution of participation in policy formulation in South Africa.

✓ Identifying and analysing participation mechanisms and transformative approaches in South Africa.

✓ Explaining the historical process that South Africa followed to ensure full participation of South Africans, especially the vulnerable communities in rural areas.

✓ Describing and outlining the different role players in policymaking processes including the role played by the social work practitioner.

## 10.1 Introduction

From the beginning of 1994, the Constitution, Bill of Rights, legislation, and a number of policies involving different government departments were formulated and implemented. Since then, a number of these policies were amended and others are in a process of being evaluated with the purpose of continuously addressing the needs of the communities. In order to do this, the participation of ordinary people, grassroots organisations, civil society, and different stakeholders in policy formulation processes is critical and important.

## 10.2 The concept participation

The term participation has evolved over time. Practitioners, researchers, institutions of higher learning, and different organisations whose main focus is the 'development agenda' have and continued to explore, describe, research, and reflect on the successes and failures of policies and projects that do or do not engage local marginalised communities, groups and organisations in decision-making processes. Development theories and approaches emphasise the importance of the role played by local communities in policymaking and developmental projects or programmes. The emphasis of participation is driven by the understanding that participation does lead to ownership, empowerment, equity, justice, and sustainability. Swanepoel and De Beers (2009: 28–30), Louw, Nel and Schenck (2010: 253–254) and the United Nations Research Institute for Social Development (UNRISD, 2014: 106) outline the critical role played by citizens or communities in shaping their own development and participating in policy formulation. The involvement of the citizens or communities in policy formulation gives them a voice and a sense of ownership in the country's policies. This means that they are making a contribution, as part of the policymaking process, to identifying solutions which will address social ills in communities and families.

Prior to 1996, and before the adoption of the Constitution of the Republic of South Africa (Act 108 of 1996), the South African black, Indian, and coloured communities never fully participated in policymaking processes. In 1994, a democratic South Africa was established with the late President Mandela as the first black president of the majority ruling party, the African National Congress (ANC). This gave the previously disadvantaged and marginalised black communities opportunities to participate in elections and to elect representatives who became Members of Parliament. The parliamentarians are elected by South African citizens who are 18 years old and above and who have registered as voters. The voters are referred to as the electorate. These voters elect the parties they believe can address their needs and represent their voice in Parliament and in policymaking processes. (Parliament document: Your Representative in Parliament)

In Parliament, each political party is allocated the number of seats which is proportional to how many votes they got in the election. Therefore, the political parties chose the people who will participate in Parliament, a lawmaking body in the national sphere of government. South Africa is a constitutional democracy. This means the Constitution is the highest law in the country and that it guarantees democracy by giving every citizen the right to vote, ensuring regular elections, and providing for a multiparty system of government. South African citizens choose their representatives for the national, provincial, and local governments by participating in the elections. Therefore, the South African Constitution makes provision for public involvement in lawmaking and other processes of Parliament. South Africa's democratic system provides for citizens to elect their representatives and allows them to have a say in matters that affect them. Chapter 4 of the Constitution outlines how Parliament facilitates public involvement in legislative and other processes. It provides for building an effective people's Parliament that is responsive to the needs of the people and driven by the ideal of realising a better quality of life for all South African citizens. This will be further discussed in the next section of this chapter.

The concept of participation has evolved over time. Arnstein (1996) as stated by Kilonzo (2013: 31) describes the three levels of participation as follows:

- **Top level:** represents **citizen power** which depicts control and high level decision-making by the citizens. It also illustrates that citizens have power to form partnerships to negotiate and engage in action.

- **Middle level**: represents the **tokenism** level which includes information provision, consultation and placation activities. At this stage, the policymakers provide advice but they maintain control over gathered information and the right to make decisions.
- **Bottom level**: represents the **non-participation** level; it covers therapy and manipulation. The activities do not involve genuine participation but just educating people about the subject matter.

Figure 10.1 below illustrates the different levels of participation adapted by Kilonzo.

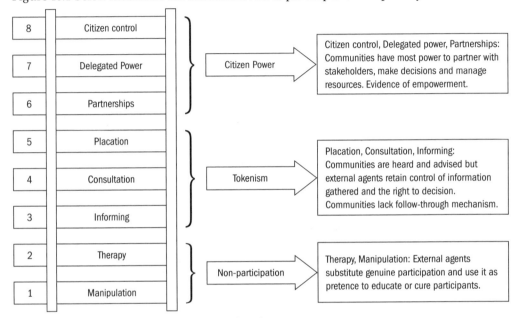

Source: Adapted from Arnstein as cited by Kilonzo (2013)

**Figure 10.1  Typology of participation**

In most situations policy formulation processes start with a felt need, social problem or a concern. Depending on the approach followed by the policymakers in developing policies or legislation, this can be an easy and quick-fix process or a tedious, time-consuming and very complex process. When an easy process is followed, the policymakers are the drivers of the process and take full responsibility. They draft the policy and present it to the communities or group after working on the documents and brainstorming without fully consulting the group. They, therefore, follow steps where they apply limited engagement processes with communities. The other method is where communities and different role players are involved. This is an in-depth consultative process. It is time-consuming and will allow different stakeholders and a number of people and institutions to give their input. Therefore, the consultative processes that policymakers choose do determine how they perceive the role of the different stakeholders.

Arnstein's typology described above outlines the three levels that policymakers can decide on to engage the communities and other stakeholders in policy formulation. The quicker and faster way to develop policy is when one uses Arnstein's lower and middle level participatory approach. At this level, only a few people are involved and the experts drive the policy formulation process. Time is a concern as this approach is not intense and consultation is superficial. This kind of approach is ineffective as it does not give the larger community members and institutions any ownership position to make decisions. The policymakers are in charge and run faster to draft policies and take the responsibility to frame the issues. Communities, therefore, miss the opportunity to define their own solutions to the identified concerns or problems. This is a challenge as many policymakers struggle with the concept of how far and how wide they should engage the larger community in policymaking processes. As Hicks (2005: 4) indicates, governance actors, activists, and political analysts around the world are grappling with this issue and with exploring how best to engage citizens in government decision-making processes.

The second approach is when policymakers follow an intense and in-depth consultative process. In this case they consult with the marginalised communities and multiple stakeholders. Participation therefore gives the marginalised, civil society, and the private sector power to participate fully in developing and making decisions on policy which affect them. The government officials also participate as equals with other stakeholders and not as the final decision makers. This process can be transformative. According to Taylor and Fransman (2004: 1), citizen participation is regarded by many as having the potential to reduce poverty and social injustice by strengthening citizen's rights and voice, influencing policymaking, enhancing local governance, and improving accountability and responsiveness of institutions. Below is a case study to help you explore what is meant by participation in policymaking. Read this case study and unpack the participation process according to Arnstein's definition.

 **OLDER PERSON'S POLICY CONSULTATIVE PROCESS**

The Eersteplaas Jubilee Church Leaders Association invited the community members, non-governmental organisations, older persons' groups, school committees, women and youth groups, business sector, social workers, teachers, nurses, and government officials who work with older people to address the challenges faced by older people. There were pockets of reports of abuse and neglect of older persons in the community. This problem was identified by the leaders of the women's group in the Jubilee church. The women leaders in the church visited a number of families and found physical and emotional abuse as a common problem among their older members. While investigating the problem, other community members came forward and reported this as a serious concern. The local police station also indicated that it had a number of cases of rape, abuse and neglect of the elderly. Many older people were found hungry and starving in their homes. The local newspapers reported incidences of missing elders. An intervention was needed to help address the needs of the Eersteplaas elders. This was a community outcry and needed immediate intervention and a long-term strategy to prevent the social problem that was growing so fast in the neighbourhood and beyond.

The different stakeholders were invited to a workshop to identify solutions towards the existing problems. The neighbouring community felt that this was a national problem and not just a concern for the Eersteplaas community. In the follow-up meetings social workers reported that this problem was alleged to be happening in different communities across South Africa. This was seen as one of challenging social ills that required immediate but a long-term solution. The idea was to develop and formulate policy to protect and prevent older person's abuse and neglect. The government developed a strategy and draft policy document on how to address these needs and concerns. The stakeholders agreed that the main goal was to develop a caring and loving environment for the older people in South Africa. The families of older persons were left out from this process as they were seen to be contributing to these social ills. Three meetings were held with stakeholders and ultimately the government officials announced that they have designed a draft policy document as a proposal for older people and will submit it to Parliament. This was a concern as some people felt three meetings were not enough to conclude on a critical policy like this. Others felt that enough consultation took place since it is the responsibility of the government to protect older persons. Social workers attended the initial meetings but could not make a substantive contribution as they had to attend to other problems.

Participating in the formulation of social policy means being engaged in a series of activities that involves a number of different players, series of discussions, debates, and dialogues. It involves establishing task teams consisting of different stakeholders that represent different groupings and individuals. The formulation process is then elevated to a stage where a team is delegated to design and draft guidelines on how to approach the policy formulation and on who should participate at what stage. A policy is a legal document binding individuals, families, communities, organisations, and political structures on how to deal with a situation or social ills in the country. Therefore, social policy addresses challenges that are related to the socioeconomic or political welfare of individuals, groups or communities.

Table 10.1 below identifies all the role players in the case study.

Table 10.1 Role players in case study

| Community members | • Older people and their families<br>• Community leaders (local, provincial, national)<br>• Church leaders (from the different churches)<br>• Community members (from rural/informal settlements and townships), all settings in South Africa. |
|---|---|
| Professionals from different disciplines | • Policemen<br>• Nurses/Doctors<br>• Social workers<br>• Psychologist<br>• Physiotherapist<br>• HIV and Aids counsellors<br>• Business sector<br>• Experts in older people issues. |
| Government officials | • Different departments (those that work with older persons). |
| Civil Society | • Unions<br>• Non-governmental organisations( NGOs)<br>• Faith-based organisations (FBOs)<br>• Community-based organisations (CBOs). |

GROUP ACTIVITY    ARNSTEIN'S MODEL OF PARTICIPATION

Use the information from the case study to draw a table showing the three levels of participation identified by Arnstein and outline the following:
1. List the groups of people who should be involved at the lower, middle and upper level?
2. Explain why they are to be involved at these levels.
3. Describe the roles they will play in formulating the older person's policy at the different levels.
4. Specifically discuss and describe the older people's role in this case study and their role in policymaking processes.

# 10.3 South Africa and the evolution of participation in policy formulation

In 1994, South Africa had undergone transformation that led to the new government establishing new systems of policymaking after the collapse of the apartheid government. This section will outline the old and new era and the role players in both eras.

## 10.3.1 The era prior to 1994

### The role of civil society during apartheid

Comparing the pre-94 and post-94 eras in South Africa, one needs to acknowledge the transformation that took place. South Africa has come a long way in its policy formulation and implementation processes. Much of the progress in this regard can be attributed to the civil society community in South Africa. Under apartheid policies were formulated based on minority rule. There was no consultation with the larger society. The approach used was that of non-participation by the majority black South African community as they had no say in the policymaking of the country. The apartheid regime applied the lower level of Arnstein's model. (1996)

During the apartheid era a number of non-governmental organisations emerged as the sector that brought huge change in the political and socioeconomic situation in South Africa. These groups of organisations were referred to as the civil society organisations (CSOs). CSOs consisted of church groups, community-based organisations (CBOs), non-governmental organisations (NGOs), unions, and the business sector. In their efforts to mobilise and change the policy setting for communities in South Africa under apartheid, they were supported by international NGOs and philanthropic foundations from the USA and Scandinavian community that funded their initiatives.

According to the Coalition of Civil Society Resource Mobilisation (2012: 10), the goal of civil society organisations was to bring down the apartheid regime as they were concerned about the discriminatory nature of the policy environment in South Africa. The issues that most concerned them were those relating to the socioeconomic and political development of black South Africans. As mentioned above, civil society organisations partnered with international non-profit organisations that funded different programmes to assist the CSOs in their fight against the unjust system of separate development and lack of participation by the majority poor black communities in decision-making processes. According to Weidman (2015: 6), in the **period 1960 to 1994**, CSOs in opposition to apartheid received extensive financial support from a variety of donors to whom they were not expected to meticulously report on their spending. As stated by the Coalition of Civil Society Resource Mobilisation (2012: 10), the CSOs contributed towards drafting the South African Constitution in 1996 and the Reconstruction and Development Programme (RDP), and participated in setting up the Truth and Reconciliation Commission (TRC). They made an invaluable contribution to the South African Constitution to the extent that it is described as one of the most advanced and progressive human rights-based constitutions in the world. As stated by Roux (2002: 418), the Constitution of the Republic of South Africa (Act 108 of 1996) paved the way for a truly democratic dispensation. This dispensation is based on principles such as freedom of speech and association, freedom of assemble and respect for life and property, as well as maintaining civilised standards and discipline. The Constitution is the supreme law of South Africa and even Parliament has to uphold the Constitution above all. This has led to total transformation in all spheres of government and administration.

### Important concepts defined

The concepts below are fundamental to the process of transformation that influenced the South African policy arena.

1. **Transformation**: According to Roux (2002: 419), transformation is when a government, and consequently all public executive institutions, virtually start from scratch, where the underlying vision, mission, and strategy is completely new and transformed. Transformation is about new mindsets and paradigm shifts.

2. **Public policy**: Maseng (2014: 1) defines public policy as when decisions of government are taken through the process of political participation involving citizens, state, and non-state actors.
3. **Public participation**: In a document by the Department of Provincial and Local Government (DPLG 2007b: 15) public participation is described as an open accountable process through which individuals and groups within selected communities can exchange views and influence decision-making.
4. **Democracy**: The word 'democracy' comes from the Greek word *demokratia* which means 'government by the people'.
   - Democracy is a balance between 'might' and 'right'. The state takes all the power (it has all the 'might'), but its power must be limited so that it does not abuse this power (to make sure it does 'right'). The Constitution guarantees the independence of the courts and establishes six independent institutions to protect citizens: the Public Protector, the Human Rights Commission, the Commission for the Promotion and Protection of the Rights of Cultural, Religious and Linguistic Minorities, the Commission for Gender Equality, the Auditor General and the Independent Electoral Commission.
   - Democracy is about balancing rights and responsibilities. Citizens can expect the government to do things for them like providing protection, health services, education and housing. Citizens also have responsibilities like obeying the law and paying tax to the state.
   - Democracy is about balancing the rights of the majority with protection for minorities.
   - Democracy is about achieving a greater balance in society so that there is greater equality for all over a period of time (Parliament, RSA).
5. **Participatory democracy**: This concept refers to citizens' participation in decision-making processes outside the structures of elected government institutions (Buccus and Hicks, 2007: 3). This kind of participation refers to democracy as a process that entitles each individual citizen to speak and be heard.
6. **Representative democracy**: It refers to when citizens' views are presented through their elected members in government. It also includes situations where the marginalised communities' voices are channelled through other representatives such as civil society organisations (CSOs) acting as external counter forces to government, or where CSOs act as co-governance with the state in service delivery and policymaking processes.

Given the transformation that has taken place, the question that arises is: With the new democratic space and the new policy environment in South Africa, are the marginalised and poor communities genuinely involved in policymaking processes? Maseng (2014: 1) argues that post-apartheid South Africa made great efforts to ensure that public policy became a democratic and an inclusive process. Thus, the public policymaking arena has continuously evolved to strengthen democracy. The government initiated and established a number of structures, processes, and systems to institutionalise public participation policymaking processes. The following subsection elaborates on some of the systems created to institutionalise public participation in a democratic South Africa.

## 10.3.2 The new democratic South Africa and government structures

After 1994, the new South African government created different structures to ensure citizen participation in policymaking in a non-discriminatory way at different levels of government.

## 10.3.2.1 Parliament of South Africa

At the highest level in the country is the Parliament of the Republic of South Africa which consists of two Houses, the National Assembly (NA) and the National Council of Provinces (NCOP).

### National Assembly (NA)

The Constitution describes the NA as the body elected to represent the people and to ensure government by the people for the people. The most important roles of the NA are to make laws and hold the Executive accountable. It passes, rejects, and amends legislation, and also plays an oversight role in ensuring that all executive organs of the state in the national sphere of government are accountable. The NA is also required to facilitate public involvement in its legislative processes. It has open sittings to encourage the media and the public to listen to their deliberations. To get the job done and for teamwork, accountability and efficiency, the National Assembly established a number of committees referred to as portfolio committees. Each committee oversees the work of a government department. The roles of the portfolio committee are to debate Bills related to the work of the specific government department, to monitor the work of the department, and to ensure public participation. Portfolio committees set up standards and norms and further monitor how departments utilize government resources for the benefit of the society. The public is also encouraged to make submissions to public hearings of the portfolio committees on matters affecting them.

An example of oversight by a portfolio committee was when the Minister of Social Development was summoned to account for the South African Social Security Agency (SASSA) saga in the Department of Social Development. The Portfolio Committee on Social Development is fully responsible for the social welfare policy issues.

Portfolio committees also look at the budget and other related matters of structure and function of the departments. However, the committees are not restricted to attending to government issues or matters only but can investigate any matter related to the relevant department. The portfolio committees are required by Parliament to present their reports to the larger plenary sitting.

> The **South African Social Security Agency (SASSA)** was established in terms of the South African Social Security Agency Act 9 of 2004 to provide efficient and effective social assistance and security services, including payments of grants, in South Africa. Despite the fact that the agency was established to administer and pay out grants to beneficiaries, amongst others, most of its functions were outsourced. One of these outsourced functions, payment of grants, was awarded to a service provider and beneficiaries complained about unlawful deductions from their grants. The Minister of Social Development has been challenged in court about awarding this contract to the service provider, which has cost the South African taxpayers billions of rand. In the end, the poor and vulnerable who rely on these social grants were the ones who suffered the most. The payment of grants was eventually taken over by the South African Post Office.

### People's participation and submission to Parliament

Sections 59 and 72 of Chapter 4 of the Constitution provide for the process to facilitate people's participation in Parliament. Parliament further established the Parliamentary Democracy Offices (PDOs) to reach out to rural and under resourced local communities to take Parliament to the people. This is a structure that allows the parliamentarians to educate and create awareness about Parliament, its role, and function. Workshops are conducted to empower the communities to understand Parliament and how it works, and to identify the needs of the communities to be able to present them to Parliament. These activities take place when Parliament is in recess. The two case studies that follow illustrate how civil society engages with specific community members regarding submissions for legislation or the changes to be incorporated in a Bill.

**Case Study** | SOUTH AFRICAN HUMAN RIGHTS COMMISSION (SAHRC): ORAL AND WRITTEN SUBMISSIONS ON THE OLDER PERSONS BILL, AUGUST 2005

The SAHRC submitted its findings on the Older Persons Bill (B68b–203) to the Portfolio Committee on Social Development at a hearing that took place on 30 August 2005. The SAHRC worked with organisations and older persons throughout the country to get their input and recommendations for changes to the Older Persons Bill (B68b–203). These submissions were taken into consideration by the portfolio committee as these were the views of the people on the ground and it reflected the participatory nature of the process. Provincial workshops were conducted by SAHRC commissioners, and an older persons' forum and the Rights of the Older Persons' Working Group were established. Many role players made substantial submissions on the Bill by attending workshops and submitting emails. The following are but a few key issues and recommendations submitted to the committee:

- The 60/65 age difference: It was proposed that this must be done away with and that the age 60 should be used in the definition of older persons.
- Older Persons Programmes: It was recommended that an institutional structure within the Department of Social Development be established to implement these programmes.
- Impact of HIV/Aids on older persons: It was proposed that HIV/Aids awareness and educational programmes for older persons should be implemented.
- Old age home: Older persons are to be supported as part of the family and community and an old age home should be a last option for the older person. The Bill should reflect a developmental approach towards ageing in which older persons are encouraged to be independent and to participate in community activities. Community care should be a priority and be separated from residential care.

 **Case Study** | SOUTH AFRICAN SOCIETY FOR THE PREVENTION OF CHILD ABUSE AND NEGLECT (SASPCAN): ORAL AND WRITTEN SUBMISSIONS TO THE SOCIAL DEVELOPMENT PORTFOLIO COMMITTEE ON THE CHILDREN'S BILL, AUGUST 2006

SASPCAN as a networking, information sharing and training organisation on abused children and families represented a number of non-governmental organisations in this field. Their submission was on three main areas:

- Resourcing: They argued for an increment in the funding for child abuse prevention and early intervention and Early Childhood Development (ECD) services.
- Appropriate balance between prevention services and early intervention for child protection services: They indicated that social workers, child care forums, and other social services professionals should work together to promote prevention services and detect instances where early intervention services should be utilised for vulnerable children and families.
- Interdepartmental co-operation and co-ordination: The recommendation was for the departments that work with children, such as the Departments of Education and Social Development, to work together and collaborate on how to address the challenges of children and families in a holistic and co-ordinated manner.

SASPCAN gave a detailed submission on the wording for sections 143, 144, 145, and 146 of the Children's Amendment Bill. They furthermore proposed new sections that deal with how local government should address the needs of families. The added section 148 will address the role of principals of public and private schools in identifying the children who are vulnerable and in need.

The SAHRC and SASPCAN case studies are just examples of how participation is encouraged in Parliament and the role of civil society in making submissions and consulting with other role players.

## National Council of Provinces (NCOP)

The main focus of the NCOP is to ensure that provincial interests and issues are taken care of at national level. It carries the mandate of providing the national forum for public consideration of issues affecting the provinces. It passes, rejects, and amends legislation for provinces. As Gumede (2008: 12) states, the NCOP is required by law to facilitate public involvement in its legislative and other processes and its committees in a regulated manner. The NCOP as a provincial structure consists of nine provincial delegations nominated by the provincial legislatures. Delegates from the South African Local Government Association (SALGA) also attend the NCOP sittings. The different political parties are represented proportionately according to the number of votes they received during the elections. The committees in the NCOP are referred to as select committees. Select committees also shadow the work of government departments, for example, the Select Committee on Social Services, the Select Committee on Education and Recreation and so on. The NCOP also has public hearings and gives the community members an opportunity to make submissions through the PDOs. *Taking Parliament to the People* is a NCOP programme where the NCOP holds sittings in provinces to encourage community participation.

The National Council of Provinces is one of the two Houses of the Parliament of the Republic of South Africa

## Joint Committees (NA and NCOP)

The National Assembly and the National Council of Provinces can also have a joint committee sitting to address a specific need. This is normally organised where there is no agreement between the NA and NCOP on a particular Bill. This will be more like a mediation committee to reach consensus.

### 10.3.2.2 Green and White Papers

According to Gumede (2008: 12), the process of lawmaking is lengthy. Before legislation is finalised by Parliament, the Green and White Paper documents are discussed and debated at community level. If there is an issue at hand from any ministry or department, they have to work on a draft discussion document known as the Green Paper. The Green Paper is then discussed by interest groups and individuals affected by the particular issues. For example, the Ministry of Social Development may look at the socioeconomic issues related to communities such as the case study above (see Eersteplaas community case study above). They will draft a Green Paper and invite all the interested parties for comment and input. After the consultative process with the Green Paper, a White Paper follows, which is a more refined discussion document. This refined discussion document is normally compiled by task teams appointed by the specific department. The department will discuss the White Paper with the task team and consult with different interest groups before it is presented to the parliamentary committee.

## 10.4 Presidency policy unit

One of the offices that also look at policy matters is the policy unit in the Presidency known as the Policy Co-ordination and Advisory Services. This unit provides research and advice, and takes care of the projects and programmes that are strategic and supporting the Presidency and government on matters related to socioeconomic development, justice, and international affairs. In the Presidency there is also a unit that takes care of monitoring and evaluation, planning and special programmes that focus on the needs and rights of women, the disabled, youth, and children.

## 10.5 Local government structures

At local level, municipalities play an important role in engaging communities in policymaking matters since they are local structures which are closer to the people on the ground. Section 152(1) of the Constitution of the Republic of South Africa (Act 108 of 1996) provides for a democratic and accountable government for local communities. The emphasis is on ensuring that there is provision of services to communities and on encouraging the involvement of community organisations in matters related to local government. This mechanism allows local communities to be involved in policymaking processes at grassroots level. This is one of the principles of democracy.

## 10.6 Outside state organisations involved in policy matters

In South Africa, the state acknowledges the role played by private sector and non-government organisations, including civil society organisations, in policymaking. There are number of active role players in policymaking, and one such role player is the National Economic Development and Labour Council (NEDLAC). This is a body through which government and organised business, labour, and community groupings join hands and come together at national level to discuss and reach agreement or consensus regarding issues related to social and economic policy matters. The following organisations are represented on NEDLAC:

- Organised business is represented by Business Unity South Africa ( BUSA).
- Organised labour is represented by the major labour federations in South Africa.
- Organised communities are represented by a number of organisations such as the South African Youth Council, National Women's Coalition, Disabled People of South Africa, Financial Sector Coalition, South African National Civics Organisation, National Co-operative Association of South Africa, etc.

NEDLAC works closely with National Treasury and the Departments of Trade and Industry, Labour, Public Works, and Finance, which are the main entities taking care of social and economic matters. Therefore, decision-making processes aimed at promoting economic growth, equity, and social inclusion are discussed at this forum.

# 10.7 Public participatory mechanisms as transformative approaches

This section describes and analyses different mechanisms that are put in place to allow communities to engage in policy-making processes. These mechanisms have also evolved over time as they were developed as part of bringing improvement to public participation, or changing the old to the new, or strengthening the existing system.

Table 10.2 Legislatures and participation mechanisms

| Mechanism | What it means | Strengths and weaknesses in relation to participation |
|---|---|---|
| Public hearings | • Government invites communities to participate in making contribution to the policy.<br>• Invitations are placed in public places such as adverts in newspapers and announcements on radio and television.<br>• Community briefings are held in different places, even deep rural areas. | • The public hearings enable the different communities to make input by attending public hearings or different briefings.<br>• The challenge is that not everyone is able to attend these public hearings so it is not the most popular public participation method. |
| Public access to portfolio committee meetings | • All portfolio committees are required to be open for the public's input in their meetings.<br>• The concept Taking Parliament to the People is when the sittings of the NCOP are held in community settings or close to rural towns for communities to attend. | • *Taking Parliament to the People* is a good concept but is not always implemented to spread it across all nine provinces.<br>• Only a select few and those who are knowledgeable of the role of the National Assembly (NA) and National Council of Provinces (NCOP) attend these open sittings. |

| Mechanism | What it means | Strengths and weaknesses in relation to participation |
|---|---|---|
| Outreach programmes and information dissemination | • Legislatures in South Africa have outreach programmes targeted at rural communities.<br>• These programmes usually take the form of educational workshops, and information is disseminated to local communities via media or community radio stations. | • This is a good way to reach out to rural communities where there is no organised civil society to provide them with information.<br>• It helps to broaden the rural communities' understanding of government resources.<br>• It makes information more readily available to rural communities.<br>• The challenge is that this is not done on a regular basis. It takes longer for information to reach rural areas and sometimes not all rural communities get the information. |
| Petitions | • Some legislatures have petition committees to receive petitions from communities or members of the public on issues of concern. | • This is an open system that allows the communities or members of the public to present their issues using the petitions which in most cases have time lines and challenge government to respond to issues.<br>• Many service delivery issues have been presented in the form of a petition. |
| Imbizo and IDP | • This form of public gathering is when a large number of people come together with different government officials to present their concerns and issues.<br>• The premiers and government departments have to participate and answer questions from community members and allow the public to debate issues with government officials.<br>• Integrated Development Planning (IDP) is facilitated through the Imbizo system.<br>• Communities are informed of the government's budget and how it will be spent in their areas. | • This is one of the interesting public meetings where government goes directly to the communities to hear their opinions.<br>• The challenge is the size of the meeting – if it is a big meeting, some people will not get the opportunity to voice their issues.<br>• Integrated Development Planning is when local government departments discuss community planning and involve different structures to give input on the needs of the local community. These needs are then aligned with the local government budgets. |
| Ward Committees | • These are committees elected at ward level and are chaired by Ward councillors to discuss community issues with politicians at ward level. | • The councillors operate differently in different wards; some have functional ward committee while others are not effective because members of the ward committees may not be able to work together. They may have differences that affect the committee's functioning which will result in the community concerns not being addressed at ward level. |

**COMMUNITY PARTICIPATION AND POLICYMAKING IN SOUTH AFRICA**

1. In your small groups discuss three mechanisms that you think are effective in South Africa to engage community members in policymaking processes.
2. Outline your observation of the role played by NEDLAC in labour or economic matters.
3. Reflect on any service delivery protest that you have observed in South Africa and discuss the effectiveness of the presentation of petitions as one of the methods of public participation. Discuss a case study of service delivery protest that you have observed or have personally experienced in the area you live in or came to know about through the media such as radio, television, newspaper, etc.
4. Pretend you are a member of one of the parliamentary portfolio committees and are giving feedback to Parliament on how 'Taking Parliament to the People' is an effective method to service the communities around understanding policy.

# 10.8 Policymaking stages and participation levels

Different authors describe the policymaking stages differently. In this section the Policy Cycle by Bridgman and Davis (1998) as cited in Spicker (2006) is discussed. Figure 10.2 provides a graphic Illustration of the cycle while Table 10.3 gives a more practical application of the various stages of the cycle.

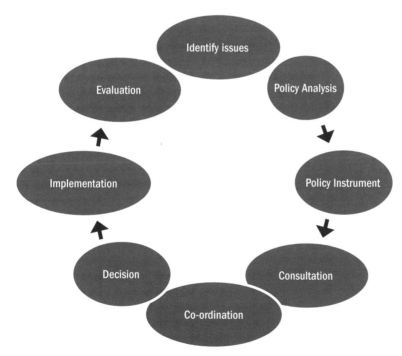

Source: Bridgman and Davis (1998) as cited in Spicker (2006)

**Figure 10.2 The policy cycle**

Table 10.3 Policymaking stages and levels of participation

| Stage | Role of stakeholders involved | Level of participation |
|---|---|---|
| Identification | • Informal concerned group is involved. They may be concerned about unmet needs or social problem, for example, unmet needs of orphans and vulnerable children. | • All community members are invited to discuss this matter; whoever is involved with children. |
| Policy Analysis | • Develop formal structured group of experts including community members to engage with the relevant government departments and officials to research the issues from all angles. | • Group leads the process and looks at theories related to this matter, researches issues, and involves a number of strategic organisations and other community members who will give relevant information. |
| Consultation | • A facilitator is elected/appointed to work with the appointed team to ensure that intense consultative processes are explored around the draft policy document. | • Facilitator's consultation digs deeper and information is still shared with different experts in the field.<br>• Goals and objectives are explored further by a team of experts in consultation with other stakeholders. |
| Co-ordination | • Task team is formed to finalise draft policy. | • Facilitator must ensure that all parties involved have been consulted for final co-ordination.<br>• This is a backward and forward consultation process before the final decision is taken. |
| Decision | • A smaller task team is delegated to consult with different officials at different levels to finalise input received from all stakeholders from the beginning to this stage. | • A decision (law or programme) is finalised at senior level in the policymaking process. This is actual enactment of law or programme. |
| Implementation | • Translating law or operational guidelines into services or programmes for services to be provided. | • Government departments involved with specific target group will be responsible to implement policy programmes be it public and private sector organisations, civic organisations and community-based organisations. |
| Monitoring and Evaluation | • Different research methods can be utilised to monitor and evaluate whether the piece of legislation or programme does address or meet the needs of the target groups.<br>• Researchers may be employed internally and externally to monitor progress and challenges.<br>• Different stakeholders are invited to participate in the evaluation process.<br>• Monitoring is during the implementation phase and evaluation is towards the end of the programme or within a specific time frame. | • Participation of all parties (stakeholders) who got involved in the beginning stage, such as beneficiaries, different departments, experts, organisations, and all target groups.<br>• Identify parties to give input in the evaluation phase. |

The stages outlined above describe the roles played by different role players in developing, formulating, implementing, and monitoring and evaluating policy. Note that it is a complex process. What is of importance is to remember that policy is not static. It changes with time depending on the concerns and demands of the society. That is why we have policy analysts to help analyse the existing policy. It is also critical to note that policy should be monitored and evaluated to establish whether it is addressing the real needs of the people concerned. Therefore, it is important for the learner to know at what stage policy should be monitored and evaluated. Hence, in government departments we have policy units which allow the staff members to plan, formulate, implement, monitor and finally, evaluate existing policies.

| GROUP ACTIVITY 3 | **WHY GOVERNMENT OFFICIALS USE DIFFERENT PARTICIPATION METHODS TO ENGAGE SOUTH AFRICANS** |
| --- | --- |

Read the conversation below and answer the questions that follow.

**Sophy:** 'Hello Peter! I hear that the social workers have convened a community meeting in the neighbourhood to talk about welfare policy. Are you going to attend? Are they not supposed to do their work silently without calling meetings? They must do their work and do it in their offices as we cannot be attending Imbizos all the time.'

**Peter:** 'I think is the right thing to be involved in all these meetings because we voted all these politicians into Parliament. They must tell us what they are doing? We are taxpayers and we need them to report to us.'

**Kgomotso:** 'I like it when we have direct discussions with all these politicians in Parliament. I like their debates in Parliament. We can see who is doing wrong things and those who don't do anything.'

**Sophy:** 'What I don't like is what is happening in Parliament. Politicians are busy fighting one another in Parliament. They must be involved, busy with their work.'

**Kgomotso:** 'Yes, they are in offices but they must also be in public to answer questions that concern us as community people. We need to tell them what we need and stop talking to one another as political parties such as the EFF and Democratic Alliance and ANC.

**Peter:** 'They never agree on anything, I am happy that we can watch debates in Parliament; we can also sometimes talk to them in the sessions that are held around our areas. This is democracy? Is this transparency? What is happening in Parliament?'

**Sophy:** 'But do people get a chance to ask them questions? The parliamentarians need to debate on matters related to policies or legislation and engage people to participate, for them to give input, instead of just arguing all the time.'

**Zulu:** 'Yes, for me, I like it when they bring Parliament to the community. It is called Taking Parliament to the People. The social workers want the government to attend to our needs and concerns. Let us support them and attend meetings when they call us; we will be able to participate in policy formulation.'

1. Many times we don't hear the voice of women in decision-making. Describe methods that you think the government can use to engage women and girls fully in policymaking processes. Give one example of how they can be engaged.
2. Disabled people also feel discriminated against as their voices are not always heard in debates on policymaking. Explain how you can get disabled people to participate in policymaking without them feeling left out.
3. Which mechanism have you (or your friend or family member) participated in to address local government matters? What did you (or your friend or family member) like or dislike about this mechanism?
4. Do you know someone who is always involved in public debate and policy? Interview her/him to understand how people view their participation in policymaking in South Africa.

## 10.9 The role of the social worker in policymaking processes

The main focus of the social work profession is to promote social change and develop social cohesion with the ultimate goal of empowering individuals, groups, and communities to drive their own development processes. Social workers are expected to adhere to the principles of social justice, human rights, and collective responsibility. The main role of the social worker in a policy-making setting is that of a change agent. King and Zanetti (2005: 120) define the role of a change agent as being involved in helping to create open, public, democratic, and dialectic processes in which all segments of society are engage in resolving social problems. Social workers, therefore, get involved in social policy issues from the first stage of the policy formation to the end. They have a role from inside and outside the agency as facilitators of change and advocates of social justice. According to Ferguson (2008: 136), the change agent works behind the scene, organising, co-ordinating, nurturing, and enabling others to be involved in democratic processes. In this case, the social worker will participate in helping to identify the need or concern, together with other team members, to a stage where she or he is part of the monitoring and evaluation process. In all these stages the social workers facilitate change and engage all parties involved. Ferguson (2008: 13) states that:

> '... social work is not a quiet profession. Social workers play an important role in the vulnerable communities' struggle for equality and their concern is social justice.'

Social policy addresses social ills, wrongs, and transformation; this is one of the responsibilities of a social worker in a policy setting. In South Africa, social workers have been involved with social welfare and policy issues for many years. They participated in the formulation of social welfare policy and the drafting of other legislation that address social injustices. Social workers play this role as staff members of the Department of Social Development and as policymakers in this department. They also help to analyse policy documents. As practitioners in the different settings, such as non-governmental organisations and the private sector, they play different roles as policy implementers and advocates. Others are academics who teach social policy as a subject matter at different levels at colleges and universities. The academic's role is to equip social work students with skills and knowledge on policy formulation, implementation, analysis, and monitoring and evaluation.

## CONCLUSION

- The transformational participation in this chapter described the different stakeholders who participate in developing policies in South Africa. It outlined the transformational participatory process and how it was established in South Africa. The involvement of the marginalised communities, including the mechanisms that were introduced in the new South Africa since 1994, through different legislatures attempt to engage all stakeholders and different communities. The challenge is genuine participation where every citizen feels that he or she is part of decision-making.

- Research is still to be conducted to prove that the different mechanisms do create opportunities for marginalised individuals and communities. Communities, at different levels, want to be engaged in and want to take ownership of policy and programme development.
- How inclusive and participatory the policymaking cycle is in South Africa is a question still to be explored further. This chapter reflected on the processes of transformation and the participatory methods that are unique to South Africa.

## QUESTIONS

1. In your own words, can you describe and give practical examples from your community of what 'real people or community participation' is all about.
2. Have you come across public servants facilitating participatory processes and engaging communities or local people? If yes, briefly write a paragraph about the highlights of your experience.
3. If no, what in your view should happen in your local community for you to feel that there is community participation that is transformative?
4. If you watch television or listen to the news, have you come across a program referring to 'people's participation'? Briefly describe in a paragraph what stood out for you in the program.
5. What in your view is a democratic society? Can you give two examples that show that South Africa is a democratic society?

## REFERENCES

BUCCUS, I & HICKS, J (2003) 'Crafting New Democratic Spaces: Participatory Policy-Making in KwaZulu-Natal, South Africa' *Transformation: Critical Perspectives on Southern Africa* Vol. 65.

COALITION OF CIVIL SOCIETY RESOURCE MOBILIZATION (2012) *Critical Perspectives on Sustainability of South African Civil Society Sector.* Auckland Park: Jacana Media (Pty) Ltd.

DE BEER, F & SWANEPOEL, H (2010) *Community Development Breaking the Cycle of Poverty* (fourth edition). Cape Town: Juta & Co. Ltd.

FERGUSON, I (2008) *Reclaiming Social Work: Challenging Neo-liberalism and promoting Social Justice.* Thousand Oaks, CA: Sage Publications.

GUMEDE, V (2008) 'Public Policy Making in a Post-Apartheid South Africa: A preliminary Perspective' *Africanus: Journal of Development Studies* 38(2) at pp. 7–23.

HICKS, J (2003) *Participatory Policy-making in KwaZulu-Natal, South Africa.* UK: Institute of Development Studies, University of Sussex (Paper compiled in partial fulfilment of MA-thesis).

IDASA (2003) Working Document Civil Society and Participatory Making in South Africa: Gaps and Opportunities pp. 1–24.

KILONZO, BT (2011) *A University and Community Driven Social Facilitation Model for Rural Development Planning in South Africa.* Thohoyandou: University of Venda (PhD-thesis).

KING, CS & ZANETTI, LA (2005) *Transformational Public Service.* Armonk, New York: ME Sharpe.

LOUW, H, NEL, H & SCHENCK, R (2010) *Introduction to participatory community practice.* Pretoria: Unisa Press.

MASENG, JO (2014) 'State and non-state actors in South African public policy'. Africa Institute of South Africa Policy Brief Number 107 at pp. 1–4.

ROUX, NL (2002) 'Public policy-making and policy analysis in South Africa amidst transformation change and globalisation: views on participants and role players in the policy analytic procedure' *Journal of Public Administration* Vol. 37 No. 4 at pp. 418–437.

SOUTH AFRICA. 1996. *Constitution of Republic of South Africa Act 108 of 1996*. Pretoria: Government Printer. [Laws.]

SOUTH AFRICA. Department of Provincial and Local Government (2007) *Participatory Democracy in South Africa Conceptual issues* at pp. 47–49 Position the analysis and framework for analysis Working Document. Pretoria: Department of Provincial and Local Government.

SOUTH AFRICA. Parliament of the Republic of South Africa 'How parliament is structured' [Online]. Available: https://www.parliament.gov.za/how-parliament-is-structured [18 May 2017].

SOUTH AFRICA. Parliament of the Republic of South Africa 'Your representative' [Online]. Available: http//www.parliament.gov.za/your representative [18 May 2017].

SOUTH AFRICA. Parliament of the Republic of South Africa 'How -our Democracy Works' [Online]. Available: www.parliament.gov.za/ how -our democracy works [18 May 2017].

SPICKER, P (2006) *Policy Analysis for Practice*. UK: The Policy Press, University of Bristol.

TAYLOR, P & FRANSMAN, J (2004) *Learning and teaching participation: exploring the role of higher learning institutions as agents of development and social change*. Institute of Development Studies Working Paper 219, March 2004.

UNITED NATIONS RESEARCH INSTITUTE FOR SOCIAL DEVELOPMENT (2004) *Social Policy Processes*. United Kingdom: Palgrave MacMillan.

WEIDMAN, M (2015) 'The changing status of Civil Society Organizations in South Africa 1994 to 2014', Hanns Seidal Foundation Background Report South Africa.

PART
04

# Working with and transforming social welfare policy

# The role of the social worker as policy implementer and advocate in South Africa

*Jean D Triegaardt*

> *'Effective policy practice requires a clear vision of social justice and the ability to operate within existing social, economic, and political frameworks to promote that vision'* (Barusch, 2002: 22).

Chapter 11 examines how the role of the social work practitioner has developed by shifting the focus from remediation to transformation. Apart from implementing existing policy through practice, the social work practitioner also has a role to play in transforming policy through advocacy. The chapter's objectives and outcomes are listed below.

## Objectives

✓ Deepening understanding of the shift required to move from remedial intervention to a more rigorous intervention integrating micro, mezzo and macro levels.

✓ Appreciating the social, political and economic context in which social workers have to intervene and effect social welfare policy change.

✓ Understanding the roles and responsibilities, particularly those of policy implementer and advocate, in effecting social welfare policy change.

✓ Identifying and discussing the skills at macro, mezzo and micro levels to effect policy implementation and change.

## Outcomes

✓ Understanding the links between the shifts from remedial intervention to intervention at the macro/micro level in transformative social welfare policy.

✓ Appreciating the context within which social workers intervene in order to contribute to transformative social welfare policy.

✓ Understanding the roles and responsibilities which give effect to a transformative social welfare policy.

✓ Gaining awareness of the macro, mezzo and micro skills at the various levels which are required for policy implementation and change.

## 11.1 Introduction

The early role of social workers is characterised by a preoccupation with remedial intervention. This remedial practice applied not only to industrial nations, but also to developing countries in the South. Social workers tended to be involved in intervening with emotional and social factors of individuals which inhibit effective social functioning. Hall and Midgley (2008: 215) suggest that although a commitment to remedial intervention has been dominating social work practice, the profession has developed other forms of intervention which include group and community social work that are more concerned with providing services and helping people to improve their social conditions and less concerned with treatment.

Colonial rule impacted directly on indigenous people in the region and this was clearly explicated in Chapter 2 of this book on the history of social welfare in Southern Africa and the region. In addition, Chapter 2 provided many insights into the socioeconomic and political situation and how these forces shaped Southern Africa's social welfare processes. Since the Southern African Development Community (SADC) countries were influenced by different colonial authorities, their respective social welfare policies were fomentedfrom different socioeconomic and political conditions. In the 1990s, structural adjustment programmes directly impacted on countries by increasing poverty levels. These heightened levels of poverty caused great difficulties for countries because of the fragile state of their economies, and as a consequence weakened welfare systems.

The situation in South Africa was further complicated by the fact that preoccupation with remedial intervention was contiguous to the racial policies and laws of the country at the time. In Chapter 4, a discussion of the social welfare and social work systems pre 1994 is provided with an indication of the fragmentation along racial lines, the inequities that existed, and the low or nonexistent standard of services for the black majority. The apartheid service delivery model was inequitable, inappropriate, and unsustainable, and relied mainly on the residual model with a focus on micro social work interventions and residential care (Patel and Hochfeld, 2012: 692). These apartheid policies and laws exacerbated the intervention of social workers who in the main focused on social and emotional functioning of individuals and groups, and the level of intervention depended on the race of the individual. White prosperity under apartheid was buttressed by public health care, education, subsidised housing, and labour market protection (Seekings and Nattrass, 2016: 168). As indicated in previous chapters (Chapter 3 in particular), extensive intervention was devoted to white people because of the 'poor white problem' in the 1930s, while minimal intervention was directed at black African people. At the time, the Hertzog's government devised state programmes with the purpose of creating work opportunities for indigent and poor white people in the areas of the railways, municipalities, and agricultural settlements (Mazibuko and Gray, 2004: 130).

The core practice methods utilised in social work intervention during the apartheid years were casework, group work, and community work. The first two methods formed a major share of practice, and the latter played a much lesser role. Casework or individual work was often viewed as portraying a remedial function, whereas group work was often viewed as promoting social work's integrative function. Community social work was believed to be best suited to promoting social work's change or developmental function (Midgley, 2010: 4). The developmental function is also realised through social work advocacy and lobbying, as well as through engaging in policy practice.

Literature and academic debates tend to differentiate between remedial or clinical social work (micro practice), on the one hand, and developmental social work or macro practice, on the other. This bifurcation of the functions of social work is unfortunate since both micro and macro practice should be linked to promote developmental social welfare.

This chapter will examine the development of the social worker as policy implementer and advocate. A policy implementer is considered to be an active executioner of all the activities required to bring the welfare policy to fruition. *Policy advocacy* may be defined as the act of defending or directly representing client(s) with the purpose of influencing decision-making in unjust or unresponsive circumstances, shifting power relations, and effecting institutional change. *Advocacy* is aimed at bringing about social policies that have specific goals, such as ensuring that all human beings have equal access to the resources, employment services, and opportunities which they require to meet their basic human needs and to develop fully (NASW, 1999, section 6.04a in Hoefer, 2009: 69). The purpose of this chapter is to examine:

- the context which fomented practice change;
- the role of social workers in effecting social, political, and economic change;
- ways of bridging the micro-macro divide;
- the skills, tactics, and roles and responsibilities required for effecting policy implementation;
- advocacy for social justice; and
- future requirements and expectations.

## 11.2 Context for affecting practice change

The broader global context with all its developments requires that practitioners rethink remedial forms of practice. Developments such as the Copenhagen Social Development Summit, the Beijing Action Platform for Women in 1995 (UN, 1996), and the adoption of the Millennium Development Goals in 2000 by the UN General Assembly had an impact on changing social workers' conceptual understanding in their approach to policy and practice. All these UN policy initiatives required social workers and community workers to be involved (Dominelli, 2010: 135). Practitioners can make use of international instruments such as the Universal Declaration of Human Rights (UDHR) to enhance citizenship rights. However, Midgley (2010:11) is of the opinion that significant differences about the nature of social development practice and the conceptual ideas which underpin different interventions persist.

Early ideas about developmental social work were influenced by the work of Paulo Freire in the 1970s. Empowerment and conscientisation were powerful concepts that influenced the discourse and the trajectory of the practice of social work, and community development in particular. The concept of conscientisation impacted directly on social workers' dialogical engagement with their clients in providing them with the space to explore and understand the power imbalances which impede their functioning, and assisting them to learn various techniques to challenge these power structures (Midgley, 2010: 14). The writings of Freire contributed to social workers taking an activist approach, and further provided insights of educational strategies to analyse class differentials. According to Freire (1972), formal schooling is arranged like a banking system in which the curriculum, that is, the official agreed-upon knowledge is deposited into the heads of school learners by teachers, which can be withdrawn when required to do so and would serve the interests of those in power.

The contribution of various liberation movements (the African National Congress and the Pan Africanist Congress), the Black Consciousness Movement, and Black Liberation Theology during the apartheid era were instrumental in the critical examination and challenging of the structural conditions in South Africa which contributed to the oppression of black people. The term 'black' here refers to all people who were discriminated against with the purpose of subjugation by the apartheid government. Fester (2015: 115) observes that black women and black men were both oppressed by apartheid and capitalism, but black and white women were exploited by most men through patriarchy. However, black women and black men were united in fighting against apartheid. The Black Consciousness Movement embarked on black community programmes in the 1970s (Bak, 2004: 84). These programmes were inspired by the work of Paulo Freire and Saul Alinsky on consciousness raising and community development. Students, social workers, and communities worked co-operatively to expand social work to include community work. In the 1970s, a women's organisation inspired by the Black Consciousness Movement, the Black Women's Federation (BWF), was formed in 1975. Social workers belonged to the BWF. The Black Consciousness Movement and women's organisations were banned in 1977.

The United Democratic Front (UDF) was launched on 20 August 1983 (Seekings, 2015). The UDF was an umbrella organisation with over 400 affiliates representing churches, civic organisations, student organisations, women's organisations, sports bodies, youth organisations, and trade unions which challenged the repressive and unjust laws, structures, and policies of apartheid.

**Launch of the UDF in Cape Town in 1983**

The UDF's Declaration opposed the tricameral parliament and the Koornhof Bills – basically, the Declaration committed members to a non-racial, democratic and unitary South Africa (Seekings, 2015: 54). In April 1985, the UDF held its first full national conference, or National General Council (NGC). The purpose was to evaluate the UDF's performance since its launch, and to plan its roles in the fast changing political landscape. The first task that the NGC had to perform was to revise the UDF's stated objectives. At the launch of the UDF in 1983, the focus was on a new constitution. In 1985, it required a broader purpose. Accordingly, the NGC revised the statement of objectives in the UDF's Working Principles to include the following (Seekings, 2015: 138):

> *'The UDF shall strive towards the realisation of a non-racial, democratic*
> *and unfragmented South Africa, and to this end shall:-*
> *3.1 articulate opposition to the legislative programme of the government*
> *in so far as such a programme conflicts with democratic principles;*
> *3.2 act as a co-ordinating body for progressive community, social,*
> *educational, political and other such organisations which subscribe to*
> *democratic principles;*
> *3.3 articulate the social and political aspirations of the affiliates of UDF*
> *and their members.*
> *...'*

The NGC issued a set of 'immediate demands' which was in concert with its wider role. These included:

- the abolition of the tricameral parliament, segregated local government, and Bantustans;
- the scrapping of the Land Acts, Group Areas Act, pass laws, and so-called security laws;
- an end to forced renewals;
- the release of political prisoners and unbanning of political organisations;
- the disbanding of the security forces; and
- a unified education system.

During the period 1985–1990, members of the UDF, United Women's Congress (UWCO), and other organisations were arrested regularly. Many of the members were on the run or in 'safe houses' in white areas, which were usually the homes of whites who were members of organisations like Black Sash or who supported the anti-apartheid struggle (Fester, 2015: 534). Similarly, UDF members who were on the run were housed in 'safe houses' in township homes of black people who were sympathetic to the cause of the UDF and opposed the apartheid government. Black Sash was a women's organisation which was well known for its activist work opposed to the unjust laws of apartheid. More discussion about the Black Sash will follow later in this chapter.

The women's movement in South Africa provided further impetus to challenge the power differentials in relation to issues of gender, and consolidated the political role of social workers in effecting change. South African women were a dynamic anti-apartheid force, challenging patriarchy and other forms of oppression. Black and white women combined their efforts in challenging both patriarchy and apartheid. These efforts were channelled through organisations. More will be discussed later about these organisations which facilitated change during apartheid. As mentioned previously, Fester (2015: 115) observes that black women and black men were both oppressed by apartheid and capitalism, but black and white women were exploited by most men through patriarchy. At the time, political activists often referred to the double oppression of black women, which implied that black women were faced with the dual challenge of oppression by the state as well as the patriarchy of their male counterparts. Despite this, black women and black men were united in their efforts to fight against the common challenge of apartheid.

The South African welfare sector was not equipped to deal effectively with structural reforms prior to 1994 because of its entrenchment in remedial practice. Lund (2008: 7) makes the observation that, in 1989, she came to the conclusion that the welfare sector was ill-prepared for engagement in macro-level, big systems reform. Since 1994, the context of South Africa demanded a change in dealing with structural issues such as poverty, unemployment, inequality, and other forms of social deprivation. These problems were exacerbated by additional challenges such as the Aids pandemic. The foundation policy document, that is, the *White Paper for Social Welfare* (1997), required a change in approach by social workers in providing welfare services to people. Policies are courses of action with the purpose of government setting goals which would fulfil human and economic development. This policy document required an expansion of remedial work to include community development work under the umbrella of the social development perspective. This latter perspective is defined as follows: 'a process of planned social change designed to promote the well-being of the population as a whole in conjunction with a dynamic process of economic development' (Midgley, 1995: 25). Patel (2015: xi) notes that it is an approach to promoting human well-being (or social welfare).

One of the key aspects of the social development perspective is the feature of harmonising social or human and economic development (this has been explained previously in Chapter 3). If more emphasis is placed on economic development and concomitant economic growth, to the exclusion of human development, then it will lead to distorted development. Economic growth is meaningless unless the standards of living of the population as a whole are improved. This requires that inclusive economic development is enhanced by government with the purpose of promoting economic participation and adopting measures that will increase employment, incomes, and educational skills and enhance standards of living (Midgley and Sherraden, 2009: 283). Social or human development implies that investment is made in human beings with the idea of promoting human capabilities.

The social development perspective is premised on certain core values. These core values have been identified in the *White Paper for Social Welfare* (RSA, 1997) as democracy, social justice, and equality. These values are explained in Chapter 3 and they form the foundation for developmental welfare policy in South Africa. Social values reflect the dominant group in society. They may exert considerable influence in shaping society and maintaining the status quo, but they are not fixed and may evolve over time (Drower, 1996: 142). Other values and principles that are identified in the *White Paper for Social Welfare* (1997) and are related to the social work profession are respect, self-determination, *Ubuntu*, and acceptance. *Ubuntu* has also been referred to as botho in Botswana. *Botho* has been described as meaning to be humble, caring, compassionate, selfless, respectful, and reliable and to love people (Rankopo, 2007: 97). The term epitomises humanity or humanness.

Developmental social welfare comprises five features which encompass a rights-based approach, harmonising social and economic policies, democracy and participation, pluralism or partnership, and bridging the macro and micro divide in intervention. These five features of developmental social welfare are explained in detail in Chapter 3. Given that there was an overall preponderance of remedial social workers, the South African welfare context with the new developmental welfare policy has evolved with its concomitant unique requirements of roles and responsibilities for social workers. The current roles and responsibilities will be analysed in response to the expectations and requirements for social workers in the twenty-first century.

## 11.3 The role of social workers in effecting social, political and economic change

McInnis-Dittrich (1994:147) notes that:

> *'As part of the social work profession's commitment to the client's well-being, it is critical to be aware of and committed to social change.'*

Social workers need to respond to the demands of society which includes the needs of individuals, families, groups, and communities. These demands include the task of advocate for the marginalised. Advocacy may be defined as those purposive efforts to change specific existing or proposed policies or practices on behalf of or with a specific client or group of clients (Mark Ezell, 2001 in Barusch, 2002: 376). Empowerment and equality are essential values for social workers interested in pursuing social justice for individuals and communities. It will include roles and responsibilities, as well as the skills and strategies required to pursue social, political, and economic change in policy.

Various academics and social work researchers observed that many social workers were complicit in the unequal delivery of social welfare services during the apartheid years (McKendrick, 1990; Patel, 2005), although this collusion was not intentional. This kind of collusion took the form of providing segregated social services, and working in racially segregated offices, programmes, and organisations. In essence, this was tantamount to supporting social welfare policies which were oppressive, discriminatory, and divisive. Certain social workers actively supported the state, informing on colleagues and clients, and aiding security police abuses (Schmid and Sacco, 2012: 293).

## 11.3.1 Advocacy during the apartheid era

Even though there were social workers who aided and abetted the apartheid security police within the country, there were social workers who were affiliated to and members of various organisations which opposed the apartheid regime. This opposition took the form of social action, and at the centre of this action was advocacy and political action. Black Sash was one such organisation that challenged oppressive laws. It was a nonviolent white women's resistance organisation that was founded on 19 May 1955. They were known for their silent protests with placards, vigils, marches, and petitions (http://www.blacksash.org.za/index.php/our-legacy/our-history). Black Sash members demonstrated against the pass laws and other apartheid legislation. Other well-known organisations included the United Democratic Front (UDF), with affiliates such as the United Women's Congress (UWCO) and Federation of South African Women (FSAW), and the South African Black Social Workers Association (SABSWA) and Concerned Social Workers (CSW) that were formed in 1945 and 1989, respectively (Mazibuko and Gray, 2004: 132).

CSW emerged with the purpose of addressing welfare policy and change processes. Both CSW and SABSWA became involved in raising awareness about unjust welfare policies and practice, advocating related issues. SABSWA was a professional organisation for (African) black social workers which made representation to the apartheid government on social welfare matters related to black communities. They also ensured that black social workers maintained a high standard of ethical conduct and integrity according to a code of ethics. One of their tasks was to promote community development and render community service (Mazibuko and Gray, 2004: 132). On occasion, joint statements and protests were provided by these organisations together with other professional associations such as the Society for Social Workers (Johannesburg) and the Durban Welfare Policy Committee which was established in 1986. These professional and social welfare agencies in and around Durban protested against the divisive and racially segregated welfare policy proposed by the government in 1985 (Mazibuko and Gray, 2004: 135). Therefore, social workers were involved in advocacy work and proposals concerning welfare policy changes during the apartheid era. The agitation against the racially segregated welfare policies gained momentum during the 1980s. In 1989, CSW together with other social work organisations such as SABSWA, the Society for Social Workers (Witwatersrand), Johannesburg Indian Welfare Association, Social Workers' Forum (Cape Town), and the Welfare Policy Committee (Durban) convened a National Social Welfare Policy Conference in Johannesburg. The purpose of the conference was to develop an appropriate social welfare policy for South Africa. Three objectives were proposed: (1) to mobilise social workers, community-based service projects, progressive social service organisations, and trade unions to reject the state's apartheid welfare policy; (2) to work towards building a united welfare movement; and (3) to commence the process of evolving appropriate welfare policy for post-apartheid South Africa (Patel, 1989). These initiatives received wide-scale support from community activists and social service organisations (Gray, 2006: S57).

There were social workers who were arrested, banished or spent time in solitary confinement as political prisoners during the apartheid era, and some were prominent leaders in the struggle against apartheid. For example, Winnie Madikizela Mandela was South Africa's first qualified black social worker.

Her political activism, leadership, and marriage to Nelson Mandela made her a primary target of the apartheid regime. She was constantly harassed, jailed, held in solitary confinement for long periods, banned, and banished to Brandford, Orange Free State.

Helen Joseph, another social worker, was the secretary of the Federation of South Africa Women (FSAW), a non-racial organisation, which was established in 1954. FSAW opposed the oppressive apartheid policies and legislation through strikes and boycotts. Helen Joseph was banned four times, jailed four times, was persecuted by police, and spent much of her life under house arrest. About twenty thousand women, including Helen Joseph, marched to the Union Buildings in

Winnie Madikizela Mandela was one of South Africa's struggle icons

Pretoria on 9 August 1956 to protest against the pass laws being extended to African women (Fester, 2015; Seekings, 2016). This was a momentous time in the history of protest against an oppressive government.

---

**EXAMPLE**     **ADVOCACY BY CONCERNED SOCIAL WORKERS (CSW)**

A central activity of CSW was its campaign called 'Dismantling Apartheid in Welfare'. With the introduction of Value Added Tax (VAT) in 1991, a CSW delegation approached the Minister of National Health and Population Development (which included Welfare) regarding the impact of Value Added Tax (VAT) on poverty. The delegation argued that the introduction of VAT would add an additional group of poverty-stricken people, people who were already struggling to make ends meet. The Minister of National Health and Population Development's response at the time was that VAT was the Minister of Finance's portfolio and not hers. Therefore, she was not interested in the CSW's arguments in advocating for a new category of poor people.

The CSW also met with the National Executive Committee (NEC) of the African National Congress (ANC) about the appointment and selection of the Minister of Welfare and Population Development in post-apartheid South Africa. The delegation's concerns were that the next Minister should be well respected and have the support of the welfare sector.

(Adapted from Schmid and Sacco, 2012: 300)

---

---

| EXAMPLE | ADVOCACY BY A SOCIAL MOVEMENT |
|---|---|

*Treatment Action Campaign and Others v Minister of Health and Others 2002(4) BCLR 356 (T)*

An example of advocacy is the case of the Treatment Action Campaign (TAC) challenging the South African government, particularly the Department of Health. The anti-retroviral drug Nevirapine offered the potential of preventing the infection of 30–40,000 children per year. The drug was offered to the government for free for five years, but the South African government announced it would introduce mother-to-child-transmission (MTCT) only at certain pilot sites and would delay setting these up for a year, thereby denying most mothers access to treatment. The Treatment Action Campaign (TAC) launched a constitutional challenge, alleging a violation of the right to access health care services, and demanding a programme to make the drug available throughout the country. Specifically, the Constitutional Court ruled that Nevirapine should be made available at those public health facilities where testing and counselling for pregnant mothers already exist. The Court ordered the government to extend availability of Nevirapine to hospitals and clinics, to provide counsellors; and to take reasonable measures to extend the testing and counselling facilities throughout the public health sector. The TAC won the case in 2002. The judgment in this case is estimated to have saved tens of thousands of lives.

Zakkie Achmat, a founding member of the TAC, campaigning for the rights of those living with HIV and Aids

The Treatment Action Campaign's victory as a result of the Constitutional Court's verdict demonstrates what an important role this NPO (or social movement) played in securing treatment for people living with HIV and Aids (Patel and Selipsky, 2010: 63).

## 11.3.2 Policy implementer

One of the roles for implementing policies is that of a policy implementer. The process of policy implementation requires that the actions need to be broken down into sub-activities. The policy process includes the following: assessment; checking the alternatives, developing an action plan; implementation; and evaluation (see Chapter 3).

Table 11.1  Skills, tactics and roles required for policy implementation and advocacy for the policy process

| Policy process | | |
|---|---|---|
| Policy implementation | | Advocacy |
| Skills | Tactics | Roles |
| Macro | Social | Developing partnerships |
| Mezzo | Political | Commonalities/differences |
| Micro | Economic | Piloting/best practice<br>Intervention in unfamiliar areas |

The above table demonstrates the skills required at macro, mezzo and micro levels. Macro skills are required to effectively engage with communities, the wider society and at a policy level with national, regional or international agencies such as the United Nations. Mezzo level skills are used to engage with formal groups or complex organisations. Micro level skills are useful in engaging with individuals, small groups and families. Tactics have been identified as social, political or economic (Kahn 1991 in Reisch, 2012: 97). There are a range of roles that social workers utilise in implementing welfare policy practice, and some of these roles are indicated in the table above such as developing partnerships; seeking commonalities or differences; piloting or use of best practice; and intervention in unfamiliar areas. These roles are elaborated on in more detail in the section under 'Roles and responsibilities for policy implementation and change'.

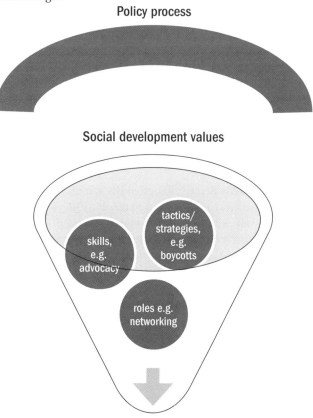

Figure: 11.1  Skills, tactics/strategies, and roles of social workers in the policy process

The above figure provides an indication of how the policy process is guided by a vision of social development values with the necessary tools such as skills, tactics or strategies, and roles of the social worker in implementing policies which will bring about transformation. In order to implement policies with the purpose of effecting change, it is necessary that social workers not only focus on the micro levels of intervention, but bridge the chasm with mezzo and macro levels of intervention. The pursuit of social justice, equity, and democracy for a transformative welfare policy would be meaningless if this chasm is not linked and integrated.

# 11.4 **Bridging the macro and micro divide**

Multi-method interventions and tactics to effect institutional change and a transformation of welfare policy are required when empowering individuals, families, groups and communities. This is linked to bridging the gap between micro and macro levels. What is essential to understand is that the dichotomy between micro interventions, which focus on individuals and small groups, and macro interventions, aimed at changing structural inequalities and injustices, needs to be recognised and acknowledged. Social work as a profession has a unique methodology that emphasises the importance of knowledge and skills in assessing the causes of needs and problems, identifying the best way of addressing them, and implementing solutions (Hall and Midgley, 2008: 215). Skills which are required to effect policy change include, *inter alia*, conflict and mediation skills, advocacy skills to facilitate building partnerships, research skills, policy scanning skills, and management and administration skills.

## 11.4.1 Macro skills for policy implementation and change

Knowledge of human rights legislation and conventions is an important component of social workers' repertoire of skills (Ife, 2001a; 2001b). Therefore, it would behove the social worker to know human rights policy and legislation such as the South African Constitution, the Human Rights Commission Act 54 of 1994, and conventions such as the Universal Declaration of Human Rights (UDHR).

- Conflict and mediation skills are advanced skills which require social workers to be empathetic and respectful, and enable them to resolve differences of opinion or disputes amongst members of a group, communities or organisations. Social workers are required to have the acumen to find and secure common ground to deal with opposing points of view.
- Advocacy is a macro level practice skill which is conducted on behalf of groups or communities who feel powerless to deal with authorities regarding issues of resources, service delivery or infrastructure.
- Facilitating building partnerships requires social workers to actively engage with individuals, groups, and communities on areas of common ground to promote policy implementation. Engagement with key stakeholders is an important component of macro practice.
- Research skills are critical to inform policy decision-making, back up arguments, and effect changes. Evidenced-based policy is a crucial consideration of policy formulation and implementation.
- Policy scanning skills are required to examine the policies and legislation that govern the existing issue or problem, the gaps that exist, the sphere of government to which the issue or problem relates, the organisation's policies and procedures in the manual, and which policies, laws and procedures impact on the services that the organisation renders.

- Management and administration skills are required to provide leadership and vision to effect policy change and implementation.

These above macro skills link with the necessary mezzo and micro skills below in policy implementation.

## 11.4.2 Mezzo skills for policy implementation and change

Mezzo skills are utilised at organisational or community level. Skills such as mediation, conflict management, and most of the above skills are used. These skills build on each other. The following skills are useful at the community or organisational level:

- Problem solving, counselling, interviewing and interpersonal skills.
- Negotiation and mediation, conflict resolution, and group work. Negotiation is a process of arriving at a mutual or agreed upon decision. Hoefer (2009: 76) suggests that before starting any negotiation, an advocate should develop an initial position, fall-back positions (that is, the minimum position), and a limit.
- Conceptual, community mobilisation, participatory approaches, entrepreneurship development, and leadership development.
- Communication (discussed below under micro skills), maintaining documentation, archiving files and documents, budgeting, management, project management, capacity-building, networking, monitoring and evaluation, time management, writing funding proposals, public speaking and presentation, lobbying, advocacy, and professionalism (Maistry, 2010: 177).
- Presentation skills. In order to present a policy issue, a social worker has to defend the argument (perhaps with research data), know the audience to which the policy will be presented, and gain support for the arguments. Presentation skills and assertiveness are valuable assets for presenting either at public hearings or other forums in order to gain support for the cause.

## 11.4.3 Micro skills for policy implementation and change

Micro skills are essential for meaningful engagement with clients and small or informal groups.

- Communication refers to written and oral communication skills which are essential to deal effectively with various stakeholders and clients.
- Respect is an essential quality in engaging with a range of clients and stakeholders.
- Confidentiality is a requirement for social workers to build trust and is required for professional engagement. Confidentiality means that the information shared by clients with the social worker will not be divulged to other people.
- Interpersonal skills are a crucial aspect of engaging with a range of clients, groups, and stakeholders. Interpersonal skills demonstrate to clients that they are respected and cared for in these engagements.

The above macro, mezzo, and micro skills are necessary skills for policy implementation and change. They are used in engaging with a range of people and target audiences. Since advocacy is such an important skill in advancing policy implementation and welfare policy transformation, a section is devoted below on advocacy practice for social justice.

## 11.4.4 Advocacy practice for social justice

Advocacy contributes to effective policy change. With advocacy skills, the required policy issue is advocated with the required goals. The necessary facts are obtained to back up the case and a strategy is developed and embarked upon. It is critical to know who are the decision makers and the key people and organisations who will be willing to support the policy issue. Thereafter, coalitions, partnerships, and allies will broaden the base of support. There are six phases of advocacy practice: (1) getting involved; (2) understanding the issue; (3) planning; (4) advocating; (5) evaluating; and (6) ongoing monitoring (Hoefer, 2009: 70).

### Phase 1: Getting Involved

Social workers do get politically involved. The history of the apartheid era provides adequate evidence of social workers who became involved in advocacy against the injustices of the government. These social workers participated and were members of various organisations (for example, UDF, FSAW, and UWCO) through which they obtained institutional support and fulfilled the social and political mandate of these organisations. Much of this discussion is covered above in section 11.3 under 'The role of social workers in effecting social, political and economic change'.

### Phase 2: Understanding the issue

Hoefer (2006) suggests a five-step process to understand the issue. These steps include the following: (a) define the issue; (b) decide who the issue impacts and how they are affected by the issue; (c) decide on the main causes of the issue; (d) explore possible solutions to the issue; and (e) review possible solutions to determine their impact on social justice.

### Phase 3: Planning

The planning phase requires that one sets out a plan to get from 'a' to 'b', that is, generating a road map. Hoefer (2009) suggests that one develop an advocacy plan which will indicate the relationship between resources, actions, and the desired outcomes. This would be an opportune time to create a plan for project management – that is, plotting time frames about when the desired outcome(s) would be achieved.

At the conclusion of the planning process, advocates should be able to answer the following four questions:

1. What do you hope to achieve?
2. Who is able to assist you to achieve what you want?
3. When can or should one act?
4. How can you act to achieve what you want?

### Phase 4: Advocating

Advocating involves engaging with the person(s) who and/or organisation(s) that need convincing of the merits of the policy issue. Preparation of the content of the advocacy message needs to be thought through very carefully, which is when political acumen or political suss is necessary. The format of the message may either be oral or written communication.

### Phase 5: Ongoing Monitoring

Monitoring is an ongoing process to ascertain whether the policy is achieving the objectives that were planned. The trajectory of the policy may need to be reviewed depending on what one is hoping to achieve.

## Phase 6: Evaluating

Evaluation is key to assessing whether policy change is required or that a benchmark has been forged. Hoefer (2006) proposes that advocates can use the advocacy maps to determine the extent of the task completion and the outcome attainment.

- Social workers may embark on advocacy on their own through their organisational work. However, other forms of advocacy can be conducted through other mediums such as professional organisations and/or social movements. These professional organisations or associations are regarded as mediums through which social workers' professional interests can be promoted and through which the profession can gain stature and recognition, depending on the association's activities. Coalitions of organisations and allies who support the policy issue may be involved in advocacy work to effect policy change. For example, children's rights organisation have come together to advocate policy and legislation that gives effect to children's rights (Patel, 2015: 168).
- Public hearings are another forum where advocacy for a policy can be conducted. Parliamentary committees call for comments on policies and legislation through public hearings, and public comments in newspapers. Refer to the case study below to see how public hearings impact decision-making in social welfare.

---

 **Case Study** | **IMPLEMENTATION OF THE POLICY OF THE CHILD SUPPORT GRANT (CSG)**

When the Child Support Grant (CSG) was first introduced in 1998, there was an outcry because of the phasing out of the State Maintenance Grant (SMG) which was allocated to impoverished families and children. The latter social grant was considered to be unsustainable, inappropriate, and discriminatory since it was provided to certain racial groups. Therefore, it had to be phased out. The replacement was the CSG which would be provided to poor children younger than seven years old and would be paid to the primary caregiver. At the time, given the resources provided by the government, the recommendation was that an amount of R75,00 per child would be paid to the primary caregiver. However, at the public hearings which were held at Parliament, organisations which included NGOs, CBOs, and trade unions campaigned and protested against the Lund Report (Lund, 2008) recommendations. These organisations objected to the proposed amount of R75,00 per child and advocated for an increased amount. Finally, it was agreed that the amount would be R100,00 per child. Therefore, the advocacy by the NGOs and some academics who worked actively with the parliamentary portfolio welfare committee was the impetus to increase the amount of the CSG to each child.

Source: Lund, F (2008); Triegaardt (2005)

---

Advocacy can be effective in contributing to transforming welfare policy, but it requires political acumen in navigating the many political agendas that opposition groups may put forward. The strategy is to find common ground which will fulfil goals that will be beneficial to achieving human rights and dignity for one's clients.

## 11.4.5 Tactics for policy implementation and change

Tactics that organisations such as the UDF, UWCO, FSAW, and others used were marches, rallies, boycotts, and demonstrations. These 'social tactics' such as marches, rallies and demonstrations were categorised by Kahn (1991 in Reisch, 2012: 97). Then there are the 'political power tactics' which can be either economic (boycotts, strikes) or political (civil disobedience). Economic tactics were certainly used by the above organisations, for example, the red meat boycott was launched in the Western Cape in 1980.

These tactics and skills are linked to the requisite roles and responsibilities which have to be carried out by the social worker to bring about policy change.

## 11.4.6 Roles and responsibilities for policy implementation and change

The roles and responsibilities of a social worker for effecting policy implementation, which are intrinsic to developmental social welfare practice, are discussed in the section below. Roles are guided by values and ethical codes of conduct.

- Within the context of developmental social welfare practice, roles that are required will be developing partnerships which will promote policy research with research centres, universities, or schools of social work.
- Networking is a key consideration since it facilitates collaborations, partnerships, and coalitions. This role may assist in reaching out to funding bodies, legislators, client groups, boards of trustees, and the public (Horton, Roland, Briar-Lawson and Rowe, 2012: 218).
- Social workers need to ascertain the commonalities and differences between individuals, groups, and communities with the purpose of reaching solutions for common problems.
- Roles of social workers, managers, and supervisors at mezzo level practice may involve piloting of a programme to test its efficacy or best practice.
- There are areas of social work which require interventions which are unfamiliar to the conventional forms of practice, for example, refugee/migrant and displaced people are still an unknown area of practice for most social workers on the continent. An important consideration for social work practice is the issue of working in the refugee/migrant and internally displaced people space. During the process of the *Review of the Implementation of the White Paper for Social Welfare* (RSA, 2016), social workers referred to the challenges they face when working with refugees and displaced people, for example, the language barriers, orphaned and vulnerable children, and economic migrants. In Chapter 8, dealing with social welfare policy in response to the risks and vulnerabilities of migrants, refugees and internally displaced people, some of these issues are identified.

## 11.4.7 Professional organisations/associations and social movements

In 2008, a new professional organisation was formed known as the National Association of Social Workers, South Africa (NASW, SA). The mission of this organisation was to serve as a united voice for the social work profession and to advance the interests and contributions of social work in its broader pursuit for human dignity and social justice (NASW, SA, 2008: 1). The objectives that underpin the mission are as follows:

- Acknowledge and promote the identity of social workers.
- Intensify education, training, development, and empowerment opportunities.
- Promote and uphold the ethical standards, quality, and efficiency of social work.
- Share best practice approaches, models, and professional techniques.
- Establish local, regional, and global networks and formalise partnerships and associations with bodies that further the interests of social workers.
- Initiate and contribute to research on any matters affecting social work.
- Seek ongoing advancement and innovation in social work.
- Seek local and global strategies and solutions toward improved services.
- Promote and market the social work profession.

- Lobby and advocate for social justice in matters that affect the social work profession.
- Facilitate the creation of conditions that are conducive to social workers' proper functioning and retention in the profession.

Affiliation to professional organisations is an important consideration for social workers to advance a political and social agenda for clients, especially in contexts of unjust and oppressive conditions.

The discussion above in section 11.3 on 'The role of social workers in effecting social, political and economic change' regarding social workers' membership of social movements is another consideration for advocacy and policy changes to advance social justice when clients, groups or communities live in oppressive conditions. For example, there are social movements such as the Treatment Action Campaign mentioned in the above discussion; the South African Unemployed People's Movement based in Durban, KZN and Grahamstown in the Eastern Cape; the Landless People's Movement in Gauteng; Equal Education in Gauteng and the Western Cape; and the Social Justice Coalition in the Western Cape. Social movements create the opportunity and space for delivery on human rights to citizens and for ensuring accountability by government.

## 11.5 Future requirements and expectations

The context in which social workers and development practitioners operate continues to evolve with complex demands in the twenty-first century, and, as a result of these complex demands, the expectations and requirements will become more complex. Moreover, developmental welfare policy envisages interventions that support and grow local community initiatives through community development, local economic development, income generation, and micro-enterprises to promote the livelihood capabilities of the poor (Patel and Hochfeld, 2012: 693). However, social workers need to find ways to ensure that individuals, groups, and communities realise their human rights to achieve their full potential. The Constitution and Bill of Rights which enshrine values and principles such as equality, social justice, and human rights provide the framework and space within which social workers can act with confidence.

## CONCLUSION

- This chapter explains certain key areas for social work and development practice. Firstly, the shift in practice from the residual intervention in the apartheid context to developmental social work in the post-apartheid context is identified. The shift demonstrates the change from oppressive and unjust welfare policies and practice to the current transformative social welfare policy and practice which has its foundations in social justice and human rights. The Constitution and human rights legislation provides the overarching framework in which social workers can operate with confidence.
- Secondly, advocacy is discussed within the apartheid era when social workers as members of social movements and/or organisations contributed to the political changes to the oppressive policies and legislation. In spite of some social workers colluding with the unjust laws of the apartheid government, there were social workers who protested against the inhumane laws and policies through their affiliation to progressive organisations like the UDF, UWCO, CSW, and SABSWA.

- Thirdly, the roles of policy implementer and advocacy in the policy process are provided substance through the use of skills and tactics. The utility of certain roles and skills will require political acumen in the light of intervention at the mezzo and macro levels. Affiliation to professional organisations and/or social movements will enhance and provide legitimacy to social workers' protests against welfare policies which violate client's rights to human dignity.
- And finally, transformative welfare policies provide both the context and the space for social workers to be effective advocates and policy implementers.

## QUESTIONS

1. What are the skills required to effect policy implementation and change?
2. How have social workers contributed to advocacy during the apartheid era?
3. Read the case study below and answer the question.

---

**Case Study  THE ROLE OF THE SOCIAL WORKER**

Mental health patients were staying in a mental health facility, namely, Sunrise (Letsatsi Le Hlabile). There were 24 patients at this facility. The Department of Health decided to move the patients to another NPO facility because of a lack of financial resources. The NPO facility where the patients were moved is unlicensed. Some of these patients have families who have stayed in touch, and others have no contact with their respective families. You are employed as a social worker at the Sunrise mental health facility.

*What would you do under the circumstances? Draw on your policy knowledge, skills and values and decide on how you would deal with this situation.*

---

4. How would you as a social worker proceed in effecting policy implementation and change in the present context of injustice against mental health patients?
5. How would you as a social worker promote transformation of welfare policies which are just and egalitarian in a context of injustice and oppression?

## REFERENCES

BAK, M (2004) 'Can developmental social welfare change an unfair world? The South African experience' *International Social Work* 47(1): 81–94.

BARUSCH, AS (2002) *Foundations of Social Policy. Social Justice, Public Programs, and the Social Work Profession.* Itasca, Illinois: F E Peacock Publishers, Inc.

BLACK SASH [Online]. Available: http://www.blacksash.org.za/index.php/our-legacy/our-history [16 November 2017].

DOMINELLI, L (2010) *Social Work in a Globalizing World.* Cambridge, UK; Malden: MA Polity Press.

DROWER, SJ (1996) 'Social Work Values, Professional Unity, and the South African Context' *Social Work. Journal of the National Association of Social Workers* 41(2): 138–146.

FESTER, G (2015) *South African Women's Apartheid and Post-Apartheid Struggles: 1980 – 2014. Rhetoric and Realising Rights, Feminist Citizenship and Constitutional Imperatives: A Case of the Western Cape.* Saarbrucken, Germany: Scholars' Press.

FREIRE, P (1972) *Pedagogy of the Oppressed.* New York: Herder and Herder.

GRAY, M (2006) 'The progress of social development in South Africa' *International Journal of Social Welfare* 15 (Suppl 1): S53–S64.

HALL, A & MIDGLEY, J: 'Social Work and the Human Services' in Hall, A & Midgley, J (eds.) (2008) *Social Policy for Development* at pp. 205–232. Los Angeles, London, New Delhi, Singapore: Sage Publications.

HOEFER, R (2006) *Advocacy practice for social justice*. Chicago: Lyceum.

HOEFER, R: 'Policy Practice and Advocacy' in Midgley, J and Livermore, M (eds.) (2009) *The Handbook of Social Policy* (second edition) at pp. 66–82. Los Angeles, London, New Delhi, Singapore: Sage Publications.

HORTON, HK, ROLAND, BD, BRIAR-LAWSON, K & ROWE, W: 'Assessment of Institutions' in Glisson, CA, Dulmus, CN & Sowers, KM (eds.) (2012) *Social Work Practice with Groups, Communities and Organizations. Evidence-Based Assessments and Interventions* at pp. 191–227. Hoboken, New Jersey: John Wiley & Sons, Inc.

IFE, J (2001a) *Human Rights and Social Work: Towards Rights-Based Practice*. Cambridge: Cambridge University Press.

IFE, J (2001b) 'Local and Global Practice: Relocating Social Work as a Human Rights Profession in a New Global Order' *European Journal of Social Work* 4(1): 515–521.

INTERNATIONAL NETWORK FOR ECONOMIC, SOCIAL AND CULTURAL RIGHTS [Online]. Available: https://www.escr-net.org/caselaw/minister-health-v-treatment-action-campaign-tac-2002-5-sa-721-cc [7 December 2017].

LUND, F (2008) *Changing Social Policy. The Child Support Grant in South Africa*. Cape Town: HSRC Press.

MAISTRY, M: 'Community Development' in Nicholas, L, Rautenbach, J & Maistry, M (2010) *Introduction to Social Work* at pp. 156–177. Claremont: Juta & Company.

MAZIBUKO, F & GRAY, M (2004) 'Social work professional associations in South Africa' *International Social Work* 47(1): 129–142.

MCINNIS-DITTRICH, K (1994) *Integrating Social Welfare Policy & Practice*. Pacific Grove, California: Brooks/Cole Publishing Company.

MCKENDRICK, B: 'The South African Social Welfare System' in McKendrick, B (ed.) (1990) *Introduction to Social Work in South Africa* at pp. 3–43. Pretoria: Haum Tertiary.

MIDGLEY, J (1995) *Social Development. The Developmental Perspective in Social Welfare*. London, Thousand Oaks, New Delhi: Sage Publications.

MIDGLEY, J: 'The Theory and Practice of Developmental Social Work' in Midgley, J & Conley, A (2010) *Social Work and Social Development. Theories and Skills for Developmental Social Work* at pp. 3–28. New York: Oxford University Press.

MIDGLEY, J & SHERRADEN, M: 'The Social Development Perspective in Social Policy' in Midgley, J & Livermore, M (eds.) (2009) *The Handbook of Social Policy* (second edition) at pp. 279–294. Los Angeles, London, New Delhi, Singapore: Sage Publications.

NATIONAL ASSOCIATION OF SOCIAL WORK, SOUTH AFRICA (2008) *Constitution*. Durban: NASW, SA.

PATEL, L (2015) *Social welfare & social development in South Africa*. Cape Town: Oxford University Press.

PATEL, L (2005) *Social welfare and social development in South Africa*. Cape Town: Oxford University Press Southern Africa.

PATEL, L (ed.) (1989) *Towards a democratic welfare system. Options and strategies*. Proceedings of the National Welfare Policy Conference, May 1989. Johannesburg: Coordinating Committee Against the Welfare Policy.

PATEL, L & HOCHFELD, T (2012) 'Developmental social work in South Africa: Translating policy into practice' *International Social Work* 56(5): 690–704.

PATEL, L & SELIPSKY, L: 'Social Welfare Policy and Legislation in South Africa' in Nicholas, L, Rautenbach, J & Maistry, M (eds.) (2010) *Introduction to Social Work* at pp. 48–74. Claremont: Juta & Co.

RANKOPO, M: 'The Micro-Macro Nexus in Community Development: Towards Reflexive Practice' in Osei-Hwedie, K & Jacques, G (eds.) (2007) *Indigenising Social Work in Africa* at pp. 90–106. Accra: Ghana Universities Press.

REISCH, M. 'Intervention with Communities' in Glisson, CA, Dulmus, CN & Sowers, KM (eds.) (2012) *Social Work Practice with Groups, Communities, and Organisations. Evidence-Based Assessments and Interventions* at pp. 81–130. Hoboken, New Jersey; Canada: John Wiley & Sons, Inc.

SCHMID, J & SACCO, T (2012) 'A Story of Resistance: "Concerned Social Workers"' *The Social Work Practitioner-Researcher* Vol. 24(3): 291–308.

SEEKINGS, J (2015) *The UDF. A History of the United Democratic Front in South Africa 1983–1991.* Cape Town: David Philip Publishers.

SEEKINGS, J & NATTRASS, N (2016) *Poverty, Politics & Policy in South Africa. Why has Poverty Persisted after Apartheid?* Johannesburg, South Africa: Jacana Media (Pty) Ltd.

SOUTH AFRICA. Department of Social Development (2016) *Review of the Implementation of the White Paper for Social Welfare Report.* Pretoria: Government Printer.

SOUTH AFRICA. Department of Welfare (1997) *White Paper for Social Welfare* in GN 1108. Pretoria: Government Printer.

TRIEGAARDT, J (2005) 'The Child Support Grant in South Africa: a social policy for poverty alleviation?' *International Journal of Social Welfare* 14: 249–255.

# Statutory role in different social welfare focus areas

*Mimie Sesoko*

Chapter 3 of this book introduces social welfare policies and programmes. The aim of this chapter is to outline the statutory role of the social welfare policies in the provision of services to vulnerable communities. The chapter looks at how transformative these policies and legislation are in the post-apartheid era.

## Objectives

✓ Briefly outlining and clarifying the different welfare legislation that are formulated, enacted and implemented to address the needs of vulnerable communities such as children, women, youth, older persons, and people with disabilities

✓ Describing and explaining the vision, mission, and objectives of the relevant legislation.

✓ Also, describing and outlining the historical processes including programmes that reflect how transformative the legislation is in the current situation in South Africa.

✓ Explaining the different role players in the implementation of the different legislative frameworks and the importance of the role played by the affected communities and stakeholders in the transformative processes.

## Outcomes

✓ Describing and analysing the different welfare legislation.

✓ Describing policy goals, objectives, and outcomes.

✓ Reflecting on the policy and programme successes and challenges.

✓ Describing the Implementation of social welfare in different settings.

✓ Outlining areas where improvement is needed in policy formulation and implementation.

✓ Analysing the role and importance of communities and other stakeholders in transforming social welfare.

## 12.1 Introduction

The Constitution of South Africa is the supreme law of the country. Therefore, all legislation (Acts and Bills) and policies in South Africa are guided by the Constitution. As part of the global community, South Africa has also ratified and signed a number of international instruments on human rights. Therefore, the *White Paper for Social Welfare* (1997), as a foundational policy document that outlines how developmental social welfare should be structured and implemented, is guided by the Constitution and the international conventions. In the light of this, welfare policy has been transformed to eradicate all the unjust and racially structured welfare systems of the apartheid era. The question is how transformative are these laws and policies?

In 1994, a democratically appointed government was established to develop a non-sexist, non-racial, and democratic society. Since then, a number of policies and legislation were formulated, amended, and reviewed to address the injustices of the past. The ultimate goal of the social welfare policies is to address the needs of the vulnerable people and to develop a caring community as stated in the Constitution of South Africa. The preamble to the 1996 Constitution describes the South Africa that we need as the one that will:

- heal the division of the past and establish a society based on democratic values, social justice, and fundamental human rights; and
- improve the quality of life of all citizens and free the potential of each person.

**statutory law:** Statutory Law is a written law made by a law-making body, which regulate a particular matter. In South Africa, statutes are laws made by Parliament, as the highest law-making body in the country. The Child Care Act 73 of 1983 is an example of a statute. A new statute can amend or even replace an old statute, for example, the Children's Act 38 of 2005 added and changed certain sections of the Child Care Act 74 of 1983.

In looking at the legislation, the chapter will refer to the international legal framework and instruments, and will utilise case studies. The Department of Social Development and other departments developed a number of policies to support the vulnerable communities and to create a caring environment. This chapter focuses on legislation and policies that involve the following vulnerable groups:

- Children
- People with Disabilities
- Older persons
- Youth
- Women.

# 12.2 Legislative framework for the care and protection of children

As indicated above, the *White Paper for Social Welfare* (1997) outlines how the welfare system should be developed to find a balance between the rehabilitative, preventative, protective, and developmental interventions for vulnerable individuals, groups, and communities. History shows that when societal challenges and problems increase, children get affected the most because they are by nature vulnerable. Children face challenges such as child abuse, molestation, trafficking, neglect, abandonment, abduction, and exploitation.

As mentioned earlier, the Constitution is the supreme law of the country. The Bill of Rights of South Africa's Constitution provides specifically for the rights of children in section 28. It states that:

1. *Every child has the right—*
   - *(a) to a name and a nationality from birth;*
   - *(b) to family care or parental care, or to appropriate alternative care when removed from the family environment;*
   - *(c) to basic nutrition, shelter, basic health care services and social services;*
   - *(d) to be protected from maltreatment, neglect, abuse or degradation;*
   - *(e) to be protected from exploitative labour practices;*
   - *(f) not to be required or permitted to perform work or provide services that—*

      (i)   *are inappropriate for a person of that child's age; or*

     (ii)  *place at risk the child's well-being, education, physical or mental health or spiritual, moral or social development;*

   (g)  *not to be detained except as a measure of last resort, in which case, in addition to the rights a child enjoys under sections 12 and 35, the child may be detained only for the shortest appropriate period of time, and has the right to be—*

      (i)   *kept separately from detained persons over the age of 18 years; and*

     (ii)  *treated in a manner, and kept in conditions, that take account of the child's age;*

   (h)  *to have a legal practitioner assigned to the child by the state, and at state expense, in civil proceedings affecting the child, if substantial injustice would otherwise result; and*

   (i)  *not to be used directly in armed conflict, and to be protected in times of armed conflict.*

(2)  *A child's best interests are of paramount importance in every matter concerning the child.*

(3)  *In this section 'child' means a person under the age of 18years.*

---

### ⓒ Case Study   ABDUCTION OF BABY SIWAPHIWE

Siwaphiwe is a one-month old baby. She was abducted from her mother while her mother was feeding her in the car. Two hijackers forced the mother out of the car at gunpoint. The car was found hours later undamaged but the baby was missing. The well-being of the one-month old baby became a priority for the state. The police searched for her. An award of R250 000 was offered. Two days later, the baby was found and the news broke that the mother was a suspect in the hijacking case of the baby.

Source: ETV news programme February 2017

Read section 28 of the Bill of Rights and the case study above and answer the questions below:
1. Which law protects the child?
2. If the mother is alleged to be the kidnapper? What should happen to her?
3. What is the role of the social worker in this case?
4. What is the role of the family?
5. What is the role of the state?
6. What is the role of the community?

---

The Department of Social Development is responsible to support and protect children. The unit that specifically deals with children is the Chief Directorate for Children. The aim of the Directorate is to facilitate and monitor the development and implementation of policies, legislation, and programmes to protect, empower, and support children. The Directorate works closely with the provincial and local Social Development units and other departments whose focus is on children's issues.. Non-governmental organisations and civil society implement these programmes. In the next subsection, the Children's Act, which is aimed at supporting and protecting vulnerable children in South Africa, is discussed.

## 12.2.1 The Children's Act 38 of 2005

The Children's Act 38 of 2005 is the statutory law that provides for the care and protection of children. It defines the different roles and responsibilities to be performed by different stakeholders. The Children's Act 38 of 2005 is, amongst others, aimed at:

- giving effect to certain rights of children as contained in the Constitution;
- setting out principles and procedures relating to the care and protection of children;
- defining parental responsibilities and rights;
- making new provision for the adoption of children;
- prohibiting child abduction and trafficking; and
- creating certain new offenses relating to children.

The Children's Act consists of 22 chapters. Table 12.1 outlines the summary section of this Act.

Table 12.1 Summary of the Children's Act 38 of 2008

| Section | Chapter | Summary | Implementation strategy |
|---------|---------|---------|-------------------------|
| General principles | Chapter 2 | Best interest of child | Need for stable family. Need for parents, care givers for the protection of the child |
| Parental responsibility and right | Chapter 3 | Parental responsibility and rights | Parenting plans |
| Children's court | Chapter 4 | Access to children's courts Matters children's court may adjudicate | Child has right to courts Legal representation |
| Partial care | Chapter 5 | Take care of more than 6 children | Temporary measure use norms and standards |
| ECD | Chapter 6 | Strategy for provision from birth to school going age | Prioritise poor communities/disabled Norms and standards |
| Protection of children Child protection system National protection register Part A & B register Protection measure and health | Chapter 7 Part 1 Part 2 Part 4 Part 3 | Child protection systems National child protection register Other protective measures Consent for medical treatment | Report abuse/neglect/ child in need of care protection Unlawful removal/child safety/child labour/ child-headed households/ Register for abused child/register for person to work with children Consequence of entry in register B Child consent at age 12 12 years access to contraceptives |
| Prevention and early intervention | Chapter 8 | Preserve child family structure Prevent and promote well-being | Parenting skill Avoid removal of child from family Strengthen families Norms and standards Court order intervention programmes |

| Section | Chapter | Summary | Implementation strategy |
|---|---|---|---|
| Inter-country adoption<br>Child abduction<br>Trafficking of children<br>Surrogate motherhood<br>Enforcement and<br>administration | Chapter 16<br>Chapter 17<br>Chapter 18<br>Chapter 19<br>Chapter 20<br>Chapter 21<br>Chapter 22 | International<br>co-operation<br>Trafficking prohibited<br>Consent of partners | Hague Convention – Force of law<br>Court confirmation<br>Agreements and termination/pregnancy<br>Inspection of facilities<br>Delegation Minister/MEC/DG/HOD |
| Child in need of care and<br>protection<br>Identification<br>Children's court process<br>Contributor order | Chapter 9<br>Chapter10 | Removal by court<br>order<br>Child investigated | Court to protect child<br>Return to parents<br>Refer to alternative care/foster care/child and<br>youth care centres and adoption |
| Alternative care<br>Foster care<br>Child and youth care<br>centres<br>Drop in centres<br>Adoption | Chapter 11<br>Chapter 12<br>Chapter 13<br>Chapter 14<br>Chapter 15 | Foster care/child care<br>centres<br>Cluster foster care<br>Children in conflict<br>with the law<br>Register adoptable<br>children | Duration of foster care 18 months<br>Norms and standard<br>Offer programmes (secure care emotional/<br>therapy/counselling)<br>Emotional and parental care support<br>Psychosocial |

## 12.3 Policy formulation and implementation strategy: progress and challenges

As outlined above, the Children's Act 38 of 2005 is very detailed and comprehensive as it covers a number of areas that were not included in previous child care legislation. The Act's objective and goals are clearly outlined. The Children's Act of 2005 was enacted after a rigorous process of consultation and participation by different stakeholders. It is a comprehensive and improved version of the Child Care Act 74 of 1983, Children Status Act 82 of 1987, and the Child Care Amendment Act 96 of 1996.

As mentioned earlier, the Children's Act was finalised after a number of consultative processes were followed to ensure that practitioners, parents, politicians, activists, and organisations working with children and families contribute to the final chapters of this Act. The consultative process also engaged children, and community participation was encouraged. Inter-governmental sectorial teams, non-governmental organisations (NGOs), and civil society all worked closely to finalise the legislation. Therefore, the step that led to the drafting and finalisation of the Children's Act 38 of 2005 was transformative. According to Roux (2002: 419), transformation is when a government and consequently all public executive institutions start from scratch, and where the underlying vision, mission, and strategy are totally new and transformed.

### 12.3.1 International machinery and the Children's Act 38 of 2005

International laws recognise children's rights, their protection, and care as a must for the government and society. On 2 September 1990,, the United Nations Convention on the Rights of the Child was incorporated into international law following its ratification by 20 states. The rights set out in the Convention define universal principles and norms for the status of children. When governments in different countries ratify a convention, they have an obligation to respect and uphold the rights set out in the convention. South Africa signed and ratified the United Nations Convention on the Rights of the Child in 1993 and 1995, respectively.

The Convention reaffirms the fact that children need special care and protection from birth and throughout childhood. In 1996, South Africa ratified the Hague Convention on the Civil Aspects of the International Child Abduction. The Organisation of African Unity (OAU) also adopted the African Charter on the Rights and Welfare of the Child (ACRWC) to reflect issues related to African culture. These issues include, amongst others, child marriages, female circumcision, the role of the child in the family and community, and the role of relatives in adoption. South Africa signed the Charter in 1997. Furthermore, in 1992, at a special children's summit held in Cape Town, the Children's Charter of South Africa was drawn up.

In South Africa, Youth Day is celebrated on June 16 every year to remember those who died during the 1976 Soweto uprising

## 12.3.2 Implementation of the Children's Act 38 of 2005 and the role of stakeholder policy

Chapter 2 of the Children's Act outlines specific roles of parents, caregivers, guardians, and family members. The role of the different institutions is defined, for example, the children's courts. Each section of the Children's Act explains the role players.

Among the services that show a significant increase in demand in communities are child protection services. As stated in the National Development Plan (NDP, 2011: 336), statistics indicate that there is a rise in violence, increasing criminality among young people, high levels of gang-related violence in schools and communities, and high levels of sexual violence against children and women, especially in economically deprived areas. Chapter 7 of the Children's Act outlines how to address child protection in communities and families. The Act therefore serves as a guiding tool for practitioners in child protection services.

## 12.3.3 Court system in South Africa

South Africa has a court system that works very well. The courts have professionals who know the law and the legal system. The courts are used when citizens break the law, or when they are involved in disputes and conflicts with one another or with the law. South Africa has different types of courts that perform different functions. The four main courts are the Constitutional Court, Supreme Court of Appeal, High Court, and Magistrates' Courts. In addition, there are other special courts such as the Children's Court. The Children's Court only deals with issues affecting children, and the social worker plays an important role in presenting her or his inquiry about the issue(s) to the presiding officer at the Children's Court.

As outlined in Chapter 4 of the Children's Act, inquiries and presentations to the Children's Court cover a broad range which include protection and well-being, care and contact, paternity, provision of ECD, prevention, alternative care, adoption, and care facilities for children. The courts now see and understand that what is important is the child's participation and best interests. Affected children can also get assistance for legal representation. Pre-hearing conferences are held with the concerned child and the family.

# 12.4 Children in conflict with the law

## 12.4.1 The Child Justice Act 75 of 2008

The implementation of the Children's Act should also be viewed in conjunction with the Child Justice Act 75 of 2008 and vice versa. The focus of the Child Justice Act is on children who are accused of criminal offences. When a crime is committed by a child, the first thing the court looks at is the age of the child and whether or not the child has criminal capacity, which means the ability to be held legally responsible for the action committed.

In formulating this legislation, one of the main principles of the Act was to minimise children's contact with the criminal justice system, and to use detention only as a measure of last resort and for a short period. Some of the aims of the Child Justice Act 75 of 2008 are to:

- establish a criminal justice system for children who are in conflict with the law;
- expand and entrench the principle of restorative justice in the criminal justice system for children who are in conflict with the law, while ensuring their responsibility and accountability for the crime committed;
- recognise the present realities of crime in the country and the need to be proactive in crime prevention by increased emphasis on the effective rehabilitation and reintegration of children in order to minimise the potential for re-offending;
- balance the interest of children and those of society, with due regard to the rights of victims; and
- create incrementally, where appropriate, special mechanisms, processes or procedures for children in conflict with the law.

## 12.4.2 Policy formulation and implementation strategy: progress and challenges

According to the National Policy Framework ( 2008: 3) , the Child Justice Act was developed based on the work conducted by government and the activists in the children's rights and child justice fields going back as far as 1996. According to the Department of Justice (2010: 3), the consultative process started in 1996 with an Inter-Ministerial Committee that recognised a need for a specialised child justice system, which was followed by a policy document. In 1997 and 1998, two discussion papers led to the drafting of the Child Justice Bill. In 2000, a national inter-sectorial steering committee on child justice comprising the Departments of Justice, Social Development, Correctional Services, Education, Health, Safety and Security (Police), and the National Director of Public Prosecution was established.

The Child Justice Act, like the Children's Act, is detailed and comprehensive. The Act consists of 14 chapters. The chapters give a clear outline of the Act and define different legal concepts. It further explains the objectives, goals, and general principles of the Act. From Chapters 2 to 14, the Act describes and explains legal procedures and processes related to handling a child in conflict with the law, looking into their criminal capabilities, detention and placement, assessment and preliminary inquiry, diversion, trial in child justice courts, sentencing, legal representation, appeals, records of convictions, and sentence . The last chapter is about the general provisions for meetings, rules of the court, inter-sectorial committee, etc.

## 12.4.3 Implementation of Child Justice Services and role of stakeholders

According to the Department of Justice and Constitutional Development's National Policy Framework (2010: 14–16), different roles and responsibilities exist for the various departments that are serving the needs of children in conflict with the law

### 12.4.3.1 The role of the South African Police Service (SAPS)
The support the child in conflict with the law requires is not purely from the Department of Justice. From the beginning when a child is arrested, the first call of responsibility is with the South African Police Service (SAPS). They have to brief the parents and the child about their rights and assist them to consult the legal representative or consult Legal Aid for help. Then they need to inform the probation officer who is under the Department of Social Development (DSD). When the child is in the hands of the SAPS, she or he needs to be treated with care and be protected and kept separate from the adults.

### 12.4.3.2 The role of the Department of Social Development (DSD)
The probation officer from DSD is mostly responsible for such cases. He or she will be guided primarily by the Children's Act and still apply the legal rules as per the Child Justice Act. After the police officer in charge conduct the preliminary inquiry, the case will be referred to the probation officer. The probation officer will do a full assessment of the child's situation. The probation officer's report will recommend different options such as diversion, home-based supervision, and release under pre-trial supervision. The probation officer will give an estimation of the child's age, express his or her views on the criminal capacity of the child, and perform duties in court.

### 12.4.3.3 Role of Department of Justice and Constitutional Development
The Department of Justice and Constitutional Development provides human resources in court for the preliminary inquiry, which include the presiding officer, interpreter, the court manager, and the clerical staff to capture and keep record of the inquiry. The department also needs to ensure that children who are sentenced are transferred within 30 days.

### 12.4.3.4 The role of the National Prosecuting Authority (NPA)
The NPA appoints and manage prosecutors in respect of the Act. The prosecutor participates in the preliminary inquiry and gives an indication, at the end of the inquiry, of whether he or she supports diversion in the case at hand. The prosecutor reviews the recommendation by the probation officer to divert to appropriate diversion programmes.If the matter is not diverted, it will be processed in the Child Justice Court.

### 12.4.3.5 The role of the Department of Correctional Services
The Department of Correctional Services (DCS) detains and manages children awaiting trail and keeps children who are in custody separately from adults. They provide educational, nutritional, health, and all other services the child requires while awaiting trial. DCS does communicate with the family and allows them to consult with the child's legal representative.

### 12.4.3.6 The role of the Legal Aid South Africa
The Act allows all children to have legal representatives. Legal Aid South Africa's responsibility is to explain to children their rights and give them information that will help them participate and discuss their matters with their legal representatives.

### 12.4.3.7 The role of the Department of Home Affairs
The Department of Home Affairs has a responsibility to provide the Child Justice Court or the magistrate with an identification document for a child when the need arises. Furthermore, it is also the department's responsibility to register the age of the child and to give this report to the probation office, family, and the court.

### 12.4.3.8 Role of the Department of Health
The Department of Health's responsibility is to provide the child with mental health facilities when the child requires to be assessed or undergo observation. The department also assists with experts to assess if the child has criminal capacity.

### 12.4.3.9 The role of non-governmental organisations and civil society
The role of NGOs and civil society as partners with the Department of Justice is very important and critical. They are the implementing agency when it comes to diversion programmes. NGOs and civil society offer different programmes that assist the child in conflict with the law in partnership with DSD. The NGOs' programmes are assessed, accredited, and funded by DSD. Regular monitoring and evaluation needs to take place to ensure that there is continuity.

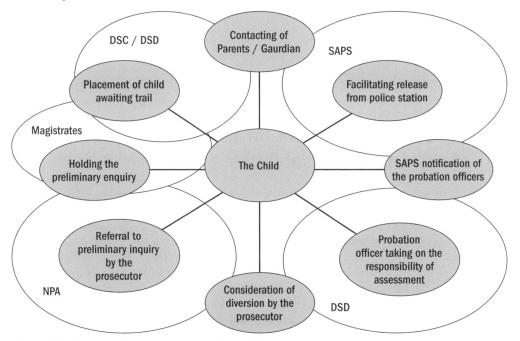

Figure 12.1  Structure of the role players in the Child Justice Services

ACTIVITY 1

## CHILDREN'S ACT 38 OF 2005 AND THE CHILD JUSTICE ACT 75 OF 2008

After studying the Children's Act 38 of 2005 and the Child Justice Act 75 of 2008, reflect on your understanding of these two Acts. Choose two of the situations in which children can find themselves as listed below, and write a paragraph describing how the Acts can be used to care for and protect a child. Outline the roles of the different role players who will be involved.
1. A blind child sitting at the corner of a street begging for food and money.
2. A girl child who was sexually abused by her mother's boyfriend for three years.
3. Refugee children who are attacked because of xenophobia.
4. A hungry teenager decided to rob a shopkeeper to get money. He used a toy gun to threaten the cashier and ran away with R500 but was arrested two days after the incident

COMMENT

## ETV NEWS BROADCAST

Read below a few opinions on some issues raised during a news broadcast on television in South Africa.

**Xoli:**    'I am so challenged by the news these days; I don't even want to watch the news or listen to the radio again. Do you people see that our country is going down? Why are the laws of this country not enforced on people who do so much wrong?

**Puleng:**  I agree with you. I am so confused by what is happening in the welfare sector. Last week, we were informed about 95 mentally ill patients at Life Esidimeni who died because they were transferred to NGOs that were not suitable for such patients. This is a human rights violation. People just die like this because the MEC did not care about the patients, but was but worried about funds and the cost of managing Life Esidimeni.

**Motho:**   And now it is the SASSA saga. We are not sure whether 17 million vulnerable individuals consisting of children, persons with disability and older people will receive their social grants. You know if these people do not get their grants it is going to be a disaster.

# 12.5 Legislative framework for the care and protection of persons with disabilities

The history of the welfare of persons with disabilities has evolved over time. In 1984, a number of organisations serving persons with disability came together to form an advocacy movement. Their aims were to address discrimination and to redefine the concept disability. Initially, the concept was defined from the perspective of a medical model, but this model had a number of limitations and weaknesses. Disabled People South Africa (DPSA) was established as an advocacy movement. It provided a voice to persons with disabilities. DPSA's role was also visible during the formulation of the South African Constitution as it represented the views of persons with disability. It contributed to many changes including the establishment of the Disability Rights movement. This movement led to the establishment of the Office on the Status of Disabled Persons in the Office of the Deputy President. This further led to the development of the *White Paper on an Integrated National Disability Strategy* published in November 1997. Therefore, the organisations for persons with disability fought for inclusion and participated in a number of policy debates and forums. Persons with disability are treated as equal citizens, like all South Africans. They demanded that they be treated with dignity, respect, and honour. Furthermore, advocacy groups and forums have continued to relook at and fight for equality in a number of areas where change has not taken place or needs to occur.

## 12.5.1 White Paper on the Rights of Persons with Disabilities

As indicated above, the definition of the concept 'disability' has evolved over time from a medical to a social perspective. The *White Paper on the Rights of Persons with Disabilities* (2015: 17) states that disability is a complex and evolving concept and defining it must take into account the following realities:

- To date there is no single definition of disability that has achieved international consensus.
- There are various definitions, however, all the rights-based definitions share certain common elements, which include:
  - the presence of impairment;
  - internal and external limitations or barriers which hinder full and equal participation; and
  - loss or lack of access to opportunities due to environmental barriers and/or negative perception and attitude of the society.
- Disabilities can be permanent, temporary or episodic.

The White Paper on the Rights of Persons with Disabilities indicates that disability can result from interaction between persons with impairment and attitudinal and environmental issues. In looking at the history of care and support for persons with disability, the White Paper on the Rights of Persons with Disabilities gives a brief synopsis of the pre and post-Apartheid era and how persons with disability were discriminated against due to the way the society defined disability. The medical approach to disability had a number of disadvantages as persons with disability could easily be viewed with pity and immediately classified as not functional.

Research conducted shows that most community members do not yet understand the rights of persons with disability. Their rights are always violated.

---

**⊘ Case Study    JOHN'S STORY: THE VIOLATION OF A DISABLED PERSON'S RIGHTS**

John is blind but has a normal life. Married with two children, he works as a manager at a cane shop. He is also studying part time at the University of South Africa (UNISA), where students and lecturers know him and treat him with respect and honour. They give him space to be independent and to do his work and cope on his own. He sees himself as a normal capable student like all the other students. John writes the same exams like other students except that he uses braille. His challenge is when he walks around in Pretoria's streets, since the roads are not disability friendly. Because his disability is exposed when crossing streets, he gets too much attention from other pedestrians. Most of the time they try to help him cross the street. He uses his white stick to manage his movement. He does not feel comfortable when people feel sorry for him. This societal behaviour and attitude towards people like him irritates him as it is disempowering and paralyses persons with disabilities. According to him, societal behaviour towards persons with disability needs to change. There is a need to create more awareness about the rights of the persons with disabilities.

---

The example above shows that there are persons with disability who can live normal lives like others. Where disabilities are different, people may need help depending on the intensity of their impairment. Society, in most cases, cannot differentiate between situations where assistance is needed or not. There is a need to the help society to change and hence a social model is the best model to help define disability (White Paper on the Rights of Persons with Disabilities, 2015: 21).

The purpose of the White Paper on the Rights of Persons with Disabilities is to broaden the scope of the persons with disability in society for them to have full involvement as capable members of society, and to look at all barriers that prevent them from participating as citizens like other people in the society. The emphasis of policy is to help society and government to remove all barriers in every sector where persons with disability are to participate even though they may have some impairment. As Article 8 of United Nations Convention on the Rights of Persons with Disabilities (UNCRPD) (as cited in the White Paper on the Rights of Persons with Disabilities, 2015: 22) states, government parties must adopt effective and appropriate measures that will foster respect for the rights and dignity of persons with disability, and that will combat stereotypes, prejudices, and harmful practices relating to persons with disability.

The main aims of the White Paper on the Rights of Persons with Disabilities are to:

- Provide a mainstreaming trajectory for realising the rights of persons with disability through the development of targeted interventions that removes barriers and apply the principles of universal designs.
- Stipulate norms and standards for removal of discriminatory barriers that perpetuate the exclusion and segregation of persons with disability.
- Provide the framework for a uniform and co-ordinated approach by all government departments and institutions in mainstreaming disability across all planning, designing, budgeting, implementing, and monitoring of services and development programmes.
- Guide gender mainstreaming to ensure that women with disabilities enjoy equitable access to all women empowerment and gender equality legislation, policies, and programmes.

The White Paper on the Rights of Persons with Disabilities is founded on the United Nations Convention on the Rights of Persons with Disabilities (UNCRPD) legal framework. According to the UNCRPD, for transformation to take place, the South African government, non-governmental organisations, and the society at large including the families of persons with disability need to change and treat the persons with disability as they treat all citizens and acknowledge their impairment but give them space to live as normal as everyone else. The policy has incorporated the strategic approach to change as consisting of three areas:

- **The rights-based approach**: This approach emphasises the social and economic development and incorporate the principle of equality and non-discrimination in policies and programmes.
- **A mainstreaming approach**: This simply means involving and supporting persons with disabilities in all government policy, programmes, and budgetary processes and ensuring that each department provides for the disabled person as required by policy.
- **Life cycle approach**: This means disability services should be offered in an integrated, collaborative, and holistically manner without discriminating against or disadvantaging any persons from birth to ageing.

The *White Paper on the Rights of Persons with Disabilities* is based on the social model approach with *nine pillars*. The pillars are interrelated and one pillar builds on the next and vice versa. The pillars are holistic and comprehensive, and address the needs of persons with disability in different settings and spaces. They cover children and women as the most vulnerable groups. This service model, as outlined below in Figure 12.2, looks at employment, education, food security, health, environment and human settlement, transport, security and safety, and participation and collaboration. International and intergovernmental co-operation is also critical as the needs of persons with disability stretch into all sectors of government. What is also critical is financial support especially funding for NGOs and Disabled Persons Organisations (DPOs).

| 1. Removing barriers to access and participation | 2. Protect the rights of persons at risk of compounded marginalisation | 3. Supporting Integrated Community Life |
|---|---|---|
| Focus areas:<br>• Built environment<br>• Transport<br>• Information and communication<br>• Reasonable accommodation.<br>Changing attitude and behaviour | Focus areas:<br>• The right to life<br>• Equal recognition before the law<br>• Access to justice<br>• Freedom from torture or in-human treatment. | Focus areas:<br>• Building socially cohesive communities<br>• Building and supporting families<br>• Accessible human settlements<br>• Access to community-based services supporting independent living. |
| **4. Promoting and supporting empowerment of persons with disability** | **5. Reducing economic vulnerability and releasing human capital** | **6. Strengthening the voice of persons with disability** |
| Focus areas:<br>• ECD development<br>• Lifelong education and training<br>• Social integration<br>• Strengthening recourse mechanisms. | Focus areas:<br>• Disability, poverty development and human rights<br>• Access to decent work and opportunities<br>• Persons with disability as owners of economy. | Focus areas:<br>• Access through self-representative<br>• Recognition of organisations<br>• Strengthen capacity of DPOs<br>• Participation and consultation. |
| **7. Building a disability equitable state machinery** | **8. Promoting international co-operation** | **9. Monitoring and evaluation** |
| Focus areas:<br>• Disability equitable planning, budgeting and service delivery<br>• Capacity-building<br>• Public procumbent and regulations. | Focus areas:<br>• Attend international conferences<br>• Learn from others. | Focus areas:<br>• Conduct studies<br>• Evaluate programmes. |

Figure 12.2 Summary of the strategic pillars for the rights of persons with disabilities

ACTIVITY 2    THE NINE PILLARS

Write a paragraph and argue for or against the concerns of persons with disability. Choose two topics below and share your view about how persons with disability should not/should be treated when it comes to the following needs:

Transport:    Should the person with disability be given special transport and travel on his or her own?

Education:    Are children with any form of disability to be treated as people with special needs and attend special schools and colleges or do they need to be separated from those who are not disabled?

Sports:    Are disabled persons supposed to play games or participate in their own special sports and why, and in which sports can they play with other abled persons?

Employment:    What should happen to persons with disability? Should they be given special treatment for special jobs?

## 12.5.2 Implementation strategy: progress and challenges

Transformation is taking place in many sectors in government and the private sector as disabled persons have voiced their rights and continue to do so. They are visible in the country as an advocacy group as the White Paper states that they have a voice, and they participate in policy formulation. Research shows that because disabled persons are still discriminated against there is still more to be done. The challenge is the funding of programmes in NGOs.

## 12.5.3 Role players supporting persons with disability

There are a number of role players to support persons with disability. The Office on the Status of Persons with Disability has a responsibility to ensure that mainstreaming disability policies and programmes happen at different departments. Leadership in this regard, therefore, needs to be provided at the top so it can trickle down from national level to provincial and local government (municipality) levels. Awareness about the rights of persons with disability needs to be co-ordinated through interdepartmental meetings and supported by programmes on the ground. The White Paper on the Rights of Persons with Disabilities (2010) describes the leadership roles that are critical to ensure that government applies the nine strategic pillars at all levels. NGOs and civil society community are viewed as partners in the service delivery process, which starts with them registering the organisation, complying with the DSD funding requirement for the facilities they use, and ensuring that activities in the organisations are in the best interests of persons with disability. Social workers are expected to monitor the facility, and the facility manager is required to adhere to the DSD reporting systems. These organisations should comply with the norms and standards established for services they provide. However, organs of states can also fail to adhere to the required policy. A case in point is what happened at Life Esidimeni, which is discussed in the case study below.

---

### ✅ Case Study    THE LOSS OF LIFE AT LIFE ESIDIMENI

The Life Esidemeni case is a clear demonstration of the violation of the rights of persons with disability. As the story unfolded in October 2015, the MEC for Health in Gauteng announced the termination of the contract between Department of Health and Life Esidemeni. Around 2000 people, who were receiving highly specialised chronic psychiatric care, were to be moved out of the Life Esidimeni to families, NGOs and psychiatric hospitals providing acute care. The reasons for closing Life Esidimeni, according to the MEC, was to save money, hence, the need to deinstitutionalize (The policy states that to do so, it should happen over several years, after developing and capacitating community care where the patients will be transferred). The MEC went against the policy. She took six months (from October 2015 to March 2016) to move mentally ill patients. This led to 105 psychiatric patients dying in the hands of NGOs, as this was a rushed process with many problems. The MEC never followed the procedures and the policy (Makgoba, 2017).

Even though policies and legislation outline the care and support, and how different role players should play their roles, incidents like this demonstrate that transformation cannot take place without compliance to the policies and statutory laws. In this case, the very people who made the law (the MEC) broke the law.

Subsequent to the **Life Esidimeni** tragedy, an inquiry was held into the tragedy headed by the former Deputy Chief Justice of South Africa, Dikgang Moseneke. The inquiry found that these patients' constitutional right to dignity was violated, and the SA government was given three months to pay compensation amounting to approximately R1 million rand to each family of those patients who survived and died in the Life Esidimeni tragedy.

# 12.6 Legislative framework for older persons

As outlined above, South Africa as a country has a responsibility to care for, protect, ensure the safety of, and provide support to children, persons with disability, and older persons. The older persons are the cream of the country since they have spent their lives contributing to their families, the community, and to organisations. Vulnerable older persons may be coming from different family settings and situations, but all of them are the responsibility of the government and those who work with organisations that support older persons. Many of the older persons who are in their sixties and above suffered a lot during the apartheid era. The effects of past injustices, discrimination, and inequality that existed during that era are still felt today. The government through the Constitution and the Bill of Rights has taken a position to care, and to support and protect the rights of the older person.

## 12.6.1 The Older Persons Act 13 of 2006

The Older Persons Act 13 of 2006, like the legislations discussed above, is specific about the rights and best interests of older persons. The Act addresses the critical primary need of the ageing community in South Africa. These are community members who were once young and energised to work in different settings in South Africa. Some may have not been employed due to a number of reasons but they contributed to South Africa in some way or another. The rights as provided in the Act apply to all older persons and the South African Older Persons' Charter further specifies the rights of all older persons. The Older Persons Act 13 of 2006 has six chapters. Similar to other Acts, it defines the relevant concepts. The Act defines an 'older person' in terms of age for both males and females. The age of 60 years gives the older person identity, and the status of ageing. Legally, one can retire at this age to access a social grant from the state. The social security grant is available to those who qualify from the age of 60 years.

The government, through the Act, takes the responsibility to care for, support, and protect the rights of older persons. The objectives of the Older Persons Act 13 of 2006 are to:
• Promote and protect the rights of older persons.
• Maintain and promote the status, well-being, safety and security of older persons.
• Shift the institutional care to community-based care in order to ensure that older persons remain in their homes within the community for as long as possible.
• Combat the abuse of older persons.

The Act specifies how these objectives must be achieved by government, communities, families, and non-governmental organisations that work with older persons. In the subsections below, some of the ways are discussed to support and care for older persons.

### 12.6.1.1 Creating an enabling and supportive environment for older persons
The Directorate for Older Persons in the Department of Social Development (DSD) is the unit with the responsibility of ensuring that the objectives, the principles, and guidelines in the Older Persons Act are implemented. They receive financial support and capacity-building to implement abuse prevention services and to promote care and support, including home-based care programmes. DSD works with a number of partners and stakeholders registered to provide services to a number of care and support programmes and activities implemented nationwide in different provinces. DSD has developed norms and standards to guide and monitor the activities implemented by these organisations, and to ensure that the rights of

older persons are respected in all areas and all institutions. The Act also stipulates that persons or institutions that provide residential or community-based care and support without being registered are guilty of an offence.

### 12.6.1.2 Residential and community-based services

Non-governmental organisations provide different programmes that are aimed at promoting independent and healthy living for older persons. Some examples of activities that relate to care and support programmes are lunch-on clubs, sports and recreation, economic activities, and educational programmes. Older persons decide on activities with the assistance of the facilitators. These activities are geared at empowering and supporting older persons holistically, and range from spiritual, cultural, medical, and social to financial programmes. Some activities require the support of professionals.

## 12.6.2 Policy implementation and challenges of older persons

Chapter 5 of the Older Persons Act addresses the need for professionals and other persons involved with the care and protection of older persons to report any form of abuse to the police or Director-General.  Through the Act, older persons are protected from different forms of abuse. Older persons experience abuse from their families and community members. Cases of neglect and abandonment are visible in communities and families. We find many older people in the streets and on corners begging. Some of the challenges are also in residential facilities like in the case study above. Most of the patients at Life Esidemeni were older persons who were not protected and some of them died as a result. The Older Persons Act clearly states that it is an offence not to report such forms of abuse. Alleged offenders who are guilty of such abuse of older persons, just like in the case of child abuse, have to appear before the courts. After investigating the case, the police can also recommend that the offenders be removed from the home if necessary. To remove them, they are given written notices and their names are then included in the offender register.

## 12.6.3 The role players in the Older Persons Act

There are number of role players to facilitate and support the care and support of older persons. In this regard, family members play a critical role as they are the expected to care for the elders. If family members are unable to do so and the elder is frail, residential care is one option. In a residential setting, the facility committee and managers are central to supporting the older person's independent living. Older persons who are staying in their homes under the care and support of families can also participate in the community and support programmes described above. Social workers, health workers, police, magistrates, and residential facility committee members play a critical role in supporting older persons.

# 12.7 Legislative framework and youth programmes

The National Youth Policy (2020) was developed to address the past and current challenges faced by the youth of South Africa. In relation to the triple challenge of poverty, unemployment, and inequality, the policy is guided by the South African Constitution, Commonwealth Youth Charter, National Development Plan (2030), African Youth Charter (2006), and the United Nation World Programme of Action for Youth (2000).

South Africa, like other countries worldwide, faces high youth unemployment and joblessness. The International Labour Organisation (ILO) estimates that, worldwide, 73,4 million young people who want to work are actively looking for jobs without finding any (National Youth Policy, 2020: 2). The goal of the National Youth Policy (2020) is to consolidate youth initiatives that enhance the capacities of young people to transform the economy and society. Table 12.2 lists the existing youth programmes.

Table 12.2 Existing youth programmes

| Programme | Purpose |
|---|---|
| National Youth Service Development Policy Framework ( 2002) | To support youth to participate in voluntarism as a mechanism to build patriotism and social cohesion. |
| Broad-based Black Economic Empowerment Act ( 2003) | To promote broad-based economic empowerment and increase effective participation of black people in the economy to promote higher growth. |
| National Youth Development Agency (2008) | To develop an integrated youth development strategy and design, co-ordinate, evaluate, and monitor programmes aimed at integrating youth into the economy. |
| New Growth Path (2011) | To develop a a three-staged approach to addressing joblessness and unemployment by government in partnership with business. |
| Youth Employment Accord (2013) Skills Accord (2011) | To support and train youth. Business, civil society, NGOs, and government supporting the skilling of youth and opportunities to find jobs. |
| DTI Industrial Policy Action Plan 2013 | To identify priority sectors in which industrial and infrastructural development opportunities can be explored in existing sectors/new areas and long-term advanced capacities. |

## 12.7.1 The success and challenges of existing youth programmes

According to the brief assessment as stated in the NYP (2020), there is a general perception that the existing programmes are failing as unemployment continues to rise and graduate employability remains very low. Youth unemployment is increasing year by year and there is no improvement. This means the existing programmes and legislative framework do not make a big difference in addressing this matter. Table 12.3 below gives a summary of some of the other challenges that youth face and suggests ways to deal with these challenges.

Table 12.3 Summary of other youth challenges and proposed solutions

| Challenges | Proposed Plan | Organisations to be involved |
|---|---|---|
| Poor health, high HIV and Aids prevalence, and teenage pregnancy. | • Support healthy lifestyles<br>• Promote sexual and reproductive health rights. | • Department of Education<br>• Family programmes<br>• Business sector<br>• Civil society<br>• NGOs. |
| High rate of violence and substance abuse. | • Provide holistic support<br>• Support guidance and second chance<br>• Health care and combatting substance abuse. | • Department of Health<br>• Department of Basic Education<br>• Civil society<br>• NGOs<br>• Department of Social Development. |

| Challenges | Proposed Plan | Organisations to be involved |
|---|---|---|
| Lack of access to sporting and cultural opportunities. | • Broadening access to sports and recreation opportunities. | • Department of Basic Education<br>• Department of Sports and Recreation<br>• Community Youth Clubs<br>• CoGTA<br>• Business. |
| Lack of social cohesion and volunteerism. | • Foster constitutional values<br>• Confront discrimination and racism<br>• Foster youth leadership and active citizenry. | • Department of Justice<br>• Department of Arts and Culture<br>• Business<br>• Faith-based organisations, NGOs, civil society. |
| Economic participation and transformation. | • Labour to absorb the youth<br>• Establish community services with income<br>• Support cooperatives<br>• Provide work exposure<br>• Grow youth enterprise<br>• Rural development and land reform for youth. | • Department of Labour<br>• Department of Small Business<br>• Department of Trade and Industry<br>• Department of Higher Education<br>• Business sector. |

The youth programmes as mentioned above require collaboration and partnership among different organs of state, civil society, and NGOs. The challenge is a lack of co-ordinated effort and inter governmental systems. Programmes mentioned in Table 12.2 above seem to be ineffective because there are no clear implementation plans. Therefore, fragmentation and a lack of integrated youth development programmes will lead to more failure.

## DISCUSSION    GENDER BALANCE ROLES

Read the discussion below. What is your opinion on this issue?

**Pinkie:** 'Today, I want us to talk about women's issues. I know we hear a lot now about having a woman as president of the country. It was the case in USA, and now in South Africa, and possibly in Zimbabwe. I am concerned that not everyone thinks a woman can lead a country. In Africa, there is only one woman president. This is a man's world and it is not easy for a woman to be elected to lead a country.'

**John:** 'I do not know if women can lead countries since they are emotional by nature. Leading a country requires toughness and hardness as you deal with many difficult issues.'

**Peter:** 'I do not agree. I think women can lead too and not only men who are tough and stubborn. As men we abuse and hurt women and children. Gender-based violence, domestic violence, and all kinds of abuse of children and women are increasing. This must stop as it is hurting the nation. Men need to respect women. Maybe a woman leader can change the country, as she will address all these forms of abuse from a woman's perspective.'

**Sophie:** 'We live in an era where gender balance is the way to go. This means women and men's roles require balance. A woman's role is no longer in the kitchen only. Today, you find them in different settings. We have women in construction, agriculture, technology, and aviation. Women are also Ministers and Deputy Ministers in government. Gender balance is the way to go.'

# 12.8 Legislative framework: women and gender mainstreaming policy

Since 1995, after the Beijing International Women's conference, South African women continue to challenge the government to prioritise the women's agenda and empowerment. This led to the development of a gender mainstreaming policy and the establishment of women structures. The Department of Women (DOW) was established in the President's office to drive and monitor gender-mainstreaming processes. Gender focal points in the departments are established to integrate gender perspectives in all policies and programmes, and to ensure that budgetary allocations are equitably distributed.

The Department of Women's goal is to lead, co-ordinate, and oversee the transformation agenda on women's socioeconomic empowerment and gender equality through the implementation of a gender-mainstreaming strategy. The Commission on Gender Equality (CGE) is a watchdog over the structures of government. Its purpose is to support the implementation of gender-mainstreaming programmes. The commission monitors and investigates cases related to the violation of women's rights, inequality, social injustice, gender imbalance, and affirmative action.

## 12.8.1 Progress and challenges

Initiatives driven by women are evident in sectors such as agriculture, construction, mining, technology, finance, health, education, etc. Women further established forums and associations in workplaces. Different groups address the needs of women in different settings. Women have performed very well in voicing and establishing activities related to their specific fields. Although this is happening on a small scale, women have made progress in voicing their needs.

Some of the main challenges that women face are crime and all forms of abuse. The Domestic Violence Act and the National Policy Guideline for Victim Empowerment are aimed at addressing such challenges. South Africa has ratified and signed the Convention on the Elimination of all Forms of Discrimination against Women (CEDAW) to support women. Despite these efforts, women continue to be the targets of sexual and other forms of assaults and abuse.

## CONCLUSION

- The chapter covered different legislation in relation to children, persons with disability, older persons, youth, and women.
- It elaborated on the different processes involved in designing legislative frameworks and the implementation process.
- The chapter further outlined the role of different stakeholders. It touched on the challenges and progress.
- It is evident that welfare policies in South Africa follow consultative and transformative processes.
- The policies outlined in the chapter are implemented in different settings. However, the challenges continue to emerge in different focus areas.

- It is evident that transformation is not fully realised while vulnerable communities continue to experience inequality and injustice.

## QUESTIONS

1. In your own words, reflect and write a summary of what you learned from this chapter?
2. What stood out for you in each focus areas?
3. What do you think needs to change in the policymaking process and/or programme implementation?
4. Do you think South Africa as a young democracy has performed well in developing social welfare policies? Write a paragraph to explain you answer.
5. Why is international machinery important for the South African government when formulating policy? Choose two international conventions in your explanation.
6. For radical transformation to occur, what should be done differently?

## REFERENCES

MAKGOBA M (2017) *Life Esidemeni Health Ombudsman Report 2017, February.* Pretoria: Government Printer.

ROUX, NL (2002) 'Public policy-making and policy analysis in South Africa amidst transformation change, globalisation: views on participation and role players in the policy analytic procedure' *Journal of Public Administration* Vol. 37 No. 4 at pp. 418–437.

SOUTH AFRICA. 1996. *Constitution of the Republic of South Africa Act No 108 of 1996* as amended on 11 October 1996. Pretoria: Government Printer. [Laws.]

SOUTH AFRICA. 1997. *White Paper for Social Welfare 1997.* Pretoria: Government Printer.

SOUTH AFRICA. 2005. *Children's Act No 38 of 2005.* Pretoria: Government Printer. [Laws.]

SOUTH AFRICA. 2006. *Older Persons Act No 13 of 2006.* Pretoria: Government Printer. [Laws.]

SOUTH AFRICA. 2008. *Child Justice Act No 75 of 2008.* Pretoria: Government Printer. [Laws.]

SOUTH AFRICA. 2013. *Broad-Based Black Economic Empowerment Amendment Act No 46 of 2013.* Pretoria: Government Printer. [Laws.]

SOUTH AFRICA. 2015. *White Paper on the Rights of Persons with Disabilities 2015.* Pretoria: Government Printer.

SOUTH AFRICA. Department of Economic Development (2011) *New Growth Path 2011.* Pretoria: Government Printer.

SOUTH AFRICA. 2013. Department of Trade and Industry (2013) *Industrial Policy Action Plan* 2013. Pretoria: Government Printer.

SOUTH AFRICA. ETV (18 March 2017) Seven o' clock News TV Programme.

SOUTH AFRICA. The Presidency of South Africa (2011) *National Development Plan 2030.* Pretoria: Government Printer.

SOUTH AFRICA. The Presidency of South Africa (2020) *National Youth Policy 2020.* Pretoria: Government Printer.

# Monitoring and evaluation: impact and outcomes

*Jean D Triegaardt*

Chapter 13 is aimed at helping development practitioners and students to get to grips with the various concepts associated with 'monitoring' and 'evaluation' of welfare policy and programmes; the kinds of evaluation; the location of evaluation and monitoring in the policy cycle process; the approaches of evaluation, and research designs which are currently available, and the value of these approaches depending on the circumstances; and, finally, the impact and outcomes of evaluation. The chapter's objectives and outcomes are listed below.

## Objectives

✓ Explaining the reasons for embarking on a monitoring and evaluation process.

✓ Discussing the kinds of evaluation and approaches that exist and their utility in social welfare policy.

✓ Elaborating on the research methods that are available in the evaluation and monitoring process.

✓ Explaining the location of monitoring and evaluation in the policy cycle process.

✓ Analysing the impact and outcomes of evaluation on social welfare policy.

## Outcomes

✓ Demonstrating knowledge and understanding of the purpose for embarking on the process of monitoring and evaluation.

✓ Demonstrating knowledge of the kinds of and approaches to evaluation which occur and the ability to be prudent in the uses of these for social welfare policy.

✓ Understanding and applying the research methods that can be employed in evaluation research.

✓ Demonstrating knowledge and understanding of the location of monitoring and evaluation in the policy cycle process.

✓ Explaining the impact and outcomes of evaluation on social welfare policy.

# 13.1 Introduction

The purpose of evaluation research is to measure the effects of a programme against the goals it set out to achieve as a method of contributing to subsequent decision-making about the programme and improving future programming (Weiss, 1972: 4). Evaluations are undertaken primarily as contributions to policy and programme formulation and modification – activities that have a strong political dimension (Rossi and Freeman, 1993: 437). Evaluations may be undertaken for a range of reasons. These may include managerial and administrative reasons; to check the accountability of welfare services to beneficiaries, funders and policy recipients; to ascertain whether programme changes or improvements are in keeping with objectives; and to identify ways to improve the delivery of services. These activities may be undertaken for planning and policy purposes, to test innovative ideas on how to deal with human and community problems, to decide whether to expand or cease programmes, or to support advocacy of one programme over another (Rossi and Freeman, 1993: 34). The main goal for conducting monitoring and evaluation (M & E) is to ensure that if the evaluation of the programme was replicated, the outcome would be the same.

The process of monitoring and evaluation is considered to be a systematic and a carefully planned process to judge whether the interventions with respect to welfare policy and programmes have been effective. Effectiveness refers to how successful the welfare programme is in providing its target population with the required welfare services and resources, and whether any benefits have accrued to its clients as intended by the organisation and its donors. Monitoring is an important component of the programme design, planning and implementation cycle. Monitoring is considered to be assessing the extent to which a programme is (1) undertaken consistent with its design or implementation plan and (2) directed at the appropriate target population (Rossi and Freeman, 1993: 2). Therefore, monitoring can be considered to be a set of 'quality assurance' activities with the intention of maximizing a programme's adherence to its design.

Generally, the kinds of evaluations can be classified as either formative (that is, monitoring) evaluation or summative (that is, impact) evaluation (Kirst-Ashman and Hull, 2012: 370). Formative evaluation is considered to be aimed at improving a programme in its foundational stages, while summative evaluation provides a final decision at the outcome stage.

# 13.2 Kinds of evaluation

## 13.2.1 Formative evaluation: monitoring

This kind of evaluation focuses on the process rather than the outcome of evaluation. Programme monitoring may be defined as the systematic examination of programme coverage and delivery (Rossi and Freeman, 1993: 164). Formative evaluation provides interim information about the programme in its implementation stage and allows for adaptations or changes to be made to the programme. Therefore, the programme plan is not engraved in stone. Since this evaluation is concerned with the process, the focus is on the programme's *service utilisation*, its *service delivery* and the *organisational support* (Rossi, Lipsey and Freeman, 2004). *Service utilisation* relates to the extent to which beneficiaries use the programme and the extent to which the programme ultimately reaches its target audience. Monitoring may be used to assess whether the programme is actually serving its intended population (Kirst-Ashman and Hull, 2012: 370). Basic data collection for monitoring may include demographics on clients (such as the name, age, gender), the reason for their contact with the organisation (emergency, food, shelter), the services rendered by the organisation (shelter arranged, food parcels arranged), and the output achieved (reports written about the client, the number of contacts). *Service delivery* is about the implementation of services being rendered according to the objectives set out at the inception of the planning of the programme. *Organisational support* is concerned with the provision of resources (such as financial resources, infrastructure and staff) to ensure that the programme is implemented as planned. An example of process evaluation is one which was conducted on street children. Two researchers (O'Donoghue and Louw-Potgieter, 2013: 547, 548) conducted such an evaluation and focused on service utilisation, service delivery, and organisational support. This process evaluation was a first attempt at evaluating a programme set up for homeless people with the intention of not only providing shelter and food, but also providing access to employment opportunities.

Therefore, monitoring can be summarised as the following:
- The purpose is to improve efficiency and effectiveness of organisations and/or projects.
- It promotes the systematic collection and analysis of data throughout the life of the project.
- It ensures that the process of the project remains on track, and alerts the team or management to any emerging challenges.
- It allows for review of activities and targets which are set in the planning phase.
- It facilitates the review of human resources, as well as financial resources for the completion of the project.
- It allows for management to continuously review the project/organisation as an overall governance tool for organisations.

## 13.2.2 Summative evaluation: impact

Evaluation is an assessment of the achievement of goals and objectives, what the issues, challenges or obstacles are in implementing policies and programmes, and how these challenges can be addressed. The purpose of evaluation is to ensure that welfare organisations are managed more effectively in order to deliver effective, productive and efficient services. These organisations are accountable to various stakeholders such as donors, communities, households, consumers of services, and government.

Donors and administrators of welfare organisations may ask the following questions:
1. Is the programme meeting the goals and objectives that it set out to achieve?
2. Should the programme be improved, expanded, reduced or abandoned?
3. Is the programme making a difference to the lives of its beneficiaries and/or what impact does it have on the beneficiaries?

Therefore, an evaluation makes an informed judgement about 'what is' compared to 'what ought to be'. It further provides an indication of corporate governance such as accountability, audits, risks, and compliance with funding requirements, serving the target audience, and achieving programme goals. Figure 13.1 illustrates the purpose of an evaluation.

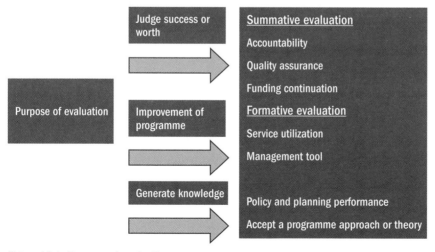

Figure 13.1 Purpose of evaluation

Programme evaluation refers to a process that is:

1. making reasonable judgements about programme effort, effectiveness, efficiency, and adequacy;
2. based on systematic data collection and analysis;
3. designed for use in programme management, external accountability; and future planning; and
4. particularly focused on accessibility, acceptability, awareness, availability, comprehensiveness, continuity, integration, and cost of services (Attkisson and Broskowski, 1978: 24).

Summative evaluations demonstrate the overall effectiveness of a programme and are critical for decision-making regarding continued funding of the programme, the success thereof, and ultimately the future of the programme (Mouton, 2014: 172).

# 13.3 Location of monitoring and evaluation (M & E) in the policy cycle

Monitoring and evaluation (M & E) is integral to the policy cycle process and has utility for management and administrative decisions. The policy cycle comprises various steps or stages which contribute to a broad conceptual understanding of the policy process. M & E is important for advocacy in policy and organisational design. The cycle starts when a problem is recognised and defined at the beginning of the policy process, for example, a concern about service delivery. Next, policy objectives are identified and options are considered. The viability of options is contemplated and this is often based on pragmatic decisions such as budgeting, what is achievable in the time frames that are available, and engagements with a range of constituencies. Finally, policy decisions are taken. Once a policy decision has been taken, government departments initiate the processes of designing a programme to achieve the policy objectives, planning the programme in detail, and implementing the programme (Public Service Commission Report, 2008). Whilst deliberating the planning and implementation of the programme, monitoring and evaluation are also considered during this phase. See Figure 13.2 below for the policy cycle which includes M & E.

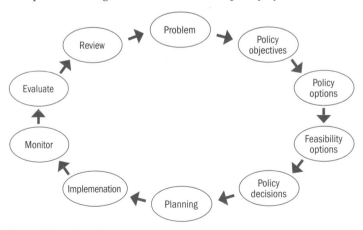

Figure 13.2: The policy cycle

# 13.4 **Research methods**

Research methods that are used include both quantitative and qualitative research designs. Quantitative designs comprise pre-experimental/hypothesis-developing/exploratory designs; quantitative descriptive (survey) design; quasi-experimental design; and experimental design (Fouche and De Vos, 2005: 133–141).

## 13.4.1 **Quantitative designs**

### 13.4.1.1 **Experimental designs**

The fundamental premise of an *experimental design* is that it uses control and experimental groups. Out of the target population, units (individuals, people) are selected randomly for the control and experimental groups, respectively. Subjects for the experimental group will be provided with the treatment or programme, while the control group will not receive the programme or treatment. Instead, a 'placebo' programme can be devised for the control group that gives the appearance but not the substance of the service. Randomised designs are effective in controlling the possibility that something other than the programme or treatment is causing the improvements that are observable.

### 13.4.1.2 **Quasi-experimental designs**

Quasi-experimental designs have features which are similar to experimental designs, but do not employ randomisation. These designs do not remove all of the threats to internal validity, but they remove the majority of them (Chen, 2015: 256). Their control of internal validity is not as reliable as a true experimental design, but they do provide important answers to cause-and-effect questions (Mark and Henry, 2006 in Rabie, 2014: 145). Factors that may undermine the validity of the quasi-experimental design include historical or seasonal events that influence observed results, maturation of subjects, the effect of the test or instruments used on the subject's behaviour, attrition of subjects from the programme, and statistical regression that would have occurred naturally without any intervention. Because of the quasi-experimental design's emphasis on cause and effect, that is, the logic of experimentation, this model seems to focus on outcome or impact evaluations with minimal attention to process and implementation evaluation questions (Mouton, 2007: 495).

### 13.4.1.3 **Survey designs**

Survey designs are discussed in section 13.5 below under 'Approaches in evaluation'.

### 13.4.1.4 **Pre-experimental/hypothesis-developing/exploratory designs**

According to Chen (2015: 253), pre-experimental designs do not resemble experimental designs. The reason that they are called pre-experimental designs is because they do not meet the scientific requirements of experimental designs. These designs do not employ randomised selection of participants nor do they include a control group (Fouche, Delport and De Vos, 2011: 145). Pre-experimental designs are used when there are insufficient resources to embark on experimental designs. There are three types of pre-experimental designs (Chen 2015: 254). These are as follows:

*One-Group Post-test-Only Design*: This design only measures the outcome after the intervention. This design is regarded as the weakest since it does not measure baseline data and cannot rule out most of the threats to internal validity. The design is portrayed as follows:

**Intervention Group: X    O**

*Static Group Comparison*: This design expands on the one group post-testonly design by adding a comparison group. The design is portrayed as follows:

**Intervention Group: X    O**

-------------------------------------

**Comparison Group:       O**

The dotted line between these two groups suggests that they are not equivalent. By adding a comparison group, the static group comparison design is a slight improvement on the one group post-test only design. Survey research is based on this design. One of the major drawbacks to this design is a lack of baseline data.

*One-Group Pre-test–Post-test Design*: This pre-experimental design is the one-group pre-test–post-test design. The design is portrayed as follows:

**Intervention Group:   X**

This design upgrades the one-group post-test only design by adding a pre-test component. However, it is still considered to be weak since it does not rule out most of the threats of internal validity. An interesting observation is that community organisations tend to use this design even though it has weaknesses.

## 13.4.2 Qualitative designs

Qualitative designs include narrative biography, ethnography, phenomenology, grounded theory, case studies, participant observation, document study, interviews, and focus groups (Fouche and De Vos, 2011: 312–389).

*Narrative biographies* refer to a story or description provided by the narrator on the life story or memoires of the individual or narrator, and this relates to both a process and a product. Biography suggests the broad genre of biographical writings (Creswell (2007) in Fouche and Schurink, 2011). These forms of research include life stories, life histories, narratives, autobiographies, and auto-ethnographies. These forms have a fundamental theme which is the unfolding of an individual's, that is, the narrator's, life experiences over time.

*Ethnography* has its genesis in anthropology. Ethnography is defined as the study of an undamaged cultural or social group based on observations by the researcher who has spent a prolonged period of time in the field.

A *phenomenological* study is an attempt to understand people's perceptions, perspectives, and understanding of a particular issue or situation.

*Grounded theory* is the effort to build substantive theory based on developing data.

Qualitative researchers are interested in studying the meaning that respondents give to their life experiences. *Case studies* are qualitative measurement designs which may make available a single case study or a small group of cases. A case study is a method of immersing the researcher in the life or activities of an individual or a small group of people in order to gain familiarity with their social worlds and to seek patterns in the respondents' lives, words, and actions in the context of the case as a whole (Fouche and Schurink, 2011: 320).

*Participation observation* is assumed to be that the real world of the participants can be understood if the words and expressions are observed and revealed in a particular situation, and these will form the qualitative data.

A range of documents is available to the researcher. Documents can be classified into primary and secondary sources. Primary sources are viewed as the original material written by the author on the author's experiences and observations, while the secondary sources comprise material that is derived from someone else as the original source (Strydom and Delport, 2011: 377). For example, an autobiography is a primary source, while a biography is a secondary source. When using secondary sources, the researcher should be prudent and carefully examine the content of the document for precision because the content is another person's interpretation of a primary source.

*Interviews* are the main mode of data collection for qualitative research. Researchers obtain information or data through the direct interchange with an individual (or a group) who has (or have) the prescribed knowledge that is sought by the researchers. Interviewing the participant or respondent involves not only a description of the interview, but a reflection of the description (Greef, 2011: 342). Qualitative studies employ unstructured or semi-structured interviews.

*Focus groups* are interviews conducted with a group of individuals who have certain characteristics in common which relate to the topic. Focus groups should be used for the following reasons:

- Seeking a range of ideas or feelings that people will express about an issue(s).
- Understanding the differences between groups or categories of people.
- The purpose is to obtain or uncover factors that influence opinions, behaviour or motivation.
- Seeking ideas emerging from the group.
- Wanting to pilot-test ideas, materials, plans or policies.
- Requiring information to help shed light on quantitative data already collected.
- The clients or intended audience place a high value on capturing the comments or language used by the target audience (Krueger and Casey, 2004: 24–25 in Greef, 2011: 362, 363).

Focus groups have revealed that people are more likely to reveal personal experiences in groups rather than in a dyadic situation.

### 13.4.3 Mixed method designs

Mixed method designs seem to be favoured in the recent practice of evaluation research designs instead of pure quantitative or pure qualitative designs since both designs have advantages and disadvantages (Rabie, 2014: 149). Mixed method designs draw on the strengths of the quantitative and qualitative designs, and discard the limitations of these designs. Combining these different designs and data sources provides the space for:

- triangulation that tests the dependability of findings obtained through different instruments to ascertain multiple causes influencing results;
- complementarity that clarifies and illustrates results from one method with the use of another method;
- development or improvement of methods where one method shapes successive methods or steps in the research process;
- initiation of new research questions or challenges where the results are obtained through one method by providing new insights on how the programme has been viewed and valued across sites; and
- expansion of the richness and detail of the study, exploring specific features of each method (Greene, Caracelli and Graham, 1989: 259 in Rabie, 2014: 149, 150).

## 13.5 Approaches in evaluation

A range of approaches may be used in making an evaluation of a welfare programme/organisation or policy. The approach will depend on the time factor and other factors such as the budget. The approaches which are available to the evaluation researcher include: surveys; the logical framework approach; the theory-based approach; rapid appraisal methods; participatory methods; and impact evaluation. These are the main approaches available to the evaluation researcher. As indicated before, the selection of these approaches will depend on the time constraints, the budget or cost factor, and the stakeholders who are involved in the evaluation.

### 13.5.1 Surveys

*Surveys* provide qualitative and quantitative data for client perceptions. Surveys provide systematic information of the population from a sample living in a community. Surveys comprise questionnaires or structured interview schedules. Respondents are usually chosen by means of randomised sampling methods (Fouche and De Vos, 2005: 137). Other types of surveys are household surveys and those for client functioning. There are certain operational stages and activities in surveys. These are presented in Table 13.1 below.

Table: 13.1 Operational stages and activities in surveys

| Stage | Activities |
|---|---|
| Planning | • Identify potential utility and relevance of information<br>• Secure commitment by potential users to use survey information<br>• Establish a steering committee<br>• Select the research project director<br>• Secure funding or budget for survey. |
| Operational planning | • Select data gathering techniques<br>• Select sampling procedures and sample<br>• Determine specific content area(s) of survey<br>• Prepare the questions and construct interview schedules or questionnaires<br>• Hire and train interviewers<br>• Pilot test to evaluate:<br>  – interviewers' skills and performance<br>  – non-response-refusal rate<br>• Check the legitimacy of the questions and the flow of these questions<br>• Select data process, data storage, and data analysis procedures. |
| Data collection | • Contact and interview respondents<br>• Edit and check-edit completed interviews<br>• Prepare instructions for the computer<br>• Prepare code book<br>• Code and check-code responses. |
| Data preparation and analysis | • Apply data analysis to procedures. |
| Presentation of findings | • Identify audience<br>• Present and interpret results of study<br>• Formulate conclusions and recommendations<br>• Submit preliminary report(s) to decision-makers, policymakers or committee members<br>• Prepare final report for wider audience. |

Source: Adapted from Bell, Nguyen, Warheit and Buhl, 1978: 280

Nussbaum (2006: 48) raises concerns about the utilitarian nature of client satisfaction surveys which does not confront issues of social justice. One of the limitations of survey research is that it can be costly and these may be a constraint for welfare organisations in a climate of financial austerity.

## 13.5.2 Logical Framework Approach

The Logical Framework Approach (LFA) is considered to be an effective strategic planning and project management tool with wide application. This approach is appealing to development donors since the activities are linked to a budgetary framework. Therefore, the accountability mechanism is built in with checks and balances and makes provision for information to be analysed and organised in a structured fashion. This approach is a core tool used in the project management cycle with an emphasis on the results or outcomes.

It is recommended to undertake a structured analysis of the existing set-up before embarking on an activity design and a construction of the log-frame matrix. LFA comprises four main analytical elements to assist in guiding the process:
- **Problem analysis**: This involves identifying the main problems and establishing the cause and effect relationships which result in and flow from these problems.
- **Stakeholder analysis**: An analysis should be done on the impact of the people who experience these problems, and the roles and interests of a range of stakeholders in addressing these problems.
- **Analysis of objectives:** Preparation of an objective tree after a problem tree has been completed. This will provide an indication of improvements in future.
- **Analysis of strategies:** Proposal and comparison of different strategies to address a particular situation (Barreto Dillon, 2010).

The logical model is a graphical representation of the relationship between a programme's operational activities and its outcomes. Evaluators who assessed the United Way of America's programme from a logic model's perspective described the *inputs* as the resources dedicated to the programme (that is, funds, staff, supplies and perhaps ideas) (Chen, 2015: 59). According to this model, *activities* can be attributed to the services which are required to fulfil the programme's mandate or mission, such as counselling of clients; referral of clients; recruiting and training of staff; and educating the community and society (Chen, 2015: 59). *Outputs* can be described as the direct products or results of programme activities; for example: the number of clients served; the number of classes taught; the amount of goods distributed; and perhaps reports produced such as annual reports. Finally, the logic model defines *outcomes* as the benefits that accrue from the programme activities such as improved health care, new knowledge, improved skills, and increased income (Chen, 2015).

As a graphic representation of this logic model, the following is proposed:

**Inputs**--------------------**Activities**-----------------------**Outputs**--------------------**Outcomes**

In Table 13.2 on the next page the LFA is applied to the problem of drug addiction that a community is facing.

Table 13.2 Drug addiction prevention logic model

| Objectives | Activities | Outputs | Outcomes |
|---|---|---|---|
| 1. To involve the community in drug prevention. | • Establish a committee to oversee drug prevention activities. | • Number of participants in this drug prevention committee. | • Number of drug-related reports to the police in the area. |
| 2. To educate the public about drug and drug prevention. | • Committee to hold quarterly or bi-monthly meetings to discuss activities and/or progress. | • Number of meetings held on an annual basis. | • Number of crimes reported to the police which are drug-related. |
| 3. Reduce the incidents of drug-related crimes. | • Community development workers from the municipality and/or local councillors invited to committee meetings to update committee on their involvement in drug prevention campaigns.<br>• Committee provides information to media/ social media on drug prevention efforts.<br>• Committee invites rehabilitated drug-free individuals to address meetings. | • Number of guest speakers invited on an annual basis.<br><br><br><br><br>• Number of media releases and reports to the media.<br><br>• Number of drug-free individuals invited to address the committee. | • Number of tips reported to the police concerning drugs. |

It must be noted that there is clear delineation between LFA and the Logical Framework matrix. The former refers to the *steps* involved in planning and designing the project. These *steps* include a *stakeholder analysis*, cause-effect analysis, objectives analysis, and alternatives analysis culminating in the design of the project. The matrix, which summarises the final design of the project, usually comprises 16 frames organised under 4 major headings.

There are two types of outcome evaluations: constructive and conclusive. The purpose of constructive outcome evaluation is to provide information for improving programme outcomes (Chen, 2015). Conclusive evaluation has the purpose of providing a formal assessment of whether a programme has a desirable effect on its goals or outcomes.

The Logical Framework matrix has four columns and four (or more) rows, which summarise the key elements of a project plan, namely:

• The project's hierarchy of objectives (project description and expected outputs)
• The key external factors critical to the project's success (assumptions)
• How the project's achievements will be monitored and evaluated (indicators and sources of verification).

| | Intervention Logic | Objectively Verifiable Indicators | Sources of Verification | Risks and Assumptions |
|---|---|---|---|---|
| Principal Objectives | | | | |
| Specific Objective | | | | |
| Results | | | | |
| Activities | | Means | Costs | |
| | | | | Pre-conditions |

Source: https://webgate.ec.europa.eu/fpfis/mwikis/aidco/index.php/Logical_framework_approach

Figure 13.3  Logical Framework matrix

## 13.5.3 Rapid appraisal approaches

Rapid appraisal approaches may be used which are quick and economical. Noyoo (2005: 231) notes that these methods are quick, low-cost ways to obtain the views and feedback of beneficiaries and stakeholders, in order to respond to decision-makers' needs for information. These approaches can be considered to be an effective way of informing decision-making.

## 13.5.4 Participatory methods

Given the present context of human rights and social justice, where citizens are expected to be involved in decision-making (which is the case in current South African welfare policymaking, that is, participatory democracy), *participatory methods* is another approach to be considered. This approach allows for a range of stakeholders to be involved at various levels with the purpose of identifying problems, collecting and analysing data, and proposing recommendations. Participation is a key principle in the policy paper, the *White Paper for Social Welfare* (1997), and therefore this type of evaluation research approach is congruent with the social development approach because of its inclusive nature. This form of research is in keeping with policy requirements (integrated development planning) at local government level.

An important aspect of the participatory method is constructivism which is concerned with participants or respondents being actively involved in the process and being equal partners in the endeavour. Creswell (2007: 20) observes that participants seek understanding of the world in which they live and work. Participants assist in formulating the measuring instrument and the strategy to be followed (Glicken, 2003 in De Vos, Strydom, Schulze and Patel, 2011). Constructivism is in direct contrast to positivism in that the philosophy of positivism subscribes to the principles of natural science whereas constructivism appreciates the complexity of human nature.

## 13.5.5 Theory-based evaluation

*Theory-based evaluation* allows for early indication of programme effectiveness. Since theory-based evaluation uses programme theory as a conceptual framework for assessing programme effectiveness, it provides information not only on whether intervention is effective, but also on how and why a programme is effective (Chen, 2015: 25, 26). Programme theory is related to logic models but distinct from them. The success of a programme can be judged by its findings, in addition to its milieu. The milieu or context such as norms, socioeconomic and political conditions will influence programme outcomes.

Programmes have a certain sequence of steps:

- conceptualising the problem, that is, a needs assessment;
- designing the appropriate methods to alleviate the problem (programme theory);
- implementing the design; and
- effecting the changes or improvements, that is, achieving the impacts.

Programme theory is defined as a specification of what must be done to achieve the necessary goals, what other important impacts may also be anticipated, and how these goals and impacts would be produced (Chen, 1990: 43).

A case study is provided below as an example of Impact Theory related to a social protection programme in Maputo, Mozambique (Buonaguro and Louw, 2014: 103–115).

 **Case Study** | **MOZAMBIQUE SOCIAL PROTECTION PROGRAMME FOR STREET PEOPLE**

In June 2011, a collaborative programme was launched as part of the National Strategy for Basic Social Security (NSBBS). This programme was called the Social Protection and Informal Work Promotion Among Street People Project (SPIWP). The SPIWP was planned as a three-year intervention programme to be implemented in Maputo, the capital of Mozambique. The programme was administered by a group of eight organisations which included representatives from civil society, Mozambican government institutions, and others such as an Italian NGO and the Development Information and Education Centre. The purpose of this programme was to reduce vulnerability, social exclusion, and poverty through social protection mechanisms. Programme documents were reviewed, and then a set of interviews was conducted with the programme designers concerning the design of the programme. As a consequence of an iterative series of interviews, a first draft of the programme impact was formulated, representing the change process as originally understood by the programme designers. The first draft of SPIWP's impact theory was presented to representatives of all the organisations and there was disagreement on what the programme needed to achieve. A working group was formed to address these discrepancies where all programme partners were represented. The group met twice and the sessions were conducted in Portuguese. Using large sticky notes, a visual representation of the programme's impact theory was built up beginning with immediate outcomes and ending with long-term impacts. The result was an organised and consensual model involving 30 different outcomes, reworked by the authors into a coherent set of outcomes, accepted by all partners as an accurate reflection of their thinking.

Theory-based evaluation is related to the Logical Framework Approach but is distinct in that it provides for a more in-depth understanding of the operations of a programme or activity. It improves the generalisability of evaluation results, contributing to social science theory, uncovering unintended effects, and achieving consensus in evaluation planning (Chen, 2015: 65).

### 13.5.6 Impact evaluation

And finally, *impact evaluation* is a systematic identification of the negative and positive effects on the welfare project, programme or policy. Impact evaluations are necessary when there is an interest either in comparing different programmes or in testing the utility of new efforts to ameliorate a particular community problem (Rossi and Freeman, 1993: 37). Impact evaluation is used to ascertain the effects of a programme which is established. If the intention of the evaluation may be to make a decision on the viability of the programme, the evaluation of this kind will be described as *summative evaluation* (Owen, 2007: 47).

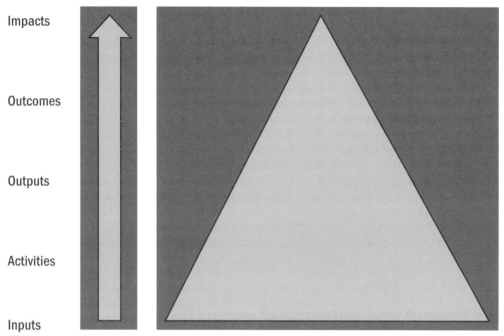

Impacts

Outcomes

Outputs

Activities

Inputs

Figure 13.4 Evaluation – the Impact Model

Evaluators may pose the following questions:
- Has the programme or policy been implemented as planned?
- Have the goals and objectives of the programme/policy been achieved?
- Have the needs of the beneficiaries of the programme/policy been achieved?
- What are the intended and unintended outcomes of the programme/policy?
- Does the implementation strategy lead to the intended outcomes?
- How do differences in implementation affect programme/policy outcomes?
- Is the programme/policy more effective for some participants in contrast to others?
- Has the programme/policy been cost effective?
- Has the programme or policy made any difference to the lives of beneficiaries? (Owen, 2007: 48).

### Why is there concern with evaluation and monitoring?
Systematic evaluation on the African continent up to the 1980s was initiated to a great extent by international organisations such as aid organisations, NGOs, and evaluators. UNICEF promoted a network of evaluation practitioners in Nairobi, Kenya in 1977 with the purpose of enhancing capacity-building for UNICEF and conducting evaluation projects in East Africa (Mouton, Rabie, De Coning and Cloete, 2014: 54). The first seminar on evaluation in Africa was held in Abidjan, Cote d'Ivoire in 1980, and was co-hosted by the African Development Bank (ADB) and the Development Assistance Committee (DAC). The objectives of the seminar included clarifying evaluation needs as identified by African countries and exploring procedures to strengthen self-evaluation capacities.

As society and the governance thereof have developed, South Africa's post-apartheid government with its concomitant context of human rights and social justice has been challenged to be more accountable to its constituents. Since many NPOs receive subsidies from the government for social welfare services, they have to account for how they spend their budgets on services and its impact on beneficiaries. In recent times, the South African government has been challenged about its implementation of policies. In 2011, Cabinet approved the National Evaluation Policy Framework which set the foundation for the National Evaluation System (NES) and the implementation of the National Evaluation Plan, an annual evaluation plan that is focusing on strategic evaluations of important government programmes (Department of Planning, Monitoring and Evaluation).

If one considers the three key questions that are directed at the monitoring of programmes, incomplete implementation or problematic implementation seems to be the main focus. These questions are as follows:

1. To what extent does the programme reach its target population?
2. Is the programme's delivery of services consistent with programme design specifications?
3. What resources are being or have been expended in the duration of the programme? (Rossi and Freeman, 1993: 163).

Many sound policies with accompanying legislation have been introduced in South Africa but the challenge appears to be the limited implementation.

## 13.6 Impact and outcome of evaluation

Impact evaluation deals with the issue of effectiveness and whether the programme made any change to the lives of the recipients, that is, whether it achieved the objectives that were planned at the inception of the programme. This could be referred to as the direct effects of a policy flowing from a programme that was devised for that purpose. Therefore, there is a considerable emphasis on the total achievements and findings. Impact evaluation is considered to be the following:

- Determining the range and extent of the outcomes of the programme.
- Determining whether a programme has been implemented according to plans and how implementation has affected outcomes.
- The provision of evidence to funders, administrators, senior managers, board members and politicians about the extent to which resources allocated to a programme has been spent wisely.
- Informing decisions about replication or extension of a programme (Owen, 2007: 253).

At the global level, impact evaluations are at the core to building knowledge about the effectiveness of development programmes by elucidating what does and does not work to reduce poverty and improve welfare (Gertler, Martinez, Premand, Rawlings and Vermeersch, 2016: 4). Impact evaluation assesses the changes in the well-being of individuals that can be attributed to a particular project, programme or policy.

For example, in South Africa, the Department of Social Development commissioned a Diagnostic Review of Early Childhood Development (ECD). The purpose of the evaluation was to evaluate the current South African ECD paradigm and policy, including the role of the state, and the implementation of ECD services and programmes. A new ECD policy was drafted in response to the ECD Diagnostic Review, including the need to target children from as early as conception. In addition, an important process outcome was an improved relationship between the three key departments involved (Social Development, Basic Education and Health).

Often evaluation research methods of policies and programmes may be driven by ideological biases. In this regard, a mixed method approach can be particularly useful. Mixed method approaches that combine quantitative and qualitative data are a key enhancement to impact evaluations based on the use of quantitative data alone, particularly to help generate hypotheses and focus research questions before quantitative data are collected and to provide perspectives and insights on a programme's performance during and after programme implementation. There are many qualitative methods, and they comprise their own research domain. Methods generating qualitative data generally employ open-ended approaches that do not rely on predetermined responses from those being interviewed. Data are generated through a range of approaches, including focus groups, life histories, and interviews with selected beneficiaries and other key informants (Rao and Woolcock, 2003). They can also include various observational and ethnographic assessments. Although the observations, views, and opinions gathered during qualitative work are usually not statistically representative of the programme's beneficiaries – and can thus not be used to generalise – they are useful to understand why certain results have or have not been achieved. Evaluations that integrate qualitative and quantitative analysis are characterised as using mixed methods.

An example of achievements was provided by provinces and districts at round table discussions in 2015, during the process of the Review of the Implementation of the White Paper (1997). Service providers in KwaZulu-Natal reported that active support, which included funding, for community projects was beginning to demonstrate positive results with projects becoming self-sustaining (DSD, *Comprehensive Report of the Review of the Implementation of the White Paper for Social Welfare* (1997), 2016: 204). An example of this was a community food gardening project.

Food gardening is one of the projects that community members embarked on

# CONCLUSION

- This chapter has demonstrated the purpose of monitoring and evaluation for social welfare policy, its utility as a tool for management, funders and its target audience.
- The location of M & E in the policy cycle is shown. The differentiation between two kinds of evaluation, that is, monitoring (formative evaluation) and evaluation (impact or summative evaluation) are discussed in detail.
- The research methods such as quantitative and qualitative methods that evaluation researchers employ are analysed.
- The evaluation approaches discussed in this chapter are surveys, the Logical Framework Approach, theory-based approach, rapid appraisal methods, participatory methods, and impact evaluation.
- The impact and outcome of evaluation demonstrates considerable emphasis on the total achievements and findings and what the programme and policy has achieved.

# QUESTIONS

1. What is the purpose of monitoring and evaluation (M & E) and does it have any relevance for management and policy decisions?
2. Discuss the approaches in M & E and which approach will be appropriate for your project? Motivate you answer.
3. What is the outcome and impact of your project or your organisation's project?

# REFERENCES

ATTKISSON, CC & BROSKOWSKI, A: 'Evaluation and the Emerging Human Service Concept' in Attkisson, CC, Hargreaves, WA, Horowitz, MJ & Sorensen, JE (1978) *Evaluation of Human Service Programs* at pp. 3–26. New York, San Francisco, London: Academic Press.

BARRETO, DL (2010) Logical Framework Approach [Online]. Available: http//www.sswm.info/content/logical-framework-approach [19 April 2017].

BELL, RA, NGUYEN, TD, WARHEIT, GJ & BUHL, JM: 'Service Utilization, Social Indicator, and Citizen Survey Approaches to Human Service Need Assessment' in Attkisson, CC, Hargreaves, WA, Horowitz, MJ & Sorensen, JE (eds.) (1978) *Evaluation of Human Service Programs* at pp. 253–300. New York, San Francisco, London: Academic Press.

BUONAGURO, L & LOUW, J: 'Case: Developing Impact theory for a social protection programme in Maputo, Mozambique' in Cloete, F, Rabie, B & De Coning, C (eds.) (2014) *Evaluating Management in South Africa and Africa* at pp. 103–115. Stellenbosch: SUN MeDIA.

CHEN, HT (1990) *Theory-driven Evaluations*. Thousand Oaks, CA: Sage Publications.

CHEN, HT (2015) *Practical Program Evaluation. Theory-Driven Evaluation and the Integrated Evaluation Perspective* (second edition) at pp. 58–93. Thousand Oaks, London, New Delhi, Singapore: Sage Publications.

CIVIL SOCIETY HELPDESK [Online]. Available: https://webgate.ec.europa.eu/fpfis/mwikis/aidco/index.php/Logical_framework_approach [3 May 2017].

DE VOS, AS, STRYDOM, H, FOUCHE, CB & DELPORT, CSL (2011) *Research at Grass Roots. For the social sciences and human service professions* (fourth edition). Pretoria: Van Schaik Publishers.

FOUCHE, CB & DE VOS, AS: 'Quantitative Research Designs' in De Vos, AS, Strydom, H, Fouche, CB & Delport, CSL (2005) *Research at grass roots. For the Social Sciences and Human Service Professions* (third edition) at pp. 132–143. Pretoria: Van Schaik Publishers.

FOUCHE, CB & SCHURINK, W: 'Qualitative research designs' in De Vos, AS, Strydom, H, Fouche, CB & Delport, CSL (2011) *Research at grass roots. For the Social Sciences and Human Service Professions* (fourth edition) at pp. 307–327. Pretoria: Van Schaik Publishers.

GERTLER, PJ, MARTINEZ, S, PREMAND, P, RAWLINGS, LB & VERMEERSCH, CM (2016) *Impact Evaluation in Practice* (second edition). Washington, DC: International Bank for Reconstruction and Development/The World Bank.

GREEF, M: 'Information collection: interviewing' in De Vos, AS, Strydom, H, Fouche, CB & Delport, CSL (2011) *Research at grass roots. For the Social Sciences and Human Service Professions* (fourth edition) at pp. 341–375. Pretoria: Van Schaik Publishers.

KIRST-ASHMAN, KK & HULL, GH (2012) *Generalist Practice with Organizations and Communities* (fifth edition) at pp. 323–357. Australia, Brazil, Japan, Korea, Mexico, Singapore, Spain, United Kingdom, United States: Brooks/Cole Empowerment Series.

LEWIS, AJ, LEWIS, MD, PACKARD, M & SOUFLEE, F (2001) *Management of Human Service Programs* (third edition) at Chapter 235. United States: Brooks/Cole.

MOUTON, J (2007) 'Approaches to programme evaluation research' *Journal of Public Administration* 42(6): 490–511.

MOUTON, J, CRABIE, B, DE CONING, C & CLOETE, F: 'Historical Development and Practice of Evaluation' in Cloete, F, Rabie, B & De Coning, C (eds.) (2014) *Evaluation Management in South Africa and Africa* at pp. 28–78. Stellenbosch: SUN MeDIA.

NOYOO, N (2005) 'Monitoring and evaluation for social development: A case for social work in South Africa' *Social Work/MaatskaplikeWerk* 41(3): 229–236.

NUSSBAUM, MC: 'Poverty and Human Functioning: Capabilities as Fundamental Entitlements' in Grusky, DB & Kanbur, R (eds.) (2006) *Poverty and Inequality. Studies in Social Inequality* at pp. 47–75. Stanford, CA: Stanford University Press.

O'DONOGHUE, K & LOUW-POTGIETER, J (2013) 'A Process Evaluation of a Programme for Street People' *Social Work/MaatskaplikeWerk* 49(4): 544–569.

OWEN, JM (2007) *Program Evaluation: Forms and Approaches* (third edition) at pp. 252–290. London, New York: The Guilford Press.

RABIE,B: 'Evaluation Models, Theories and Paradigms' in Cloete, F, Rabie, B & De Coning, C (eds.) (2014) *Evaluation Management in South Africa and Africa* at pp. 116–164. Stellenbosch: SUN MeDIA.

ROSSI, PH & FREEMAN, HE (1993) *Evaluation. A Systematic Approach*. Newbury Park, London, New Delhi: Sage Publications.

ROSSI, PH, LIPSEY, MW & FREEMAN, HE (2004) *Evaluation. A systematic approach*. Thousand Oaks: Sage Publications.

SOUTH AFRICA. Department of Planning, Monitoring and Evaluation Report.

SOUTH AFRICA. Department of Social Development (DSD) (2016) *Comprehensive Report of the Review of the Implementation of the White Paper for Social Welfare, 1997*. Pretoria: Government Printer.

SOUTH AFRICA. Public Service Commission Report (2008). Basic Concepts in Monitoring and Evaluation. Pretoria: Government Printer.

STRYDOM, H & DELPORT, CSL: 'Information collection: document study and secondary analysis' in De Vos, AS, Strydom, H, Fouche, CB & Delport, CSL (2011) *Research at grass roots. For the Social Sciences and Human Service Professions* (fourth edition) at pp. 376–396). Pretoria: Van Schaik Publishers.

WEISS, CH (1972) *Evaluation Research. Methods of Assessing Program Effectiveness*. Englewood Cliffs, New Jersey: Prentice Hall.

# Lessons of experience in transforming social welfare policy

*Viviene Taylor*

Chapter 14 focuses on the main themes and messages relevant to the processes of transforming social welfare policy in Africa. These themes and messages emerge from a critical analysis of the history, the politics, the economics, and social conditions in Africa as well as experiences drawn from preceding chapters in this book. The objectives and outcomes for this chapter are listed below.

## Objectives

✓ Analysing social welfare policy issues within the broader political economy context of Africa.

✓ Reviewing the main themes that emerge in each chapter and providing a critical analysis of these themes.

✓ Highlighting some of the main lessons of experience in transforming social welfare policy in sub-Saharan Africa.

## Outcomes

✓ Analysing critically social welfare policies within Africa's political economy context.

✓ Examining the main themes and providing a critical analysis of these themes.

✓ Describing key lessons in transforming social welfare policy in sub-Saharan Africa.

## 14.1 Introduction

In the contemporary world, debate and controversy continue to surround social welfare policy as a concept and approach to social development, its origins, its underpinnings and constituent parts, and its relevance for countries in Africa.

Some theorists argue that this is because the intellectual traditions of social work dominate the field of social welfare policy and that social work's historic vocation is more consistent with an approach that is reactive, piecemeal, and ameliorative (Lee and Raban, 1988) rather than transformative and emancipatory. Is this because social work as a profession and related social service professionals aim to integrate individuals, families, and communities into existing unequal structures and systems? Is the social integration role of social work and social welfare policy designed to reproduce inequities in access to resources, power, and privilege because of the dominance of its colonial heritage in countries in Africa? These are critical questions that remain a focus in this concluding chapter.

Answers to these questions inform the analysis in this chapter in the context of lessons of experience on the political economy of transforming social welfare policy in Africa. Social welfare policy and practice, despite its chequered colonial history, have a central role in ensuring that basic social welfare rights are accessible to all. Making human rights a reality for the millions of historically disenfranchised people is part of a transformative[1] social welfare policy agenda (Taylor, 2014). The political economy of Africa is complex and rooted in a long history of conquest and struggles against imperialism, colonial, and postcolonial processes. The Balkanisation (breaking up of Africa into territories according to colonial requirements) of the continent has led to regions that remain strongly influenced by economic and political relations with former colonial powers. These influences create fractures among countries and fuel language, economic, political, and territorial divisions. Africa, today, not only reflects the historical features of colonial struggles but also has huge differences and variations in its social and economic systems.

Part of the complexities influencing the continent are the old and new compacts of power among economic and political elites within countries and within the international multilateral system that reproduce patterns of ownership and power and that reinforce the subjugation of the majority in the interests of elite capture of power. Although leading theorists such as Ake (1976) and Bienefeld (1988) analysed the political economy of Africa more than four decades ago, the features that shape the continent's development trajectory or path remain stubborn challenges. These challenges prevent countries in the region from transcending their historical and economic legacies and advancing a transformative vision of social welfare policy to ensure the human development of Africa's people.

Among the challenges highlighted by Ake (1976) are intense ethnic conflict, the single party system, the high incidence of efficiency norms in political competition, recurring military coups, and political repression with poor economic development performance (Ake, 1976). While the seeds of these challenges predate colonialism according to Ake (1976), the periods of colonial rule and postcolonial governance fuelled ethnic conflict, competition, and government through coercive force to repress dissatisfaction of the people with the regimes in power.

Navigating these complex challenges to advance a transformative and emancipatory social welfare policy agenda and process may seem difficult, yet lessons from experience provide markers that can guide social service professionals and policymakers. The next section highlights some of the lessons from experience and analyses the main themes that emerge in the chapters of this book.

# 14.2 Lessons of experience in transforming social welfare policy in Africa

Historical and theoretical analyses (Ake, 1976; Bienefeld, 1988) of the political economy of Africa link policy responses from governments to the crises of capitalist development during colonial and postcolonial periods, as well as the political and economic consequences of national governance in an international context dominated by a world economic system that privileges those with control over resources. Analyses of the experiences in the various chapters of this book, as well as using a political economy lens to critique the social welfare policy responses of countries in the region, provide some lessons of experience. Taylor, in Chapter 1 of the book, makes a compelling argument for the study of social welfare policy as a discipline and field of professional practice in Africa. She asserts that there are compelling reasons for a renewed urgency to respond to conditions of extreme poverty and the realisation that traditional support systems such as the family, community, and kinship support systems are no longer able to cope with the heavy burden of care imposed on them. The systematic and violent disruptions to black family life as a deliberate project of political and economic subjugation of the majority during colonial and postcolonial rule in Africa and white rule, especially in South Africa, continue to limit the life chances and well-being of the majority of people as illustrated in Chapters 1 and 4 by Taylor and Chapter 2 by Noyoo. The effects of recurring social crises such as structural unemployment, chronic conditions of poverty, and epidemiological crises as a result of diseases such as HIV and Aids, famine, and food insecurity make social welfare policy as a response as critical as the need for economic development. This is a lesson that most governments in Africa recognise because both economic and social development are interdependent and prioritising one area above the other undermines human development as well as the sustainability of socially inclusive economic development.

The next sections provide a more detailed analysis of the main themes and lessons of experience in the chapters of this book.

## 14.2.1 Conceptualising transformative social welfare policy using a political economy perspective to change power relations

Using a political economy analysis in Chapter 1, Taylor asserts that transformative social welfare policy goes beyond a conventional social welfare approach that aims to integrate individuals and families into oppressive economic and social systems. She explains that transformative social welfare policy ensures that all people living in a given country are able to participate in economic activity (production) and political activities irrespective of their race, gender, status, sexual orientation, geographical location, or disability. Importantly, reproductive functions of social welfare are transformative when care is provided to ensure that women are supported and empowered through antenatal and postnatal processes, as well as when the bodily integrity of women and children is protected from all forms of violence and abuse.

The basis of transformative social welfare policy and practice is social justice and human rights. A human rights approach to social welfare policy in Africa, and especially in South Africa, links directly to addressing inequalities, discrimination, and multiple deprivations that people experience as a result of oppressive regimes and systems. Social and economic rights are integral to transformative social welfare policy and constitute the basis to protect the bodily integrity of girls, women and boys against violence and ensure that girls and women have the freedom to make choices about their reproductive health and care.

There are two main themes that emerge in Chapter 1. Firstly, social welfare policy is transformative when it enables the equitable redistribution of services, provisions, and income to members of society who are the poorest, most vulnerable, and at risk. It is redistributive and socially just in applying the principle of equity or fairness. This principle enables redress to ensure gender equity and race-based equity, and it also addresses spatial differences that arise from rural-urban bias and apartheid spatial planning. Secondly, social welfare policy and provisions should empower those who have been historically excluded from the benefits of society so that there is a real shift in power relations.

The conceptual understanding of social welfare policy is influenced by the values and ideologies that governments adopt as Triegaardt explains in Chapter 3. She shows how theories and approaches that underpin welfare policy reinforce the values and ideological views of dominant political parties, which can vary from conservative and liberal to radical perspectives. Governments' approach to social welfare policy and provision is on a policy continuum and includes major interventions that are characteristic of a welfare state or institutionalism. At the other end of the continuum are conservative states that adopt an approach that is minimal and narrow state intervention because the belief is that individuals should take responsibility for their own well-being or acquire services through the market, and the state steps in to assist in a residual way when all else fails. The assumption is that the structures of society are working well and the problem lies with the inability of the individual to cope.

Recognising the limits of the residual approach, Triegaardt affirms a state-centred developmental approach as well as a feminist lens through which this approach should be applied. This approach, she argues, has relevance for transformative social welfare policy because the political, economic and social well-being of women and their families, and the structural forces and collective processes that contribute to the oppression and disempowerment of women and poor people can be better addressed through this approach. Experiences and analyses of social welfare policy approaches in countries in sub-Saharan Africa show that most countries take a narrow and minimal approach to welfare provision because the governance systems as well as the financial capacities adopt an incremental and gradual model of policy decision-making.

## 14.2.2 States gain political legitimacy during social and economic crises through the use of social welfare policies

Chapter 1 by Taylor provides a historical overview of the main features of the evolution of social welfare policy in Africa, and uses South Africa as an example to highlight the links among social welfare policy and political and economic processes. Taylor (Chapters 1 and 4), using a political economy analysis, shows how policy discourses on social welfare crystallised in Africa and, more recently, in South Africa during periods when the political legitimacy of states was challenged by popular uprisings for improvements in the quality of life, especially of previously disenfranchised people.

Noyoo (Chapter2) traces and discusses the development of social welfare policy especially focusing on the Southern African region. His analysis points out that contemporary social welfare policy trends in Southern Africa are shaped by the political and economic forces and social welfare processes that dominated the region from precolonial, colonial, and postcolonial periods. Social welfare policy in Africa therefore evolves in response to and is a by-product of a political economy and a specific welfare regime that exist in a country. Africa is not homogeneous and each country inherited and assimilated into different colonial traditions that continue to shape and influence present-day governance and administrative styles as well as institutional, policy, and legislative frameworks.

Sub-Saharan Africa's context is underpinned by conditions of chronic poverty and a very high disease burden. HIV and Aids and malaria are still the main contributors to its high mortality rates. Besides chronic poverty, insecurity is a feature of the lives of people as a consequence of conflicts in countries such as Uganda, Sudan, and the Democratic Republic of the Congo (DRC). Reflecting on the trends in the region, in Chapter 2, Noyoo argues that Southern Africa is facing major challenges relating to undemocratic political regimes, bad governance, and human rights violations, which are eroding the social and economic development prospects of the region.

A key lesson from Chapters 1, 2 and 4 is that social welfare policies and, more generally, social policies are outcomes of political processes through which a state responds to people's demands to address conditions affecting them and their unmet social needs.The chapters in this book explain how social welfare policies and the systems that result from these change over time, and they analyse these changes against changes in political and economic regimes in countries. It is also clear that social welfare policy as a professional field of study and as a field of practice has many dimensions and can be applied narrowly or comprehensively to improve the well-being of people. However, from a transformative social welfare policy perspective, the preferred option is to adopt a comprehensive approach that includes the social and economic rights of individuals and families.

## 14.2.3 Continuing crises and social upheavals highlight structural flaws in economic and political systems

Postcolonial and post-independent countries in Africa are still going through a period of political, ideological, and social upheaval. The roots of these upheavals are many and are interwoven with the dramatic changes that have taken place in the late twentieth and early twenty-first centuries. Changes in political ideologies of states as well as advances in technology, in mechanisation, and in the ability to move finances across countries at a speed never before experienced have made countries in the twentieth and twenty-first centuries more interdependent and linked even as inequalities between countries grew.

The dominance of markets through the transnationalisation of production processes underpinned by a neoliberal economic and trade agenda has led to a world in which the few that have wealth and privilege have been able to amass even greater individual and corporate wealth. (Transnationalisation took off during the late 1980s. It means that corporations locate their manufacturing industries in parts of the world where they can use cheap labour without complying with minimum wage regulations and health and safety standards for workers and where they can access other resources such as land, raw materials, energy at preferential rates). The flip side of this accumulation of wealth and privilege is that postcolonial countries, that were lagging behind because of the effects of distorted colonial development processes, remain impoverished and mirror the growing inequalities that are a feature of all market-led countries.

At the same time, technological innovations and the use of new information and communication technologies create a demand for a more educated and skilled workforce. Health crises due to HIV and Aids and preventable diseases also reinforced the need for improved health provision. The demands of the markets for healthy, educated and skilled labour and natural resources have increased. Governments in Africa now recognise that to become a part of the global economy, social welfare policies help to meet the basic needs of people and create conditions for their integration into the market or economic system. Deprivations in health, education, and in wages and income threaten the lives of millions of people and also reduce the revenue earning capabilities of African states. It is these contexts that prompted governments to use an approach to social welfare policy and provision that initially was politically expedient and that responded in an ad hoc, incremental and residual way to people's needs, so that the worst effects of deprivations could be contained and the state would be seen as benevolent and acting in the interests of people.

Lessons of experience across most countries in Africa highlight that formal sector waged work is declining and of those in employment the majority work in the government civil service sector or are employed by business in the private sectors. Such workers in the formal sector are a small minority of the economically active population in all regions in Africa. Another important lesson in Africa is that even those with formal waged employment are exposed to risks and are vulnerable because of HIV and Aids. In most countries the statutory retirement ages for salaried workers exceed (or are very close to) the life expectancies of especially males who generally have lower life expectancies than females. Formal employment is not a predictor of well-being if it does not include adequate social insurance including health care. The majority of the economically active population who are not in waged formal or informal work eke out an existence in the survivalist sector and rely on subsistence farming or family networks of support.

Social welfare policy interventions cushion the worst effects of market economies. Most countries in Africa have market-led economies and in such contexts the status of social welfare policy is very low or virtually nonexistent. The realisation that market systems fail people, especially in contexts in which chronic poverty and systemic inequalities are a feature of the global economy,was reinforced through the financial and economic crises in 1998 and 2008, and the declines experienced in their wake. This realisation led governments to focus on the added value of introducing social protection measures that would provide a minimum floor or basket of goods and services to all citizens.

## 14.2.4 The influences of colonial administrative systems in prescribing and limiting the role of social welfare policy

During different periods, systems of government have played an important role in determining the direction, role, and functions of social welfare. As Noyoo reflects in Chapter 2, colonial administrations adopted a community development approach that was based on the principles of self-help and limited state intervention. In contemporary societies, deprivations in health, education, and in wages and income threaten the lives of millions of people, and environmental disasters as well as state repression and militarisation of states in Africa make the lives and security of people precarious.

Despite the urgency to provide alternatives to the current approach to social welfare – and to address both the root causes and symptoms of social conditions –many countries are stuck within a framing of policies that retain the historical traditions of colonial and postcolonial regimes. Policies are introduced when families and kinship systems are unable to provide for the needs of their members and when the market system is unable to include the workforce into waged employment. In Chapter 2, Noyoo provides a historical overview of the precolonial and colonial influences that shape governments' responses to social welfare policy in the region. He discusses some of the impacts of precolonial and colonial policy influence on societies in Africa, especially in Southern Africa, and argues for social welfare policy responses that are more contextually relevant and appropriate and that affirm the cultural and social histories of people in the region.

The limited and residual policy approach that remains in use in most countries (refer to Taylor in Chapter 1 and Triegaardt in Chapter 3) is just sufficient to muffle the voices of the disaffected and marginalised and to legitimise the state. Social work intervened to help people to integrate into existing unequal structures and the limits of their interventions were prescribed and set by governments. This situation is changing and professionals are adopting approaches to social welfare policy and provision that moves away from an ad hoc, incremental and residual one towards an approach that addresses the needs of people within a human rights approach. As Triegaardt points out in Chapter 3, policy approaches adopted in industrialised countries in the early days influenced social welfare in countries in Africa. She argues that a more developmental approach achieves better outcomes for people. In Chapters 1 and 4, Taylor refers to such an approach as transformative because it ensures that social welfare policy embeds human rights of people in accordance with internationally approved norms and standards.

Analyses of the politics, economics, social, cultural, and environmental contexts of countries in Africa, from the perspective of a transformative social welfare policy approach as analysed by Taylor in Chapters 1 and 4, show that notable continuities exist with past undemocratic and discriminatory policies and practices. Adjustments made to address increasing poverty and vulnerabilities have led to new policies and pieces of legislation without addressing the root causes (structural) causes of the conditions that keep people in poverty, expose them to risk, and make them vulnerable. A key lesson is that governments respond to crises within the limits set by existing economic and social structures. The gradual changes in social welfare are typical of a residual and reformist approach rather than a transformative and developmental one.

At best the policy changes introduced post-independence were thus designed to maintain the status quo and reduce the worst effects of absolute poverty without addressing the inequities in the distributionof benefits, services, and access to rights that would change existing structures and power relations. The main lesson of experience is the need for governments to play an enabling institutional and regulatory role, creating the space for people to understand their rights and entitlements to social welfare. The institutional and developmental role of government should be complemented by a regulatory and policy framework for private sector social welfare provision, not-for-profit provisions, and community support systems to ensure equitable social welfare provision.

## 14.2.5 Impetus for policy change in response to demographic and social challenges is increasingly influenced by regional policy actors

Shifts in social welfare policy approaches were also driven by changes in demographic and social and economic conditions as discussed by Taylor in Chapters 5 and 6. Recognising the complexities of such contexts, governments in Africa were also strongly influenced by regional actors from intergovernmental agencies as well as international non-governmental organisations. A United Nations agency – the United Nations Educational, Scientific and Cultural Organisation (UNESCO)– established a Management of Social Transformation (MOST) programme in 1994 to assist governments to utilise research to change their policy approach and direction. The aim was primarily to provide social science research findings and data to policy decisionmakers and other stakeholders across all regions of the world. UNESCO used this programme to facilitate regular meetings of Ministers of Social Development or Social Welfare to share knowledge that would strengthen the link between social science research and policymaking and would be used especially to address poverty and social issues and conditions (Ministry of Community Development and Social Services (Zambia) & Department of Social Development (South Africa), 2009).

The process that was used to assist governments in Africa to manage social transformation is instructive and provides relevant lessons of experience for the region. The MOST programme facilitated an initial Forum of Ministers of Social Development or Social Welfare for countries from the Southern African Development Community (SADC) in Cape Town in November 2004, which was hosted by the government of the Republic of South Africa (RSA). During January 2006, the government of Mali hosted the first Forum for Ministers representing countries of the Economic Community of West African States (ECOWAS) under the MOST programme. At a second meeting convened with Ministers of Social Development and Social Welfare of SADC in Johannesburg in November 2006, there was recognition of rising poverty levels and social exclusion faced by most people in African countries and the inadequacy of existing policy responses to these conditions. This process was followed by another forum held in

Livingstone in November 2009 which was jointly hosted by the Ministry of Community Development and Social Services of Zambia and the Department of Social Development of South Africa (Ministry of Community Development and Social Services (Zambia) & Department of Social Development (South Africa), 2009).

People participating in transforming legislation and policies in South Africa

Nyerere discussing lessons of experience in Africa

These forums created the space for reflexive (reviews and assessments) policy analysis and practice in the African region. It also enabled governments to share common and unique experiences and challenges in the social welfare and social development policy field. For example, a key lesson that emerged from shared experiences in Africa was the significance of social cash transfers in the fight against poverty and vulnerability. Experiences were shared on the contribution cash transfers make to the empowerment of women, and those infected by HIV and Aids and other debilitating diseases. Evidence from pilot cash transfer programmes sponsored by donors and operated by non-governmental agencies in Eastern and Southern African countries and in Ethiopia illustrated the potential of cash transfers and employment programmes to make a difference in the lives of the poorest people. Such donor supported pilot programmes provide lessons of experience for governments so that with strategic government interventions these programmes can be scaled up and produce multiplier social and economic effects.

## 14.2.6 Changes in policy approaches and interventions are more likely to emerge through discourses and sharing experiences

Regional and national forums for policy debates and discourses, especially among senior government officials and policymakers as shown through the MOST programme initiative, are likely to change perceptions about social welfare policy. Such processes created the space for policy discussions among member states on common and unique social welfare conditions and the challenges they experience in trying to achieve better social outcomes. Through policy debates and discourses, policymakers and government officials in the region realised that a paradigm shift was necessary. The conceptual frameworks for social welfare policy derived from industrial models and colonial and postcolonial administrative systems were critiqued as inappropriate for the conditions countries in Africa experience. A turning point was achieved through such engagements when a definition was agreed that perceives social (welfare) policies as interventions designed to promote the well-being of citizens and address structural inequalities in wealth, ensure greater equality for all, correct market shortcomings, reduce poverty, and promote social inclusion (Ministry of Community Development and Social Services (Zambia) & Department of Social Development (South Africa), 2009: 8–9).

This thinking shifted how social welfare policy was understood, its perceived role and functions, and how it should be implemented in countries to address poverty, inequalities, and vulnerability. The African Union, through its Department for Social Affairs, played a decisive role in shaping the social policy agenda when it launched a Social Policy Framework for all member states at a meeting of Ministers of Social Development in 2008 in Namibia (www.au.int). During the last two decades, shifts in thinking on social policy and the role and place of social welfare were also influenced by the International Labour Organisation's (ILO) initiatives on social protection and decent work (www.ilo.org), the Economic Commission on Africa (ECA) (www.uneca.org) and the African Development Bank (www.afdb.org). Together with these actors there were many international non-governmental organisations, research think tanks, and policy experts who influenced and shaped critical discourses on social policy and social welfare policies as paths to social development.

In similar vein, Chapter 4 by Taylor highlights how understandings of social welfare policy and its impacts on the provision of social welfare services in Africa, and more specifically in South Africa, have changed over time. As in other postcolonial countries, South Africa's social welfare policy journey towards an approach that is transformative – and that protects and empowers individuals, families, households, and communities to develop with dignity – remains a site of contestation. An important lesson from experience in South Africa is that transformative outcomes are being shaped and influenced through the alignment of post-1994 social welfare policy and legislation with the Constitution (1996) and with the National Development Plan (NPC, 2011). These macro policy frameworks provide the basis for policy coherence and integration into processes that not only address the rights and needs of people but importantly also restructures the systems and processes to ensure people's participation in policymaking.

Chapter 4 (Taylor) analyses how the social welfare policy agenda in Africa is shifting as new normative regional instruments for the progressive achievement of human rights and welfare are established. The introduction of the African Charter on Human and People's Rights (OAU – AU, 1981) and the African Charter on the Rights and Welfare of the Child (OAU – AU 1990) are analysed as policy frameworks that can be used to hold governments and other actors to account in the absence of democratic and accountable systems of governance. Using a case study as an example, Taylor provides an analysis in Chapter 4 that shows how South Africa's experiences of transformation also provides lessons in how concepts such as developmental social welfare, social protection, and social development can take on new meanings and be applied in ways that reclaim human development for the most deprived while transforming power relations. At a conceptual level the links among transformative and developmental social welfare, social protection, and social development are clarified, and at an operational level the roles of government, the private sector, and the not-for-profit sector in the design and distribution of transformative social welfare services are discussed. Just as different approaches to social welfare policy exist on an ideological and value base spectrum so too do various definitional concepts of social welfare policy. Chapter 4 brings these concepts together and maps them into paths to social development underpinned by transformation and social justice.

## 14.2.7 Macro policy and strategic challenges determine the role and functions of social welfare policy

As the chapters in this book show, especially Chapters 4, 5 and 6 by Taylor and Chapter 7 by Noyoo, inadequate systems of governance with ineffective policies can lead to economic and political unrest that affects the most deprived sectors of communities. When governments fail to regulate the social dimensions of mining – as in the case of the Marikana uprising (Chapter 7) – and of industrial development and agricultural developments effectively, the potential for political and economic unrest are ever present. The absence of appropriate macro policy frameworks to address the social dimensions of neoliberal economic globalisation processes and the threats posed by these processes for poor individuals, families and households is a key theme that runs through many chapters in the book. However, where countries have included social welfare policies, and social protection measures and programmes into their national development plans, they are better able to integrate needs and rights of people into macro policy frameworks and to lobby for the necessary resources to address social welfare needs and rights of people.

As Chapters 5 and 6 reveal, poverty, growing inequalities, and continuing social marginalisation remain features of the social and economic landscape in Africa. The recognition that macroeconomic and social policy goals and processes must be integrated so that the coping abilities and resilience of individuals, households, and societies are not undermined is an important lesson of experience for governments in the region. Macro social welfare policies as well as policies on the design and use of new technologies and information systems also need to take account of the new risks and vulnerabilities spawned by such technological innovations. The changing nature of work as a result of increased mechanisation of mining, agriculture, and services and the impact on people without the necessary skills threaten the livelihoods of many (Taylor, 2013). The use of social media and new communication technologies also creates new platforms for violations and abuse of people's rights, especially those of women and children.

## 14.2.8 Linking macro social welfare policies to evidence-based strategic programme interventions to address poverty, inequalities, risk and vulnerabilities

Framing social welfare policies and legislation within a human rights and constitutional approach that protects the social and economic rights of people in Africa is the beginning of the process of transformation and not the end. A lesson from practice is that, for transformative changes to be implemented, policymakers and social service professionals have to understand what is wrong with the existing frameworks and provisions. This knowledge comes through the use of appropriate evidence and data from the field. As Chapters 5 and 6 by Taylor highlights, it is essential to understand the relationships among evidence-based knowledge, professional social service practice, and the demographic and social and economic conditions in which people live. Social welfare policies that do not have their basis in evidence, and do not reflect the actual conditions and circumstances in which people live, are unlikely to have the desired impacts on the lives of people.

Countries in Africa recognise the importance of reliable evidence and data in policymaking but lack the capacity to collect evidence, analyse data, and provide such information in ways that policymakers can use to amend or transform policies. It is especially difficult, as

Taylor points out in Chapter 5, to get reliable data on the range and quality of social welfare services being delivered to people by the state and non-state service providers. This poses a continuing and strategic challenge because the range of services available to people, the accessibility or reach of such services, the distribution of services,and demand for specific services are unlikely to be linked to demographic trends or to needs and rights of people.

The lack of evidence and demographic data on gaps in provision related to people's needs and entitlements obstructs the transformation process and undermines principles of fairness in the distribution, access, adequacy, and quality of services. An important lesson from experience is that to make strategic social welfare policy choices and programme interventions, it is essential for every countryto develop the capacity and resources to collate, analyse, and use evidence-based knowledge to influence policy changes in the design and distribution of social welfare services. This capacity will enable a transformative social welfare policy approach that, as Taylor indicates in Chapters 5 and 6, is responsive to people's needs and conditions and the context in which people live.

Another lesson of experience is that policies and legislation on social welfare should include benchmarks as well as targets for the delivery of social provision that prioritise the needs of all, especially those currently excluded. Countries in Africa (Mauritius, Botswana, Ethiopia, Lesotho, and Seychelles, among others) that have universal as opposed to means-tested criteria for the allocation of social welfare benefits and services are better able to reach those who need benefits and services in the most efficient ways. If the delivery of services is available to all on a universal basis, there is less likely to be administrative obstacles, less chances for discrimination on the basis of gender, sexual orientation, race, or ethnicity, and less room for bureaucratic and administrative blockages due to value judgements of administrators (Taylor, 2013).

People's exposure to risk and vulnerabilities also emerge in the context of experiences of forced and voluntary migration as discussed by Schenck in Chapter 8 of this book. She provides a glimpse into experiences of refugees, migrants, children and others, and describes the conditions within which they struggle to live. She also explains the rights and international guidelines for the treatment and care of refugees and migrants and compels social work professionals to reflect on the services that are required to protect and promote the rights of migrants and refugees.

The use of evidence and demographic trends to introduce policy changes also provides policymakers and social service providers with data on whose needs and rights should be prioritised. This evidence-based prioritisation of needs, rights, and entitlements enables policymakers and administrators to make strategic programme choices in the design and the sequencing of reforms or transformation and the time frames for delivery of social provision. A cross cutting theme and lesson from countries is that institutionsand programmes must be underpinned by strong government commitment and policy leadership from a dedicated top government department or interdepartmental task team working across sectors within and outside of government.

A key lesson from the field discussed in Chapter 5 shows that a country's ability to care for those who are vulnerable and exposed to risk and living in multidimensional poverty is dependent on the reliability of its demographic data acquired through either census or surveys. Governments in Africa do not always have the resources to make adequate provision for all those who need social development services. Using demographic data and profiles to guide their decisions on which parts of the population require urgent social welfare policy interventions can make a difference in the lives of those who are most deprived and at risk.

Analysing the persistence of poverty and inequalities in Chapter 6, Taylor finds that two aspects influence how policymakers deal with poverty. The first is how they understand poverty, its causes, and its relationships with other social development concerns such as vulnerabilities and risks people experience during different stages of their lives. The second aspect is the relationship between poverty and the ownership of assets, the distribution of assets as well as the type of exchange transactions people are able to make in a market economy. In contemporary societies in Africa, there is increasing recognition that responses to poverty must go beyond addressing deprivations in basic material needs and include other dimensions. For example, the powerlessness people experience in their daily lives as a result of their systemic exclusions from social and economic processes of development also requires urgent attention.

## 14.2.9 Erosion of the family as an institution and provider of mutual support

The effects of brutal colonial and post colonial regimes on the family as an institution have eroded and reduced its role. The assumption that members of families provide support and mutual aid to one another no longer holds true. As Noyoo explains in Chapter 7, the concept of family in contemporary society is malleable and quite difficult to define. He also notes that ideological and conservative positions creep into family discourses all over the world and that despite these issues the family is a fundamental and complex component of all human societies. Social welfare policy responds to risks and vulnerabilities of families and introduces measures and interventions to protect families and members of families from adversities in society. When families are affected by social and economic crises, it influences the organisation of sexual relations and reproduction of human beings. It also affects how members of families engage in economic activities, the gender division of labour, the (re) distribution of property, the transfer of culture, the socialisation of children, and how they provide for the care of older people.

As political, economic and social institutions change, these have an impact on the structure and functions of the family. Although families share similar features that characterise them, Noyoo notes that South African families differ from those in most of sub-Saharan African countries. This is because they are defined by various characteristics including race-based categories as well as the indigenous ethnic groups which make up South African society, and as a result South African families are multiracial and multi-ethnic. South Africa reveals significant changes over the years brought about by the impact of colonisation and apartheid on traditional African family systems. There are also new and different family types that have emerged in the country such as those of same-sex partners which are protected by South Africa's legal system. Also, single parent families are on the rise as well as child-headed families. These new family types pose challenges to welfare service provision because of the diversity of needs that should be taken into account when providing social welfare services. Social welfare policy and provision in this context have to be responsive to the changing structure of family life and the changing needs of families across the continent.

## 14.2.10 Balancing social and economic expenditure to pursue a socially inclusive and redistributive social development agenda

Lessons of experience in Africa (Taylor, 2009) revealed that most countries are allocating very small budgets to social welfare services and social development but are increasing expenditure on social protection services, especially for social grants in the form of cash transfers, for specific categories of people living in extreme or absolute poverty. Small island states such as Mauritius and Seychelles were able to reduce poverty and inequalities through balanced financial allocations made from revenue collected through taxes. National budgets need to prioritise expenditure on social welfare policy priorities in similar ways in which they prioritise allocations to provide incentives for economic growth to encourage private sector investments. Another lesson of experience with regard to financing of social welfare provision is the need to reprioritise expenditure among social programmes so that those that are designed to reach the most deprived are increased and other priorities can be phased in gradually.

Some countries in Southern Africa and East Africa that have been reliant on donor funding to finance social welfare programmes experience many challenges in sustaining such programmes even when these are making positive impacts on the well-being of people (such as pilot cash transfer programmes). Other countries in the region, especially those coming out of conflicts, are more reliant on humanitarian aid for post-conflict social welfare provision.

## 14.2.11 Applying democratic and participatory processes in analysing and formulating social welfare policy and laws

Social welfare policies and legislation in most countries are approved and enacted by governments through parliamentary processes. They are directly influenced by the values and principles of the political regime in power and by the economic approach to development that governments adopt and promote. As Chapters 9, 10 and 12 note, the formulation of policy usually takes place within the context of the prevailing political, economic, and social and cultural environment. As we note from policy experiences in the region, contexts in which there have been major conflicts, civil wars, and internal disruptions influence and shape social welfare policies, programmes, and interventions directly as in the case of the Democratic Republic of the Congo (DRC). This country's social welfare policies were conceived, designed, and implemented within the context of a post-war/conflict environment since the 1960s.

In the post-1994 period, South Africa's social welfare policies were strongly influenced by the social and economic rights entrenched in the Constitution. These rights are embedded in the Constitution as a response to the denial of civil, political, social, and economic rights to the majority of South Africans. As noted by various authors in preceding chapters, social welfare policies and programmes are put into place when governments make decisions about whose needs should be addressed and the programmes and processes that should be established to provide for these needs. A significant aspect of social welfare policy includes making decisions about the resources that should be allocated to finance social welfare services, benefits, and other forms of provision to address needs, issues, and social problems.

The choices governments make about these dimensions of social welfare are part of the broader political and economic process as noted by Taylor and Triegaardt in Chapter 9 and Sesoko in Chapters 10 and 12. A central theme that runs through Chapter 10 by Sesoko is the significance of people's participation in the policymaking process. This affirms the democratic principle that people affected by a situation or condition be involved in its resolution through policy processes. Sesoko outlines these participatory processes from the initial phase of policymaking through to the implementation and monitoring and evaluation phases. She frames these processes by providing definitions and theoretical understandings of key concepts used in Chapter 10 such as participation, public participation, democratic, representative democracy, and transformation. Using case studies, Sesoko provides snapshots of different scenarios where participation took place and highlights the successes and failures of the transformational participatory processes. These lessons of experience underscore the significance of the role played by local communities in policymaking and in developmental projects as well as the difficulties in managing such complex processes.

According to Sesoko and others in this book, lessons from history adequately demonstrate that without people's involvement in recently established post-1994 democratic spaces in South Africa, marginalised communities will continue to be deprived from the benefits and opportunities in the country. The participation of people in formulating social welfare policy means being engaged in a series of activities that involves a number of different players, series of discussions, debates, and dialogues. It also involves providing information and knowledge to all those involved so that they are able to become meaningfully engaged in task teams consisting of different stakeholders representing different interest groupings and individuals.

Arising from experiences in South Africa, Sesoko highlights how policies, laws and legislation are guided by the Constitution of South Africa and by a number of international instruments on human rights to which the country is a signatory. She acknowledges that social welfare policy and laws post 1994 should be designed to address the unjust and racially structured welfare system that was established under apartheid. Sesoko, however, questions the extent to which these laws are transformative. Using various legislation in relation to children, persons with disabilities, older persons, youth, and women she describes and discusses the processes followed in designing these statutory requirements and the implementation process. Despite social welfare policies and legislation in South Africa being outcomes of consultative and transformed processes for engagement and implementation in different statutory and social welfare settings, she concludes that there are many challenges that continue to influence the lives of the poorest. The main theme that emerges from her discussion is that transformation is not fully realised if the vulnerable communities continue to experience inequality and injustice.

## 14.2.12 The roles of social service professionals in policy advocacy and social movement activism

An interesting lesson emerges from Chapter 11 in which Triegaardt traces the roles of social workers in policy advocacy. She takes a historical perspective and looks at how the early role of social workers was confined mainly to a preoccupation with remedial intervention. According to Triegaardt, social workers were involved in intervening to address emotional and social factors affecting an individual's effective social functioning. Her view is that in the early days of the profession there was a commitment to remedial intervention and this dominated social work practice. As the profession evolved, other methods such as group work and community development were also used to help people improve their social conditions.

Recognising that social and economic systems or institutions and the policies and laws that regulate these institutions needed to be changed, social service professionals were prompted to develop policy implementation and advocacy roles. Triegaardt provides a useful perspective on policy advocacy. Policy advocacy, according to Triegaardt, is the act of defending or directly representing people who are being served so that they can influence decision-making to change unjust or unresponsive policies and laws and in so doing they are able to shift power relations and effect institutional change.

She links the changes in the roles of particularly social workers to the changes in the broader global context that compelled practitioners to rethink remedial forms of practice. Some of the impetus for changes she attributes to UN policy initiatives and the use of international instruments such as the Universal Declaration of Human Rights (UDHR) to enhance citizenship rights. Social movement activism through involvement in various liberation movements (the African National Congress and the Pan African Congress) and the Black Conscious Movement during the apartheid era also highlighted the links among oppressive systems and structural conditions in South Africa and the realities of people's lives. Social movement activism provided the space for social service professionals to advocate for the rights of people they served as well as their own rights.

Besides the advocacy roles, social service professionals, as part of the social welfare policy process, are increasingly required to monitor and evaluate welfare policy and programmes. Triegaardt discusses these techniques in Chapter 13. She focuses on different types of evaluation, the location of evaluation and monitoring in the policy cycle process, the approaches to evaluation, and research designs which can be used. The significance of monitoring and evaluation is primarily its contribution to policy and programme formulation and modification, which Triegaardt indicates are activities that have a strong political dimension. She concludes that the purpose of monitoring and evaluation for social welfare policy lies in its utility as a tool for management, funders, and its target audience. A central message with regard to the role of evaluation is that professionals and policymakers should review the context in which policies and legislation are crafted and the structural and systemic conditions affecting people so that recommendations for change – drawn from the evaluation process – would enhance the policy relevance and responsiveness.

## CONCLUSION

- The lessons of experience and main messages drawn from an analysis of countries in sub-Saharan Africa reveal that in postcolonial, post-modern (the early period of the 1920s during which industrial development became mechanised) and post-development contexts (the period from 2000 that was influenced by transnational production processes and new information technologies) social welfare policy and provision is part of a shifting terrain. The chapters in this book highlight that for many countries the emancipation of people from poverty and inequalities remains ephemeral. The politics and economics that determine social welfare policy processes and outcomes continue to be shaped by a status quo that ensures the accumulation of privilege and wealth for a few and increasing poverty and inequalities for many.
- In many cases on the continent, the lessons point to governments in the region adopting a reformist and incremental approach to social welfare policy with an emphasis on responding to what is politically expedient or needs that determine survival issues. This approach differs from the perspectives that argue for a transformative social welfare policy process that entrenches human and constitutional rights of people to social and economic development. The analysis in this chapter and others also reinforces democracy as an organising principle for transforming policy processes. Furthermore, the effective and accountable management of institutional arrangements for the distribution and delivery

of social services and benefits is a cross-cutting issue that emerges from experiences and evidence. Linked to institutional arrangements and the distribution of social welfare services is the imperative to ensure that financing and resources for social welfare services and benefits are given the same attention as are issues of economic development.

- The integration of social and economic development of people who have been historically excluded through unjust systems will not take place without deliberate social welfare policy interventions that promote their integration into social and economic processes. This can be done by ensuring contextual relevance of social welfare policy and building professional capabilities for a transformative agenda through the five strategies below:

  1. Embedding human rights and social justice in social welfare policy and professional practice to ensure transformative and developmental outcomes.
  2. Reinforcing knowledge that links micro and macro development processes so that the needs and lived experiences of people on the ground are reflected in macro policy and financing arrangements.
  3. Using evidence to integrate demographic, social, and economic data in analysing the relevance and adequacy of social welfare policies and services.
  4. Linking individual welfare and capabilities with human well-being and distributive justice in social welfare provision.
  5. Using regional (Africa) and international human rights instruments to monitor and evaluate the progressive achievement of universal access to social welfare services that address the root causes of poverty and social inequalities as well as the symptoms.

- All chapters in this book highlight that for social welfare policy to play a transformative role an important criterion is a responsive and accountable government that adopts an integrated approach to both social and economic policies and that uses universal social welfare provisioning as a redistributive measure to ensure inclusion and social justice. Effective social welfare policies and provision is possible in either open or closed market economies. However, the type of public-private mix is important and the regulatory role of government is essential to ensure equity and access in provision. Progress in eliminating poverty, reducing inequalities, and addressing the needs of the most vulnerable and at risk is possible using transformative and developmental policies. A significant lesson of experience is that there are many paths to achieving equitable social development and that these paths are neither a singular nor a linear process. Strategies adopted may be varied and diverse and each country is shaped by unique experiences (such as history, politics, economics, culture, social conditions) and there may be periods of accelerated development and even setbacks. As noted in the following statement by Taylor:

  *'Decades of struggle, recurring crises, structurally embedded inequalities and poverty should spur discourses in ways that make social justice more than a concept or mirage in the wastelands in which millions of the poorest people on the African continent live'* (Taylor, 2013: 23).

## QUESTIONS

1. Discuss some lessons and experiences of social welfare policy in your country and suggest ways through which you can apply a transformative and developmental approach.
2. Discuss critically the significance of political, economic and governance environments in Africa for the transformation of social welfare policy and social service provision.

# REFERENCES

AFRICAN DEVELOPMENT BANK (2017) 'Indicators on Gender, Poverty, the Environment and Progress toward the Sustainable Development Goals' *African Countries* Volume XVIII [Online]. Côte d'Ivoire: Economic and Social Statistics Division. Available: https://www.afdb.org/en/documents/publications/gender-poverty-and-environmental-indicators-on-african-countries/ [Accessed 2017].

AKE, C (1976) 'Explanatory Notes on the Political economy of Africa' *The Journal of Modern African Studies* Vol. 14 No. 1 (March 1976) at pp. 1–23. Available: http://www.jstor.org/stable/159645.

BIENEFELD, M (1988) 'Dependency Theory and the Political economy of Sub-Saharan's Crises' *Review of African Political Economy* No.43 1988 [Online]. Available: http://www.tandfonline.com/doi/abs/10.1080/03056248808703791 [Accessed 2017].

INTERNATIONAL LABOUR ORGANISATION (ILO). Available: www.ilo.org. [Accessed 2017].

SOUTH AFRICA. National Planning Commission (2011) *National Development Plan: Vision for 2030*. Pretoria: Government Printer. Available: http://www.gov.za/sites/www.gov.za/files/devplan_2.pdf.

TAYLOR, V (2008) 'Social Protection in Africa: An Overview of the Challenges' Research Report prepared for the African Union [Online]. Available: www.eprionline.com/wpcontent/uploads/2011/03/Taylor2008AUSocialProtectionOverview.pdf.

TAYLOR, V: 'Social Justice: Reframing the "Social" in Critical Discourses in Africa' in Tangen, S (ed.) (2013) *African Perspectives on Social Justice*. Kampala: Friedrich-Ebert-Stiftung.

UNITED NATIONS (1948) *Universal Declaration of Human Rights* General Assembly Resolution 217A adopted by the General Assembly on 10 December 1948. France: Paris.

UNITED NATIONS DIVISION FOR ECONOMIC AND SOCIAL AFFAIRS (UNDESA) (2001) *Report on the World Social Situation* 2001. New York: UNDESA.

UNITED NATIONS ECONOMIC COMMISSION FOR AFRICA (UNECA). Available: www.uneca.org [Accessed 2017].

UNITED NATIONS UNITED NATIONS EDUCATIONAL, SCIENTIFIC AND CULTURAL ORGANISATION (UNESCO) 'The Management of Social Transformation (MOST) Programmes' [Online]. Available: http://www.unesco.org/new/en/social-and-human-sciences/themes/most-programme/ [Accessed 2017].

ZAMBIA & SOUTH AFRICA. Ministry of Community Development & Social Services (Zambia) & Department of Social Development (South Africa) (2009) *Report of the Southern African Departments and Ministers of Social Development and Social Affairs* Regional Social Policy Round Table. Livingstone, Zambia, 22–25 November 2009. Available: http://www.dsd.gov.za/index2.php?option=com_docman&task=doc_view&gid=131&Itemid=3.

## Endnote

1 Transformative social welfare policy embeds principles of human rights, equity, universal access and provision, and social justice in its content and practice.

# Index